Jurists and Legal Science in the History of Roman Law

Clifford Ando, Massimo Brutti, Oliviero Diliberto
Giuseppe Falcone, Detlef Liebs, Andrea Lovato, Dario Mantovani
Valerio Marotta, Fara Nasti, Aldo Schiavone, Emanuele Stolfi

Jurists and Legal Science in the History of Roman Law

Edited by
Fara Nasti and Aldo Schiavone

Translated by
Peter Christie

Routledge
Taylor & Francis Group
LONDON AND NEW YORK

G. Giappichelli Editore

First published 2022
by Routledge
4 Park Square, Milton Park, Abingdon, Oxon OX14 4RN

and by Routledge
605 Third Avenue, New York, NY 10017

Routledge is an imprint of the Taylor & Francis Group, an informa business

British Library Cataloguing-in-Publication Data
A catalogue record for this book is available from the British Library

Library of Congress Cataloging-in-Publication Data
A catalogue record for this book has been requested

ISBN: 978-0-367-33333-1 (hbk-Routledge)
ISBN: 978-0-429-31926-6 (ebk-Routledge)
ISBN: 978-1-032-04757-7 (pbk-Routledge)
ISBN: 978-88-921-3588-8 (hbk-Giappichelli)

Typeset in Simoncini Garamond
by G. Giappichelli Editore, Turin, Italy

The manuscript has been subjected to a peer review process prior to publication.

CONTENTS

ABBREVIATIONS

To the usual abbreviations indicated in the *Année Philologique*, add the following list:

AARC – *Atti dell'Accademia Romanistica Costantiniana*
AG – *Archivio Giuridico "Filippo Serafini"*
ANRW – *Aufstieg und Niedergang der römischen Welt*
AntAfr – *Antiquités Africaines*
AUPA – *Annali del Seminario Giuridico dell'Università di Palermo*
BCH – *Bulletin de correspondence hellénique*
BIDR – *Bullettino dell'Istituto di Diritto Romano "Vittorio Scialoja"*
CIL – *Corpus Inscriptionum Latinarum*
DizEp. – *Dizionario Epigrafico*
DNP – *Der Neue Pauly*
ED – *Enciclopedia del Diritto*
ILS – *Inscriptiones Latinae Selectae*
MAL – *Atti della Accademia Nazionale dei Lincei. Memorie. Classe di scienze morali, storiche e filologiche*
Materiali – *Materiali per una Storia della Cultura Giuridica*
MedAnt – *Mediterraneo Antico. Economie Società Culture*
Mefra – *Mélanges de l'École Française de Rome. Antiquité*
NNDI – *Novissimo Digesto Italiano*
PWRE / RE – *Paulys Realencyclopädie der classischen Altertumswissenschaft*
QF – *Quaderni Fiorentini per la storia del pensiero giuridico moderno*
RAL – *Atti dell'Accademia Nazionale dei Lincei. Rendiconti. Classe di scienze morali, storiche e filologiche*
RDR – *Rivista di Diritto Romano*
REL – *Revue des Études Latines*
RIL – *Rendiconti. Reale Istituto Lombardo di scienze e lettere*
RISG – *Rivista Italiana per le Scienze Giuridiche*
RHDFE – *Revue Historique de Droit Français et Étranger*
TvR / RHD – *Tijdschrift voor Rechtsgeschiedenis / Revue d'Histoire du Droit*
ZRG / ZSS – *Zeitschrift der Savigny-Stiftung für Rechtsgeschichte – Romanistische Abteilung*

CONTRIBUTORS

The Editors

Aldo Schiavone – Principal Investigator of the ERC Project, Advanced Grant, '*Scriptores iuris Romani*'. Member of the Institute for Advanced Study, Princeton, and of American Academy of Arts and Sciences. Among his books: *The End of the Past*, Harvard U.P. Cambridge 2000, *The Invention of Law in the West*, Harvard U.P., Cambridge 2012.

Fara Nasti – Professor of Roman Law, University of Calabria, Senior Staff of the ERC Project

The Authors

Clifford Ando – Professor of Classics, History and Law, University of Chicago

Massimo Brutti – Professor Emeritus of Roman Law, Sapienza, University of Rome

Oliviero Diliberto – Professor of Roman Law, Sapienza, University of Rome, Senior Staff of the ERC Project

Giuseppe Falcone – Professor of Roman Law, University of Palermo

Detlef Liebs – Professor Emeritus of Roman Law, University of Freiburg (Germany)

Andrea Lovato – Professor of Roman Law, University of Bari

Dario Mantovani – Professor of Droit, culture et société de la Rome antique, Collège de France

Valerio Marotta – Professor of Roman Law, University of Pavia, Senior Staff of the ERC Project

Emanuele Stolfi – Professor of Roman Law, University of Siena, Senior Staff of the ERC Project

The quotations from Italian authors have all been translated into English, as have those from non-Italian authors quoted in Italian translation. The quotations in French, German and Spanish have been left in the original version.

PREFACE

This book is connected with the project *Scriptores iuris Romani* (P.I. Aldo Schiavone), funded by the European Research Council, and still in progress at the Sapienza University of Rome. Its aim is to provide a new textual and interpretative basis for the history of Roman law and Roman legal thought. No longer the Justinian codification, the formidable mosaic of the *Corpus iuris*, but the single jurists – profile by profile and work by work – in their dual function as inventors of a science and as creators of a legal system that oriented a global empire.

Thus far, seven volumes have been published by 'L'Erma di Bretschneider' of Rome: Quintus Mucius Scaevola. *Opera* (by J.-L. Ferrary, A. Schiavone, E. Stolfi); Iulius Paulus. *Ad edictum libri I-III* (G. Luchetti, A.L. de Petris, F. Mattioli, I. Pontoriero); *Antiquissima iuris sapientia, saec. VI-III a.C.* (A. Bottiglieri, A. Manzo, F. Nasti, G. Viarengo, V. Marotta, E. Stolfi); Aelius Marcianus, *Instititutionum libri I-IV* (D. Dursi); Callistratus, *Opera* (S. Puliatti); Domitius Ulpianus, *Institutionum libri*; *De censibus* (J.-L. Ferrary, V. Marotta, A. Schiavone); Iulius Paulus, *Decretorum libri* (M. Brutti).

At least ten other works are due to appear before the conclusion of the research in January 2022, including one on P. Mucius Scaevola, M'. Manilius, M. Iunius Brutus (S. Barbati), one on Pomponius, *Enchiridion* (F. Nasti), and one on Cervidius Scaevola, *Quaestionum libri* (A. Spina).

Here we present some articles, both on methodology and the history of historiography, and on the profile of certain jurists, which we partially discussed in a meeting in Rome, at the beginning of our research. These contributions can be considered a useful approach to a type of historical enquiry not very familiar to an English-speaking audience, but which has played a role in the revitalization and new fervour of contemporary studies on the ancient world.

Fara Nasti, Aldo Schiavone

Part I

METHODS AND PATHS

Chapter 1

SINGULARITY AND IMPERSONALITY IN THE THOUGHT OF ROMAN JURISTS

Aldo Schiavone

SUMMARY: 1. Our project. – 2. From Code to jurists. – 3. Singularity and impersonality. – 4. The authoriality of Roman jurists.

1. Our project

The aim of the *Scriptores iuris Romani* Project is to introduce and spread – not only among specialists, but to a broader audience of scholars or even those merely curious about law and history – what we can define as a still uncommon and almost unknown way of viewing Roman law, or at least its most important part. This is a manner that is no longer focused, as is usual, on the Justinian codification – the monumental structure of the *Corpus Juris Civilis*, and in particular the *Digesta* – but directly on the Roman jurists, their single and definite profiles, considered for what they really were: the authentic protagonists of a long and grandiose intellectual journey, which would become a key feature of the West.[1]

With our work – which we have been carrying out for years, long before it became a European Research Council Project, and which had already involved various institutions, including the Istituto Italiano di Scienze Umane, the Scuola Normale Superiore and the University of California, Berkeley – we wish to present a solid textual and interpretative basis for this drastic change in perspective.[2] We have brought out

[1] What I say in these pages is based on my *Ius. L'invenzione del diritto in Occidente. Nuova edizione* (Torino 2017), English translation of first edition, 2005, *The Invention of Law in the West* (Cambridge [Mass.]-London) 2012.

[2] An account of these beginnings can be found in F. Amarelli, A. Schiavone, E. Stolfi, 'Corpus Scriptorum iuris Romani. Nascita di un progetto', in SDHI 71 (2005) 4 ff.; V. Marotta, E. Stolfi, 'L'inizio dei lavori', in SDHI 72 (2006) 587 ff.; C. Giachi, P. Giunti, 'I lavori di Berkeley', in SDHI 73 (2007) 597 ff.; F. Tamburi, 'Montepulciano: una settimana di verifiche e confronti', in SDHI 74 (2008) 923 ff.

a series of volumes through the publisher L'Erma di Bretschneider, each one dedicated to the reconstruction of the work of a jurist (or a part of the work in cases in which we have more ample documentation).

For each author, we have provided: a broad introduction to his life and his thought; reproduction of the Latin (or Greek) text of his writings, rearranging the fragments handed down by the Justinian *Digesta* or by other sources according to the original design – as we are able to reconstruct it today – accompanied by a measured critical apparatus grounded in the Mommsen edition; an Italian translation with a historical-juridical commentary; and finally a complete collection of the quotations made by ancient authors useful to outline the biography of the jurist considered.

An indispensable point of reference is, of course, the work of Lenel, truly pioneering for the era in which it was conceived: a beacon that still stands alone, after almost a century and a half, illuminating a path incredibly neglected, or never even perceived, by subsequent studies on Roman law.[3] Obviously, after such a long time, many results of the German scholar's extraordinary research should be re-examined: and we will not fail to do so when the opportunity arises – even if our main aim is not to replicate his *Palingenesia* but to continue on the road that he foresaw.

2. From Code to jurists

From the point of view of historiographic theory, the enterprise we are undertaking requires the acquisition of a very important preliminary datum: the separation, in the most radical way possible, of the real history of Roman law from the history of its tradition and its fortune from the Justinian age to the twentieth century: a phenomenon of almost incalculable proportions that has still not ceased to influence the legal culture of the West.

At the origin of the tradition is the Justinian codification, the formidable mosaic of the *Corpus Iuris*. Instead, the core of the history of Roman law consists of the jurists in their dual, but almost inextricably interwoven, function as inventors of a science and as creators of a legal system that guided a global empire.

---

[3] O. Lenel, *Palingenesia Iuris Civilis*, I-II (Lipsiae 1889; reprint Roma 2002); L.E. Sierl, *Supplementum* (Graz 1960).

The success of the medieval and especially modern tradition of Roman law has decisively contributed to the establishment in the West of the individualistic form of private subjectivity as an intrinsically juridical form: a hugely important result that has accompanied and favoured the triumph of the capitalist organization of the world. Captivated by the force of such an outcome, we have ended up projecting the model of the Code, the basis of that tradition, not only – as was completely legitimate – onto the events subsequent to its formation, that is onto the history that it initiated, but also – which instead was quite misleading – onto those that preceded it, i.e. the real history of Roman law, as if the latter were nothing but its prelude, the anticipation of its realization.

That is how the shadow cast by the Justinian codification obscured the Roman jurists, hiding them for millennia. For too long, their history – which is, in its strongest sense, the actual history of Roman law – has never been told: and this omission, concealing a decisive point of our past, has removed from us a very part of ourselves. While the late medieval and especially modern tradition of Roman law, from the Bolognese masters to the German Pandectists, was developing right before our eyes – and left Europe with a legacy that is unique but whose appraisal has now definitively been made, and there is nothing more to add – the authentic Roman genealogy of that knowledge, so utilized and reworked, has remained a largely unexplored territory from which we still have much to learn.

Today, contemporary juridical thought must perform a crucial task: a leap beyond itself and its old confines to succeed in thinking and disciplining the reality emerging from the great transformation in the last decades of the twentieth century: to construct a legal system of the new global world worthy of the name. But this will be impossible without coming to terms completely – without lacunae – with our past, without first having written all of our history. In this sense, the function of present-day legal historians could be much more important than one might imagine; and it certainly does not consist – as some still insistently believe – in attempting to continue, in an ever more tired manner, a tradition that has now ceased forever. Rather it is to bring to light a part of the past that we had buried without knowing it: to understand it and finally – freer, because to understand is to change – to be able to look ahead.

3. Singularity and impersonality

In the twentieth century, each time some scholar of Roman law tried to deal with the ancient jurists in order to more carefully trace their characters and profiles, it was sooner or later objected that, although the effort was commendable, the history was impossible to recount. According to widespread opinion, two particular obstacles would have hindered it.

The first concerned the state of the texts. It was said that of the works of the ancient jurists, with the sole exception of Gaius, there remained only fragments – those making up the plan of the *Digesta*. Moreover, they were strongly altered by the intervention of the Justinian compilers, when not (according to more recent hypotheses, culminating in the reconstruction by Franz Wieacker)[4] already modified from the originals by the editors who had transcribed them after their first publication (especially by those who had worked between the second part of the third century and the first decades of the fourth).

Today this barrier seems anything but insurmountable. The use of a less destructive philology, less conditioned by classicist prejudices, has left us much more confident about the good preservation of the writings of Roman jurisprudence. After an unprejudiced examination, the great majority of what were thought to be Justinian, or even late antique ('post-classical', as was preferred at the time), interpolations and falsifications turned out to be non-existent, suspected merely on the grounds of very weak evidence, or of a priori *petitio principii*, based on ignorance of the writing styles of the jurists and the richness of their conceptual worlds. Not to mention that the more we carefully study the late antique legal culture, as we have begun to do for some time now, the more we discover that it had other objectives, perspectives and expressive means, that it was not a plan for the systematic rewriting of the works of the old masters.

As for the fragmentary condition of the texts, this is certainly an incontrovertible fact. Yet, we are now able to reconstruct even very complex intellectual histories starting from collections of documents far more incomplete than the ones we have for Roman legal thought: this is what occurs in the history of science, of philosophy, of religion, of material culture. It is sufficient to pose the right questions, using the appropriate tools.

---

[4] *Textstufen klassischer Juristen* (Göttingen 1960, reprint 1975).

The second objection raised against the study of the thinking of Roman jurists is much more insidious. Indeed, it leads us directly to the heart of the most important problem posed by this type of historiography.

According to a belief that was widely held in twentieth-century Roman studies, and which we can trace back to an intuition by Lorenzo Valla, and later to a line of studies from Savigny to Schulz,[5] the Roman jurists were intrinsically indistinguishable from one another; in other words, they were all 'fungible people', according to an expression by Savigny himself[6] which then remained exemplary of this position. The specificity of their intellectual work, let us say also the peculiarity of their science and its manner of developing in time, would have meant that those figures lost all definiteness. Their voices would overlap and merge into a single sound, in which it would be impossible to distinguish the contribution of each one: the choir would be their unique destiny.

There is some truth in this statement that cannot be ignored but rather valued if we wish to take a step forward.

The problem that it raises seems to me to be that of the authoriality of the texts of the Roman jurists as literary texts and of its particular condition. Clearly, this question evokes an even broader horizon: the authoriality (in general) of all ancient writing (and not only juridical writing), which, although changing in relation to the different eras and different literary genres, is very far from the modern one, to which we are long accustomed. Indeed, modern writing constitutes its own condition in very close relation to the birth of modern individualism – first Renaissance, then Cartesian and Enlightenment, up to its culmination in the construction of the bourgeois 'I': a form of conscience without

---

[5] L. Valla: in the preface to the third book of *Elegantiae*, in E. Garin (ed.), *Prosatori latini del Quattrocento* (Milano-Napoli 1952) 607-609; F.C. Savigny, *Vom Beruf unserer Zeit für Gesetzgebung und Rechtswissenschaft* (Heidelberg 1814, 1840³, reprint Hildesheim 1967) now also in H. Hattenhauer (ed.), *Thibaut und Savigny. Ihre programmatischen Schriften* (München 1973) 95 ff., and in J. Stern (ed.), *Thibaut und Savigny. Ein programmatischer Rechtsstreit auf Grund ihrer Schriften* (Berlin 1914, reprint Darmstadt 1959) 69 ff.: an Italian translation is in G. Marini (ed.), *Thibaut-Savigny, 'La polemica sulla codificazione'* (Napoli 1982) 87 ff.; F. Schulz, *History of Roman Legal Science* (Oxford 1946, 1953²) German translation *Geschichte der römischen Rechtswissenschaft* (Weimar 1961) Ital. transl., *Storia della giurisprudenza romana* (Firenze 1968).

[6] *Vom Beruf*, ed. Hattenhauer (n. 5) 189 (but see also 114), Ital. transl., 194 (and 110).

equal in the ancient world, which did not even know the word 'individual' (Aristotle says 'each one of us', the Romans *singulus* or *privus/privatus*, which have completely different meanings in terms of the constitution and recognition of subjectivity – and it is a point that carves out an abyss between ancient and modern).

In the texts of the Roman jurists – beyond differences which nonetheless should not be underestimated, with the change in eras and types of works – the singularity of the authors (hence, I will not say their 'individuality', but the condition of their authoriality as ancient writers) is constantly influenced, as if compressed, by the presence, in the very core of their work, of an irrepressible element of impersonality: the perception of which made Savigny speak, in an improper but shrewd way, of 'fungibility'. An inclination to the impersonal that had a precise explanation: it developed, I believe, from the common awareness of the jurists (or at least of the most important of them, the only ones for whom we have information) that they were participating, with their own intelligence, decision after decision, writing after writing, in the collective formation of a grand ontological architecture, a true metaphysical scheme, in which the social reality they faced – the living set of the 'private' relations of imperial Rome – was transcribed into a world of figures, proportions and abstract and quantifiable (however invisible) measures, provided with their own density and consistency, spectral but unquestionable (*res incorporales* in the language of Gaius, who revisited Seneca).[7] In other words, and in short: an inclination to the unveiling of the law as a form of being, inevitably reflected in what we might call the 'juridical state' of the human mind (I am reworking an expression of James Hillman).[8]

Yet, this was an ontology that developed a metaphysics very different from that which had dominated Greek philosophy from Parmenides to the Stoics: a metaphysics that hypostatized, transfiguring it into archetypes, social relationships rather than naturalistic elements or ethical and cognitive models, as in Greek thought; only relationships of the coexistence among men, observed from the point of view of their regulation. A knowledge of bare facts, pure experience of life, which became an ontological construction: a *phronesis* transformed into an

[7] Gai. 2.12; Sen. *ep.* 58.14. On this point in particular, see *Ius*^{2} (n. 1) 197 ff. [these pages are not present in the first edition, Torino 2005, and thus they are not included in the English translation *The Invention* (n. 1)].

[8] J. Hillman, *A Terrible Love of War* (London 2004, reprint 2005), 1: "the martial state of soul".

episteme; *prudentia* changed into *rationes iuris*. Thus, the Roman jurists discovered their theoretical vocation (according to a luminous intuition of Vico),[9] albeit concealing it in the shadow of a merely practical end.

However, the common awareness of an entire group that it was participating in the progressive creation of this grandiose design, accompanied by the sharing of a rigorous specialist vocabulary at the service of an increasingly technicalized and powerful conceptual apparatus – the transcription of the whole universe of private relations spread out under their gaze into a kind of ontological cartography of the sociality of the empire – inevitably ended up attenuating the authoriality of the single jurists, of any particular contribution, tempering the specificity of each impression the more the strictly practised specialism became demanding. In short, there was, in the work of those masters, truly something irreducibly anonymous, linked to the growth – which we could call choral-like – of the ontological structure of *ius* fortified by an almost endless series of cases, accumulated and conserved over time as an encyclopaedia (from the juridical perspective) of human sociality in its relationship with nature and with the production of wealth: whose function was not knowledge, but rules, the uninterrupted creation of norms, which no event could escape.

4. The authoriality of Roman jurists

Nevertheless, concealed under the thickness of this impersonal blanket – the collective knowledge of a group that acted as a very powerful regulating machine – the singularities endure, albeit at a level that we would not call deeper but more decentralized – muffled, and in part as if having changed colour, but preserved. In no intellectual tradition – ancient or modern – does the knowledge it elaborated manage to liberate itself from the historical specificities of its protagonists, which inevitably accompany its formation and growth. Roman juridical thought is no exception: it is only a matter of discovering the functioning of dialectics – which varies in relation to the circumstances and the subjects involved – between singularity and impersonality, between permanence and variability.

Thus, the authoriality of the jurists can finally emerge, dampened but

[9] 'Philosophi autem Romanorum ipsi erant iurisconsulti', as in chapter XI of *De nostri temporis studiorum ratione*, in G. Vico, *Opere*, I (ed. Gentile, Nicolini) (Bari 1914) 101.

not cancelled behind the shield of shared constructions and solutions: it is merely necessary to seek it and find it. And it does not emerge only in the open contrasts between the single persons – the so-called *ius controversum*. Often the latter shows only the most superficial side of the differences. Instead, it is better revealed in the network of connections linking the profile of each author to an environment, to a time, to a world and a circulation of ideas; to a general view of his duties and his role, and of those of the science he cultivates; to a peculiar relationship with political power: all elements that determine and condition even the most technical choices – their axis and their specific curvature, we might say – in a subtle but always decipherable interplay between knowledge merely received and new knowledge personally produced.

At this point, it is clear that rediscovering the jurists is not an exercise in intellectual archaeology, to trace a lost but all in all insignificant context. Instead, it is the only possible way to underline the historical importance of a set of disciplinary devices and the ontological apparatus underlying them, which otherwise were destined to appear – as they have often done and continue to do today in many respects – as structures outside of time, almost as if the social metaphysics that founded them was not – as it is – only the result of a historically determined cultural operation, but proved to be truly an archetypal system over and above history: a fallacy from which we have not yet completely escaped.

Certainly, modern Western law is based on concepts and categories that precede and go beyond modernity: but mistaking this fact for a tendentious projection of the juridical form as such onto the eternal and the absolute of an ahistorical necessity of a vaguely naturalistic flavour is a misunderstanding with catastrophic consequences, which unfortunately does not belong only to our past. Rediscovering the Roman jurists in all their concealed historicity – passing from the system they eventually constructed, highlighted by the architecture of the *Digesta*, to the genealogies that allowed its early development – is the most important way to avoid such a trap.

What is the origin of that character of the West that we call legal science, first singled out by Roman thought? What is the secret of its birth and the extraordinary duration of its syntax? Why was law constituted as a separate rationality, and what are the connections that, despite everything, bind it to the geography of the social powers that accompany it – the economy, technology and above all politics?

These questions, the basis of the historian's work, presume the passage of the interpreter from the plane of forms that seem to overwhelm and cancel history, to that of the forces that permitted their creation: because the historical transmutation of the forces does not coincide with the history of the forms, even if the two levels continuously refer to each other.

The Roman jurists had a vague but pervasive awareness of the exceptional nature of their work. The coherent dialogue that intertwines the one with the other through the centuries, which establishes the particular compactness of the historical temporality of their thought – no other ancient knowledge ever had anything comparable – with thousands of quotations (but in the whole of their writings there must have been many more) knotted along the thread of a single, interminable discourse; the continuous counterpoint between the cold abstractness of ontology and the burning concreteness of the case history perpetually evoked by them; the jealous defence of one's separate rationality, and at the same time the no less constant search for a direct relationship with politics: all this tells us about their awareness of being at the turning point of an entire civilization, the place in which power – the power of an empire that had unified the world – becomes order, rule, discipline; the flowing line that transforms force into consensus, and justifies it. The intersection where force becomes (can become) form, as I said before.

And it is exactly on these passages and on these intertwinements that today we must interrogate the Roman jurists: it is this lesson – and not others, older and worn out by use and time – that we wish to hear from them, and that we must discover in the impersonality of their knowledge, finally evaluated by the singularity of their persons. The genealogy of a type of equation between order and power which today is certainly outdated but which nonetheless continues to indicate a path: the search for a global rule whose legality opens up, on the one hand, onto the science underlying it and, on the other, onto the consensus that measures its efficacy and effectiveness.

And this – I believe – is the only way to restore to our studies the place they lost, and to return them to the centre of our present thinking.

This is what we are attempting to do.

Chapter 2

STORIES OF LEGAL DOGMAS, STORIES OF ROMAN JURISTS: AN UNCOMPLETED TRANSITION

Massimo Brutti

SUMMARY: 1. Continuity and abstractions. – 2. The history of jurists as 'external' history. – 3. Singularity denied. – 4. Individualizing studies. – 5. Fritz Schulz: autonomy and unity of *iurisprudentia.* – 6. The study on the jurists. – 7. The historiography on Roman legal thought at the end of the twentieth century.

1. Continuity and abstractions

Even today, following a tenacious habit, legal historians often represent the multiplicity of juridical forms by means of a set of concepts constituting a totality, a 'system'. The evolution of law is part of a unitary discourse, which links together disciplines, moments and places that are different and distant in time. The idea of a linear relation between past and present and of a continuity of fundamental juridical schemes, starting from Roman law, concerns especially the relationships between private individuals.

The juridical constitution of persons and the acts contributing to the economic circulation of goods are more or less consciously identified as the basis for an analogy between the ancient and modern experiences of law: for a reflection of images that lends potent legitimacy to the disciplines of today. If there is a distant past that confirms them, this means that they have a force able to go beyond their own time and project themselves into the future. Thus, Ulpian's *utilitas singulorum* is associated with the modern market system. [1]

A quietistic orientation prevails in the doctrines that share continuity. Anchored in tradition, they are incapable of problematically interpreting and conceiving the social rifts and conflicts in which they are participants.

The key concepts of the historiographic narrative are assumed to be

[1] Ulp. 1 *institutionum*, D. 1.1.1.2: ... *publicum ius est quod ad statum rei Romanae spectat, privatum quod ad singulorum utilitatem* ....

invariant: they are current categories of thought; they belong to the historical milieu of the authors and the theoretical currents that elaborate them, but they are constructed so as to corroborate a consistency with the past. Within the context of studies of Roman law, they become the reference points of every description. The *iurisprudentia* of the Romans, which is the point of origin of the tradition, is considered en masse, as the basis of subsequent developments. This was a very clear methodological approach in the nineteenth-century European-continental culture and its essential premises were derived from the preceding centuries, which saw the establishment of systematic visions of science starting from late humanism. I would mention, among other works in this direction, *De Systemate Iuris Romani* by Gottfried Wilhelm Leibniz (written between 1680 and 1682). The text already contains the constitutive traits of the systematic thinking that would develop with Pandectism: antinomies, dissonances, solutions that cannot be reduced to the dimension of regularity are set on the same plane as the errors committed by the *conditores iuris* and the interpreters.[2]

In roughly the same years, the work of Jean Domat concentrated, with a similar procedure, the content of the sources into *leges* arranged according to an order different from that of the Justinian compilation and selective with respect to the materials that make it up: an order de-

[2] See G.W. Leibniz, *De Systemate Iuris Romani* (published by G. Mollat, *Mittheilungen aus Leibnizens ungedrückten Schriften*, II edition [Leipzig 1893] esp. 103 f.), cited in L. Raggi, 'Storia esterna e storia interna del diritto', in BIDR 62.1 (1959) 199 ff., published again in Id., *Scritti* (Milano 1975) 73 ff. This work deals with the lines of systematic thinking within which the European-continental science traditionally constructed the 'internal history of law'. With this expression, Leibniz meant the study of normative contents, the very *substantia* of jurisprudence. Instead, to him the 'external history' coincided with the *adminicula*: it was the history of everything that did not participate directly in the juridical system, even though contributing to its formation. Cf. G.W. Leibniz, *Nova methodus discendae docendaeque iurisprudentiae ex artis didacticae principiis* (Frankfurt 1667), in *Variorum opuscula ad cultiorem jurisprudentiam adsequenda* (Pisis 1769) reproduced in Id., *Sämtliche Schrifte und Briefe, herausgegeben von der Preussischen Akademie der Wissenschaften*, VI, I (Darmstadt 1930) 259 ff.: ... *Historia externa ad Jurisprudentiam necessaria est: Historia Romana ad intelligendum Jus civile; Ecclesiastica ad intelligendum Jus Canonicum; Media ad intelligendum jus Feudale; Nostrorum temporum ad intelligendum Jus Publicum ...* The relationship between contemporary external history and *ius publicum*, which is – according to a statist view – the space within which private law is formed, should be underlined. In *De Systemate Iuris*, Leibniz related the juridical construction of *ius privatum* to Roman models, but its rationality depended on the novelty of the systematization, which placed the contents of this *ius* in a generally ahistorical position. It was the systematic juridical thought that defined the *regularia iuris*.

fined as 'natural', coinciding with 'written reason'.[3] Behind this convergence between the German and French thought were the treatises of the 'cultured' jurists, who had favoured the theme of *ius civile in artem redigere*, drafting systematic forms including the entire juridical phenomenology. Insisting on *ars iuris* and on *ratio* led to a weakening of the philological components.

The reconciliation between description of invariant structures and historical narrative is a problem that permeates the entire modern juridical culture. It would lead to the unifying perspectives (where system and history tended to become one) inspired, between the nineteenth and twentieth centuries, by conservative historicism and positivistic evolutionism. Perspectives that were often challenged, due to their misleading abstractness, and which nonetheless maintain the ability to fascinate.

The narrative of continuity is often referred to as 'history of dogmas', with a phrase borrowed from theological language, widely used in nineteenth-century German science and adopted in Italy.[4] In translat-

---

[3] See J. Domat, *Les Lois civiles dans leur ordre naturel* (Paris 1689-1694) edition *Oeuvres complètes de J. Domat* (in four volumes), edited by J. Remy (Paris 1835). In particular, *Traité des lois*, in *Oeuvres*, cit., tom. I, cap. XI, § 19, p. 42: "… Mais pour les lois naturelles, comme nous n'en avons le detail que dans les livres du droit romain, et qu'elles y sont avec peu d'ordre, et mêlées avec beaucoup d'autres qui ne sont ni naturelles, ni de notre usage, leur autorité s'y trouve affaiblie par ce mélange, qui fait que plusieurs on ne veulent ou ne savent pas discerner ce qui est sûrement just et naturel, de ce que la raison de notre usage ne reçoivent point …". And again § 24, p. 46, concerning the subtleties that must be rejected, even if they came from Roman law, "parce qui'il n'est reçu en France que comme la raison écrite, et que ces subtilités, blessant le droit naturel, blessent la raison …".

[4] See K.R. Hagenbach, *Lehrbuch der Dogmengeschichte* (Lepzig 1857); A. Von Harnack, *Lehrbuch der Dogmengeschichte*, 3 voll. (Freiburg 1886-1890): these are studies related to German Lutheranism. Here the historical dimension introduces a balance to the fixity of the theological system. In contrast, in the field of law, there is an inverse procedure that attributes an indisputable character to the concepts, as if they superimposed, upon the concrete forms of law, the construction of principles and ideas detached from reality but capable of governing it, from the height of its generality and abstractness: a kind of "overworld" (this is the name used by E. Paresce, *Dogmatica giuridica*, in *Enciclopedia del diritto*, XIII (Milano 1964) 681 ff., esp. 692, republished in Id., *La dinamica del diritto. Contributi ad una scienza del diritto* (Milano 1975) 7 ff.). The juxtaposition of the statements of law and the postulates of a positive religion had a strong influence on the jurists. Cf. in this regard C.A. Den Tex, *Encyclopaedie Jurisprudentiae* (Amsterdam 1839) 520 ff.: … *Dogmatum nomina, cum in theologia, tum in iuris disciplina, intelleguntur ipsa placita, quae iuncta integram doctrinam efficiunt.* The *doctrina integra* is equivalent to Savigny's totality, which I will discuss further on. See R. Orestano, *Introduzione allo studio del diritto romano* (Bologna 1987) 288; F. Galgano, *I dogmi nel diritto* (2008), in Id., *Dogmi e dogmatica nel diritto* (Padova 2010) 7 ff., esp. 11. The subject of the unquestionability and ahistoricity of dogmas (impermeable to any

ing passages from Leibniz's *Nova methodus*, Gustav Hugo used (in

---

discourse on the politics of law) is in R. Orestano, *Introduzione allo studio storico del diritto romano*, II edition (Torino 1961) rist. 1963, 244 f. (these pages are not reproduced in the strongly reworked text of the *Introduzione* published in 1987). In the opposite sense, it is necessary to remember the defence of the ordering and selective function of the abstractions termed 'dogmas' proposed by N. Luhmann, *Rechtssystem und Rechtsdogmatik* (Stuttgart 1974) Italian translation by A. Febbraio (Bologna 1978) 43 ff. The meaning that he gives to the term deriving from theological language is consistent systematic thought (above all see Savigny). Luhmann proceeds from the widespread thinking that considers to be arbitrary the legal propositions distanced from criticism and assumed to be incontrovertible, but he upends this point of view, affirming the necessity of a legal science detached from the norms that attains a conceptual universe sure of its internal order. In his opinion, it is only through abstractions that an autonomy of interpretation is attained: "According to the usual way of interpreting the concept of dogmatics, the most important characteristic of this concept is the prohibition of denial, the non-deniability of the starting points of the argumentative chains. These starting points are distanced from criticism ... Instead, sociologists well know that in social life there is nothing that is 'arbitrary per se' and they also know that all of human communication presupposes 'undeniable' elements. From the sociological perspective, the problem can thus be simply the following: 'At what level, to what degree of abstraction are the undeniable elements arranged when they are given the form of dogmatics? And on what socially introduced and established prohibitions of denial are these elements based?'... The positive function of dogmatics should reside in the fact that, through the manner of organizing the prohibitions of denials, the exploitation of texts and experiences is brought to the level of flexibility that is from time to time necessary" (transl. from the Italian text). Therefore, the jurist inflects the norms by means of dogmas. It is an image congenial to the primacy of science that has long characterized the German experience. For my part, I cannot fail to see an authoritarian influence in the 'prohibition of denial'. In my opinion, the starting points of argumentative chains cannot belie the principle of justification (which governs the theory of argumentation); they cannot rest on a command nor on a postulate distanced from discussion, but only on premises to be justified on the basis of reasonable statements and on a consensus, which may not even be unanimous and may occur within conflicting situations. What does it mean that prohibitions of denial are socially established? There seems to me a strong risk that dogmatics would result in a conformism of the science, in a single interpretation according to the dominant social mores (ideologies and interests). Finally, it is easy to see what distortion can be produced by dogmas, conceived thusly, when they become the framework and referent of the historical narrative. If – as I believe – the juridical concepts considered undeniable are the reflection of an ideological choice (the 'socially established prohibitions of denial'), there is an evident self-projection which derives from it and which precludes an individualizing historiography (even with respect to the present) able to focus on the conflicts or able to understand the discontinuities that distance the past from us. Further on I will show how the uses of the concept of dogmatics were originally related to systematic thinking and how this connection was present in the nineteenth century in Germany and in Italy. Yet, dogmatics would also have a broad use in the twentieth century. In this regard, I will mention the positions of Emilio Betti. They are theoretical developments all connected with the events of the study of Roman law. In this regard, see notes 46-47.

1791) the term *Dogmatik* as equivalent to *didactica*, while in 1814 Christian Gottfried Haubold related it to the notion of system.[5] My underlying hypothesis is that this scheme reflects and together determines the dominant historiographic method in the study of Roman law of the last two centuries, still capable today of influencing our studies.

Dogmas are linguistic propositions, or summary categories of linguistic propositions, linked to the idea of authority or to that of reason. They govern juridical narratives. They anchor them to an order that can be defined outside of and independently of the various historical situations. Singularities and possible innovations are all imagined within dogmas, moments of a development.[6] Therefore, the scope of the details and of the contradictory motivations behind the practice is cancelled or strongly attenuated.

The weakest synonym of dogmas is 'institutes': a term that has a central place in the discourse of Friedrich Carl von Savigny and of which I will shortly examine a few uses. The term seems to refer most closely to the being, to the reality of law, but in juridical discourse it translates – like dogmas – into propositions and into stable theoretical categories.

The vision of law separated from life and the consequent prevalence of the technical element over the political element are closely related to the reworking of normative materials of the ancient *ius*, dehistoricized and adapted to the present. Dogmatics was born civilistic, it revolved around subjective rights but soon surpassed the original confines and was adapted to public law. The repositioning took place within nineteenth-century constitutional thought. Once again, the science constructed a network of technical schemes, of which it preached truth (i.e. cognitive function), and which were such to assure a depoliticized representation of the state mechanisms.[7]

---

[5] Hugo's translation is in the journal Civilistische Magazin 1 (1791) 23 ff. I cited earlier (in note 2) Leibniz's *Nova methodus*. Also see C.G. Haubold, *Institutionum iuris romani privati historico-dogmaticarum lineamenta* (1814) (Lipsiae 1826) 16 ff., on the identification of *dogmatics* with *ordo systematicus*. Cf. Orestano, *Introduzione allo studio del diritto romano* (Bologna 1987) 283 ff., esp. 287 (it marks the first medieval and humanist juridical uses and then the connection with the historical study between the eighteenth and nineteenth centuries).

[6] The notion of 'development' ('Entwicklung') presupposes a referent, a subject: a logical set of mutually related categories that are the subjects of a historical movement; yet, it is never a movement that subverts the models of the past.

[7] I am thinking especially of C.F. Von Gerber, *Über öffentliche Rechte* (Tübingen 1852) 36 f., Italian translation, *Diritto pubblico*, ed. by P.L. Lucchini (Milano 1971) 34 f. (The book includes two translations: that of the 1852 version and that of a later work: *Grundzüge des deutschen Staatsrechts* [Dresden 1880]): "Zunächst

2. The history of jurists as 'external' history

Using some examples, I will summarize the doctrinal events revolving around the systematic visions of law and their impact on the description of the past. A synthesis is possible, and this does not seem arbitrary to me, because of the surprising insistence with which European juridical thought in the modern age has described the history of law as a sequence of abstract entities, overshadowing other possible forms of narrative.

All this emerged very clearly in the science (and the erudite memory) of the eighteenth century. The contents of jurisprudence were in the foreground, summarized in axioms,[8] while the history of their formation, i.e. the history of jurists and their works, was confined to the margins of theoretical discourse.

In this regard, I wish to recall – it is the first of my examples – a 1764 text by Daniel Nettelbladt explaining the separation and opposition between the world of rules and that of jurists.[9] The law, as a set of normative data, and jurisprudence, identified as the *auctores*, their biographies, their works, were the subject of different treatments. These treatments dealt with both the experiences from the Middle Ages to the eighteenth century, drawn without interruption, and the more remote relationship between *iura* and *prudentes* in the Roman world.

Nettelbladt's jusrationalist vision provided a theoretical framework destined to influence subsequent legal studies. He defined the history of jurisprudence as *historia litteraria iuridica*, part of a more general literary history. Its characteristic was an understanding of the *veritates singulares* of the jurists: empirical data concerning the authors, their

---

ist es das ganz Formelle, die juristische Construction, welche das Staatsrecht vom Privatrechte entlehnt. Die ganze Summe allgemeiner juristischer Begriffe, welche im Privatrechte in ihrer Einfachheit und ursprünglichen Reinheit zergliedert werden, braucht auch das Staatsrecht, und zwar in ganz gleicher Weise …". The passage reveals the debt to Pandectism. Also see P. Laband, *Das Staatsrecht des deutschen Reiches*, in *Handbuch des öffentlichen Rechts der Gegenwart* (Tübingen II.1, 1883) 20 (it theorizes the freeing of public law from politics and the logical unity of the concepts imposed with respect to rules). Enlightenment on this perspective and on the Gerber-Laband convergence comes from W. Wilhelm, *Metodologia giuridica nel secolo XIX*, ed. by P.L. Lucchini (translation of the German edition of 1958; Milano 1974) 143 ff.

[8] *Axiomata* is the word used, along with *theoremata*, by Heineccius. See further on, note 29.

[9] See D. Nettelbladt, *Initia historiae litterariae iuridicae universalis* (Halae Magdeburgicae 1764).

succession, the influences and disagreements that could be discerned.[10] Clear within Roman thinking was the differentiation between the *sectae* of the Principate (Sabinians and Proculians); their genesis consisted of the contrast, political as well as theoretical, between Labeo and Capito.[11] It was here, starting from the singular truths (in which the concept of biography appears), that the destinies of jurisprudence could be observed, while the discourse on law followed another path. Nettelbladt wrote:

> The history of jurisprudence is not to be confused with the history of rights and obligations constituted through positive laws; this, if it were not generally accepted that the history of laws is called the history of the law, could be defined properly as the history of the law, assumed, without any possibility of doubt, in the sense of moral faculty of behaving. In fact, this history does not concern the destinies of the discipline called jurisprudence, but rather the destinies of the rights and obligations constituted by means of positive and thus changeable laws, while it seeks its origins and recounts their events.[12]

Rights and obligations appear to be subject to change, and yet the German jurist considers them a unitary notion, the foundation of *historia iuris*: he establishes the main referent and the boundaries. The representation of private law revolves around the guiding idea of *facultas*

---

[10] Nettelbladt, *Initia historiae* (n. 9) 3 f., § 1: "... *Quae sub nomine* historiae litterariae iuridicae, *der juristischen gelehrten Historie, venit disciplina, est pars historiae litterariae, quae continet veritates singulares de iurisconsultis, iurisprudentiae positivae fatis et scriptis iuridicis* ...". Also the division to which the *Historia litteraria iuridica universalis* is subjected demonstrates the centrality of the information and studies concerning the jurists: "... *Historia litteraria iuridica universalis abit in tres partes, quae sunt Notitia Iurisconsultorum seu Biographia iuridica, die Kenntnis der Rechtsgelehrten; Historiae iurisprudentiae, die Geschichte der Rechtsgelehrtheit, et Notitia scriptorum iuridicorum, seu bibliographia iuridica, die Kenntnis der juristischen Schriften, juristische Bücherkunde. Illa circa Iurisconsultos seu auctores iuridicos; illa circa fata iurisprudentiae positivae; haec circa scripta iuridica versatur* ...".

[11] Nettelbladt, *Initia historiae* (n. 9) Tit. III, *De sectis inter Iurisconsultos*, 32 ff., §§ 39-43. Also see 49 ff., *De singulis iurisconsultis*, and §§ 66-93 on the Roman jurists.

[12] Nettelbladt, *Initia historiae* (n. 9) ... § 195: "... *Nec confundenda est historia iurisprudentiae cum historia iurium et obligationum per leges positivas constitutarum, quae, nisi receptum esset historiam legum dici historiam iuris, proprie historia iuris, nimirum pro facultate morali agendi sumti, dici posset. Haec historia enim non disciplinae eius, quae sub iurisprudentiae nomine venit, fata concernit, sed potius fata iurium et obligationum per leges positivas constitutarum, sicque mutabilium, dum inquirit in originem earum et quas subierunt vicissitudines recenset*". On this passage, see Raggi, *Storia esterna e storia interna* (n. 2) 87.

moralis agendi. Grotius's definition comes to mind, in which *ius* is understood as an immediate attribute of the person: *qualitas moralis*, whether an *obligatio* corresponds to it or whether it becomes a real right.[13] And it was Leibniz again, in 1667, who defined *ius* as *potentia moralis*, identifying the person as *subiectum qualitatis moralis*.[14]

These are the presuppositions of juridical knowledge based on subjective rights. The matter of *ius* is trapped in the mesh of individualism. The spheres of freedom of private subjects derive from nature or from reason before being recognized by statutory laws.

Nettelbladt dealt with laws as regulators of rights and of their practice, thus guarantors of appropriation and exchange between formally equal subjects; but he excluded from the systematic treatment the study of jurists, the singularity of their lives and their works.

The same separation between literary history and juridical discourse was the basis of a collective volume introduced by Johann Gottlieb Heineccius[15] and published in 1735. The *historia iuris* under discussion was in reality only external history (based on the Leibnizian approach) or history of *iurisprudentia* (according to the taxonomy that would be established by Nettelbladt). In the foreground were reflections on the long fragment of the second book of the *Digesta*, drawn, according to the *inscriptio*, from Pomponius's *liber singularis enchiridii*.[16]

This is a humanistic theme, as shown by the essay by Cujacius[17] and as we can see in a similar article by Zasius.[18] The volume consists of various contributions, including one by Heineccius himself (an author

---

[13] Hugonis Grotij (H. Van Groot), *De iure belli ac pacis libri tres* (1625), edition Amstaeledami 1735, I, 1, 4.

[14] Leibniz, *Nova Methodus* (n. 2) II, 15 ff.

[15] Born in 1681, died in 1741. The German surname is Heinecke.

[16] *Opuscula ad historiam iuris et maxime ad Pomponii Enchiridion illustrandum pertinentia collegit I. L. Uhlius. Praefationem praemisit Io. Gottl. Heineccius*, Halae 1735.

[17] At the beginning of the volume: Iacobi Cuiacii (J. Cujas), *Commentarius ad Pomponii L. 2 D. de origine iuris*, in *Opuscula ad historiam iuris* (n. 16) 1 ff.

[18] See Ulrici Zasii (U. Zaesy), *In legem secundam ff. de origine iuris (D. 1, 2, 2)*, in Id., *Opera Omnia*, Lugduni 1550, coll. 270 ff. A first version of this text is in Id., *Lucubrationes, aliquot sane quam elegantes nec minus eruditae …*, Basileae 1518. Zasius was born in 1461 and died in 1535. Cf. C. Ghisalberti, 'Il commentario dello Zasio al Dig. 1, 2, 2', La parola del passato 107 (1966) 81 ff. Zasius highlights the *dissentiones* amongst the jurists (an aspect that would be dealt with by Nettelbladt). He gathers information from various sources for each of the persons examined. On the different *sectae* he observes: "… Ex quodam naturae nixu fit ut homines facile dissentiant …" (see *In legem secundam*, cit., col. 352). The tendency to arguments becomes *morbus litterarius* (*ibidem*, col. 355). On the contrast between Labeo and Capito, he prefers the former.

whose works would circulate widely until the mid-nineteenth century). The common historiographic picture concerns the Roman jurists, roughly following the method of *successio prudentium* according to Pomponius.

Heineccius outlined the idea of a reconstruction of Pomponius's work based on the partial sources available.[19] This was a project based on the philological instances of humanism. Along the same lines, Cornelius van Bynkershoek[20] passed from *Enchiridion* and focused on Labeo's *qualitas ingenii* (with a notation that we could call individualizing), underlining the connection between the innovative doctrines of the jurist and his erudition in fields different from *scientia iuris*.[21]

---

[19] See Heineccius's *Praefatio* to the *Opuscula ad historiam iuris* (n. 16) I ff., in particular XIX f. It reports the *civitatis leges earumque rationes* as a subject of juridical study. Fundamental operations are *definire, partiri, discernere*. He continues: "*... Haec sane ita cadunt in iurisperitum, ut si absint, ille iurisperitus esse desinat, et nomen hoc in se praeclarum ac venerabile non sine dedecore ferat. Itaque non vagamur extra oleas, si quos profectus in his studiis fecerit Pomponius, diligenter dispiciemus. Quemadmodum enim, qui in diffractam aliquam et suis membris mutilatam statuam incidunt, quamvis ex totius operis contemplatione illius pulchritudinem multo facilius esse perspecturi, tamen ex partibus, quibus tempus pepercit, de totius simulacri praestantia non infeliciter iudicant: ita et nobis, quibus per fatorum iniquitatem non nisi particulae quaedam ac fragmenta operum Pomponii supersunt, vel ex iis de eius ingenio et doctrina iudicare, et, quod in proverbio est, ex ungue leonem aestimare licebit*". The metaphor of the statue, whose physiognomy must be uncovered, means to think of the work of the jurist, to appreciate its ingenuity, the doctrine according to a truly individual dimension. In a broad synthetic juridical dissertation, which follows the order of the Justinian institutes (with a very wide use of historical notations), Heineccius deals with the theme of *interpretatio* by focusing on the dissident jurists: the individualities that create the movement of law. Cf.: Jo. Gottlieb Heineccii, *Antiquitatum Romanarum Jurisprudentiam Illustrantium Syntagma secundum ordinem Institutionum Justiniani digestum* (1719; IX edition Napoli 1764) (in two volumes), lib. I, tit. II, §§ 24-36, p. 117 ff. In this regard, I would point out that the theme of *ius controversum* continues to be present in the romanistic tradition. See Nicolai Vigelii (N. Weigel), *Methodus iuris controversi in quinque libros distincta*, Basileae 1579; and still S. Cocceius (Samuel Von Cocceji), *Jus civile controversum, Ubi illustriores Juris controversiae breviter et succincte deciduntur, difficiliores materiae explicantur, objectiones solide solvuntur, et Legum dissensus nova saepe ratione, ubi hactenus satisfactum non videtur, conciliantur* (I edition 1713, IV edition, Francofurti et Lipsiae 1779). I observe that, while Vigelius's work on the same topic proposed a very clear method for jurisprudential discussion, here there returns the goal (already programmatically stated by Justinian) of the conciliation of contrasts. Thus, the attention to pluralism is sacrificed.

[20] 1673-1743. He was a lawyer and magistrate. Information in Orestano, *Introduzione* (n. 5) 82.

[21] C. Van Bynkershoek, *Praetermissa*, in *Opuscula ad historiam iuris* (n. 16) 33 ff. and 151.

In a recent article, Jean-Luis Ferrary highlighted how the first palingenetic approaches to texts by Roman jurists date to the sixteenth century: to the same years in which Cujacius and Zasius were writing.[22] He first recalled the studies by François Bauduin on Cato Licinianus and the Mucians,[23] and then the *Index legum* by Jacques Labitte, the *Commentum* by Cujacius on the fragments by Africanus. Later (in the seventeenth century) were the writings of Jacques Godefroy, and in the early eighteenth century by Everard Otto, on Servius, Alfenus and Papinian, and by Abraham Wieling on *iurisprudentia restituta*.[24]

Eighteenth-century culture knew a wide-ranging palingenetic work written by Karl Ferdinand Hommel (an author to whom Nettelbladt attributed great merit).[25] Nevertheless, considering this literary production as a whole, it must be observed that it remained on the periphery of the science of law. This was appreciated by Christof Adam Rupert: "*... Super est historia prudentum, quam describere quidam agressi sunt, sed parce ac timide*".[26] It is a field of study that has not spread and does not influence the true scientific construction aimed at rethinking and updating the material of Roman origin.

Nettelbladt perfectly captured the distance separating the philological approach from the systematic one (a potential divergence was already lurking in the humanistic union between *ars iuris* and philology)[27] and explained it based on the opposition between the 'singular truths' related to jurists and the vicissitudes of subjective rights.

Thus, the two planes were rather distinct also in Heineccius. Studies on jurists (we can recall *De Salvio Iuliano, iurisconsultorum sua aetate*

---

[22] See J.-L. Ferrary, 'La palingénésie dans les travaux des juristes jusqu'à Lenel', in D. Mantovani, A. Padoa Schioppa (eds.), *Interpretare il Digesto. Storia e metodi* (Pavia 2014) 535 ff.

[23] F. Balduini (Bauduin), *Cato sive commentarium ad regulam Catonianam* (Argentorati 1555); Id., *Commentarius de iurisprudentia Muciana* (Basileae 1558).

[24] Citations of each of these works, which contain plans or examples of textual restitution or comments on the texts, are in Ferrary, 'La palingénésie' (n. 22) 538 ff.

[25] See in particular the *Praefatio* in Nettelbladt, *Initia historiae* (n. 9). Published three years later was the palingenetic work by K.F. Hommel (1722-1781), *Palingenesia librorum iuris veterum, sive Pandectarum loca integra ad modum indicis Labitti et Wielingi oculis exposita et ab esemplari Taurellii Fiorentino accuratissime descripta*, 3 voll., Lipsiae 1767-68.

[26] Christophori Adami Ruperti, *In Enchiridion Pomponii ICti De origine iuris Animadversiones*, in *Opuscula ad historiam iuris* (n. 16) 33 ff. and 151.

[27] See Orestano, *Introduzione* (n. 5) 153 ff.; 582 ff.; 606 ff.

coryphaeo)[28] remained on the margins. Yet, he clearly changed his tune when he described the subject of the science in his *Elementa iuris civilis secundum ordinem institutionum* and spoke of *systema iuris*, consisting of *definitiones*, *axiomata*, *theoremata*.[29] It is the same epistemological approach that we will find in Savigny. The conceptual order is based on a consequential and uniform method that the good jurist adopts. Mathematics is evoked as something divine (*divinae et sublimiores mathematum disciplinae*): it is the premise of a conceptual similarity between axioms and dogmas.

3. Singularity denied

The theme of jurisprudence, which eighteenth-century elaborations had placed in parentheses, took on a new centrality with Savigny's writings of 1814-15, from which the German Historical School arose. It now assumed a different meaning. The particular truths of jurists disappeared. The dichotomy between the system and individual elaborations was abandoned, since the latter were contained within a historical totality centred upon the unity between past and present, which does not allow any internal pluralism. It was a model of the science, which Savigny contrasted with the design of a unitary civil code for the German states, supported by Anton Friedrich Justus Thibaut. The science, anchored in Roman law, must provide the principles, the conceptual models that order the existing normative data and orient their interpretation. The doctrine is linked to the past: there where it constructs a law for the present there is no room for philology, which if anything can function as an external aid in understanding the ancient texts.

---

[28] Halle 1733.

[29] J.G. Heineccii, *Elementa juris civilis secundum ordinem institutionum* (1727), new edition, Venetiis 1797, 6 ff.: "… *Omnium sane scientiarum ratio in principiorum intelligentia, et conclusionum cum iis cohaerentia posita est: et quemadmodum, qui divinas illas et sublimiores mathematum disciplinas tradunt, non iubent auditores aliquot millena problemata ediscere: sed definitiones, axiomata, theoremata illa inculcant et demonstrant, quibus perspectis ipsi facultatem quaevis problemata promte solvendi consequantur … Eam ego Jurisconsulti laudem puto maximam, si ita percepta habeat artis suae praecepta, ut iurium singulorum rationes et principia intelligat, eaque in promtu habeat axiomata, ex quibus quaestiones omnes enodare possit, ut, obveniente bella aliqua specie, non opus ei sit, responsum ex Bartoli cortina petere*". The science based on the system (the term occurs several times in these pages and the sentences I have cited explain its meaning) is conceived in opposition to the style of the medieval jurists: to Bartolism and to the *horridum dicendi genus* of the glossators (*ibidem*, 10).

Outlining a manifesto of the historical school, Savigny rejected the French models and the legislative innovations related to the Enlightenment idea of code. Unification of the local laws in Germany and the production of common rules must be based on existing ones and on tradition (in which *usus modernus pandectarum* carries weight).[30]

A surprising self-projection intervened at this point. The conservative formula found a legitimizing reason in the imitation of Roman jurisprudence.

---

[30] Cf. F.C. von Savigny, *Vom Beruf unsrer Zeit für Gesetzgebung und Rechtswissenschaft* (Heidelberg 1814, II edition Heidelberg 1828, III edition Heidelberg 1840) now in J. Von Stern (Hrsg. und eingel.), *Thibaut und Savigny. Ein programmatischer Rechtsstreit auf Grund ihrer Schriften* (Berlin 1914, reprinted Darmstadt 1959); Italian translation G. Marini (ed.); A.F.J. Thibaut, F.C. von Savigny, *La polemica sulla codificazione* (Napoli 1982) 99 f., in which the "organic connection between the law and the essence and character of the people" is identified (transl. from the Italian text). Immediately afterwards there is: "the true seat of the law is the shared conscience of the people"; it is an aspect of life, a 'political element' and contemporaneously a 'technical element'. The special function of the technical element opens a path to the assumption of a systematics deriving from jusrationalism, which with incisive adaptations is referred to the practice of juridical relations and acquires historical importance. On this background, a model of law created by science is advanced, as it is in the "connection between common law and local rights" in force in most of the German-speaking regions (p. 164). See also p. 122: "A dual aptitude is indispensable to the jurist: he must possess a historical sense to clearly understand what is peculiar to each age and each form of law, and a systematic mind to consider each concept and each principle in its deep relationship and interaction with the whole, that is, in the single real and natural context". These words are revealing: in pointing out a one-to-one relationship between historical identification and systematic framework, they end up identifying the system as an essential form of knowledge. The same perspective is seen in the editorial with which Savigny introduced the first issue of a new journal in 1815, promoted to give voice and provide original contributions to the 'historical school'. Cf. F.C von Savigny, 'Ueber den Zweck dieser Zeitschrift', in Zeitschrift für geschichtliche Rechtswissenschaft 1 (1815) 1 ff., now Id., *Vermischte Schriften* (Berlin 1850) I, 105 ff.: "The historical school believes that the juridical material is provided by the nation's entire past, albeit not by arbitrariness, such that it could be of one kind or another at random, but rather that it derives from the most intimate essence of the nation itself and from its history. The thinking of each age should, however, be focused on discovering this material produced by an intimate need, on rejuvenating it and on keeping it alive. In contrast, the non-historical school believes that the law is produced at all times by the people who have legislative power, in a manner completely independent of the law of the past and according to what is considered best at the present moment. Therefore, this school can explain the fact that all of the law is not, in every moment, renewed and organized in a manner completely different from the previous time only by the inertia of the legislator in the correct exercise of his office or because he, purely by chance, has retained as true the legal conceptions of the previous time".

> It was said above that in our science success depends on the patrimony of fundamental principles, and it is on this patrimony that the greatness of Roman jurists is founded. The concepts and principles of their science did not appear to them as products of their own arbitrariness, but instead were real beings whose existence and genealogy became known to them through long, intimate custom. Thus, their whole procedure acquires a certainty not found elsewhere if not in mathematics, and it can be said without exaggeration that they calculate (*rechnen*) with their concepts (transl. from the Italian text).[31]

These are words that would profoundly influence studies on Roman law, also present-day ones.

Here we see a dual idealization, corresponding to two historically convergent ways of understanding the science. On the one hand, it is considered a set of abstract determinations with which a type of calculation can be performed. On this point, Savigny followed in the footsteps of Leibniz.[32] *Rechnen* indicates calculation, deducing the discipline of cases from pre-established principles and rules, according to a procedure considered to be certain; and it contemporaneously designates enumeration, understanding. It is a verb used in reference to procedures for constructing the system.[33]

On the other hand, juridical concepts were considered data of reali-

---

[31] Thibaut, Savigny, *La polemica sulla codificazione* (n. 30) 110 f.

[32] Leibniz, *Nova methodus* (n. 2) Tom. II, 155 ff.; and cf. *Opera omnia*, edition Deutens, Genéve 1768, vol. IV, ep. 1, 254 and 257: "… *coeteroquin ego, digestorum opus vel potius auctorum quae excerpta sunt labore admiror, ne quidquam vidi, sive rationis acumen sive dicendi nervos species, quod magis accedat ad mathematicorum laudem. Mira est vis consequentiarum certatque ponderi subtilitas*". The praise is directed to the *auctores*, similar to mathematicians.

[33] An example given by Savigny in *Beruf* refers to the concept of calculation: "… In every triangle, … there are certain data from the ratio of which all other data are necessarily derived: for example, from two sides and the angle between them, the triangle is derived. Similarly, each part of our law possesses such elements, from which all others are given: we can call them the guiding principles (*wir können sie die leitenden Grundsätze nennen*). Bringing them to light and reconstructing, based on them, the internal relationship and the kind of affinity between all the concepts and juridical rules, is not only one of the most difficult tasks of our science, but it truly constitutes the element that confers the nature of scientificity on our work" (in Thibaut, Savigny, *La polemica sulla codificazione* [n. 30] 106 f; transl. from the Italian text). The metaphor of the triangle is valuable for an understanding of the jurist's intellectual activity. His first task is to extract the guiding principles of each part of the law. This identification or discovery makes use of historical study. In the principles, which the jurist reveals, every other regulatory norm of concrete cases is implicit (and deducible by means of science).

ty. This ontological structure would be very clear in the *System of Modern Roman Law*: an exemplary work of construction of private law, all based on abstractions deriving from ancient thought and pervaded by the same restorative and quietist spirit animating the programmatic writings of 1814-15.[34]

Based on such premises, it is not difficult to conceive the schemes making up the legal order as dogmas: indisputable products. It would be the path followed by the Pandectists.

The method of calculation, a deductive method based on principles and their internal order, dominates *iurisprudentia*. It is not – continues Savigny in the *Beruf*

> the exclusive property of one or a few great authors, but rather the common heritage of all; whatever the difference in the degree of mastery of application, the method is always the same. Even if we possessed their complete writings, we would find much less individuality than in any other literature; all are working, so to speak, on the same great endeavour, hence we cannot entirely reject the idea that it is the basis of the compilation of the Pandects (transl. from the Italian text).

Now the ancient jurists are being idealized and considered as a single block; the individualities appear to be irrelevant. Indeed, they are 'fungible persons'; their knowledge is the archetype of systematic thought.

These pages constituted an example and a theoretical watershed. Viewed as a class and at the same time as a set of intellectual constructions affecting practice, *iurisprudentia* was the product of a separation of the technical element from the popular consciousness; it was the root and model of European science.

In the first volume of his *System* (1840), Savigny wrote that juridical interpretation, in addition to recalling the thought from which the law is derived, must always sufficiently consider, for each problem it deals with, "the idea of the entire set of historical and dogmatic relations".[35] The use of the concept of 'dogmatic relations', referring to notions and principles within the system, recalls the definitions by den Tex and by Haubold.[36] He thinks of the autonomous totality of law, which goes beyond the norms to be understood and whose systematic construction

---

[34] F.C. von Savigny, *System des heutigen Römischen Rechts*, Berlin 1840-49 (in eight volumes), Italian translation V. Scialoja, Torino 1886-96.

[35] Savigny, *System* (n. 34) I (1840) 215 ff. (transl. from the Italian text).

[36] See above, notes 4 and 5.

is the device and revelation. It is on this terrain that the concept of 'institutes' acquires significant meaning: organizations of the system, able to compose groups of rules and juridical relationships, and of which the historical development can be described:

> ... also the legal rule, like its integration into the law, has its deepest foundation in the intuition of *juridical institute*; and the organic nature of this is also manifested in the strong correlation of its constituent parts, as in its progressive development ....[37]

In the second half of the nineteenth century, romantic organicism would be mixed with positivistic representations. The institutes, whose evolution will be described, would increasingly resemble physical entities. The illusion of objectivity related to juridical concepts would leave a profound imprint on the ways of thinking about the history of law.

In 1857, not many years after Savigny's propositions mentioned above, Rudof von Jhering explained how dogmatics (for him synonymous with juridical knowledge) introduces abstractions into the historical narrative that transcend the empirical objects of the description and link the past to the present in a relationship of homogeneity and continuity. By means of such abstractions one can study the content of the works of Roman jurists and their law. Jhering meant above all abstractions not adhering to the sources, but constructed, invented today by the modern jurists, who conceptualize the work and history of ancient jurisprudence, capturing elements enclosed within the realities of the past, inferable from them but not expressed in the sources, indeed concealed from the conscious mind of the jurists who lived and worked in those times.

> As the scientist uses the fossil remains of an ancient era of the world, in that they make him aware of problems around which they do not immediately express anything; as often the smallest pieces provide him with the most important conclusions: a bone tells him about an entire animal, and a tooth teaches him the means of feeding to which the animal was destined; this is how things go also with regard to the remains of an era in the past history of law. Thus, if before – to put it in a paradoxical manner – it was customary to measure the value of expositions and historical-juridical discoveries based on their *adherence to the sources*, in the new approach the merits would, in contrast, be condi-

[37] Savigny, *System* (n. 34) I, 9 ff.: "... all the juridical institutes are connected in a system and they can be fully understood only in the great cohesion of this system, in which their organic nature is manifested" (transl. from the Italian text).

> tioned by *non-adherence to the sources*, and the most important future historical-juridical discoveries will consist of such principles and thoughts, which no Roman jurist has expressed. In this sense, one can also speak of a *productive* activity in the history of law ....

This is how what Jhering called dogmatics works. It discovers something that is beyond the sources and helps to interpret them according to an order alien to them; but by this way it does not misunderstand them, but rather fully comprehends their meaning, which can appear to today's observers.[38]

Thus, a complex theoretical apparatus established the approach which, after Savigny, would be defined as historical, evolutionary or historical-dogmatic. There is a trait of continuity to be mentioned with respect to jusrationalism: the vision of law constructed, using ancient materials, around the primacy and regulation of the spheres of freedom of private individuals[39] shifts philological study to the margins but does not exclude it. Indeed, with the interpolationist critique, we will witness the development of philological research suitable for systematic construction, capable of distinguishing two juridical structures, both endowed with internal consistency, the classical and the Justinian, corresponding to different developmental phases of the institutes.

All this presupposes a unitary image of jurisprudence. Yet, the renewal of philological studies, the interest in the social and political forms of antiquity, the increasing tendency between the nineteenth and twentieth centuries to promote historical works not directly aimed at dogmatic elaboration, provided – albeit slowly and amongst many contradictions – a framework that was richer and irreducible to the traditional images of so-called 'classic' law.

The history of jurisprudence that elaborated *ius* was no longer merely a history of concepts that spanned time (therefore ahistorical). It was progressively converted, first through isolated formulations and then

---

[38] R. Von Jhering, 'Unsere Aufgabe', in Jarbücher für die Dogmatik des heutig. röm. u. deutsch. Privatrecht 1 (1857) 1 ff. (transl.). The idea of a science that discovers a deep and non-explicit meaning in past history is already in F.C. von Savigny, 'Ueber den Zweck dieser Zeitschrift', 1 ff., ora in *Vermischte Schriften* (n. 30) I, 105 ff.: "... The historical school believes that the juridical material is provided by the nation's entire past, albeit not by arbitrariness, such that it could be of one kind or another at random, but rather that it derives from the most intimate essence of the nation itself and from its history. The thinking of each age should, however, be focused on discovering this material produced by an intimate need, on rejuvenating it and on keeping it alive. ..." (transl.).

[39] In this aspect, we see the permanence of the category 'subjective right'.

with more ambitious working hypotheses, into a history of the authors and their ideas: in a more precise and free account of discussions arising from cases, of particular normative solutions that succeeded one another and were often contrasted, in the broad horizon that went from the second century BCE to the first decades of the third century CE.

However, there was a limit, destined to persist until the present day. A literature on jurists that contradicted romantic and positivist organicism was certainly being formed; but it – although strengthened, as we shall see, during the second half of the twentieth century – failed to acquire a central place in the study of Roman law. The conviction that the singularity of the jurists was irrecoverable or substantially of little importance for the description of law carried weight.

Also for these historiographic events I will limit myself to some examples.

4. Individualizing studies

In the context of late nineteenth-century studies on Roman law, Lenel's *Palingenesia*, published in 1889, marked a caesura: it was a qualitative leap forward in philological instrumentation and appeared in a phase of relative revival of research. It carefully considered the results achieved by the interpolationists, especially Eisele and Gradenwitz. The space for investigations of jurists was more ample than at the time of Hommel.

Lenel himself, in writings such as *Das Sabinussystem* in 1892 and *Afrikans Quästionen* some decades later, proposed an individualizing approach to the single jurisprudential works. Among the books before and after *Palingenesia* expressing this tendency, we can recall above all the volume by Hermann Fitting, *Alter und Folge der Schriften römischer Juristen* published in 1860, whose second edition appeared in 1908, and also H. Buhl, *Salvius Iulianus*, 1886, and W. Kalb, *Roms Juristen, nach ihre Sprache dargestellt*, 1890.

Along with these I would place *Papiniano* by Emilio Costa (1894), which is a useful read even today.[40] The breadth of biographical references, the examination of the work, the comparison with other *condito-*

---

[40] Cf. H. Buhl, *Salvius Iulianus* (Heidelberg 1886) (critically reviewed by Ferrini, in AG 1887); H. Fitting, *Alter und Folge der Schriften Römischer Juristen von Hadrian bis Alexander* (Basel 1860; also see the II edition, Halle 1908); W. Kalb, *Das Juristenlatein. Versuch einer Charakteristik auf Grundlagen der Digesten* (Nürnberg 1888; reprinted Aalen Scientia 1984). Also see E. Costa, *Papiniano. Studio di storia interna del diritto romano* (2 voll. Bologna 1894) I, 1 f.

res iuris provided the occasion to describe a historical period. Especially with respect to Iulianus, Costa marked a discontinuity, also related to the influence of elements extraneous to the Roman tradition, with the expansion of the empire:

> … Finally, Papinian marks the point at which, these fundamental organizations having been relaxed and dissolved because of the changed social and political conditions and the prevalence by now of lively and vigorous external influences, there arose also in the law the need for new configurations grounded in a new freedom of relations, and the detachment from the law, that determined on the classical Roman bases by Iulianus, was solemnly and stridently pronounced. The way delineated by Papinian, conforming to the needs of his time, was then continued by the jurisprudence of the following age, and finally by the Justinian jurisprudence … (transl.).

These notations indicated the force of the Oriental components, not external but internal to jurisprudence. It was an interpretation different from that of the interpolationists. The discontinuity was not postclassical or Justinian but emerged at the end of the second century.

Between 1885 and 1901, there were numerous writings on jurists by Contardo Ferrini, a scholar whose education was influenced by German authors such as Mommsen and Dernburg. His works revealed his closeness with Zachariae von Lingenthal (Byzantine law was a common interest) and Alfred Pernice, author of a vast treatise on Labeo (the first volume had been published in 1873).

Ferrini's orientation was averse to the extreme points of interpolationism, of which he recorded the diffusion.[41] He basically gave credit to the passages of the *Digesta*.[42] He examined individual works by illus-

---

[41] Cf. C. Ferrini, 'Atilicinus', in ZSS 7 (1886) 85 ff.; Id., 'De Iustiniani Institutionum composizione coniectanea', in ZSS 11 (1890) 106 ff.; Id., 'Die juristischen Kenntnisse des Arnobius und des Lactantius', in ZSS 15 (1894) 343 ff.; Id., 'Ein unbekannter Codex rescriptus der Basiliken', in ZSS 17 (1896) 329 ff.; Id., 'Die processualische Consumption der 'actio de peculio'', in ZSS 21 (1900) 190 ff.; Id., 'Beiträge zur Kenntniss der sog. römischsyrischen Rechtsbuches', in ZSS 23 (1902) 101 ff.

[42] This caution guides his interpretation of the sources (placing him close to Lenel), although he is convinced of the influence of Greek and Oriental components in the compilation. Cf. C. Ferrini, *Pandette* (Milano 1900; II edition 1904, reprinted 1917) 4 f.: in the *Digesta*, "albeit amongst the many interpolations, the word of the mighty jurists of the classical age has been passed down to us" (transl.). This approach is in C. Ferrini, 'Saggi intorno ad alcuni giureconsulti romani (Fabio Mela – Plauzio – Q. Elio Tuberone)', in RIL 18 (1885) 865 ff.; 900 ff.; Id., 'Sesto Pedio', in RISG 1 (1886) 34 ff.; Id., 'Aulo Cascellio e i suoi responsi', in RIL 19

trious jurists or minor figures that presented original ideas. He looked at the peculiarity of the cases: this seemed to him the way – he wrote – to analyse juridical dogmas "in their function and in their development". But he was little influenced by dogmas. He concentrated on single turning points of jurisprudence; he renounced an overall view; he proceeded by small samples, along the margins of the classical sources included in the sixth-century compilation. What he wrote in 1890 on the use of texts other than that of Gaius in the elaboration of Justinian's *Institutiones* should be highlighted. He corrected Lenel, proposed a study on the nature and scope of Marcian's *Libri institutionum*. Yet, he limited himself to particular acute and rhapsodic notes.

Instead, the above-mentioned work on Labeo by Alfred Pernice, published between 1873 and 1895, was still linked to *Dogmengeschichte*. He overlaid the investigation of the biography and writings of the Augustan jurist with a reconstruction of the so-called 'classical' Roman institutes, which did not differ from the Pandectistic schemes, conceived as a device to be applied to the past, essential to translate Roman law into a current language.[43] The first scheme is 'das Rechtssubject', a key word central to systematics between the eighteenth and nineteenth centuries; the second is 'das Vermögen' (a Savignian notion covering rights

(1886) 395 ff.; Id., 'Viviano – Prisco Fulcinio', *ivi*, 735 ff.; Id., 'Atilicinus' (n. 41); Id., 'Ottaveno e le sue dottrine', in RIL 20 (1887) 332 ff.; Id., 'Sulla palingenesi delle Istituzioni di Marciano', in RAL 6 (1890) 326 ff.; Id., 'Intorno all'ordinamento dell'editto pretorio prima di Salvio Giuliano', in RIL 24 (1891) 560 ff.; Id., 'Intorno ai Digesti di Alfeno Varo', in BIDR 4 (1891) 1 ff.; Id., 'I libri ad Plautium di Paolo', in Memorie della R. Accademia di Sc. Lett. ed Arti di Modena 10 (1894) Sez. Scienze, 169 ff.; Id., 'I libri di Paolo ad Neratium', *ivi*, 295 ff.; Id., 'I commentarii di Ulpiano e di Paolo 'ad legem Iuliam et Papiam'', in RIL 34 (1901) 394 ff.; Id., 'I commentarii di Terenzio Clemente e di Gaio 'ad legem Iuliam et Papiam'', *ibidem*, 303 ff.; Id., 'Intorno alle Istituzioni di Marciano', *ibidem*, 736 ff.; Id., 'Sulle fonti delle Istituzioni di Giustiniano', in BIDR 13 (1901) 101 ff. All these works are in *Opere di Contardo Ferrini*, II (Milano 1929).

[43] See A. Pernice, *Labeo. Römisches Privatrecht im ersten Jahrhundert der Kaiserzeit. Alles Erschienene in 5 Teilen*, I. (Halle 1873-1895, reprinted Scientia Verlag Aalen 1963). After an *Introduction* on the personality and work of Labeo, the German professor's treatise assumes a systematic configuration. It goes beyond the specific work of the Augustan jurist and disregards the structure of his thought, of his writings. The three parts that make up the 1873 volume have the following titles: first, *Das Rechtssubject* (a key word and fundamental concept in systematics between the eighteenth and nineteenth centuries); second, *Das Vermögen* (this is a Savignian notion, which embraces the law of things and that of obligations); thirdly, *Die Rechtsgeschäfte* (juridical acts: another scheme typical of Pandectism). There is a clear propensity to establish a general theory nourished by jurisprudential materials. Later, the 1895 volume would be dedicated to *dolus malus* and *bona fides*.

on things and credits); the third is 'die Rechtsgeschäfte' (juridical negotiations: a category of eighteenth-century origin). Hence, the historical perspective was overtaken by the primacy of abstractions.[44] An attempt at a program, inspired by Ferrini's notes and some points of biographical history proposed by Pernice with regard to Labeo, can be found in a text by Ludwig Mitteis from 1917.[45] Starting from the 'Gaius prob-

---

[44] Hints of greater confidence in the novelties are found in a work of 1887 by Antonio Longo, a young lecturer in the History of Roman law, who then went on to study Administrative Law. Cf. A. Longo, "Titius Aristo'. Contributo alla storia della giurisprudenza romana nell'età traianea', in Antologia giuridica 2, fasc. 45 (Catania 1887). I quote from the extract, included in the library of V. Scialoja. The author, born in 1862, was twenty-five years old and was already a lecturer in the History of Roman law in Modena. See p. 1: "... Hence, a new and very vast horizon has been opened for today's scholar of Roman law, so that Roman juridical thought no longer consists in an anonymous collection of fragments tantamount to an equalization that excludes diversities, but rather in a large organic elaboration contributed to by many, very different jurists; so that by attributing to each one that which is his, one could appreciate the importance of the principles established in relation to the development of the legal institutes, the place that each one of them held, his intrinsic value as a jurist and as a writer ...". The individual contribution was defined in relation to the development of the institutes. This did not forget the traditional concept and was the weak point here. In reality, the history of the institutes was dominant in those years. Clear in this regard and related to positivistic evolutionism is the vision of V. Scialoja, *Diritto romano. Diritto successorio, Lezioni dettate nella R. Università di Roma*, anno scolastico 1886-1887, 24 ff.: "... It is a principle of philosophy of history, which can now be taken as a scientific fact, that institutes arise by way of so-called evolution from previous institutes; and that when a new institute has arisen by way of the previous institutes, it can also perfectly become the opposite of that from which it originated. Moreover, and this is true not only for the historical sciences but also for the natural sciences, since it is a very general datum of positive science, when a given effect occurs, this effect becomes in turn the cause of new effects, even when the cause that originated it has been destroyed ... Thus it is for the testamentary succession arising from the need to make a stranger a member of the family, when there is no son or nephew, so he will continue the existence of the family line. Hence, the will begins to be acknowledged in order to preserve the family succession; but soon it begins to live a life of its own and starts to become the means by which all the principles of individual freedom are infiltrated into the succession, until the head of the family comes to obtain the free disposition of his goods, and the principle of family succession comes to be killed ..." In this regard, see M. Brutti, *Vittorio Scialoja, Emilio Betti. Due visioni del diritto civile* (Torino 2013) (in the first part I tried to focus upon the historicism-evolutionism relationship, the organicistic metaphors and more in general the individualistic concept that inspires all of Scialoja's work).

[45] Salvatore Riccobono would promote the publication of this work in Italy. The program outlined in it seemed to him an antidote to the excesses of interpolationism. Cf. L. Mitteis, *Storia del diritto antico e studio del diritto romano* (1917), Italian translation in AUPA 12 (1929) 492 ff.

lem' and the contents of the Verona manuscript, he set a goal for future studies:

> Pernice's idea to write a *Labeo* was undoubtedly a good one, but the author became bogged down in the details.
> The important work of following the gradual rise of juridical concepts and their evolution from one generation to another, thereby demonstrating the individual activity of the single jurists, and thus to present a biographical juridical history of Roman antiquity, in the same way as individualities are recorded in the history of art, this task is still before us. (transl. from the Italian text).

This was an ambitious proposal (a prosopography of jurists), which for many years would remain unfulfilled.

Instead, the history of institutes prevailed in the study of Roman law. To trace out this history, concepts drawn from the Roman lexicon were added to the self-projection of modern schemes. They were also understood as substances, as "real beings": as Savigny called them. Moreover, his system consisted largely of conceptual schemes that had Roman names. Yet, when names are understood as referents of a development, of an evolutionary sequence, it is clear that we leave the precise narrative of ancient thought. An organism, as Scialoja would say, is constructed outside of it, an organism with its own identity (made up of concepts and guiding principles) and which in time undergoes variations and adaptations.

Therefore, in the illustration of Roman institutes, there is the same tendency to the production of schemes that do not coincide with those of jurisprudence but which refer to it; they do not summarize it and instead add something, as Jhering had highlighted. They are the result of tradition, the image of a conceptual order conceived in the present.

These were theoretical categories which, in the Italian science, were rigorously arranged in a plan by Emilio Betti.[46] If the classical Roman law cannot but be viewed in the light of tradition, of which it is the moment of origin, then it can also be linked to the current dogmas, since they are expressions of that tradition that unites us to antiquity: dogmas suitable to represent different eras, provided that – following

[46] Cf. E. Betti, 'Diritto romano e dogmatica odierna', in AG 99 (1928) 129 ff.; and in AG 100 (1928) 26 ff., now in Id., *Diritto Metodo Ermeneutica. Scritti scelti*, ed. by G. Crifò (Milano 1991) 59 ff. Cf. once again my *Vittorio Scialoja, Emilio Betti* (n. 44) 116 ff.

the Pandectistic style – they are formulated with a high degree of abstraction.[47]

In reality, Betti's theory is not far from the dominant historiographic practices of the twentieth century. It can be said that it expresses their basic orientation with an unusual awareness. Let us take the exegetical terrain constituted by what remains of the works of the ancient jurists. The models usually assumed as general referents (even if designated by Roman terms, for example *dominium*, *possessio*, *successiones*, *contractus*, *culpa*) are extracted from the discursive contexts of which they were a part and of the argumentative procedures with which the jurists made reference to them; they become something else. They overlap and replace the concrete establishment of normative solutions: they relate them to an architecture external to the cases on which Roman jurisprudential law was based.[48] The ancient lexicon is subtracted from the concrete dynamics of which it was a part and is used to designate categories whose particulars reveal the weight of tradition. The overlap is even more evident when the Roman terminology is abandoned and modern juridical notions are used directly, on the assumption that they were 'implied' in classical thought. Thus, hypostasis of concepts becomes easy, which – as far as Italian studies on Roman law are concerned – is a nineteenth-century inheritance: it derived from the Pandectistic style that replaced the French one after unification of Italy.[49]

---

[47] Betti criticizes the contents of the Pandectistic treatises (for example the 'dogma of will' in the theory of the juridical act) and not the forms of the conceptual production.

[48] An example, in late nineteenth-century literature, of theoretical construction taken from the context and the particularities of cases in Roman jurisprudential elaboration can be found in F. Gallo, *Synallagma e conventio nel contratto. Ricerca degli archetipi della categoria contrattuale e spunti per la revisione di impostazioni moderne. Corso di Diritto romano*, I (Torino 1992) 18 f. The author deals with the contributions of single Roman jurists in the field of contract law and draws something else from them: an archetype, a general category of the tradition: "... In the adopted perspective, there emerges in the field of contract law, the contributions of two very different jurists: Labeo, endowed with great genius and penetration, and Ulpian, a very skilled compiler with systematic ambitions. These jurists are responsible for the systems of greatest importance in this field within the above-mentioned tradition, from the Justinian age to the present day. It is no exaggeration to say that they represented, in this milieu, the guiding ideas, the archetypes of the contractual category. Still today they constitute, in our experience, the core of the conception and discipline of the contract" (transl.).

[49] A model for this widespread way of thinking is in V. Scialoja, *Negozi giuridici, Corso di diritto romano nella R. Università di Roma*, anno accademico 1892-93, raccolto

5. Fritz Schulz: autonomy and unity of *iurisprudentia*

I will now read a passage from Fritz Schulz's *History of Roman Legal Science*, first published in England in 1946 (the second edition is from 1953, the German edition from 1961). Despite the leap in time with respect to the writings of Mitteis, it almost seems that the author totally rejected his proposal. For Schulz, the refusal of the prosopographic approach had strong roots. He assumed, again in Savigny's footsteps, the image of a *iurisprudentia* without significant transformations and without marked individualities.

In 1946, he wrote:

> The task before us is clear. We must resolutely set aside purely biographical questions; we must concentrate on the history of the lawyer's art to the exclusion of the history of its individual exponents. The field of biography has already been harvested. The crop could not, from the nature of the case, be heavy; the personalities of the Roman jurists are hidden from us for good and all. The biographies of the individual jurists, with their fragmentary personal details and bare catalogues of works, must be left in the background and the first place must be given to their mistress, Roman legal science herself ... [50]

In 1934, he had written:

> One can gather linguistic peculiarities of this or that jurist, enumerate the doctrines that one or the other advanced; yet, all this does not alter the observation that there were no transformations in the method of Roman jurisprudence, that the legal language largely remained constant until the middle of the third century, that all in all the scientific individuality was little developed. [51]

---

dai dottori Mapei e Nannini, III ristampa, con *Prefazione* di S. Riccobono, 28 ff.: "... The general theory that we make juridical acts is not properly a Roman theory, in the sense that Roman jurists knew this theory as part of their legal science: instead it is a theory that was being formed from elements of Roman law by way of abstraction ..." (transl.). Scialoja accepts that this is an a priori construction. Yet, it cannot be said to be false. In short, the conceptualization draws upon a truth outside the historical datum.

[50] See F. Schulz, *History of Roman Legal Science* (Oxford 1946, II ed. 1953) 4; and Id., *Geschichte der römischen Rechtswissenschaft* (Weimar 1961, expanded edition), on which was based the Italian translation by G. Nocera, *Storia della giurisprudenza romana* (Firenze 1968) 12 f.

[51] F. Schulz, *Prinzipien des römischen Rechts* (Berlin 1934; Engl. transl. by M.

Roman law can still be represented in the forms fixed by the nineteenth-century science: this is the fundamental idea in Schulz's *Classical Roman Law* of 1951. In a page of this work, the author states that classical private law, i.e. formed with jurisprudence, "the true Roman private law", is "a uniform, original and quite unique system". He considers it "today still alive" and its history still open. And he states that he has entirely followed the "Pandecten-System": that of the German books.[52]

If we look closely, the fundamental concepts of Schulz's *History of Roman Legal Science* were not detached from the impersonal image of *scientia iuris*, defined in the *Prinzipien* and in *Classical Roman Law*. In this regard, he wrote:

> If we cannot among the classical jurists discover personalities of pronounced scientific originality, it is because none such existed. With this the tone of the classical discussions is in harmony … The atmosphere is one of strict and composed objectivity which, even at the cost of a certain monotony, eschews all verbal adornment. There is no attempt to be persuasive, no contentiousness, no advocacy. Legal witticisms, and strong and malicious criticisms such as even Aristotle at times indulged in, are excluded. It strikes us into surprise when Celsus occasionally describes another jurist's opinion as ridiculous. In their dealings with one another these great gentlemen did not stoop to polemics fit only for rhetoricians.[53]

Arnaldo Momigliano recalled Schulz's intolerance toward any historiographic contamination between rhetoric and *scientia iuris*.[54] As if – also in the study of the past – the purity of the law should be respected. Or better, the idea of purity that guides *iurisprudentia* and is its prerogative.

This is not merely a theoretical model; indeed, we are dealing with a description of real events. The "strict and composed objectivity" reflected by the science – according to Schulz – was a historical result of the aristocratic culture that surrounded the jurists. Yet, in his account – albeit precisely supported by an examination of the sources – I believe

Wolff, Oxford 1936; Italian translation, *I principii del diritto romano*, ed. by V. Arangio-Ruiz, Firenze 1949) 11 and 93 ff.

[52] F. Schulz, *Classical Roman Law* (Oxford 1951) 1 ff. Cf. M. Bretone, *Tecniche e ideologie dei giuristi romani*, II edizione (Napoli 1982, rist. 1984) 349 f.

[53] F. Schulz, *History* (n. 50) 125.

[54] Cf. AA.VV., *Le conseguenze del rinnovamento della storia dei diritti antichi*, in *La storia del diritto nel quadro delle scienze storiche. Atti I Congr. Società it. di storia del dir.*, Firenze 1966, 33 f.

that the idealization (completely modern) of jurisprudence is undeniable. To him, this appeared able to govern its practice, to give itself authority, to reproduce itself uniformly over time and thus to maintain its independence from political power.[55] It is the guardian of tradition and legality: a role often denied to jurists by twentieth-century politics.

I draw attention to the novelties and the results of the work. Despite his choice not to give significance to the biographies of the individual jurists, Schulz provided a key, original in the European debate of the mid-twentieth century, to explain the sequence of events of the law defined as classical and the development leading from it to Justinian's compilation. The chosen plan was the history of literature – by types and not by authors: hence, still an impersonal history.

He did not limit himself to duality, between the classical *ius Romanum* and the Justinian one, but posed a specific historiographic problem, different from the one with which the interpolationists troubled themselves. First of all, he wondered what are the meaning and the results of the post-classical versions, which handed down the jurisprudential texts and which subjected them to significant changes.

Responding to the question means opening a new field of research and investigating a series of textual events, which involve changes prior to the compilation. In the end, there remains a representation of the "classical juridical style", marked by the freedom of the science and the compactness of the method.

There are numerous examples. I will only mention the reading of Pomponius's *Enchiridion*, from which emerges a hypothesis of continuity between the republican and imperial jurisprudence, while *ius respondendi* was weakened.[56] Here is the significance of freedom and the importance attributed to the autonomous manifestation of *publice respondere*. Here is the prestige of the jurist related to the rigour of his intellectual work.

Or, one can cite, with reference to the Severan age, the diagnosis of the non-genuineness of Paulus's *libri decretorum*, which removed from

[55] Cf. M. Bretone, *Tecniche e ideologie* (n. 52) 333 ff. Also see AA.VV., *La giurisprudenza romana nella storiografia contemporanea. Testi di un seminario raccolti da A. Schiavone e A. Giorgio Cassandro*, Bari 1982 (although the seminar was in 1977); in particular, on Schulz's political positions (he belonged to German social democracy, was banned from teaching in the initial phase of Nazism, while jurists in the service of the regime increased in importance and degree), see the intervention in the seminar by G.G. Archi, 98 ff.

[56] F. Schulz, *History* (n. 50) 112 ff.

the scene a text of singular force, all within the work of the *consilium principis* and the controversies that pervaded it. Here Paulus's role seems to emerge clearly before our eyes, but we are dealing with a neutralized source within Schulz's reconstruction,[57] precisely because the complexity of the variants appearing in it appear too little classical.

In short, the singularities were lost. The rewriting of the texts between the third and fourth centuries involved radical interventions to the original versions, such as to render – in his opinion – a realistic intellectual biography of the jurists virtually impossible.

Ultimately, we can see two distinct profiles in Schulz's approach. He rejected the individual dimension because of an ideological choice: he defined Roman jurisprudence as a collective entity, without strong internal differences: hence, in the footsteps of Savigny. He traced the sequence of events of this class and its doctrinal elaboration, anchoring them overall to the republican models. On the other hand, he considered the information necessary for the biographies irretrievable due to the vicissitudes of the texts (in the context of the transformations between the third and fourth centuries). Hence, the meaning of each one's contributions was lost.

Schulz's treatise would be widely used in European historiography. Clear and rich in contributions to knowledge of the *prudentes*, it would long be the subject of debates and the basis of new investigations. As I tried to demonstrate elsewhere, Schulz would influence Vincenzo Arangio-Ruiz, and the contacts with Mario Lauria[58] and the convergences with Siro Solazzi, both professors in Naples, are well known. Then there is the influence on Giovanni Pugliese (regarding the isolation of jurisprudence) and Mario Talamanca (the propensity to underline the aristocratic atmosphere in which the jurists operated and the scepticism about the relations between Greek thought and *studium iuris*).[59]

6. The study on the jurists

After Schulz, I arrive at the examples of historiography that follow him and are closer to the present day. In many of the studies, we observe a

[57] *Ivi*, 154 ff.

[58] About whom, see the review of *Prinzipien* in SDHI 1 (1935) 219 ff.

[59] On Schulz's influence, and on the Italian authors who accepted his ideas, see M. Brutti, 'Costruzione giuridica e storiografia. Il diritto romano', in RISG n.s. 6 (2015) 55 ff., esp. 115 ff. and 121.

progressive detachment from the German Romanist: a shift in the research from jurisprudence as a literary apparatus to the role and choices of the single authors of normative formulations. At the same time, research on the jurists is intertwined with a theoretical rejection of the history of dogmas (or of institutes).

In 1952, a book was published in Germany which was, in many respects, the antithesis of that of Schulz: *Herkunft und soziale Stellung der römischen Juristen* by Wolfgang Kunkel.[60] The individualizing perspective and the prosopographic analysis were explicitly related to social history. Kunkel recalled the teaching of Matthias Gelzer[61] and Friedrich Münzer.[62] In those authors, there was an openness to sociology, albeit connected to an elitist theoretical vision, all considered not dissimilar to certain of Schulz's images of jurisprudence, especially the republican one (viewed as an admirable oligarchy).

However, Kunkel decisively opened the way for the historiographic rejection of the depictions of the *prudentes* as members of authoritative minorities, separate, by reason of their profession, from political dynamics: that is, committed to cultivating the autonomy of the jurist. Indeed, not even the pontifical college, in which he saw the roots of the *Rechtswissenschaft*, could be said to be separate; instead, it was part of social life, it exercised a political power. Thus, also the secularization and heterogeneous social composition of the legal experts, who would render judgements and write books, were phenomena of political importance. The republican jurists and those of the Principate would become participants in the powers governing the system or would oppose them.

I recall in particular the portrait that the author painted of Ulpian: the Syriac milieu of his education, the Hellenistic philosophical culture, the extraordinary influence he exerted on politics, on the 'Staatsführung'. Precisely because of the importance he assumed, outside of the world of books, the Severan jurist ended up assassinated during the conflicts within the imperial apparatus.[63]

However, the sociological approach to jurisprudence did not deal with the issue of relationships among the life, family roots, cultural contacts and

---

[60] Weimar 1952.

[61] M. Gelzer, *Die Nobilität der römischen Republik* (1912; II edition Stuttgart 1983).

[62] F. Münzer, *Römische Adelsparteien und Adelsfamilien* (Stuttgart 1920).

[63] Put to death in front of the emperor. See Kunkel, *Herkunft und soziale Stellung* (n. 60) 245 ff. More recently, see R.A. Bauman, 'The Death of Ulpian, the Irresistible Force and the Immovable Object', in ZSS 112 (1995) 385 ff.

political positions of the jurists and their work in the juridical experience. Examination of the resolution of controversial cases, of the writings, of the fragments of ideology that can be comprehended in them was lacking.

Instead, some authors, who also used the lesson of Kunkel, were moving in this direction (the jurisprudential contents next to the biographies). Some suggestions of this were already in John Crook's book on the *consilium principis*, three years later.[64] Mobile and informal colleges of jurists flanked the emperors: between them and the political power there was collaboration, confrontation, sometimes tension.

There followed *Gaius* by A.M. Honoré,[65] with a timely recognition of the works of the Antonine jurist and all the biographical notes that could be drawn from them. The same year saw a contribution on the Severan jurists.[66] A work by Schindler from 1957 (on the contrast between Iulianus and Celsus)[67] and above all the book by Elmar Bund on Iulianus's method[68] dealt, by means of an analytical approach free of dogmatic reminiscences, with the juridical literature of the second century.

The logical method that Gaius employed when he dealt in the *Institutiones* with the subject of obligations was analysed in a 1959 article by Riccardo Orestano.[69] The relationship that this author established with some dialectical procedures, whose outlines were repeatedly sketched in Roman thought, from Cicero to Quintilian, served to account for the particularity of Gaius's discourse. Not a definitive discourse, but a problematical one. *Species* and *genera* were relative categories, as they did not indicate ontologically fixed structures.[70] The realities they were

---

[64] J. Crook, *'Consilium principis'. Imperial councils and counsellors from Augustus to Diocletian* (Cambridge 1955).

[65] A.M. Honoré, *Gaius. A Biography* (Oxford 1962). The value of this jurist lies – according to Honoré (ibid., 127) – in his simplicity, which explains the fortune of the *Institutiones* in the late empire. They would constitute a barrier to Orientalization.

[66] T. Honoré, 'The Severan Lawyers. A Preliminary Survey', in SDHI 28 (1962) 162 ff.

[67] K.H. Schindler, 'Ein Streit zwischen Julian und Celsus. Zum Problem der überholenden Kausalität', in ZSS 74 (1957) 201 ff.

[68] E. Bund, *Untersuchungen zur Methode Julians* (Graz 1965). See, among other things, the attention that the author (21 ss and 190 f.) gives to the use of arguments that can be called authoritative, starting from consolidated acquisitions of *interpretatio prudentium.*

[69] R. Orestano, ''Obligationes' e dialettica', in Jus 10 (1959) 18 ff., now in Id., *Scritti*, with an interpretative note by A. Mantello (Napoli 1998) III, 1341 ff.

[70] Cf. R. Martini, ''Genus' e 'species' nel linguaggio gaiano', in *Synteleia V. Arangio-Ruiz*, I (Napoli 1964) 462 ff.

meant to describe were investigated on the basis of *topoi*. Rhetoric entered into the dialectical procedures.[71]

The common horizon is that of discussion. In Gaius's text there is an arrangement of arguments corresponding to the *rationales quaestiones* set by Hermagoras (the first of which is *coniectura*, based on the questions underlying the legal text, *sitne aliquid, unde ortum sit, quae id causa effecerit*).

Likewise, in the *Libri rerum cottidianarum*, the passage on obligations, which *aut ex contractu nascuntur aut ex maleficio aut proprio quodam iure ex variis causarum figuris*,[72] is attributed to the overlapping of two questions, included in the Hermagorean scheme of *coniectura*: that is, *unde ortum sit* and *quae id causa effecerit*. Orestano concluded:

> … the word *causae* from the phrase *ex variis causarum figuris* must be taken in the precise meaning it has in the question *quae id causa effecerit*, i.e. in the particular sense that this word has in *coniectura*. That here we are dealing with dialectical use seems to me to be confirmed by another statement, namely that also the term *figura*, with which we find combined the word *causa*, is typical, in many of its uses, of logical and dialectical language. (transl.)[73]

The reading of Gaius's text does not take for granted a reproduction of dialectical schemes. Rather, it presupposes an adaptation, within a discursive space that is not philosophical but responds to a practical and regulatory need.[74] The hypothesis according to which the master, often seen as a mere teacher of little or no originality, knows and uses *topoi* and the logical thought of his time is not easily accepted for the traditional fields of study. It is alternative to the isolation of the jurists, to the completely endogenous formalization of *ius*.

---

[71] One must keep in mind a book not specifically on Roman Law, which is theoretically important since it contrasts topical knowledge with axiomatic and deductive knowledge: the former appears to respond to the manner Roman jurists operated; the second emerges in the tradition of the studies in Roman law and is that found in the dogmatic proposals. See Th. Viehweg, *Topik und Jurisprudenz* (München 1953, Italian translation by G. Crifò, Milano 1962).

[72] D. 44.7.1pr.

[73] Orestano, 'Obligationes' (n. 69) 1355 f.

[74] The deviation and the differences between ancient juridical knowledge and philosophical currents are dealt with at several points, especially with regard to diairetic techniques, by M. Talamanca, in *La filosofia greca e il diritto romano*, II Roma 1977, 3 ff.

More clearly oriented toward the intellectual biography was the article by Paolo Frezza, *La cultura di Ulpiano.*[75] In some passages of the Severan jurist most oriented toward theory, there was a non-superficial contact with the Neoplatonic scholastic tradition, dominant in Syria at least since the time of Origen. And in the reference to the *vera, non simulata philosophia*, which the *sacerdotes iuris* cultivated, there was a claim to the formative function of the schools of law.[76]

Franz Horak's book on the history of theoretical forms can also be traced back to the *Entscheidungsbegründungen* of jurisprudence.[77] It analysed the particularity of the arguments and considered the literature on ancient rhetoric, also advancing hypotheses on the unspoken motivations of the judgements, perceived through analysis and comparison of the texts. The research shifted so decidedly from the normative contents to the procedures constituting the individual solutions and the framework of the juridical texts.

After this heterogeneous series of writings, a fixed point, a first collection motivated by the intention to carry out a complete survey of the jurists, appeared in a 1976 volume of the *Aufstieg und Niedergang der römischen Welt.*[78] I mention among others the work by Dieter Nörr on Pomponius, the expression of a point of view that had by now clearly surpassed Schulz and which on the one hand dealt with the relationship between the science of law and fields of knowledge external to it and on the other hand opened up to a consideration of the 'historical conscience' of the Roman jurists (what they thought of the future, what had passed, the impact of memory).

An example of research on the contributions of jurisprudence to the

---

[75] SDHI 34 (1968) 363 ff., now in Id., *Scritti*, ed. by F. Amarelli, E. Germino (Romae 2000) II, 645 ff. Also see P. Frezza, 'La persona di Ulpiano', in SDHI 49 (1983) 412 ff., now in *Scritti*, III, 527 ff. On a single controversial work by the Severan jurist, see B. Santalucia, *I 'libri opinionum' di Ulpiano*, 2 voll. (Milano 1971).

[76] Ulp. 1 *inst.*, D. 1.1.1.1.

[77] F. Horak, *Rationes decidendi. Entscheidungsbegründungen bei der älteren römischen Juristen bis Labeo* (Innsbruck 1969). See 1 f. and note 3, references to previous writings on the method of the jurists.

[78] II.15, herausg. von H. Temporini, W. Haase, Berlin-New York 1976. These are substantial contributions (W. Waldstein, B. Schmidlin, F. Casavola, J. Kodrebski, D. Liebs, R. Düll, H. Hausmaninger, E. Bund, A. Wacke, D. Noörr, G. Diósdi, V. Giuffré, C.A. Maschi, G. Crifò). In most cases, these studies go beyond jurisprudence, no longer thought of as a sort of logical-historical unity, and they explore the lives of the jurists, the relationships with the cultural and social milieu of which each was a part, the argumentative procedures they used.

imperial regulatory production, related to the practice rather than to the forms of knowledge, is in a book by Tony Honoré, whose first edition appeared in 1981.[79] The jurists appear as collaborators of the *principes*, but not yet subjected to the bureaucracy, up until the first decades of the third century CE; then their work is devoid of independent effect and they are absorbed in the apparatus of the absolute empire.

The dual approach – politics and theoretical elaboration – was the basis of the latest book by Tony Honoré on Ulpian, in which the dimension of this jurist's work, directed toward the provinces and the large population of subjects who had become *cives*, was related to the empirical meaning inherited from his predecessors. He made use of a centuries-old literary heritage, a network of relations between abstractions and cases, continually visible in the course of *iurisprudentia*. At the same time, he utilized philosophical cues deriving from Cicero and from Neoplatonic thought.[80]

[79] T. Honoré, *Emperors and Lawyers* (Oxford 1981, II edition 1994) in particular on the Principate and the centuries in which a relative autonomy of jurisprudence (expressed through literary activity) coexisted with collaboration with the imperial power, see 1-70. Cf. F. De Marini Avonzo, *Rec. a T. Honoré, Emperors and Lawyers* e Id., *Ulpian*, in IURA 33 (1982) 194 ff.: "Wishing to respect the republican legality, even if adapted to the new constitutional situation, the prince could not refuse to act as the praetor, whose function had been to conform the state of law with the notions of equity, justice and usefulness current in the ruling circles. This need gave rise to the new practice of assigning equestrian officials to archival research of jurisprudential precedents useful to guide the emperor in his decisions; with the increase in demand, the officials were charged with writing minutes to be submitted for the imperial signature ..." (transl.). The collaboration stemmed from the accordance to jurists of the role of guarantors of continuity. In this regard, Crook, *Consilium principis* (n. 64) 29 ("It may seem paradoxical that if continuity was the great contribution of the *amici* to the Empire, they should not have been organized into an official privy council ...") insists on the informality of the organization of the *amici principis*, who included jurists, and on the multiplicity of the experiences borne by them.

[80] See T. Honoré, *Ulpian. Pioneer of Human Rights* (Oxford 2002; a first edition, without the winning reference to *Human Rights*, was published in 1982). The part concerning "the cosmopolitan and egalitarian movement that culminated in the Antonine constitution" is not exempt from apologetic tones on the recognition of human dignity, within a context of which these pages underestimate the class-conscious structure and the tyrannical elements (ibid., 76 ff.). More historicizing is the chapter entitled *The Empirical Method*, 94 ff. On Ulpian's constitutional thinking, cf. V. Marotta, *Ulpiano e l'impero*, I (Napoli 2000; II, Napoli 2004).

7. The historiography on Roman legal thought at the end of the twentieth century

Some of the most significant contributions of Italian historiography, from the 1960s onward, dealt with the jurisprudence of the second century CE. First of all, the return to a crucial topic, Pomponius's *Enchiridion*. Its diachronic story and the genealogy of the *prudentes* were discussed by Mario Bretone (the first draft of this article was in 1965, later supplemented) and Franco Casavola (in 1976).[81]

Leaving behind Schulz's scepticism about the fragments known to us, the two authors analysed the theoretical and ideological features of the work. According to Bretone, Pomponius's theme was the juridical order in its historical continuity, in contrast to the unitary idea of the *iura* outlined by Gaius. The *ius respondendi ex auctoritate principis*, undervalued by Schulz, would indicate – in the commemoration of the Roman jurist – an alliance between the *princeps* and a part of the *prudentes*: political support for the *responsa*, which did not change the methods of their formation. Thus – Bretone argued – Pomponius understood imperial *beneficium* as a reinforcement of the autonomous value of *respondere* and of the science. Not a compression then. The *Enchiridion* excluded an authoritarian upheaval.

According to Casavola, Pomponius's model was marked by the advance – in the time of *civitas* and its growth – of a formal conception of the law. From self-organization of society to the norms to 'direct imperativity': in this, the diachrony of *ius* was resolved. Moreover, going beyond Pomponius, Casavola saw a common Hadrianic style, a cosmopolitan and moderate exercise, which appeared through *scientia iuris*. This referral of different juridical profiles to the figure and politics of a *princeps*, who had achieved stability and reforms, bridged the gap between external history and internal history, between normative data and affairs of the empire.

The jurists were read, studied, within a context which was no longer apriorism or the evolution of the institutes: both topics lucidly advanced by Scialoja as obligatory paths in the study of Roman law in the

[81] See M. Bretone, *Tecniche e ideologie* (n. 52) 209 ff. The book's seventh chapter, entitled *L'Enchiridion di Pomponio*, reproduces an article in Labeo 11 (1965) supplemented with observations made during the course *Linee dell'Enchiridion di Pomponio* (Bari 1965, II edition, Torino 1974); F. Casavola, *Cultura e scienza giuridica nel secondo secolo d.C. Il senso del passato*, in *Aufstieg und Niedergang* (n. 78) 131 ff., republished in Id., *Giuristi adrianei* (Napoli 1980) 1 ff. The book contains various other writings on the history of the jurists.

time of systematic thought. Now it was a matter of probing a history of social and cultural morphologies, with means of knowledge, with heuristic schemes more complex than those of traditional juridical exegesis, which usually drew abstractions from the texts and rendered them independent of the dimension of cases.

Casavola's objective was "to reconstruct the mentalization of the pre-juridical in the juridical": [82] in this sentence, we perceive the reflection of a scission, which instead historical investigation should resolve.

Bretone wrote:

> What the historian can no longer do, contrary to what Mitteis and Schulz believed, is to insist on continuity rather than on a gap. Comprehension of Roman jurisprudence, and of the law it (directly or indirectly) helped to produce, passes through criticism of the modern Roman law tradition. That jurisprudence ... moves in a precedent-problematical manner and uses argumentative and definitional techniques which, categorized differently *per se*, are all rather far from the axiomatic and conceptualistic-deductive procedure transmitted to modern legal science by late jusnaturalism; the law, advanced or formulated by jurisprudence, is in its most profound nature the sediment of a "professional routine" ... (transl.). [83]

In the writings of these two scholars (albeit very different), there were no longer dogmas to support the historical narrative, and through the years their language became free of any subordination to the old dominion of juridical abstractions outside of time. [84]

The early work of both scholars was flanked by Aldo Schiavone's first book, in 1971, *Studi sulle logiche dei giuristi romani*. His methodo-

---

[82] Casavola, *Giuristi adrianei* (n. 81) 104.

[83] Bretone, *Tecniche e ideologie* (n. 52) 350.

[84] Federico d'Ippolito, a participant in the Neapolitan cultural milieu, contributed to the history of the jurists with a series of studies with original ideas from the end of the 1970s, dealing among other things with the difficult reconstruction of the individual work of the more ancient *auctores*, of whom we know little. See F. d'Ippolito, *Ideologia e diritto in Cassio Longino* (Napoli 1969); Id., *I giuristi e la città* (Napoli 1978); Id., *Giuristi e sapienti in Roma arcaica* (Bari 1986); Id., *Sulla giurisprudenza mediorepubblicana* (Napoli 1988); Id., *Del fare il diritto nel mondo romano* (Torino 2000); Id., *Saggi di storia della storiografia romanistica* (Napoli 2009). See the intervention by d'Ippolito in the 1977 seminar, cited above in note 55, on the need to go beyond Schulz, researching the presence of events external to jurisprudence (which involves a convergence with the antiquists, similar to the one theorized by Momigliano).

logical intention was to consider the history of the discourses, the works, the arguments and the logical structures of the books dating to the *prudentes* and fragmented by the compilers as an alternative field with respect to the history of the institutes: precisely the one whose development and limits I mentioned earlier.

> The role that this book is intended to play within the problematical horizon of our historiography is to open up discussion, for which the time is ripe, on the history of the reasonings of the Roman jurists … (transl.).[85]

This involved a shift for studies on Roman law: from the legal order to the jurists. Yet, he made a critique of the articles and books devoted to this subject, which would also return at a later date. It is not enough to describe episodic aspects, ideas of intellectual biography or segments of thought attributable to the concept of ideology. Value choices cannot be separated from procedures of juridical qualification and regulation. The distinction between techniques and ideologies leads to the outlining of the general ideas of the authors, but without focusing upon the formation of the normative solutions and the notions within them.

The notion of *contractus*, already discussed in the first book, would be the central subject of his research: a recurring point for over thirty years. I will try to summarize the historical characteristics of the uses to which this conceptual and terminological scheme was put, with changing features. In some theoretical practices, it was an instrument to dictate the discipline of uncertain cases, of juridical problems not assimilable to *ius receptum*. In other contexts, it was the conceptualization of consolidated principles. It was an abstraction within the instruments to govern the cases; or it was a scheme that classified and defined. The origin of the classification was the work of Quintus Mucius, while Labeo introduced the word συνάλλαγμα in order to name situations not falling within the types.

In both fields of discourse, the reasonings had a material impact. In the books subsequent to that first work, the perspectives changed and became richer,[86] up to the volume *Ius. L'invenzione del diritto in Occi-*

---

[85] A. Schiavone, *Studi sulle logiche dei giuristi romani. 'Nova negotia' e 'transactio' da Labeone a Ulpiano* (Napoli 1971) 1 ff.

[86] See A. Schiavone, *Nascita della giurisprudenza. Cultura aristocratica e pensiero giuridico nella Roma tardorepubblicana* (Roma-Bari 1976); Id., *Giuristi e nobili nella*

dente published in 2005. In my opinion, the itinerary does not present radical differences. The common thread with the research carried out in the past consists in an analysis of the modalities and historical reasons for which the *ius* is considered a form disembodied from material relations, which it nonetheless requires and which it regulates. The *ius* is set within a theoretical sphere distinct from the cases. The connection between the single normative solutions seems to me – according to this view – paratactic. In each judgement, in each textual junction, there was a form that the jurist elaborated or discussed, which allowed him to pass from one case to another, to construct an equality of juridical treatment, even if abstract.[87]

Therefore, the logical structures, permeable and able to be compared with other knowledge, go far beyond the biographies. In the impulse to destructure the juridical discourses, there is perhaps in Schiavone an echo of the French philosophers. The decomposition of the plans used to construct the interpretation of a text, the search for novelties, for the ideal and theoretical turning points in the history of the texts, make one think of Althusser. This is seen in the second book, dedicated to Quintus Mucius Scaevola, in which the recourse to dialectics, within the *libri iuris civilis*, was seen as an "epistemological schism" in the fabric of republican knowledge.[88] According to the author, formalization of the *ius* began precisely from there.[89]

Bretone concluded a 1977 article on Schulz, pointing out the two aspects which, in his opinion, cannot be eliminated from studies on Roman law:

> To what extent can a historiographic sensibility directed at the 'institute' (in the broadest sense of the word), at the typical forms of action and of

Roma repubblicana (Roma-Bari 1987); Id., *Linee di storia del pensiero giuridico romano* (Torino 1994); Id., *The Invention of Law in the West* (Cambridge [Mass.]-London 2012).

[87] See the concept of *aequabilitas* in Cicero's oration *Pro Caecina*.

[88] Schiavone, *Nascita della giurisprudenza* (n. 86) 90 ff.

[89] On all these topics, on the rethinking of the Pomponian model, which leaves behind the same critical review by Schulz, already assimilated, see E. Stolfi, 'Il modello delle scuole in Pomponio e in Gaio', in SDHI 63 (1997) 1 ff.; Id., 'Per uno studio del lessico e delle tecniche di citazione dei giuristi severiani: le 'sententiae prudentium' nella scrittura di Papiniano, Paolo e Ulpiano', in Rivista di diritto romano 1 (2001) 345 ff. A theoretical reflection, in which there emerges the theme of processes of formalization of *ius*, is in the volume *Il diritto, la genealogia, la storia. Itinerari* (Bologna 2010).

occurrence and at their change over time, can take no interest in the single man, struggling with his own life, with his own destiny? (transl.).[90]

Two further questions arise from these words. What is the level of typicality and the itinerary through which the forms are defined within the historiographic work? And where does one seek, how does one suppose the individual life, given that the basic object of our studies is the scarce literature concerning law?

There is only one answer: return to the discourses of the jurists. I would mention the search for the singularity of the jurists according to the systematist Nettelbladt. While confining the lives and works of the authors in *historia litteraria*, he had emphasized the writings as a research subject. Well, each analysis of the biographies and intervention strategies of the jurists must, in practice, be based on the words contained in those writings. Here we discover, if possible, the individual footprints (the traces of life, the politics), here the concepts that give structure to the single juridical reasonings.

The historiography of Roman law in the age of jurisprudence, if it leaves dogmas, is translated into a molecular investigation of normative solutions, of the forms in which they are transmitted and discussed. I recall a 1948 article by a German Romanist which strongly influenced the Italian debate. The author was Andreas Schwarz and the subject was *ius controversum*.[91]

The syntagma *ius controversum*, invented by the orators, was given a broad acceptation, to describe the internal movement of jurisprudence. "We speak of controversial law when different points of view within a juridical order and on the same problem are in opposition" (transl. from the Italian text).[92] In the cases dealt with by the jurists, variety of

---

[90] Bretone, *Tecniche e ideologie* (n. 52) 353.

[91] See A. Schwarz, *Das strittige Recht der römischen Juristen*. The article appears in *Atti del Congresso Internazionale di Diritto Romano e di Storia del Diritto* (Verona, 27-29 September 1948; a revised and expanded version is found later in H. Niedermeyer, W. Flume (Hrsg.) *Festschrift F. Schulz*, Bd. II (Weimar 1951) 201 ff., from which I took the quotations (the *Atti* of Verona were edited by G. Moschetti [Milan 1953]). For the Italian translation, see A. Lovato (ed.), *Itinerari di lettura per un corso di diritto romano* (Bari 2011) 171 ff. Schwarz's writing influenced M. Bretone, "Ius controversum' nella giurisprudenza classica', in MAL serie IX, vol. XXIII, fasc. 3 (Roma 2008) 755 ff. Also see M. Brutti, 'Il dialogo tra giuristi e imperatori', in V. Marotta, E. Stolfi (eds.), *'Ius controversum' e processo fra tarda repubblica ed età dei Severi* (Roma 2012) 97 ff.

[92] These are Schwarz's initial words.

opinions was a normal and very frequent occurrence, as was the emergence of novel problems, outside of the commonly accepted normative orientations.

Using the concept of *ius controversum*, we place in the forefront the constant problematicalness of the *ius quod sine scripto venit compositum a prudentibus*: the law of experts, which arises outside of authoritative documents.[93] It is marked by an opening up to discussion and by the connection of every solution with the process.[94]

The lesson that can be learned – and I am convinced of its validity – is that the abstractions that the jurists used must all be perceived and measured within this problematical dimension. Otherwise they lose meaning. Their nature is intrinsically ideological, since they are bearers of choices exposed to contrast.

Therefore, problems and solutions, negations and confirmations. The *historia litteraria* describes their geography.

I will try to explain what this means, recalling a passage by Michel Foucault. In *The Archaeology of Knowledge*, he briefly defined what he called "analysis of the discursive field".[95] Well, Roman jurisprudence is this: a large 'discursive field', in which we look for sequences and correlations of individual normative statements. Foucault wrote: "... we must grasp the statement in the exact specificity of its occurrence; determine its conditions of existence, fix at least its limits, establish its correlations with the other statements that may be connected with it, and show what other forms of statement it excludes" (transl. from the Italian text). The normative statements of the Roman jurists – I would add – are composed in books, each with its own time and with a language that can refer to other languages. Personal biographies, however difficult and incomplete, help provide a glimpse of the authors. But the

---

[93] Pomp. *sing. enchir.*, D. 1.2.2.5.

[94] On the 'problematical consistency' in the jurists (to use a formula proposed by Viehweg in the above-mentioned book, note 71), and on the alternative to systematic thinking, which is manifested in the case dimension of jurisprudential work and in the use of abstractions useful for the reasonings in which they are formed (examples within a field of discussion) and which are not impermeable to the surrounding culture (for example, dialectics or rhetorical tools) but rather participate in it, cf. L. Raggi, *Il metodo della giurisprudenza romana*, corso 1967-68, in *Scritti*, Milano 1975, 165 ff., now reprinted with a preface by M. Campolunghi, S.-A. Fusco (Torino 2007): a work that still today retains its programmatic strength.

[95] M. Foucault, *L'archeologie du savoir* (Paris 1969, Italian translation, *L'archeologia del sapere. Una metodologia per la storia della cultura*, Milano 1971, reprinted 1997) 38 ff.

challenge is the molecular history of the jurisprudential contributions, piece by piece, book by book, and without generalizations or overlapping categories.

The concrete individuality from which we begin is that of the juridical writing. The metalanguage to be used will only be conventional and related to specific objects. An example: the summary determination of the conditions of feasibility of a means of judicial protection, according to the statements of one or other jurist, and the repetitions or related changes, from one opinion to another, from one book to another.

This research perspective, although entirely sensible and congenial to the purposes of our studies, is still largely to be explored. Therefore, the palingenetic work that is beginning today, starting from Lenel's approach and accompanied by an analytical re-evaluation of the works and fragments,[96] is – I believe – a very useful endeavour. The reasoned translation of the texts is the other goal. It can be used to perceive in the jurists the linguistic regularities, the anomalies and at times the breaks not concealed by the compilers. It is in the proper sense an interpretation, which is measured with the history of words and their combinations.

Thus, if we immerse ourselves in the materiality and singularity of the jurisprudential discourses, eliminating any apriorism, we make the paths of a new critical historiography clearer and more solid.

[96] Which is added to the foundation formed by Lenel and can induce corrections to it.

Chapter 3

'KUNSTGESCHICHTE' AND 'KÜNSTLERGESCHICHTE'. THE PROBLEM OF LITERARY GENRES IN THE ROMAN LEGAL LITERATURE

Emanuele Stolfi

SUMMARY: 1. An inescapable turning point: on Fritz Schulz's 'postulates'. – 2. Which biographies? – 3. Four other questions.

1. An inescapable turning point: on Fritz Schulz's 'postulates'

If – as Pasolini [1] wrote – discussions about books always come down to "descriptions of descriptions" (since each book is per se a description of something), my intervention could be considered, at least in its beginning, a description of third (or fourth) degree. Even in its title, it evokes the formulas that can be read in one of the studies with the greatest impact on research on Roman jurisprudence (I refer of course to Schulz's *History of Roman Legal Science*). [2] However, the methodological guideline that Schulz enunciated in the *Introduction* with those

[1] See P.P. Pasolini, *Descrizioni di descrizioni* (ed. by G. Chiarcossi) (Torino 1979) esp. 457 ("... 'descrizioni' di cosa? Di altre 'descrizioni', che altro i libri non sono ... Nella vita accadono dei fatti, i libri li descrivono: ma in quanto libri sono anch'essi dei fatti: e quindi possono essere anch'essi descritti: dalla critica".

[2] F. Schulz, *History of Roman Legal Science* (Oxford 1946) = *Geschichte der römischen Rechtswissenschaft* (Weimar 1961) = *Storia della giurisprudenza romana*, Italian translation (Firenze 1968). For an overview of the historiographical debates aroused by this work, see at least (and in the perspective that most interests us here) L. Lombardi, 'La nave di Teseo. A proposito della riedizione tedesca della Storia della giurisprudenza romana di F. Schulz', in AG 161 (1961) 55 ff.; *La giurisprudenza romana nella storiografia contemporanea. Testi di un seminario raccolti da Aldo Schiavone e Anna Giorgio Cassandro* (Bari 1982) (in which practically every relationship and intervention was based on a rediscussion of that book); L. Lantella, *Le opere della giurisprudenza romana nella storiografia* (Torino 1979) 125 ff. (which dealt with the 'systematic model' which in Schulz was outlined with regard to the writings of the Roman jurists); A. Mantello, *Per una storia della giurisprudenza romana. Il problema dei Miscelliones* (Milano 1985) 199 ff. Cf. also *infra*, note 4.

expressions – aimed at clearly favouring the perspective of 'Kunstgeschichte' over any reconstruction of 'Künstlergeschichte'[3] – drew, terminologically and conceptually, upon lines of thought extraneous to the historiography of Roman law scholarship: Winckelmann's lexicon and certain profiles of Croce's theory of history, recalled in two strategic quotations (one in the epigraph and the other in a concluding note of the *Introduction*), both absent in the *History* but (re-)introduced in the *Geschichte*, and upon which it will be necessary to return. That declaration of intent cannot be reconsidered except by passing through other now classic pages: those that Bretone dedicated to 'postulates and aporias' of the *History*.[4]

These are well-known things, but I will try to proceed in order. The need to concentrate on a 'juristische Kunstgeschichte' was indicated by Schulz in programmatic terms, at the beginning of his book, as the authentic 'task' that now had to be carried out, after – he wrote – the studies of Roman law between the nineteenth and twentieth centuries had not substantially shifted the focus of their interests from Roman law to Roman legal science – and here I would say that, with reference to some names he mentioned (Pernice, Ferrini and, even more, Lenel), the judgment was ungenerous even to the point of being a falsehood – and after "the field of biography has already been harvested" and the crop "could not, from the nature of the case, be heavy". Therefore – he continued – "the biographies of the individual jurists, with their fragmentary personal details and bare catalogues of works, must be left in the background, and the first place must be given to their mistress, Roman legal science herself".[5]

Thus was determined – not to be substantially belied in the concreteness of the investigation – the "rejection of the biographical approach" that Bretone[6] had identified as the first of three 'postulates' of Schulz's work (followed by the "isolation of Roman legal science with respect to other techniques or sciences and to other areas of ancient culture" and the "notion of 'style' as a canon for an analysis of the legal literature").

What was behind Schulz's so radical rejection (to me not due mere-

---

[3] I use, for obvious reasons, the terminology of the German version: cf. Schulz, *Geschichte* (n. 2) 4.

[4] See M. Bretone, 'Uno sguardo retrospettivo. Postulati e aporie nella History di Schulz' [1978], in Id., *Tecniche e ideologie dei giuristi romani*[2] (repr. Napoli 1984) 335 ff.

[5] All the quotations are from Schulz, *History* (n. 2) 4 (= *Geschichte* [n. 2] 4 f.).

[6] *Tecniche e ideologie* (n. 4) 335 ff.

ly to an objective scarcity of data available in the sources)?[7] How had he arrived at that conviction – openly stated, although not always fully followed – of the absolute uselessness of an approach that also involved the prosopographical data of the single *prudentes*, more significant than the knowledge they practised (their "origin and social position", in the words of Kunkel;[8] the public roles covered and the interweaving of relationships of power in which they played a part; the cultural, physical or ideal environments they frequented, and so on)? And whence came to him such marked hostility for "purely biographical questions",[9] to end up gathering (and then dismissing) many elements pertaining to the specifics of various jurisprudential personalities, but on a scientific much more than existential level? This last point[10] is one to which we must return, just as some thought should be given, with regard to the presumed marginality of those "purely biographical questions", to the reference to Croce,[11] of whom we well know (at least since the times of Chabod)[12] the striking discordance, almost a fertile contradiction, be-

---

[7] As maintained for example by C.A. Cannata and B. Santalucia, in their respective 'interventions' in *La giurisprudenza romana* (n. 2) 80 ff.; unlike M. Talamanca, 'Intervento' (*ivi* [n. 2] 86), according to whom that of Schulz is only "a topos that justifies a decision based on other crucial moments" (transl.).

[8] Naturally the reference is to W. Kunkel, *Herkunft und soziale Stellung der römischen Juristen* (Graz-Wien-Köln 1967²). The fact that Schulz himself was not insensitive to these aspects (see *Storia* [n. 2] 185 ff. [= *History* [n. 2] 102 ff.]) only partially lessens the methodological distance between his approach and Kunkel's research: cf. also *infra*, § 3 and note 91.

[9] Thus Schulz, *History* (n. 2) 4.

[10] Already understood by, among others, Lombardi, 'La nave di Teseo' (n. 2) 68 and Mantello, *Per una storia* (n. 2) esp. 204 and note 106.

[11] Of which Schulz, *Storia* [n. 2] 12, note 2 (= *Geschichte* [n. 2] 4 note 3) cited *Nuovi saggi di estetica* (Bari 1962) 225 ff. (where, moreover, the strictly biographical data, almost always irrecoverable and considered not crucial, were well distinguished from "other orders of historical knowledge", such as those concerning the context in which the work was written, the cultural influences and the social scenarios that more or less strongly affected it: such as to tone down, but not eliminate, each reconstruction dedicated to the 'personality of the artist', to be understood as 'aesthetic personality' rather than 'biographical personality'. Of Croce the theoretician and historian of aesthetics, Schulz was careful not to recall other reflections, such as those dedicated to the authentic "error that takes the name of the theory of artistic and literary genres", also in view of the fact that "each true work of art has violated an established genre" (thus B. Croce, *Estetica come scienza dell'espressione e linguistica generale. Teoria e storia* [1902¹], rist. [ed. by G. Galasso] (Milano 1990) 45 ff., esp. 47 f., 565 ff.).

[12] Of whom see especially *Lezioni di metodo storico* (L. Firpo ed.) (Roma-Bari

tween theory of history on the one hand and historiographical practice on the other: the former completely focused on the primacy of processes of universal forms, vast reconstructive, cohesive and almost impersonal outlines; [13] the latter, vice versa, marked by an attention to particulars, the individual details, the concreteness of the lives (not only "of adventures of faith and of passion"). [14]

Certainly, there was in Schulz a distancing from Krüger's *Geschichte* [15] (with his interest in the personalities of the jurists and their literary productions, which in fact precluded him, in the logic of the *History*, from achieving an authentic history of the Roman legal science). But above all what seems very plausible, albeit per se impossible to prove (as explicit references are lacking in Schulz's pages), is the conjecture [16] that there emerges here a silent polemic against Mitteis, guilty of having pointed out, in an intervention of 1917, a possible new work itinerary in the "biographical legal history of Roman antiquity, in the same way individualities in the history of art are revealed". [17]

I find this last analogy truly significant: not only because it seems to confirm the polemic implicit in Schulz (with the centrality he assigned

1969) 184 ff., esp. 192 ff. (where the Aostan scholar questioned how "questo senso dell'umano, anzi del singolo uomo, così profondo nel Croce storico, ... si concilia con le ripetute affermazioni del Croce teorico contro il 'biografismo'") and 210 (where there was still understood, "tra alcune affermazioni teoretiche ... e le opere concrete di Croce storico", an evident "iato: che è poi un riflesso dello iato più generale ... fra il provvidenzialismo storicistico e il senso storico del Croce"). He insists on these profiles of Croce's work, precisely to introduce some turning points in the studies on the Roman law, in the Naples of the 1950s, also M. Bretone, 'La perla nella conchiglia' [1993], now in Id., *Diritto romano e coscienza moderna. Dalla tradizione alla storia. Scritti nomadi* (Madrid 2011) 123 ff. Cf. also *infra*, note 14.

[13] Since "history is thought, and, as such, thought of the universal, of the universal in its concreteness": thus B. Croce, *Teoria e storia della storiografia* (Bari 1927³) 49.

[14] The allusion is obviously to B. Croce, *Vite di avventure di fede e di passione* [1935¹] (G. Galasso ed., Milano 1989). There are insightful comments, in the *Nota del curatore* of this volume (p. 441 ff. with other bibl.), on that "sorta di gusto nativo" which, "per la biografia, e per la biografia storica in particolare", emerges from many places in Croce's production.

[15] See P. Krüger, *Geschichte der Quellen und Litteratur des römischen Rechts* (München-Leipzig 1881 and 1912²). The observations of Mantello, *Per una storia* (n. 2) 170 ff., on this work are especially deserving of consideration.

[16] Advanced by Bretone, *Tecniche* (n. 4) 336 f.

[17] Thus L. Mitteis, 'Antike Rechtsgeschichte und romanistisches Rechtsstudium', which I know from the Italian translation ('Storia del diritto antico e studio del diritto romano'), in AUPA 12 (1929) 477 f. (the quotation is taken from p. 492).

instead to 'Kunstgeschichte'),[18] but above all because it refers to a historiographical field in which, at least from the times of Winckelmann (whose words, taken from the *Geschichte der Kunst des Altertums*, opened Schulz's *Einleitung* to the *Geschichte*), the exaltation of harmony and the measure of the artistic manifestations of certain Greek and Roman seasons had been translated into a complete idea of the 'classical', destined to spread to other areas of antiquity. A perspective that took away, or at least strongly compressed, space and meaning from each reconstruction of the biography of the protagonists (and also of the characteristics of their work that deviated from that paradigm). "It is exactly the opposite of the individualizing art that would be proposed as a model by Mitteis", Massimo Brutti[19] correctly pointed out with regard to the "reconstruction of the classical" in Winckelmann, returning[20] to consider the intervention by Mitteis.

And it is also, I mention incidentally, the umpteenth illustration of how the category of 'classical'[21] operates. Assuming the generalized respect of a uniform and timeless canon, it cancels and hides the individualities and each manifestation less in compliance with the model, and it inhibits reconstruction of the peculiarities of the single jurists. It induces us to speak, within our field, of a jurisprudential law, but then in fact assimilates the operation of the *prudentes* to the characteristics of a single metahistorical legislator, with his cohesive and coherent design, immune to antinomies and gaps (a phenomenon not only historiographical but also historical, established at the time of the first 'actual-

---

[18] A similar lexicon would be used by S. Riccobono in reviewing the *History* (in BIDR 53-54 [1948] 403), where he encouraged the study of the individual contributions of the *prudentes*, since "si conosceva il monumento portentoso e non gli architetti. Ma nessuno può negare l'esistenza degli artefici".

[19] 'I romanisti italiani in Europa', in *Il diritto italiano in Europa (1861-2014). Scienza, giurisprudenza, legislazione* (in Annuario di diritto comparato e di studi legislativi 5 [2014]), ed. by M. Bussani, 235, note 88 (but see also p. 228).

[20] After Bretone (*supra*, note 16) and also R. Orestano, *Introduzione allo studio del diritto romano* (Bologna 1987) 544. See, more recently, G. Santucci, 'La scienza romanistica tedesca vista dall'Italia: il 'dogma' della fungibilità dei giuristi romani', in C. Baldus, M. Miglietta, G. Santucci, E. Stolfi (eds.), *Dogmengeschichte und historische Individualität der römischen Juristen. Storia dei dogmi e individualità storica dei giuristi romani. Atti del Seminario internazionale (Montepulciano 14-17 giugno 2011)* (Trento 2012) 148 f. and note 58.

[21] On which it is sufficient here to refer to the substantial and suggestive reflections of M. Bretone, *Diritto e tempo nella tradizione europea* (Roma-Bari 1999^4) 179 ff., esp. 188 ff. Cf. now also Brutti, 'I romanisti italiani' (n. 19) esp. 235 ff.

izing' revisitation of that production of knowledge, with the Justinian *permutatio legum*).[22] All in all, I believe we can identify here the most striking point of junction and interaction between the myth of the 'classical' and that of the 'fungibility' of the Roman jurists,[23] as well as certain assumptions of interpolationism[24] and the Schulzian orientation of which we are speaking. It is no coincidence, for example, that in the work of Gustav Hugo[25] there is the first, most complete arrangement by genres of the jurisprudential literature of each period of the Roman experience,[26] as well as an image that to some extent anticipates the "fungibel Personen" of Savigny's *Beruf*:[27] that of the *Digesta* as a theat-

---

[22] Insisting on this, dealing with the crucial repercussions it had on the vision of law of all the Western tradition, is F. Gallo, 'La permutatio legum giustinianea rivoluzione giuridica ignorata dalla nostra tradizione', in *Estudios Jurídicos en Homenaje A. Guzmán Brito*, II (Alessandria 2011) 527 ff. On the peculiar physiognomy which, precisely in the Justinian conception, the problem of antinomies assumed, I can refer to E. Stolfi, 'Dal ius controversum alle antinomie', in Legal Roots 6 (2017), esp. 382 f. with other bibl.

[23] See *supra*, note 21 and *infra*, note 27 f.

[24] Whose development can obviously not be outlined here, not even briefly. I have tried to isolate some aspects of it that to me are most important, and to provide some historiographical orientation (also regarding the decisive effect of the 'classical' category on the premises and objectives of interpolationism), most recently in 'Studio e insegnamento del diritto romano dagli ultimi decenni dell'Ottocento alla prima guerra mondiale', in I. Birocchi, M. Brutti (eds.), *Storia del diritto e identità disciplinari: tradizioni e prospettive* (Torino 2016) 19 ff.; 'Protagonisti e percorsi dell'interpolazionismo. A proposito di una recente indagine su Gradenwitz e Riccobono', in SDHI 84 (2018) 325 ff.; 'Attorno a critica del testo e storia del pensiero giuridico. Alcune riflessioni', in AUPA 62 (2019) 247 ff. esp. 256 ff.

[25] I refer to *Lehrbuch der Geschichte des römischen Rechts, bis auf Justinian* (Berlin 1826[10] [1790[1], 1799[2]]), concerning which cf. at least L. Raggi, 'Storia esterna e storia interna del diritto nella letteratura romanistica' [1959] in *Scritti* (Milano 1975) 89 ff.; G. Marini, *L'opera di Gustav Hugo nella crisi del giusnaturalismo tedesco* (Milano 1969) esp. 67 ff.; A. Schiavone, *Alle origini del diritto borghese. Hegel contro Savigny* (Roma-Bari 1984) esp. 29 ff.; Mantello, *Per una storia* (n. 2) 130 ff.; Bretone, *Diritto e tempo* (n. 21) 213 ff.

[26] It is, with respect to the historiographical tradition of which we can largely consider Schulz to be the heir, an important historiographical turning point, which has been studied and valued above all by Lantella, *Le opere* (n. 2) 125 ff.

[27] See in particular *Von Beruf unserer Zeit für Gesetzgebung und Rechtswissenschaft*, (Heidelberg 1840[3] [1814[1]]) 157. As pointed out by G. Marini, *Savigny e il metodo della scienza giuridica* (Milano 1966) 81 ff., the idea of fungibility of the jurists was implied in many other of Savigny's pages, despite (or perhaps because of) the central role he assigned to scientific elaboration within the history of law – essentially perceived as a cultural flow, marked (as observed by A. Mazzacane,

rical work whose author (Justinian) never speaks directly, to conceal himself behind various characters, all participants of the same drama.[28]

2. Which biographies?

We must ask ourselves what it actually means to reject a biographical approach. Does this exclusively involve the intention not to be distracted by small prosopographical details of little significance, to be consigned exclusively to what once would have been called 'external history', and to give value instead to the overall morphology of a form of knowledge, to the salient features of its work protocols consolidated between one generation and another? Obviously we can also discuss this (and appropriately Bretone has already done so),[29] since sometimes many of those presumed details turn out to be anything but marginal, especially after the (second) postulate, that of 'Isolierung', went decidedly into crisis, and we learned to understand and value – although many, unfortunately, still only in word – also the fecund 'impurity' of the law.[30]

I think, however, that in Schulz that methodological guideline (expressed, not by chance, at a crucial point of the *History*) was not limited only to this. It ended up involving other data – more directly attributable to the technical contribution, rather than the personal experience, of each jurist – all to the benefit of a more compact representation (the only one by which – Schulz stated – "the Roman legal science can be completely understood"),[31] organized by long periods ('archaic', 'Hellenistic', 'classical' and 'bureaucratic') but revolving around gen-

---

Savigny e la storiografia giuridica fra storia e sistema [Napoli 1976^2] 28) by literary traditions and sequences of books. On the lack of an authentic "taste for interpretation of the single ancient jurist" in the great German scholar, cf. F. De Marini Avonzo, 'La filologia romanistica di Savigny', in QF 9 (1980) 261. Formulations comparable to Savigny's perspective can also be found in Humanism: cf. D. Mantovani, 'L'elogio dei giuristi romani nel proemio al III libro delle Elegantiae di Lorenzo Valla 'Per quotidianam lectionem digestorum semper incolumis et in honore fuit lingua Romana'', in *Studi per Giovanni Nicosia*, V (Milano 2007) esp. 171 f. and note 60, 198 ff.

[28] See Hugo, *Lehrbuch der Geschichte*^{2} (n. 25) 352 f., which I dealt with in *Studi sui 'libri ad edictum' di Pomponio. I. Trasmissione e fonti* (Napoli 2002) 10, note 11.

[29] In *Tecniche* (n. 4) 337 ff.

[30] In the sense of R. Orestano, *'Diritto'. Incontri e scontri* (Bologna 1981) esp. 558 ff.

[31] Thus in *Storia* (n. 2) 13.

eral characters and tendencies, with a particular slant (I would like to discuss this further) also in the analysis of the literary production.

All in all, it was a rhetorical expedient (or, if we like, a sort of bluff): in the *Introduction*, there was designated with dismissive terminology ('fragmentary personal details') a set of aspects that effectively would have remained at the periphery of the exposition, but which properly do not belong to 'biographism', shoddy or not. Help in revealing it – provided, of course, that Bretone's conjecture is accepted – also comes from reinterpretation of the pages of Mitteis to which I referred, where he identified in Pernice's *Labeo* a useful model (even if in many ways not fully realized) and indicated "the important task of following the gradual emergence of legal concepts and their evolution from generation to generation", convinced that it was possible to "demonstrate with this the individual activity of the single jurists"[32] (although it is true that Mitteis's discourse had its incongruities, to the point of setting on two parallel lines the sequence of events of the jurists in time and "a private law fixed in its perfection").[33]

Here then is, in his eyes, what the "biographical legal history of Roman antiquity" should have been: not a collection of extrinsic minutiae, on the verge of the merely anecdotal, but a series of investigations aimed at restoring depth and order to the abstract and unitary picture of 'classical law', bringing to light the plurality of its jurisprudential protagonists and their contributions. This involved a more or less defined and complete plan of destructuring certain monistic images of the Roman juridical experience, which had some similarities with the aim of reinterpreting the latter in the framework of a general 'antike Rechtsgeschichte'; this had been proposed in previous decades by (in truth Wenger, even more than) Mitteis himself and was destined to gain little success in the following years (it is sufficient to think of the radical criticisms that Koschaker would address to what he called 'neo-humanistic orientation').[34]

---

[32] Thus Mitteis, 'Storia del diritto antico' (n. 17) 492.

[33] As mentioned by the same Bretone, *Tecniche* (n. 4) 349 (the quoted words are his).

[34] The reference is to P. Koschaker, *L'Europa e il diritto romano* (Italian translation, Firenze 1962) esp. 909 ff. In regard to that field of study, aimed at reconstructing an 'antike Rechtsgeschichte', very critical tones can also be found in M. Talamanca, 'Gli studi di diritto greco dall'inizio dell'Ottocento ai nostri giorni', in *Scintillae iuris. Studi in memoria di Gino Gorla*, I (Milano 1994) 901 ff., 909 ff. Cf. also, always in the name of basic scepticism, F. Wieacker, *Storia del diritto privato moderno*, II (Milano 1980) esp. 110 and Orestano, *Diritto, 'Incontri' e scontri* (n.

Obviously I do not mean that in Schulz the scientific personalities had no way of emerging, albeit certainly much less so than what might have been expected from a *History* of their science – so much so that we can largely accept the harsh judgment of Schiavone,[35] according to whom, in the *History* "the Roman jurists (...) continued to appear as cardboard cut-outs, the abstent protagonists of an evasive and disappointing reconstruction" (an almost equally severe assessment had been expressed by Raggi,[36] involved in turn in a generally unitary treatment, at least in appearance,[37] of the 'method of Roman jurisprudence'). Nor do I wish to suggest that Schulz's reconstruction of certain fundamental and long-lasting traits is devoid of historical plausibility: we have all dealt with multiple and incisive manifestations of the 'traditionalism' of the Roman jurists,[38] with their strong class spirit, the tendency to work in adherence to shared and persistent canons, with peculiarities that helped make the *ars iuris* a form of knowledge separate from other fields of ancient culture, in the perception of their contemporaries even before modern observers.[39]

---

30) 246. Significant caution regarding the ways and forms in which an 'antike Rechtsgeschichte' should have been practised were in the same Mitteis, 'Storia del diritto antico' (n. 17) esp. 478 and 489 (where we read: "the history of ancient law is a concept as erroneous as would be the vision of a general star system because today we must suppose that the starry sky consists of an infinite number of systems of suns distinct from each other"). On the different positions of Mitteis and Wenger, E. Höbenreich, 'À propos 'Antike Rechtsgeschichte': Einige Bemerkungen zur Polemik zwischen Ludwig Mitteis und Leopold Wenger', in ZSS 122 (1992) 547 ff.

[35] *The Invention of Law in the West* (Cambridge [Mass.]-London 2012) 36.

[36] See L. Raggi, *Il metodo della giurisprudenza romana* ([1968], rist. Torino 2007) esp. 163.

[37] But it is necessary to consider, in this regard, the appropriate comments of M. Campolunghi, S.-A. Fusco, *Prefazione* to Raggi, *Il metodo* (n. 36) 16 ff.

[38] In regard to which, reference must be made above all to: D. Nörr, 'I giuristi romani: tradizionalismo o progresso? Riflessioni su un problema inesattamente impostato', in BIDR 84 (1981) 9 ff.; but also see, more recently, M. Bretone, *Storia del diritto romano* (Roma-Bari 1993^8) esp. 61 ff.; T. Giaro, 'Diritto come prassi. Vicende del discorso giurisprudenziale', in *Fides Humanitas Ius. Studii in onore di Luigi Labruna*, IV (Napoli 2007) 2254 ff., esp. 2260; G. Valditara, *Lo stato nell'antica Roma* (Soveria Mannelli 2008) 240 ff.; M. Bretone, 'Ius controversum nella giurisprudenza classica', in MAL, serie IX, vol. XXIII, fasc. 3 (Roma 2008) 755 ff., 765 ff. with other bibl. Also to be considered concerning the meaning of tradition – in which an attitude very different from mere 'conformity' was identified – are the contributions now available in G. Grosso, *Tradizione e misura umana del diritto* (Milano 1976) 25 ff., esp. 55 ff.

[39] This has been elucidated mainly by A. Schiavone, 'Sapere giuridico e identità romana. Un'interpretazione', in M. Citroni (ed.), *Memoria e identità. La cultura*

I mean to say that the propensity to focus upon 'jurisprudence' at the expense of the 'jurists' (to overcome which one must avoid[40] the risk of a simply inverse choice)[41] is a decision by the interpreter, discretionary to the point of arbitrariness, and it is certainly not imposed by the condition of the witnesses that have come down to us: it has, because of its one-sidedness, high costs and not insignificant implications. We measure it clearly in regard to the topic (I would prefer to speak of 'problem') that I evoked in the second part of the title of this intervention: that of 'literary genres'.

Since he intended to distance himself from Krüger's *Geschichte* (where the subject of literary genres had its importance),[42] Schulz was not interested in the Roman legal science "only in so far as … it is involved in a history of the sources and literature".[43] Therefore, examination of the jurisprudential writings occupied a final position and relatively limited space in the various sections of the *History* (and we should also reflect on this, considering among other things that it is from the fragments of those works that a large part of the material used in the previous analysis was inevitably drawn). In particular, 'the literature' was always addressed in the last chapter of each section: the fourth in those relating to the 'archaic', 'Hellenistic' and 'classical' periods, which repeat the same structure; the third in the

---

romana costruisce la sua immagine (Firenze 2003) esp. 65 ff. Also see Id., *The invention* 37 f., where the critical rethinking of Schulz's orientation does not exclude the idea that, in effect, Roman legal science ended up becoming opaque already "in the eyes of contemporaries, plunging it into a rigorously specialized and almost initiatory dimension; distant, after Cicero (...), from the interest of the great figures of the age", since "in general, in the mirror held up by the educated, the philosophers, the historians, and the erudite men of Latin culture, legal matters were perceived as a distant world – an isolation that was both its greatness and its downfall".

40 As observed by Bretone, *Tecniche* (n. 4) 351.

41 In any case, it is difficult not to agree with G. Pugliese, 'Storia dei giuristi e storia del diritto', in *La giurisprudenza romana nella storiografia contemporanea* (n. 2) 55, where he deemed a history of jurisprudence impossible without a history of the jurists.

42 Although Schulz's approach can be considered (also in view of the time span to which we are referring: from Lenel's *Palingenesia* to the present) our first, and inevitable, term of comparison, it is necessary to consider at length also the history of the reconstructions which, prior to him, were dedicated to the literary genres of Roman jurisprudence, starting at least from Gustav Hugo (on which supra, § 1 and notes 25 f.) and passing to books such as Krüger's *Geschichte*. Among the few scholars who have studied these subjects in depth, albeit within a peculiar perspective (and with a closer examination, as ascertained, only of Hugo's *Lehrbuch*), is Lantella, *Le opere* (n. 2) 125 ff.

43 Thus Schulz, History (n. 2) iii.

part on the 'bureaucratic' period, where the examination of jurists and *munera iuris peritorum* is incorporated into a single initial chapter.[44]

The exposition was never organized by authors (as in Krüger's *Geschichte*) but according to the type of works (only within this arrangement do we meet the various jurists in chronological order). This basic choice emerges in terms that are progressively more precise and defined: from the trichotomy among 'literature of sacral law', 'of private law' and 'of public law' which completes the 'archaic' age and then returns to the 'Hellenistic' one (but to give space, in the production of private law, to various *genera scribendi*) up to the more complete arrangement by literary forms of the 'classical' age, the authentic acme of the whole narrative.

I will, of course, not go into further details, even though there are aspects deserving of specific attention – such as the very broad scope of Schulz's groupings, which include, even in the 'isagogic literature', writings with different titles (and also, in many ways, with different characteristics), up to uniting, in the 'problematic' literature, works with a visibly unequal structure.[45] And there are other truly surprising data, starting with the absence, for the Imperial period, of a type of works that takes due account, grouping them all in a distinct (sub)class, of the writings on *ius civile sensu stricto* (that 'civil law tradition' that

---

[44] And the title of the chapter that concerns us is also slightly altered, since for 'the literature of the period' there is no mention (as instead in the case of the previous periods) of 'its forms and transmission': arguably a small indication of the basic uniformity that Schulz tended to evoke in his account of the legal science from the pontifical period to the third century CE, to underscore then, vice versa, a clear discontinuity.

[45] Criticisms are not lacking regarding this particular heterogeneous type of writings (in the English and German versions, respectively, 'Literature of Problemata' or 'Problematic Literature' and 'Literatur der Problemata': cf. Schulz, *History* (n. 2) 223 ff. = *Geschichte* [n. 2] 281 ff. = *Storia* [n. 2] 401 ff.), such as by G. Negri, 'Prolegomeni ad una ricerca sui generi letterari nella giurisprudenza romana', in *Seminario romanistico gardesano. 19-21 maggio 1976* (Milano 1976) 26; Lantella, *Le opere* (n. 2) 78 f.; F. d'Ippolito, *Saggi di storia della storiografia romanistica* (Napoli 2009) esp. XXXII. Explicit acceptance, at least in principle, is instead found in C.A. Cannata, *Lineamenti di storia della giurisprudenza europea*. I. *La giurisprudenza romana e il passaggio dall'antichità al medioevo* (Torino 1976^{2}) 58 f., which however suggests keeping the *libri digestorum* distinct from the 'case-problematic literature', which in his opinion would be, in many respects, closer to the *libri ad edictum* than to the *responsorum* ones. G. Negri, 'Appunti sulle 'antologie casistiche' nella letteratura giuridica dell'età dei Severi. I libri disputationum di Ulpiano', in *Cunabula iuris. Studi storico giuridici per G. Broggini* (Milano 2002) 265 believes that the 'literary genres' of the quaestiones and the disputationes "do not per se define the structural peculiarity of the contents".

long preserved structural homogeneity[46] and appeared to the Justinian compilers to merit an autonomous space, reserved precisely for the mass of Sabinian works). Indeed, Schulz chose instead to ascribe Sabinus's *libri tres* to 'isagogic literature' – and also on this there would be much to discuss – and to completely omit Cassius's much vaster work and then attribute all the *ad Sabinum* (along with the works dedicated to Cassius's *libri iuris civilis*!) to the overall genre of 'Commentaries, Epitomae, and Notae on juristic works'.[47]

3. Four other questions

The fundamental problem – which the just-mentioned phenomena help to emerge but do not exhaust – seems to me something else: the function that this category of 'literary genre' fulfils in the whole of Schulz's exposition. I find at least four aspects worthy of attention in this regard: naturally, I will keep them separate for clarity, but they are strongly interrelated.

Firstly, the objective that Schulz, by assigning such a crucial role to this notion, aimed to pursue, also with respect to the historiographical approaches he intended to deal with. Secondly, the historical validity of such a choice, i.e. its correspondence, or not, to the idea that the ancient authors had of the diversity amongst jurisprudential works, and of the weight that this eventually assumed in their writing. Thirdly, and

---

[46] The best known is the option (arguably expressing an overall view of society, centred on the role of the *familia* and of the transmission of its patrimony over time, as shown, at least for Quintus Mucius, by Schiavone, *The Invention of Law* (n. 35) esp. 194 f.) according to which, from the late Republican era onward, the works of *ius civile sensu stricto* opened with the treatment of wills and bequests, continuing then with that of *ab intestato* inheritances. Insisting on this aspect was above all G. Scherillo, 'Il sistema civilistico', in *Studi V. Arangio-Ruiz*, IV (Napoli 1953) 446 ff.; but see also M. Lauria, *Ius Romanum*, I, 1 (Napoli 1963) esp. 57 f. Also not to be neglected are the differences which, in terms of expository style (above all in the setting of legal problems and solutions), emerge in this tradition with respect to the strictly case works: perceptive, in this regard, are the remarks of A. Magdelain, *De la royauté et du droit de Romulus à Sabinus* (Rome 1995) 188.

[47] A genre of works which, in truth, requires further definition, in view of the conspicuous lack of uniformity of the works attributed to it by Schulz. Cannata, *Lineamenti* (n. 45) 60 ff., for example, insisted on the distance between the 'treatises' *ad Quintum Mucium* and *ad Sabinum* and the *Notae* (characterized by a style that he instead tended to liken to that of the *libri regularum*). Cf. also, and more generally, J.-L. Ferrary, 'Les titres des textes juridiques', in *Titres et articulations du texte dans les œvres antiques. Actes du Colloque International de Chantilly. 13-15 décembre 1994* (Paris 1997) 245 ff.

independently (at least in part) of this second aspect, the historiographical fecundity of this approach, i.e. the ability of the category in question to assume a real heuristic value, providing adequate keys for analysis and understanding to modern scholars. Fourthly, the success of that perspective, i.e. the repercussions it has had in our studies, in the seventy years separating us from the *History*.

I will proceed more rapidly with regard to the first aspect, since its explanation tends to be provided by what has thus far been recalled about Schulz's clear predilection for a 'juristische Kunstgeschichte'. Precisely where, dealing with the literary production, he could not avoid facing the individuality of the jurists, the category of literary genre allowed him to play down that pluralistic element, recovering (or preserving) the image of a collective work in which persistence in time and uniformity prevailed – imposed, above all, by a datum largely extrinsic to the scientific personality of each author.

An attitude that reveals, it seems to me, all of the German scholar's disciplinary narrow-mindedness (and obviously not only his), which a long tradition of 'modernizing' analyses of *Digesta* fragments, aimed at studying the jurists not as 'intellectuals' but as 'literature',[48] as mere sources from which to draw information about this or that institution, led to the treatment of their works in a manner quite different from how literary and philosophical criticism had long dealt with other types of texts. I will limit myself to recalling the orientation that Foucault, twenty years later in an article significantly entitled *What is an Author?*, would describe as still dominant in those areas:[49] the "notion of 'author' constitutes the strong point of individualization in the history of ideas, of knowledge, of literature. ... Still today [we are in 1969], when we trace the history of a concept or a literary genre or a certain type of philosophy, I think that such units are in any case considered relatively weak, secondary and superimposed interpretations with respect to the original, solid and fundamental unit of the author and the work".[50]

---

[48] According to the polarity which, undoubtedly tending toward the opposite work guideline, was highlighted above all by F. Casavola, *Giuristi adrianei* (Napoli 1980) 101 ff., largely followed, for example, by Mantello, *Per una storia* (n. 2) esp. 235, and V. Marotta, 'I giuristi romani come 'intellettuali': la cultura di Callistrato', in Ostraka 1 (1992) esp. 287.

[49] To set it, however, radically in discussion in order to destructure the "author-function", understood as "one of the possible specifications of the subject-function": thus M. Foucault, *Scritti letterari* (Italian translation, Milano 1984) 20.

[50] In these terms, again see Foucault, *Scritti letterari* (n. 49) 2 f. On the literary genre as 'convention', but able to influence the author, see, G. Pagliano, *Profilo di*

In Schulz, the centrality assigned to literary genres contributed to a better explanation, by reducing the essential complexity to the minimum, of his idea of 'style' (concerning which Bretone identified the *History*'s third 'postulate'). Also in this regard the emphasis on a classical homogeneity dominated – since all the jurisprudential contributions between the late Republic and the period of the Severans were characterized by simplicity, clarity, precision, objectivity, purity –[51] not too different from Beseler's image of the *prudentes* as "strictly observant Atticists".[52] However, there was little space to describe diversified expressive modules, and this space was largely covered by the literary canons of each genre of works (although it is true that the types of the latter were directly identified more according to the contents than to structural and stylistic criteria).[53]

Therefore, the broad peremptory observations with which Schulz concluded the discussion of the 'Hellenistic' period also had to be valid concerning the production of the jurists. Indeed, in his view, from the latter period "to the end of antiquity, the power of the literary tradition remained unbroken", so that – he concluded, drawing on a formula of Cicero's *Orator*, whose projection onto the jurisprudential *genera scribes* was rightly criticized by d'Ippolito –[54] "to each category of literature, its own style".[55]

Hence, I come – also in the light of this connection, in many ways neuralgic, between literary forms and ways of writing (and thus also of juridical analysis and argumentation)[56] – to the other points I indicated above. I would be rather determined about the first of them, more cau-

sociologia della letteratura (Roma 1993) 123 ff. Negri, 'Prolegomeni' (n. 45) 25 even maintains – with prevalent, but not exclusive, attention to the Roman juridical works – that "once established, the genre acquires, in the subsequent evolution, a pre-eminent function, which transcends the author's individuality". This author however moves in a very different perspective from that of Schulz (and also, in truth, from that commonly assumed), already in the sense in which is understood jurisprudence, and thus the related literature, which he considered to include laws, edicts, *negotia*, etc.

51 Thus, in particular, Schulz, *History* (n. 2) 98.

52 On this judgement by Beseler (dating to 1913), and on certain congruities that emerge with respect to Schulz's approach (but also Eduard Norden's), see Bretone, *Tecniche* (n. 4) 342 ff.

53 Cf. Negri, 'Prolegomeni' (n. 45) 26 and T. Masiello, *Le Quaestiones di Cervidio Scevola* (Bari 1999) 96.

54 In *Saggi di storia* (n. 45) XX f., note 20.

55 Thus, in *History* [n. 2] 98 [where, however, the quotation from Cicero does not appear] (*Storia* [n. 2] 178 = *Geschichte* [n. 2] 116).

56 With all that obviously follows in the collective and often controversial creation of the normative cores of (above all) private law.

tious about the second, while on the last I will limit myself to a few annotations.

From the perspective of the Roman jurists, did the category of literary genre have the same crucial function as Schulz assigned to it? I would say no, as indeed it has long been ascertained. As Masiello observed,[57] "An awareness of literary genre in the scientific production ... of Roman jurisprudence ... is lacking, or imperceptible". In particular, according to Lantella,[58] there emerges from the quotations of the *prudentes* (who were certainly not bound to recall only opinions expressed in works of the same type as that in which the quotation was made[59] and often only mentioned the name of the author they were drawing upon, or to whom they were dedicating the entire work, in the form of a comment on a previous writing)[60] an authentic 'disinterest in literary genres' – and to a certain extent also "in the work as an autonomous artefact", according to an attitude essentially attributed[61] to 'cultural concreteness' and the 'principle of authority' that would have oriented the jurisprudence, with an 'explanation'[62] I consider not completely satisfactory.[63]

---

[57] *Le Quaestiones di Cervidio Scevola* (n. 53) 96.

[58] *Le opere* (n. 2) 63 ff.

[59] It is sufficient to think of the role of the references to the *Digesta* of Celsus and, even more, of Iulianus in Ulpian's *ad edictum* – with a presence so frequent and incisive as to induce us to consider the work of the last Cassian scholarch as one of the preferred sources of Severan commentary (no less, for example, than the *libri ad edictum* by Labeo, Pedius and Pomponius): cf. T. Honoré, *Ulpian. Pioneer of Human Rights* (Oxford 2002^2) esp. 128 ff. Also see, for some specific profiles of Ulpian's techniques of reference, qualification and assembly of Iulianus's thought, E. Stolfi, 'Per uno studio del lessico e delle tecniche di citazione dei giuristi severiani: le 'sententiae prudentium' nella scrittura di Papiniano, Paolo e Ulpiano', in RDR 1 (2001) 345 ff.

[60] Thus according to Lantella, *Le opere* (n. 2) 65 f. The prevalence (or at least the extreme frequency) with which he thought to use this method of citation should however take account of the many and delicate problems – of dislocation, meaning, more or less high recurrence depending on the cited person and referent etc. – raised for example by the use of accurate quotations (i.e. with indication of the writing and/or book from which they are taken), especially in works that are large and of more assiduous reproposal of the jurisprudential debates such as the commentaries on the Severan period edict (especially that of Ulpian, which I discussed, with particular regard to one of his 'sources', in *Studi sui 'libri ad edictum' di Pomponio*, I [n. 28] 31 ff. with bibl.). Cf. also Ferrary, 'Les titres des textes juridiques' (n. 47) esp. 238.

[61] From the same Lantella, *Le opere* (n. 2) 66 ff.

[62] In the sense attributed to the term by Lantella, *Le opere* (n. 2) 66 f.

[63] Above all, the impact related to the *auctoritas* of the jurists – and thus to the

Above all d'Ippolito, in some of his last pages, acutely illustrated the reasons by which to doubt that the Roman jurists had "the awareness of having drawn precise typological boundaries for the form of their writing", even affirming that "the categories of genre, literary form, typologies ... were not those of Roman jurisprudence".[64] The first two arguments mentioned by d'Ippolito seem to me to be especially relevant: on the one hand, the fact that it is not always true, looking at the writings of the *prudentes*, that "the genres are intransigent and poorly support the inclusion of different arguments", since, in our field, "between matter and form there is no exclusive relationship ... of internal rigidity"; on the other, the point that "not all the jurists ordered their materials into literary forms specifically intended for them", since, for example, "arguments advanced by a certain jurist under the title of *Epistulae* can be deployed, by himself or by another author, in a different type such as *Responsa*".[65]

To these considerations I would add only one other: the absence of a perspective 'by literary genres' in the representations of the Roman jurists, even where they expressly took on the role of historians of their own *ars*. Obviously this is the case of Pomponius in his *Enchiridion*, in which at most he was prompted (in retracing what I have suggested to call[66] the

---

weight of the personal prestige (scientific, but also social and political) that distinguished some of them, even affecting the forms of reception of their doctrines – constitutes a rich and complex subject, which seems to be missing from unequivocal and undifferentiated keys of interpretation with respect to the various jurisprudential seasons. I have tried to provide at least an outline of the problems and distinctions that I deem necessary in 'Brevi note su interpretatio e auctoritas fra tarda repubblica ed età dei Severi', in Interpretatio prudentium 1 (2016) 159 ff., esp. 169 ff. with bibl.

[64] Thus d'Ippolito, *Saggi di storia* (n. 45) XXVIII and XXXX.

[65] Again see d'Ippolito, *Saggi di storia* (n. 45) XXX ff. Concerning the second argument, it should be pointed out that, where we still were to assume Schulz's perspective, we would always find ourselves in the same type of writings, i.e. in what he called 'problematic literature' (albeit with all the objections that, legitimately, this category has aroused: *supra*, note 45), so that what would vary is only the title of the jurisprudential writings. The two arguments referred to in d'Ippolito's text were followed (p. XXXI f.) by a further one (in my opinion, less conclusive and perhaps with some questionable assumptions), consisting in the "rapid weakening of this or that literary type" that we observe in the production of the Roman jurists (the example given is that of the *libri epistularum*), with a perception of 'instability' that we can draw from them, so as to exclude "any value 'useful' to the style" (transl. from the Italian text).

[66] From the time of my *Studi sui 'libri ad edictum' di Pomponio*, I (n. 28) 330 ff. up to "Plurima innovare instituit'. Spunti esegetici attorno al confronto tra Labeone e Capitone in D. 1.2.2.47 (Pomp. lib. sing. ench.)', in *Studi per Giovanni Nicosia*,

'phase of the literarization' of legal knowledge, up to, but in this case not including, Labeo) to mention the titles of the works composed by each one. And if he ever went so far as to deal with profiles of style (such as the *antiquus sermo* displayed by Tubero the Younger,[67] which so harmed the success of his books),[68] he did so without relating it to the types of works carried out. I would certainly agree with the point[69] that, in the entirety of Pomponius's manual, a "history of the jurists" was effectively outlined rather than a "history of the juridical literature", while I find truly weak the traces he identified concerning[70] a "latent presence of a history of the literature" and even of "a (historicist) theory of the literary genres".

This does not mean that, for a jurist, it was irrelevant – in the choice of subjects, in their arrangement, in the forms of case analysis, in the type and origin (from school or practice) of problems he faced and of methods of solution he adopted, in the density of references to previous doctrines, and so on – to devote himself to the writing of a commentary on the edict or *ad Sabinum*, of *libri institutionum*, *quaestionum* or *responsorum*. Nor does it mean that the titles assigned to the respective works (by themselves or by others) do not deserve attention – even though I find truly 'partial', and almost always problematic, the "correspondences between 'microtypes' of titles and types of works" that Lantella sought to extrapolate.[71]

In any case, adherence to certain canons – let us think only of the use of quotations, so infrequent in Schulz's 'problematic literature', or of the different relationship established with the text of the praetor in the *ad edictum* with respect to the *digesta*, which also in the first part were based on the sequence of praetorian predictions – seems to emerge only in tendentious terms. Certainly, no one can argue (to re-

VIII (Milano 2007) esp. 59 ff.; 'Cunabula', in AUPA 54 (2010-2011) 265 ff.; 'Dissensiones prudentium, dispute di scuola e interventi imperiali', in V. Marotta, E. Stolfi (eds.), *Ius controversum e processo fra tarda repubblica ed età dei Severi. Atti del Convegno (Firenze, 21-23 ottobre 2010)* (Roma 2012) 290 ff. with other bibl.

67 A "borderline case" – according to Lantella, *Le opere* (n. 2) 44 – in relation to the variety of types of concurrent information offered by Pomponius.

68 Cf. D. 1.2.2.46: "*...Tubero doctissimus quidem habitus est iuris publici et privati et complures utriusque operis libros reliquit: sermone etiam antiquo usus affectavit scribere et ideo parum libri eius grati habentur*".

69 Formulated by Lantella, *Le opere* (n. 2) 47.

70 By the same Lantella, *Le opere* (n. 2) 48 ff. and 54 ff.

71 *Le opere* (n. 2) 74 ff. esp. 77 ff. Concerning the titles of the writings of Roman jurisprudence, also see, more recently (and from a different perspective), Ferrary, 'Les titres des textes juridiques' (n. 47) 233 ff., esp. 238 ff.

main within the context of the just-mentioned literary types) that there is uniformity in the manners of describing and resolving cases in the *digesta* of Alfenus, Celsus, Iulianus and Cervidius Scaevola;[72] nor can one deny the different scope of the jurisprudential references (not only in quantitative terms, but also those of assembly and writing strategies) in works so close to each other in period, audience and objectives such as the commentaries on the edict by Paulus and Ulpian.[73]

This is obviously the reason for the caution necessary regarding the third point, concerning the effective heuristic value the category of literary genre can assume for us. Over and above the doubts always raised by the adoption of notions conceived exclusively by the interpreters but never found explicitly in the witnesses of the historical period under study (doubts that I would be far from dispelling by recourse to the image of the 'name' and the 'thing', judging that the ancient authors lacked only the first and not the second),[74] we can certainly not deny that including a fragment, or an entire work, in a tradition of writings provides useful interpretative keys. Above all, it seems to me that this can contribute to an assessment, in the correct perspective, of their peculiarities (of structure, expository style, argumentation techniques), forcing us to consider only those exclusive to a series of texts or to an author, where others will be mainly attributable to the conditionings of the genre and its regimen (such that the specificity of the jurist will mainly be understood priorly, in the very choice of having engaged in that type of writings).

---

[72] For some further comments in this regard, cf. E. Stolfi, 'I casi e la regula: una dialettica incessante', in L. Vacca (ed.), *Casistica e giurisprudenza. Convegno ARISTEC. Roma, 22-23 febbraio 2013* (Napoli 2014) 24 ff. with bibl.

[73] I have tried to bring this to light – albeit with prevalent attention to the methods of referencing, on their part, specific works or doctrines – in *Studi sui 'libri ad edictum' di Pomponio*, I (n. 28) 29 ff., esp. 40 ff. and 'Per uno studio del lessico' (n. 59) 347 ff.

[74] I use deliberately Betti's terminology. The legitimate search for the 'thing', even in a historical context where the 'name' was absent, was for example invoked by Betti in reference to the topic of subjective law (against studies, such as those of Villey, centred on the terminological datum): cf. E. Betti, *Falsa impostazione della questione storica, dipendente da erronea diagnosi giuridica* [1952], now in Id., *Diritto metodo ermeneutica. Scritti scelti* (ed. by G. Crifò) (Milano 1991) 397 ff. Moreover, this is a recurrent and almost obsessive image in his production, dealt with above all by A. Schiavone, *Storiografia e critica del diritto. Per una 'archeologia' del diritto privato moderno* (Bari 1980) 111 ff., and Id., 'Un'identità perduta: la parabola del diritto romano in Italia', in Id. (ed.), *Stato e cultura giuridica in Italia dall'unità alla repubblica* (Roma-Bari 1990) 294 ff. Cf. also E. Stolfi, 'Riflessioni attorno al problema dei 'diritti soggettivi' fra esperienza antica ed elaborazione moderna', in Studi Senesi 118 (2006) 126 ff.

However, the interpretative keys thus acquired must be used with extreme prudence. Firstly, because we must never lose the awareness that – as has been observed[75] – "a classification of genres of works always presents elements of uncertainty and even artificiality. Not only is there uncertainty about the type, in which to include one and the other work, but each has an individuality, a reality of its own, which is only partially defined when forced into the abstract schemata of a classification." I would add that the inclusion in a literary form will never be able to account – alone – for the characteristics of a jurisprudential writing and of the scientific personality of its author. If anything, the opposite is true: when we stop at that datum, we will again consign ourselves to the myth of 'fungibility',[76] albeit in a singular declension, obscuring or ignoring the traits less easily ascribable to the dictates of the genre. What deserves to be investigated more carefully is not so much how it follows the model (which is more historiographical than historical) but rather how much it deviates from or exceeds it.

Therefore, the correct historiographical use of our notion – its fertile transformation, if we prefer, from 'category' to 'problem' – must be oriented towards a study aimed at verifying and analysing (and not compressing) the peculiarities in works and jurists, and it requires that we proceed by constantly making comparisons: amongst writings of the same title (or pertaining to the same type, or included in a specific tradition), amongst authors and works of a certain period, amongst several works by the same jurist, and also amongst the different contexts (in a formal and content sense) in which we find proposed a series of cases or a similar elaboration (given the notoriously topical scope of many jurisprudential doctrines, and also of some definitions).

Let us consider one example relating to the work that, with Jean-

---

[75] From C.A. Maschi, 'La conclusione della giurisprudenza classica all'età dei Severi. Iulius Paulus', in ANRW, II.15 (Berlin-New York 1976) 677. In this regard, see also M. Talamanca, 'Per la storia della giurisprudenza romana', in BIDR 80 (1977) 222 ff., note 47 (in defence, in disagreement with Maschi's approach, of the 'heuristic' value of the notion of literary genre, with the resulting classifications) and d'Ippolito, *Saggi di storia* (n. 45) XXXI and note 35. He believes that "a literary type" cannot be "understood as a rigid classificatory design", but nonetheless has "a heuristic value", even that of "not ... imprisoning research within impassable boundaries" (transl.), Bretone, 'Il testo giuridico', in *Lo spazio letterario di Roma antica* [1989], now in Id., *Diritto romano e coscienza moderna* (n. 12) 184. See also Id., *Storia* (n. 38) 275 (according to which, with respect to the production of the *prudentes*, "forms and genres are not a simple classification scheme") and Ferrary, 'Les titres des textes juridiques' (n. 47) 240 ff.

[76] Cf. *supra*, § 1 and note 27 f.

Louis Ferrary and Aldo Schiavone, we conducted in a volume of the *Scriptores iuris Romani* Project. In the study of the *libri iuris civilis* by Quintus Mucius, what can we draw from his mere inclusion in the genre of civil law works *sensu stricto* (a category surprisingly lacking in Schulz)? Certainly something useful, at least at the structural level – although, besides the initial treatise on law of successions,[77] it is difficult to establish how and how much of the thematic sequence inaugurated by Quintus Mucius survived in the literature between the first and third centuries CE; moreover, the inferences we have sought to make (at the level of the sequence of the *capita*) from the order of subjects and sections of Sabinus's *libri tres* (and relative commentaries, from Pomponius to Paulus and Ulpian)[78] must be used with caution, merely as clues and conjectures.

Ever more profitable elements of analysis become accessible only through the comparisons I have just mentioned: exiting from the 'genre' *sensu stricto* (but remaining in the same 'civil law tradition'), i.e. looking at that of 'Commentaries, Epitomae, and Notae on juristic works'.[79] The preferred role is obviously assumed by Pomponius's *ad Quintum Mucium*, whose examination – conducted also in the light of what we learn elsewhere of the style of this jurist, so distant from the incisive and preceptive bearing (almost always in the form of maxims and judgements) of the ancient *pontifex* – has been crucial in the identification of possible nuclei of Mucian thought conserved in places other than those presenting the explicit arrangement among lemmas coming from the *libri iuris civilis* and their examination by Pomponius.[80] Yet,

---

[77] Which clearly emerges from the palingenetic reconstructions of Lenel and Bremer, and is widely comprehensible in the light of the reasons highlighted especially by Schiavone: *supra*, note 46. Cf. also E. Stolfi, 'Tithasus', in *Signa amicitiae. Scritti offerti a Giovanni de Bonfils* (Bari 2018) 64 ff. and 'I libri iuris civilis. Introduzione', in J.-L. Ferrary, A. Schiavone, E. Stolfi (eds.), *Quintus Mucius Scaevola. Opera* (Roma 2018) 104 f. with other bibl.

[78] Essential in this regard is the reconstruction by R. Astolfi, *I libri tres iuris civilis di Sabino* (Padova 2001^2).

[79] To use the terminology of Schulz, *History* (n. 2) 204 ff.

[80] As just one example, it is sufficient to recall the very high probability, now commonly acknowledged, that a Mucian elaboration underlay the discourse of Pomponius – who probably added further ideas and additions, so as to make the approach more complete and more pertinent to his times – in the note (4 *ad Q. Muc.*) D. 46.3.80. More generally, he had pointed out on various occasions the possibility of attributing to the Republican jurist the first formulation of doctrines appearing in Pomponius's commentary; S. Di Marzo, *Saggi critici sui libri di Pomponio 'ad Q. Mucium'*, I-II (Palermo 1899-1900) (partially republished in Labeo 7 [1961]

no less important information has come from other works attributed to Quintus Mucius – with sometimes illuminating results arising from the comparison with the fragments taken from the *liber singularis horon*, in regard of which I do not share the more radical doubts about the effective paternity[81] nor the hypothesis of its strict affiliation with isagogic

---

218 ff., 352 ff.). Similar orientations, and often with even more cogent arguments, have emerged in analyses dedicated, from then onward, to this or that passage of the *ad Quintum Mucium*, and which we have tried to consider in our volume of the *Scriptores iuris Romani* (see now Ferrary, Schiavone, Stolfi [eds.], *Quintus Mucius Scaevola. Opera* [n. 77]).

[81] A notoriously controversial point, since there have long been discussions both on whether that brief collection of definitions (and rules) was compiled by Quintus Mucius – or rather by a later author, though probably using Mucian materials – and on the relationship of this writing to the *libri iuris civilis*. Among the many interventions in this regard, see at least O. Lenel, *Palingenesia iuris civilis*, I (Lipsiae 1889) 762 f. note 7; F.P. Bremer, *Iurisprudentiae antehadrianae quae supersunt. Pars prior. Liberae rei publicae iuris consulti* (Lipsiae 1896) 50, 103 f.; G. Lepointe, *Quintus Mucius Scævola. I. Sa vie et son oevre juridique. Ses doctrines sur le Droit pontifical* (Paris 1926) esp. 40 ff.; G. Scherillo, 'Note critiche su opere della giurisprudenza romana', in Iura 3 (1952) 180 ff. (with a strong, well-argued defence of the attribution to Quintus Mucius, whereas I find it impossible to demonstrate, and difficult to follow, the conjecture according to which multiple passages of juridical content in Cicero's *Topica* should be attributed to the *liber singularis horon*); P. Stein, *Regulae iuris. From Juristic Rules to Legal Maxims* (Edinburgh 1966) esp. 36 ff. (who also undoubtedly supports the Mucian paternity of the work); Schulz, *History* (n. 2) 94 and 296 (who instead has many doubts); B. Schmidlin, *Die römische Rechtsregeln. Versuch einer Typologie* (Köln-Wien 1970) 126 f. (with significant cautions); G. Crifò, 'Ex iure ducere exempla. Gaio Trebazio Testa ed i 'Topica' ciceroniani', in *Studi C. Esposito*, II (Padova 1972) 1109 and note 33; A. Watson, *Law Making in the Later Roman Republic* (Oxford 1974) 157 with other bibl. (in the name of marked scepticism, even more accentuated in previous studies, such as where [Id., *The Law of Property in the Later Roman Republic*, Oxford 1968, 190] the same scholar had suggested the possibility that the work was none other than "a later collection from Scaevola's *Ius civile* or from Pomponius' *libri ad Quintum Mucium*"); B. Schmidlin, 'Horoi, pithana und regulae – Zum Einfluß der Rhetorik und Dialektik auf die juristische Regelbildung', in ANRW, II.15 (Berlin-New York 1976) 107 ff.; Bretone, *Tecniche* (n. 4) 78; F. Wieacker, *Römische Rechtsgeschichte. I. Einleitung-Quellenkunde-Frühzeit und Republik* (München 1988) 599 f.; F. Lamberti, *Studi sui 'postumi' nell'esperienza giuridica romana*, I (Napoli 1996) 124 ff. with other bibl.; Ferrary, 'Les titres des textes juridiques' (n. 47) 248 (who rightly observed in the same Greek title an argument against the hypothesis of a later and apocryphal writing); C.A. Cannata, *Per una storia della scienza giuridica europea. I. Dalle origini all'opera di Labeone* (Torino 1997) 253. The last author believes, in particular, that the *liber singularis horon* was written before, as "a kind of preparatory work", the larger work; in an inverse manner, Bremer, *Iurisprudentiae antehadrianae*, I (n. 83) 103. Scherillo, 'Note critiche' (n. 83) 185 f., in his turn, hypothesized that Quintus Mucius "deduced some of his aphorisms from his larger work, or in contrast introduced some of his aphorisms into the larger work".

literature[82] – or from reconsideration of the basic characteristics, and some specific elaborations, of the production of Publius Mucius or Servius (above all where ascribable to the *Reprehensa Scaevolae capita*)[83] or of what Mantovani has indicated as "the beginnings of the *ad edictum* literary genre" (recording the attestations of a jurisprudential interest in the *verba edicti* already in the pre-Servian period and noting how, in this regard, "with Q. Mucius the witnesses become more frequent").[84] Therefore, I would not be too distant, whilst adopting a not entirely concurring view, from the conviction of Negri[85] that "it is necessary ... to study each work, each stylistic institute, each content type in the context of the genre understood as a diachronic structure" (although, in his opinion, a 'formal continuity' cannot be excluded).

Finally, a few words on the impact that Schulz's 'construction by genres' has had on our studies (speaking of Quintus Mucius,[86] the play on words is inevitable!). Perhaps the affirmation will be surprising, and

---

See also M.A. Messana, 'Sui libri definitionum di Emilio Papiniano. Definitio e definire nell'esperienza giuridica romana', in AUPA 45 (1998) 96 ff. with other bibl., and Schiavone, *The Invention of Law* (n. 35) esp. 215, according to which "the *Horoi* must have been a sort of synthetic recapitulation" of the *iuris civilis* books. On the surprising use of this work by the compilers, Scherillo, 'Note critiche' (n. 83) 181 f. and F. Wieacker, *Textstufen klassischer Juristen* (Göttingen 1960) 142 and 168; on the relationship, in the work of the same Justinians, between the *liber singularis horon* and (obviously not the *libri iuris civilis* of Quintus Mucius, but) the *ad Quintum Mucium* of Pomponius, D. Mantovani, 'Aggiornamenti sull'Appendix e i tempi di compilazione del Digesto', in *Fides Humanitas Ius. Studii L. Labruna*, V (Napoli 2007) 3186 f. with bibl. See, lastly, E. Stolfi, 'Il liber singularis horon. Introduzione', Ferrary, Schiavone, Stolfi (eds.), Quintus Mucius Scaevola. Opera (n. 79) 161 ff.

[82] As maintained, in particular, by Schulz, *History* (n. 2) 93 f. In the rightly critical sense, among others, Ferrary, 'Les titres des textes juridiques' (n. 47) 249. Bretone, *Storia* (n. 38) 275 included Mucius's Horoi in a late-Republican "theoretical-didactic literature" (further examples of which were however not indicated).

[83] An attribution which, again, appears likely for a much larger number of fragments than those which, at the time, Lenel and Bremer attributed to Servius's work. On the *Reprehensa Scaevolae capita*, see, recently, Schiavone, *The Invention of Law* (n. 35) 262, and A. Castro Sáenz, 'Notata Mucii: contextualización de un problema', in *Estudios Jurídicos en Homenaje A. Guzmán Brito*, I (Alessandria 2011) 655 ff.; Stolfi, 'I libri iuris civilis. Introduzione' (n. 79) 107 with other bibl.

[84] Cf. D. Mantovani, 'Gli esordi del genere letterario ad edictum', in Id. (ed.), *Per la storia del pensiero giuridico romano. 1. Dall'età dei pontefici alla scuola di Servio* (Torino 1996) respectively 97 ff. and 104.

[85] Thus in 'Prolegomeni' (n. 45) 29.

[86] And of what, concerning his scientific work, Pomponius observed in his very well-known D. 1.2.2.41: ... *Quintus Mucius Publii filius pontifex maximus ius civile primus constituit generatim in libros decem et octo redigendo.*

perhaps unacceptable, but I think that, concerning this specific aspect, the influence of the *History* has been limited, indirect and latent.

I will attempt to explain myself better. The expository model as a whole was crucial for a long time, albeit practically unrepeatable (nor repeated), with the basic themes underlying also the role played by the category of literary genres, with that 'rejection of the biographical approach' from which I have proceeded. Schulz's methodological perspective has, paradoxically, been more a brake than a stimulus for the development of a mature historiography on Roman legal thought: it has lessened, rather than enhanced, the enormous importance of Lenel's *Palingenesia* (which Schulz did not like, and not only for reasons of juridical philology),[87] which long remained on the periphery of the Roman law scholar's workbench. Schulz's work has often operated as a dialectical pole for new orientations, in Italy (starting from the late 1950s)[88] and in Germany itself (Schwarz's *Das Strittige Recht* and Kunkel's *Herkunft* were rightly considered[89] "the most adequate response to Schulz's methodology").

However, the predominance, in the study of the jurisprudential literature, of a perspective characterized by types of works has played an appreciable role only in increasing the awareness that the analysis of a series of witnesses (a work, a section of it, single texts) cannot ignore the tradition of thought and writing of which it was originally a part, and that certain characteristics might not have been a feature exclusive to them, because they corresponded to a consolidated and to some ex-

[87] As emerges also (but not only) from the less than enthusiastic comments expressly dedicated to Lenel's *Palingenesia* by Schulz, *History* (n. 2) 141. On this point, among others, M. Talamanca, 'Otto Lenel e la 'Palingenesia'', in O. Lenel, *Palingenesia iuris civilis*, I (rist. Roma 2000) IX and d'Ippolito, *Saggi di storia* (n. 45) esp. XVI f. I discussed some aspects of Lenel's methodology, which could be amongst the most significant in this regard, in *Studi sui 'libri ad edictum' di Pomponio*, I (n. 28) 207 f. and note 4 with bibl., and in 'Attorno a critica del testo' (n. 24) 265 f. with other liter.

[88] For some orientation in this regard, I refer the reader to E. Stolfi, 'Il contesto culturale', in Baldus, Miglietta, Santucci, Stolfi (eds.), *Dogmengeschichte* (n. 20) 253 ff. and Id., 'Diritto romano e storia del pensiero giuridico', in L. Vacca (ed.), *Nel mondo del diritto romano. Convegno ARISTEC. Roma, 10-11 ottobre 2014* (Napoli 2017) esp. 115 ff. both with bibl. See also d'Ippolito, *Saggi di storia* (n. 45) esp. XX ff. and, lastly, C. Masi Doria, 'La romanistica italiana verso il terzo millennio: dai primi anni settanta al duemila', in Birocchi, Brutti (eds.), *Storia del diritto e identità disciplinari* (n. 24) 184 ff. (who rightly believes [p. 187] it "un errore interpretare come biografismo" the approach adopted in that line of research).

[89] From d'Ippolito, *Saggi di storia* (n. 45) XVII.

tent unavoidable regimen. And yet, it does not seem to have gone beyond this result (acceptable, but also rather generic and predictable).

It is not by chance that monographs and essays on single jurisprudential works have flourished, especially in recent decades,[90] with attention to the prerogatives of their style, structure, form of argumentation, and not only to the strictly normative contents. However, very little has been produced concerning the history of the literary genres: I do not mean at the level of considerations of historiographical method (I have been able to refer to many of them), but of concrete analysis of a *genus scribendi* as practised by more than one jurist (one of the few exceptions that comes to mind is the brilliant work by Frezza on *responsa* and *quaestiones*).[91]

It seems to me a confirmation – albeit with the prudence with which such data must always be assessed – of the dead-end street into which Schulz's perspective risked leading us, when not supplemented by those further guidelines and that combination of comparisons to which I have referred and which we must be able to put to use, today more than ever. Not to suppress or inhibit an overall reconstruction of Roman jurisprudence, but to be able to understand its multiform richness, finally restoring a complete and distinct scientific physiognomy to its protagonists: our *Scriptores iuris Romani*.

[90] I have tried to provide a list – undoubtedly incomplete, and in any case limited essentially to Italian and German studies – in Diritto romano e storia del pensiero giuridico (n. 88) esp. 107 ff.

[91] I am referring to P. Frezza, "Responsa' e 'Quaestiones'. Studio e politica del diritto dagli Antonini ai Severi' [1977], now in Id., *Scritti*, III (Roma 2000) 351 ff. Also to be mentioned is A. Dell'Oro, *I 'libri de officio' nella giurisprudenza romana* (Milano 1960). I would add the pages, certainly not of a manualistic nature (despite the title of the book), with which Bretone, *Storia* (n. 38) 274 ff., outlined 'the literary forms' of Roman jurisprudence, not without demonstrating, however, that this exposition must intersect with that dedicated to the individual jurists and their respective production.

Chapter 4

HISTORICITY OF LAW AND *IUS CONTROVERSUM* IN ITALIAN HISTORIOGRAPHY OF THE TWENTIETH CENTURY. THE WORK OF RICCARDO ORESTANO AND LUIGI RAGGI

Andrea Lovato

SUMMARY: 1. Genesis of a method. – 2. Teachers and students. – 3. From practice to science. – 4. Ideology or ideologies of the jurists? – 5. "An enormous gymnasium of opinions".

1. Genesis of a method

In Riccardo Orestano's long scientific reflection, a basic conviction was that, when 'methodology' is discussed in the juridical field, we are not dealing with anything different from our personal conception of law.[1] In other words, the method used in analysing a problem always depends on the initial perspectives, on the heuristic tools used. According to this scholar, the only valid method for a serious approach to law was historical investigation: in one of his best-known works (I am referring to the *Introduzione*),[2] there is no expression used more than 'historicity of law'. It was "the problem of problems",[3] a question perceived as so

[1] R. Orestano, *Introduzione allo studio del diritto romano* (Bologna 1987[3]) 12.

[2] A famous and intensely studied work, upon which remains indelible the judgment formulated by P. Grossi, 'Storia di esperienze giuridiche e tradizione romanistica (a proposito della rinnovata e definitiva 'Introduzione allo studio del diritto romano' di Riccardo Orestano)', in QF 17 (1988) 534: "The secret of a book is to have a soul almost as if it were a living creature; and it is well to add, if someone were to believe the contrary, that it is the privilege of few, of very few books, especially in the steppe territory of our legal sciences (…)". A book that is identified – observed Grossi – with the same line of research of its author, research that is experimentation of a methodical canon.

[3] Cf. Orestano, *Introduzione* (n. 1) 175.

weighty as to render it, from the very first pages, the guiding criterion of the investigation, with the intention to contribute to the education of jurists, for whom tradition – any tradition – was not an inevitable constraint to be passively abstracted, but rather constituted the object of a continuous critical examination.[4]

To present-day historiographical sensibility, this approach may seem obvious; it was not so when Orestano, not yet 30 years old, began to deal with the historical-juridical science of the time. This was toward the end of the 1930s – in 1937 to be precise – and the young scholar, destined to become an undisputed master, took part in the competition for a chair announced by the University of Cagliari and won it, but not without strong opposition: negative evaluations came from some commissioners, who criticized the candidate from a methodological perspective, accusing him of 'insensitivity' to the systematic aspects of law and to the essence of legal institutions.[5]

Evident from his earliest works, focusing on the genesis of the Augustan Principate, is the basic element of the method that would characterize Orestano's entire existence: the constant link with the world of 'facts', with the concrete experience of life: an indissoluble connection, the only one considered suitable to deal with the problems without falling into abstract legal categories, often the result of schematizations incapable of penetrating the reality of a phenomenon in constant motion. For Orestano, it was necessary to ask the sources new questions, to rethink methods

[4] Orestano, *Introduzione* (n. 1) 14. This explains why the teacher considered pleonastic – a 'useless tautology', he wrote – the adjective *historical* in front of 'study', omitted in the passage from the previous editions to the third, the definitive one, of 1987. Retaining that adjective could have generated the misunderstanding – he specified – that there could be a 'study' that was not 'historical' of Roman law as of any other law: an absurd and unacceptable conclusion, since a law, by the mere fact of having existed or of existing, cannot but be uniquely and necessarily 'historical': cf. Orestano, *ibid.* (n. 1) 11. However, see the critical remarks in this regard by Grossi, 'Storia di esperienze giuridiche e tradizione romanistica' (n. 2) 538.

[5] Cf. M. Campolunghi, *s.v. Orestano*, in *Dizionario Biografico dei Giuristi Italiani (XII-XX secolo)*, ed by I. Birocchi, E. Cortese, A. Mattone, M.N. Miletti (Bologna 2013) 1462. Orestano's victory was accompanied by violent polemics that were included in a more profound contrast, writes F. De Marini Avonzo, 'Riccardo Orestano (1909-1988)', in SDHI 54 (1988) 556, between those who wished to maintain the atemporal value of 'classical' Roman law and those who maintained its historicity. The following reflection is incisive: "We live in a time in which the question risks becoming topical once again: I sense danger in certain nostalgias for the era in which the generalized use of dogmas in describing Roman law was an undisputed instrument of academic power for our discipline".

and perspectives, to be emancipated from the Pandectistic tradition, with the aim of replacing "dogmatic constructivism" [6] with empirical observation. Only in this way could scientific research renew itself and attain a vision, whose characteristic trait would be "the dissolution of systematic necessity". [7] To achieve this aim, it would have been necessary to preliminarily abandon positions "of haughty certainty and marked immobility" – as the master called it [8] – and endeavour to dispel the illusion that the sciences, in every field of human knowledge, could arrogate to themselves the pretence of being based on possession of absolute truth.

Another lucid approach of Orestano involves the problem of awareness of the historicity of law. This delicate question concerns both the ancient and modern jurists, if it is true – as it is – that it consists in being aware that what they transmit to the future does not come from themselves, and that they possess it only in a fragile and provisional manner. [9] With respect to ancient jurisprudential thought, Orestano rejected the prevalent doctrine of his time, which maintained the absence in the *prudentes* of any thinking in that regard. The master made a distinction: meditations on the historicity of law did not constitute a salient feature of the scientific physiognomy of the Roman jurists, but only in the sense that they did not come to the surface, i.e. they did not amount to 'expressed' problems. As we read in the *Introduzione*, "For Roman jurisprudence, the true manifestations of an awareness of the historicity of law must be sought in the ways in which it concretely operated and in its realizations" (transl.). [10]

---

[6] The expression is that of M. Brutti, 'Rileggere Orestano. Teoria e storiografia del diritto', in RISG 4 (2013) 4.

[7] Cf. Orestano, *Introduzione* (n. 1) 32-33 and note 14, in which the author reports a verbatim quotation of N. Abbagnano, 'La metodologia delle scienze nella filosofia contemporanea', in AA.VV., *Saggi di critica delle scienze* (Torino 1950) 15.

[8] Orestano, *Introduzione* (n. 1) 32.

[9] I summon up a formulation of D. Mantovani, 'Il diritto romano dopo l'Europa. La storia giuridica per la formazione del giurista e cittadino europeo', in AA.VV., *Scopi e metodi della storia del diritto e formazione del giurista europeo. Incontro di studio* (Padova, 25-26 novembre 2005), ed by L. Garofalo (Napoli 2007) 77. It seems useful to recall here a thought by P. Grossi, 'Testimonianza per un maestro: Riccardo Orestano', in QF 39 (2010) 922, according to which in Orestano's conception the present and the past are not separable dimensions: instead they are placed in a strict dialectic, so that through comparative analysis the result of a complete historicization can be achieved. Among more recent authors, a summary is in M. Nardozza, 'Analisi del discorso giuridico e coscienza storica nel pensiero di Riccardo Orestano', in A. Briguglio, R. Martino, A. Panzarola, B. Sassani (eds.), *Scritti in onore di Nicola Picardi* (Pisa 2016) 1823 ff.

[10] Orestano, *Introduzione* (n. 1) 181; also see *ibid.*, 597 ff. The question was speci-

In the work of the *veteres*, the 'historical conception' of law was experienced and operated concretely "with a full and constant, almost absolute, consistency".[11] Not by chance, in the daily 'creation' of law of which Pomponius spoke, Orestano identified one of the most lucid manifestations of self-awareness of an entire class of experts: there can be no *ius* if there is not some *iuris peritus*, whose effort serves to advance, to improve *cottidie* law.[12] In this famous enunciation, he saw engraved in stone the task and the responsibility of the jurist of *every* time,[13] thus agreeing with Schulz on the idea of the *prudentes* as protagonists of an assiduous work, thanks to which through the centuries the law of Rome remained fluid, adaptable, ready to satisfy new needs.[14] The controversiality intrinsic to it[15] prevented any risk of 'petrification', being translated into a continuous flowering of ideas and solutions, albeit often in contrast with each other: Schwarz had spoken of "a state of constant vibration" ("*ein Zustand immerwährender Vibration*")[16] in which the permanent problems and provisional nature of

fically addressed by the scholar in 'Storiografia e coscienza della storicità del diritto', in IURA 9 (1958) 240-249 = *'Diritto'. Incontri e scontri* (Bologna 1981) 339-347.

[11] Orestano, *Introduzione* (n. 1) 182.

[12] Pomp. *l. s. enchir.*, D. 1.2.2.13: ... *post hoc deinde auctorum successione dicemus, quod constare non potest ius, nisi sit aliquis iuris peritus, per quem possit cottidie in melius produci.* Orestano dealt with the symbolic value of Pomponius's text in, among other things, 'Idea di progresso, esperienza giuridica romana e 'paleoromanistica'', now in *Edificazione del giuridico* (Bologna 1989) 255 f. More generally, very important pages on the activity of elaboration of *scientia iuris* by the jurists are contained in the chapter which, with the title 'Il 'metabolismo' dei giuristi', closes *'Diritto'. Incontri e scontri* (n. 10) 723 ff.

[13] Orestano, *Introduzione* (n. 1) 55-56. The italics are those of the author.

[14] Cf. Orestano, *Introduzione* (n. 1) 57, in which the author shares the opinion formulated by F. Schulz, *History of Roman Legal Science* (Oxford 1953²) 286.

[15] I underline this idea, intending to highlight controversiality as a 'founding' element of the science of the Roman jurists: naturally, not a sterile and abstract set of conflicting opinions but a variety of solutions, the result of selective operations carried out on 'factual' (juridically relevant) data emerging from the case investigated in a specific context. As observed C. Beduschi, 'Il 'ius controversum' fra razionalità e giustizia', in V. Marotta, E. Stolfi (eds.), *'Ius controversum' e processo fra tarda repubblica ed età dei Severi* (Roma 2012) 29, "the jurisprudential discourse developed fundamentally as a cognitive path, foreordained to bring to light the optimal structure of a controversial relationship, an expression of the common feeling present in the civitas".

[16] Cf. A.B. Schwarz, 'Das strittige Recht der römischen Juristen', in *Festschrift Schulz* 2 (Weimar 1951) 202 = *Il diritto controverso dei giuristi romani*, Ital. transl. by A. Lovato, in A. Lovato (ed.), *Itinerari di lettura per un corso di diritto romano*² (Bari 2011) 174.

the arguments did not clash with the security of the method. In this regard, there are no differences between the ancient and modern intellectual dimension, since no scientific investigation, in the past or in the present, has been conducted or can be conducted without dealing with its history, [17] and this constantly validates the equation: historicity = *scientia iuris*.

On the intrinsic historicity of the investigated subject, as well as on other questions of method – from analysis of the language to attention to the socio-political and economic contexts in which law is generated – Orestano's teaching was transmitted to students such as Giovanni Tarello, Gino Giugni, Enrico Zanelli and Emanuele Somma (to name just a few). I wish to recall here, in particular, Luigi Raggi. The convergences between teacher and student were manifold, starting with the interest in the sociological approach to the study of law, [18] and the custom – which Orestano had inherited in turn from his teacher, Salvatore Riccobono – to work directly on the sources. Another point in common was awareness of the need for a constant interweaving, in the scientific investigation, between the 'internal' and 'external' moment of the historical reconstruction: starting from Bauduin – one of the first advocates of the need for a deep connection between historical and juridical knowledge [19] – and from Leibniz, Raggi insisted, in a famous article, on the concept of 'legal history' "as an awareness of the development of law due to needs and characteristics inherent in it". [20] In this respect – he observed – modern historiography has refined its analytical tools: it has abandoned the distinction between external and internal history of

---

[17] The identification of historicity of law with *scientia iuris* was a fixed point for the scholar: among the very many pages he dedicated to the subject, we recall those of *'Diritto'. Incontri e scontri* (n. 10) 18, where the identification becomes 'absolute' according to M. Bretone, *Diritto e tempo nella tradizione europea* (Roma-Bari 2004 new ed.) 185, note 37. See also Grossi, 'Storia di esperienze giuridiche e tradizione romanistica' (n. 2) 540 f.

[18] Cf. M. Brutti, 'Antiformalismo e storia del diritto. Appunti in memoria di Riccardo Orestano', in QF 18 (1989) 712 f.

[19] In the programmatic work *De institutione historiae universae et ejus cum jurisprudentia conjunctione*, published in 1561, in which Bauduin tended to favour the search for the genuine jurisprudential text, independently of its juridical use, thus intending to recuperate its full historical reliability. See lastly M. Brutti, 'Dal Digesto ai giuristi', in D. Mantovani, A. Padoa Schioppa (eds.), *Interpretare il Digesto. Storia e metodi* (Pavia 2014) 616 ff.

[20] L. Raggi, 'Storia esterna e storia interna del diritto nella letteratura romanistica', in BIDR 62 (1959) 199 ff. = L. Raggi, *Scritti* (Milano 1975) 73 ff. The cited point is on p. 83 of the *Scritti*.

law and turned its attention to the ways in which the Romans fell back on their experience, discovering the *Roman* science of law, *Roman* legal historiography, and beginning to study the ideological components and the instrumental coordinates used by the jurists in the specific socio-economic contexts of their time.[21]

This explains the title given to this presentation: in the thought of Orestano and that of Raggi, historicity and controversiality appear as two attributes of law, since the true jurist works in the constant awareness of the historicity of the phenomenon under investigation and of the necessary dialectical dimension of his work.[22] In this way, aiming at the solution of conflicts of interest with case analysis, he produces *cottidie* law, according to the above-mentioned Pomponian image.

2. Teachers and students

In the 1950s, Orestano taught in Genoa, in the chair previously held by scholars of the stature of Fadda and Bensa, working on points central to the thought of Scialoja and Jhering, condensed – as recalled by Franca De Marini Avonzo – in famous phrases such as "Roman law is dead", "through Roman law, beyond Roman law".[23] On the basis of ideas behind expressions such as these, a method of teaching and study was developed which was capable of conditioning the historical-juridical research of entire generations. Original impulses emerged, new lines of research opened up: the overcoming of the normative conception of the *Corpus Iuris*, the fight against the abstractions of modern dogmat-

[21] Raggi, 'Storia esterna e storia interna del diritto' (n. 20) 99. The italics are those of the author.

[22] With regard to this dimension, it is known that the path toward consideration of *ius controversum* as a general category of the work of the *prudentes* was opened by the conference held by Andreas B. Schwarz at the International Congress of Roman Law and History of Law held in Verona in September 1948, later published, with additions, in 'Das strittige Recht der römischen Juristen' (n. 16) 201-225 = 'Il diritto controverso dei giuristi romani' (n. 16) 173-197. On Schwarz's contribution in focusing on a series of fundamental elements of the category (in particular, the descriptive function of the 'internal movement' of jurisprudence, the links with judicial practice and concrete cases), see for all M. Brutti, 'L'indipendenza dei giuristi (dallo 'ius controversum' all'autorità del principe)', in F. Milazzo (ed.), *'Ius controversum' e auctoritas principis. Giuristi principe e diritto nel primo impero. Atti del Convegno internazionale di diritto romano (Copanello, 11-13 giugno 1998)* (Napoli 2003) 403 ff. (esp. 405 f.).

[23] Cf. F. De Marini Avonzo, 'Rileggere l''Introduzione' di Orestano', in Labeo 34 (1988) 210.

ics, the clarification of the notion of 'juridical experience', "with its potential to overcome formalism to link instead the techniques and thought of jurists to reality and facts".[24]

On these broad topics, Orestano's thinking inspired that of Raggi. And apart from the scientific influence, some characteristics of a shared human journey remain indelible. In the preface to Raggi's *Scritti*, the commemoration by his teacher is vivid and emotional.[25] The "long communion of life" between the two had lasted 18 years;[26] and they had been fruitful years, because it was necessary to ensure that Roman law was discussed – it could be said, paraphrasing Mantello[27] – not simply as a 'historical' law, but above all because it was able to 'say something' to the contemporary jurist. On this central point, Raggi turned the problem around: it is not correct to ask whether Roman law can still contribute to the jurist's education, but whether it is legitimate to imagine law without history. We read:

> Scholars of Roman law certainly cannot prevent scholars of positive law from celebrating their liberation from Roman law, understood as a liberation from the Pandectistic rationalism that forced new realities into old schemata. Indeed, scholars of Roman law must take part in such celebration, since it is to their merit that they have contributed, with their results, to that liberation. If anything, their current objective is to prevent that, in the law studies, the 'liberation from Roman law' degenerates into liberation from historical knowledge. (transl.)[28]

---

[24] Thus De Marini Avonzo, 'Rileggere l'"Introduzione"' (n. 23) 210.

[25] R. Orestano, *Prefazione* to L. Raggi, *Scritti* (n. 20) V-XXIV (= R. Orestano, *'Diritto'. Incontri e scontri* [n. 10] 693-710; R. Orestano, *Scritti*, 3 [Napoli 1998] 1685-1706).

[26] From the time of his university studies in Genoa, where Raggi graduated under Orestano in 1955, until his death in Macerata on 5 November 1968: a period of time marked by the scholar's incessant struggle against the incurable disease that killed him at only 38 years of age.

In the 'Prefazione' (n. 25) VIII, Orestano recalled the sufferings of his student affected by the disease that was devastating him but of which – "due to a natural reticence that marked his character and a sort of shame about the ailment, which he always maintained" (transl.)– he hardly ever spoke, not even with his teacher.

[27] A. Mantello, 'Futuro del passato o futuro attraverso il passato?', in Labeo 34 (1988) 228.

[28] L. Raggi, 'A proposito di studio e insegnamento del diritto romano', in Rivista di Diritto civile 4 (1958) 327 = *Scritti* (n. 20) 113. These last words are very

He had written a few lines earlier that, concerning the conceptual constructions of the moderns jurists, scholars in Roman law cannot counterpose the construction of another rationalism in competition with it; and it would have been vain to exalt the 'perenniality and universality' of Roman law. Rather, their fundamental contribution could have been that of the offense "that historical research continually brings to the tranquil immobility of dogmatic results";[29] however, it would have been necessary to include the problem within the broader question of legal historiography as a function of knowledge of law.[30]

Therefore, a conception pervaded by awareness of historicity provides nourishment to the conviction, common to the two scholars, of a law in the service of concrete life and of the infinite problems arising from it; thus the vision of the jurist as 'interpreter', 'mediator' – in the full sense of the term – "between the reality that exists and the reality that one wishes existed";[31] hence the need to study techniques and methods used in antiquity by a class of specialists, with the caution – on this point, Raggi was very clear from the beginning of his final course of lessons[32] – that each investigation on the method of the Roman jurists also has value as an approach, from a historical perspective, to the very problem of juridical methodology.[33]

Raggi returned to this subject often, focusing on the topical method

current, especially in times like ours, dominated by a pseudo-cultural bureaucratic technocracy and informed by parameters anything but respectful not only of history in general but also and above all of historicity as a specific attribute of many scientific disciplines, among which the legal ones. The thought of D. Mantovani, 'Il diritto romano dopo l'Europa' (n. 9) 60, can be shared when he states that we must all feel the responsibility of not wasting the tradition that has led us to possess the educational role that the teaching of legal history has played thus far.

[29] Raggi, 'A proposito di studio' (n. 28) in *Scritti* (n. 20) 113.

[30] Raggi, 'A proposito di studio' (n. 28) in *Scritti* (n. 20) 115.

[31] Mantello, 'Futuro' (n. 27) 223.

[32] These are, as is known, the lessons given by Raggi in the last course on the history of Roman law that he taught at the University of Macerata during the 1967-1968 academic year. The scholar died a few months later. Gathered together by the students in the summer of 1968 in the form of typewritten notes and then mimeographed (cf. M. Campolunghi, S.-A. Fusco, 'Prefazione' to L. Raggi, *Il metodo della giurisprudenza romana* [Torino 2007] 2), these lessons were initially included in Raggi's *Scritti* (n. 29) 165-254; although aimed at first-year students, and thus essentially institutional, they represent – in addition to an original educational proposal – a text that is exemplary in its method and innovative scientific contents.

[33] Raggi, *Il metodo* (n. 32) 31.

as a *technique of thinking by means of problems*:[34] a procedure intrinsic to the work of the Roman jurists, aimed not at the search for absolute truths, but for plausible solutions, forged by the continuous critical comparison of ideas, theories, doctrines. The original spirit of the sources – he would say in the final lesson – can be identified in the controversy, in the constant acceptance of comparison among opinions;[35] and this explains why jurisprudential techniques are nourished by the contents of other disciplines, from rhetoric to philosophy.[36]

An opposite position, not infrequently emerging over the centuries, was taken by those who desired a Roman law set "sotto una campana di vetro" – the metaphor is again by Raggi – made to conform to a unitary and falsely homogeneous reconstruction, "... in cui tutti i particolari si legano tra loro in una visione organica perfetta, senza la minima sbavatura".[37] Orestano echoed these words, affirming that he no longer believed in the universality of the juridical experience (even though this – he added – could be "gratifying and consolatory"), understood as a 'totalizing' reality in which all the particular experiences were to be included, unified, absorbed and dissolved, "... senza limiti spaziali e temporali, dal passato più remoto al futuro più lontano".[38] And further:

> However, when one descends from the empyrean of abstraction – and the jurist, if he wishes to be such, must of necessity descend – to discourses and reasonings on the 'reality of the real', in its concreteness, these must always and only be performed with precise reference to *single* experiences, which have materialized and materialize in individual formations, well defined – I repeat – in their spatial demarcation and temporal dimension. (transl.)[39]

---

[34] Raggi, *Il metodo* (n. 32) 35. The italics are those of the author.

[35] Raggi, *Il metodo* (n. 32) 162.

[36] The problem represented by the points of contact, but also of divergence, between Roman legal thought and rhetoric was a subject dear to Raggi and often turned up in his lessons, cf. in particular Raggi, *Il metodo* (n. 32) 46 ff., 56, 70 ff., 81 f., 106 ff.

[37] Raggi, *Il metodo* (n. 32) 162. This obviously does not exclude the existence of "individualizing points in juridical Humanism and beyond": this is considered by Brutti, *Dal Digesto* (n. 19) 614 ff., to whom the cited expression belongs, which provides the title of the section.

[38] Orestano, *Introduzione* (n. 1) 367.

[39] Orestano, *Introduzione* (n. 1) 366-367. The italics are those of the author.

Underlying these historiographical conceptions – on the one hand that conforming to the idea of Roman law as a 'model of perfection', on the other that maintained by Orestano and Raggi – are, obviously, antithetical visions on how to interpret that very rich and boundless patrimony, consisting of lively and concrete experiences brought to fruition through the centuries. Naturally, the difference is manifested in many ways, but the first consists in the manner in which to perceive the ancient witnesses: as blocks of a compact and granitic building or, in contrast, as a 'precipitous writing' of needs, interests, problems cropping up in daily practice and juridically relevant. The *Ventotto pagine necessarie*, which served as an introduction to a well-known study on matrimony, provided the author with the occasion to acknowledge the scientific travail that had led him to a clear methodological transformation.[40] When he began that labour – he said – matrimony in the conception of the Romans was for him a topic to be faced with the usual instrumental baggage of the Romanist: consultation of the existing literature on the subject, collection and exegesis of the sources, search for possible interpolations, until reaching the 'dogmatic' classification of the legal regime both for the classical period and for the Justinian one. Then – wrote the scholar – "it never even entered my mind that for such a topic there could be other ways: a kind of obligatory schema, which ended up providing a common physiognomy to much of the concerning the history of Roman law in the last few decades".[41] Matrimony – he continued – was presented to him as the institution,[42] an abstract entity of related norms organized in a 'system', for which historical study was admissible, of course, but only to the extent that it identified and combined the rules that had to make up the current general discipline. It would be interesting to investigate more thoroughly the process of maturation that led Orestano to a radical inversion of the method; here, however, we must limit ourselves to highlighting some important points, undoubtedly including the one constituted by the intent, considered imperative, not to deal with the texts of the *Digesta* as if they were elements of positive legislation, and to consider them instead for what they really are: fragments of scientific elaborations to be repositioned each in its own time.[43] In contrast, the opposite

[40] R. Orestano, 'Ventotto pagine necessarie. Introduzione a *La struttura giuridica del matrimonio romano dal diritto classico al diritto giustinianeo*' I, Milano 1951, VII-XXXIV (republished in *'Diritto'. Incontri e scontri* [n. 10]) 115-143.

[41] Orestano, 'Ventotto pagine' (n. 40) in *'Diritto'. Incontri e scontri* (n. 10) 118.

[42] The spacing is that of the author.

[43] Orestano, 'Ventotto pagine' (n. 40) in *'Diritto'. Incontri e scontri* (n. 10) 129.

methodology erred in creating a series of multiple conceptualizations, 'normativizing' both the facts of the cases investigated by the jurists and their opinions on them.[44]

Moving in the direction indicated by Orestano was research that still seems to have been pioneering around the middle of the last century. Inspired by Capograssi, the scholar advanced a new idea of the history of law, as a history of multiple experiences dictated by the pulsating reality of life.[45] Raggi learned the lesson, focusing on essential methodological aspects. The single text – he wrote in a point in which the master's influence is clearly felt – should never be considered a unit *per se*, but must always be included within a dense network of relationships with the cultural environment that expressed it.[46] This idea also involves the physiognomy of juridical reasoning. Like authors such as Schwarz, and against Savigny's approach shared by Schulz, Raggi maintained that an absolute coherence could not exist *a priori* in the jurisprudential sources, since it was not through a mere 'calculation of concepts' that the argumentations of the jurists were developed. He rejected the rationalistic and mathematical logic that had its roots in Descartes and Leibniz: the latter's *Corpus Iuris reconcinnatum* – he wrote – is ultimately the *Corpus Iuris* "reduced to shreds and recomposed into an entire new systematic arrangement".[47] In contrast, according to the scholar, intuition plays an important role in identifying the most appropriate solution to the specific case:[48] underly-

---

[44] Cf. Orestano, 'Ventotto pagine' (n. 40) in *'Diritto'. Incontri e scontri* (n. 10) 134.

[45] A fundamental point, on which we will insist later. However, in the meantime, see Grossi, 'Testimonianza (n. 9) 925 f., as well as the bibliographical indications provided by E. Stolfi, 'Il contesto culturale', in *Dogmengeschichte und historische Individualität der römischen Juristen – Storia dei dogmi e individualità storica dei giuristi romani. Atti del Seminario internazionale* (Montepulciano, 14-17 giugno 2011) (Trento 2012) 252, note 3.

[46] Cf. Raggi, *Il metodo* (n. 32) 154. A point of confluence with Orestano's thought, cf. Brutti, *Antiformalismo* (n. 18) 717.

[47] Raggi, *Il metodo* (n. 32) 162. On the Leibnizian ancestry of Savigny's thought, see Brutti, *Dal Digesto* (n. 19) 626 and note 74.

[48] Cf. Raggi, *Il metodo* (n. 32) 41. Contrary to the opinion of those who underestimated this aspect, Raggi maintained that the Roman jurists often arrived spontaneously at the solution of a problem submitted to them by means of an 'immediate' understanding of the case, without the need to resort to 'a rational argumentation'. The affirmation, although somewhat strong, intends to explain one of the aspects of the work method of the *prudentes*, as do the reflections given in the following pages (see Raggi, *ibid.* [n. 32] 42 ff.), tending to highlight the lack, frequent in the texts that have come down to us, of motivation, i.e. the centrality of the *auctoritas* of the jurist as a

ing the science of the *prudentes* was the ability to grasp, within the internal dynamics of things, the starting point for a more adequate, more valid direction, perhaps in contrast to the existing juridical datum. In any case, a fundamental point is represented by the fact that the arguments of the jurists were problematical and provisional – and as such susceptible to being questioned, sometimes using rhetorical motivations [49] – since there was no final objective, but a permanent and inexhaustible activity of approximation resulting from the 'doubt' that is the lifeblood of every cognitive process. A possible origin of this thought is in the position taken by Hegel who, in a bitter polemic with Hugo, had appreciated the 'non-consequentiality' of the Roman jurists as one of their greatest virtues. [50]

The diffidence, or better intolerance, of Orestano and Raggi toward abstract categories of thought and universal dogmatic constructions fully rejected also the expression 'Roman legal order', often used in the literature as a synonym of Roman law: "a much more dangerous myth" – stated Orestano in a lecture delivered in Rome on 23 March 1961 [51] – "since scientific support could make it seem correspondent to a reality, behind which men would disappear, to bring forth an abstract framework of rigid and necessary structures, absolute and unalterable, looming over the organized collectivity". [52] This would end up in the con-

premise upon which to base – or with which to strengthen – a certain interpretative line. This obviously does not detract from the circumstance that the 'controversial' nature of the Roman *scientia iuris* allowed the jurists – as highlighted by Beduschi, 'Il 'ius controversum'' (n. 15) 3 – to declare the law in terms of a substantial (because inspired by contexts of life) and formal (since developed through logical schemata) rationality. These are complementary and not antithetical aspects.

[49] Thus Brutti, 'L'indipendenza' (n. 22) 403-404.

[50] Cf. G.W.F. Hegel, 'Introduzione' (§ 3) to *Lineamenti di filosofia del diritto*[5] (= *Grundlinien der Philosophie des Rechts*, Berlin 1840[3]) (Roma-Bari 1996 new ed. rev. (con le aggiunte di E. Gans) ed. by G. Marini, 1999, 26. Hegel's polemic was directed against the *Manuale di storia del diritto romano* by Gustav Hugo. This position was dealt with by Brutti, ' L'indipendenza' (n. 22) 415-416 and note 22, with stimulating observations.

[51] Published with the title 'Concetto di ordinamento giuridico e studio storico del diritto romano' in Jus XIII (1962) 35 ff., subsequently (with additions) in Orestano, *'Diritto'. Incontri e scontri* (n. 10) 395 ff., and in the *Scritti*, 3 (n. 25) 1557 ff., finally in RISG 4 (2013) 35 ff. (from which are taken the quotations).

[52] Orestano, 'Concetto' (n. 51) 53 (transl.). In the course of the scholar's long scientific activity, it is possible to observe significant transformation in this regard: from the initial acceptance of the notion of 'system' according to the conception of Santi Romano to the distancing himself from it, as it was too narrow – albeit convenient as an interpretative schema in an 'ordering' function – and therefore inade-

ception of the history of the complex juridical events of ancient Rome as a single corpus, experienced for fourteen centuries from its origins to Justinian, thus reintroducing, in a surreptitious manner, "those evolutionist representations which, with so much effort and only recently, are being overcome".[53] It is necessary instead to distinguish specific historical moments, so as to highlight not only the elements that give the impression of continuity between periods but also those that are different, a sign of sometimes profound transformations.

3. From practice to science

The methodological approach based on rejection of the notion of ordering, understood in an institutional sense, to make way for the flexible and concrete conception of 'experience',[54] allows, like no other, considera-

quate to explain all the facets of the juridical phenomenon, which is above all, as noted Grossi, 'Storia di esperienze giuridiche e tradizione romanistica' (n. 2) 542, "… before being form and order, a dimension of life". Hence the acceptance of the concept of "juridical experience", which Orestano borrowed from the jurist and philosopher Giuseppe Capograssi, interpreting it – thus Grossi, *ibid.* (n. 2) 542 – "... as a specific and singular way of experiencing law in history, of perceiving it, conceptualizing it, applying it in connection with a certain vision of the social world and certain cultural presuppositions ...". It should be borne in mind that Orestano later re-elaborated this notion, moving away from the universalizing and generalizing vision of the philosopher to accept the idea of an 'experience' conceivable only in the plural, that is in an individualizing sense. On this point, see A. Calore, 'La romanistica italiana dal 1945 al 1970: tra storia e dogmatica', in I. Birocchi, M. Brutti (ed.), *Storia del diritto e identità disciplinari: tradizioni e prospettive* (Torino 2016) 134, note 183. Valuable reflections on the relations with Capograssi were formulated by Orestano in the essay 'Della 'esperienza giuridica' vista da un giurista', in *Scritti*, 3 (n. 25) 1756 ff.

[53] Orestano, 'Concetto' (n. 51) 50. We should recall the judgement of Grossi, 'Testimonianza' (n. 9) 926, when he observed that Orestano's conception of the history of law as a history of juridical experiences, spelled out in various synchronic moments rather than in a diachrony slipping into 'continuity', allowed the teacher to remain unaffected by "that clinging vice of continuity, on which many historians of not great methodological competence had slipped". Still topical on the relationships between legal dogmatics and historical study, with radical criticism of the vision of a modern private law in close connection and continuity with the ancient one, are the pages of M. Brutti, 'Storiografia e critica del sistema pandettistico', in QF 8 (1979) 317 ff.

[54] Another page (cf. Orestano, 'Concetto' [n. 51] 51) contains the significant expression "legal system *per momenta*", also used in another important work, *I fatti di normazione nell'esperienza giuridica romana arcaica* (Torino 1967) 26, to express the inseparable connection between the datum provided by phenomenal reality and

tion of jurisprudence as intimately connected to every other aspect of legal phenomenology.[55] Indeed, because of its ability to grasp the individuality of single historical events, the thought of the *prudentes* appears to be the only way capable of representing the complex world of law in its true dimension, consisting not only of organizational structures, precepts and logical relations but also of contradictions, ambiguities, arbitrary decisions and conflicts. "On the opposite side of this subtle network of choices and historical determinations which make up the juridical experience" – writes Brutti – "are the concepts that the science of law places outside time; the abstractions that do not move, closed and separated from one another. In short, the systematic superstitions".[56]

But there is more. According to Orestano, in its self-reflection carried out since ancient times, jurisprudence has accumulated an experience composed of an infinite series of facts, by means of which the thinking of the jurists has been constructed through the millennia.[57] A continuous *fieri* has enriched the instrumental expertise of *prudentes*, even though – noted the scholar – many have claimed and claim to fix its rules and schemata: "like someone who wishes to freeze a flight of butterflies within the display case of a natural sciences museum".[58] On the basis of the conviction that the juridical is manifested in the concreteness of facts sooner than in norms,[59] he intended, with this acute metaphor, to highlight the process of mummification to which a very mobile thought had been subjected through the centuries for the purposes of the formation of 'systems', seeking – unsuccessfully – to cancel the *diversitates*.

The perspective illuminated by Orestano and Raggi overturned the current methodological approach.[60] If law is opened to history, then the juridical experience becomes an integral part of the historical expe-

---

the descriptive schema that constantly, and as much as possible, seeks to adapt to it. Cf. Calore, 'La romanistica' (n. 52) 126 and note 146.

[55] Orestano, *Introduzione* (n. 1) 354.

[56] Brutti, 'Antiformalismo' (n. 18) 723. The author (*ibid.*, 702 ff.) also highlighted another fixed point of Orestano's thought, the impossibility of a complete definition of 'juridical experience': the 'continuous setting' of relations between the present and the past, relived through the interpretation of various sources, forces the historian to experience the flexibility and relativity of each schema.

[57] Orestano, *Introduzione* (n. 1) 356.

[58] Orestano, *Introduzione* (n. 1) 356.

[59] Orestano, 'Concetto' (n. 51) 39.

[60] See lastly Calore, 'La romanistica' (n. 52) 126 f., 134 f.

rience and must, consequently and necessarily, abandon any dogmatic and 'constructivistic' desire in order to anchor itself to reality, to the 'facts' of life, to the demands and interests to which law continually attempts to provide answers within its specialistic viewpoint. The indissoluble connection between the factuality of human experience and the elaboration conducted by the *prudentes* poses a problem often faced by the interpreters, which we could define as 'self-awareness' of the legal science. Raggi dealt with this question at the beginning of one of his lessons: he resolved to investigate the time and manner in which a case analysis, with aims limited to the solution of specific cases, was able to translate into a reflection on its methods, procedures and results.[61] Raggi identified this turning point in the later Republican period and saw in Cicero an exceptional witness, if not protagonist, of the establishment of new speculative needs.[62]

It is of no interest to discuss here the validity of the theory, but rather to focus attention on the phrase in which, interpreting the Ciceronian perspective, the scholar maintains that knowledge of *ius civile* is essentially achieved through practice: "one ends up mastering the subject through the very activity of the jurist".[63] The *prudentes* are seen as the only individuals able to elaborate a synthesis of the various data borrowed from experience, thus realizing that *ars* which for Cicero was synonymous with *scientia*. I seem to sense a common ground between the thought of Raggi and an idea of Orestano, according to which the science of law, like any other, *is self-constructed* from within, "through an incessant critical review of its procedures".[64] This can be adjudged a trait common to the ancient and modern legal science, if it is true – as has been observed[65] – that the object of historiography cannot consist only of systems, since in that way it would ignore the creative function of the science of law, the influence that it is able to exert on juridical structures and on their development.

Through the awareness of its function and the re-elaboration of the tradition behind it, Roman jurisprudence was able to elevate itself from a technically based practice to *ars*, to *scientia iuris*, operating in the world of facts from a hermeneutical perspective. I recall a well-known

---

[61] In the ninth lesson: cf. Raggi, *Il metodo* (n. 32) 86 ff.

[62] Raggi, *Il metodo* (n. 32) 87.

[63] Raggi, *Il metodo* (n. 32) 90.

[64] Orestano, *Concetto* (n. 51) 37. The italics are those of the author.

[65] Brutti, 'Rileggere Orestano' (n. 6) 23.

definition by Gadamer: 'hermeneutics' as the art of disclosing, of acting as interpreter, of explaining and interpreting. Naturally, it also embraces the underlying art of understanding, which is required when the meaning of something is not clear and unequivocal.[66] Legal hermeneutics – added the philosopher – clearly has the function of creating law,[67] and the hermeneutical effort is successful whenever an elucidation, a penetration, an appropriation takes place.[68] There is a clear distance separating this perspective from the one outlined by Schulz's *Isolierung*, which presupposes instead – wrote Brutti – a formal representation of the juridical phenomenon and the law-norm equation.[69]

We must deal with this outline. Schulz is an author to whom both Orestano and Raggi gave great attention, but from whom they often distanced themselves. If on the one hand – stated Orestano – one must agree with the German scholar concerning the evaluation of the 'creative' role played by the *interpretatio prudentium* – tending to combine certainty and elasticity of law[70] – on the other the difference of opinions in many aspects is clear. Firstly, on the question of the historical sensitivity of the Roman jurists, denied by Schulz, for whom they demonstrated a stubborn aversion to the study of history.[71] Secondly,

---

[66] Cf. H.G. Gadamer, *Ermeneutica*, in *Enciclopedia del Novecento*, II (Roma 1977) 731.

[67] Gadamer, *Ermeneutica* (n. 66) 735.

[68] Cf. Gadamer, *Ermeneutica* (n. 66) 738.

[69] Brutti, 'Antiformalismo' (n. 18) 677. Cf. also Stolfi, 'Il contesto' (n. 45) 254 ff., as well as by the same author – in particular on the distancing from the Schulzian *Isolierung* of many subsequent studies – 'Diritto romano e storia del pensiero giuridico', in *Nel mondo del diritto romano. Convegno ARISTEC Roma, 10-11 ottobre 2014*, ed. by L. Vacca (Napoli 2017) esp. 105 ff.

[70] Cf. Orestano, *Introduzione* (n. 1) 57, with reference to Schulz, *History* (n. 14) 286.

[71] Cf. Schulz, *History* (n. 14) 70, 134, discussed by Orestano, *Introduzione* (n. 1) 178 ff., 596 ff. See also *supra* note 10. Schulz had maintained the complete absence of historical reflection in Roman jurisprudence also in another famous work, *I principii del diritto romano* (= *Prinzipien des römischen Rechts*, München 1934) Firenze 1946, 89 ff. The scholar admitted that a certain interest in history was present in Gaius, but only occasionally and to an insignificant extent. Critical of Schulz's position was, as is known, C.A. Maschi, *Il diritto romano nella prospettiva storica della giurisprudenza classica* (Milano 1966^2) *passim*. This is not the place to thoroughly examine this delicate question, but we should recall at least the judgement – in my opinion completely acceptable – formulated by G. Crifò, 'Ulpiano. Esperienze e responsabilità del giurista', in ANRW II.15 (Berlin-New York 1976) 710, who observed that with the elimination of the historical perspective and with the homoge-

(here the distances increased) concerning the research methodology. Orestano accused Schulz of using heuristic tools consisting of abstract conceptualizations, as well as of employing such entities as tesserae to compose a mosaic detached from reality, through a process he called "reification of abstractions".[72] The central point concerns the method followed in the scientific elaboration of the data provided by the sources. Many manual discourses, as well as those on specific topics, are based on a 'classical dogmatics' which is pure abstraction: "an ideal mosaic, composed of materials selected and ordered according to presuppositions and concepts in which the thought of today often overlaps with the ancient one, overpowering it".[73] In this way, it is inevitable to lapse into the vision of a linear development of ancient juridical thought, imagining a paradigm of perfection thanks to a jurisprudence conceived as homogeneous and coherent, at the cost of ignoring or underestimating (or attributing to later periods) the dissonant testimonies.

Thus, in a scenario purged of differences and fluctuations of thought, the basis of the law of the *prudentes*, controversiality, ended up being cancelled. Orestano's criticism was radical. The broad historiographical debate on 'method' – he observed – had merely created "un groviglio sempre più arruffato, il quale dimostra unicamente l'evaporazione e direi addirittura l'inconsistenza del concetto stesso di 'diritto classico'".[74] Raggi echoed these harsh words: once again in reference to Schulz's *History*, he concluded his course of lessons with a drastic and cutting judgment:

> Therefore, this work, valid on an instrumental level, is essentially to be rejected in the manner it deals with the problem of jurisprudential law, bringing into it a vision of Roman law as a source of modern abstractions and formalistic techniques to which they refer. (transl.)[75]

---

nization of the various personalities of the jurists there is the risk of falling into a juridical ontology beyond time and history; and he adds, with reference to Ulpian (*ibid.*, 713), that he was not only a 'systematizer' of the law in force in his time, but also a historian of law, "both in the sense of having sought and indicated causes and developments of the institutions and doctrines that he expounded in his works, and in the other sense, which seems to us of great importance and modernity, of having used history as an argument" (transl.).

[72] Orestano, *Introduzione* (n. 1) 399.

[73] Orestano, *Introduzione* (n. 1) 550.

[74] Orestano, *Introduzione* (n. 1) 551.

[75] Raggi, *Il metodo* (n. 32) 163.

4. Ideology or ideologies of the jurists?

The vision of jurisprudential law as an organic unit, composed of fungible jurists, found a fierce opponent in Mitteis in the second decade of the twentieth century.[76] Orestano followed his methodological approach, developing the theory that Roman jurisprudence was formed by many individualities, each of which made a personal contribution to the science of law. He decisively rejected the impersonality of legal interpretation,[77] maintaining that the only manner of study suitable for a serious approach to the thinking of the *prudentes* was the individualizing one: over and above the subject, it was the science itself that should be seen as a sum of individualities.[78]

Several currents of thought, generated by schools and doctrines of continental Europe starting from the sixteenth century, contributed to the construction of dogmas and legal systems. However, it was particularly with Savigny and Puchta that the ontological dimension of juridical phenomenology was accentuated. Orestano's vision was clear. It is true that for Savigny law and legal science were history,[79] but this does not mean that he should not be considered one of the greatest theorists of the systematic method in the legal sphere. His very famous and monumental work, the *System*, is its evident proof. In the second half of the nineteenth century, the reconstructive efforts of the prevailing jusrationalism multiplied, tending to discover affinities, connections and relations linking concepts and relationships. 'Structural units' were outlined, institutions and groups of institutions were clarified, followed by entire branches of law. The 'constructors' sometimes spoke of the 'pyramid of concepts' (*Begriffspyramide*), and this *modus procedendi* was described by the master in these terms: "effort is made to ensure that the bricks are well squared, with firm joints, in order to cement them together in overlying orders of increasing generality: the aspiration and goal is a single

[76] However, the new historiography concerning Roman jurisprudence, proposed by Ludwig Mitteis in the second decade of the last century, did not achieve the desired developments. Also in Mitteis, there remained strong – wrote Brutti, *Dal Digesto* (n. 19) 633 – "the primacy of systematic thinking in the description of law".

[77] Cf. Brutti, 'Antiformalismo' (n. 18) 722. It is evident that in this perspective the traditional image of a full homogeneity of the jurists was demolished: cf. Brutti, *ibid.* (n. 18) 707.

[78] So Brutti, 'Antiformalismo' (n. 18) 722. See also *ibid.*, 719.

[79] R. Orestano, 'Edificazione e conoscenza del giuridico nel 'Sistema' di Savigny. Tre motivi di riflessione', now in *Edificazione del giuridico* (n. 12) 182.

pyramid that includes and summarizes all the others".[80] In operations of this type, in which dogmatics serves to realize both operational functions (the easy attainment of a solution for each case) and cognitive ones (recomposition of the data of every experience, of the present as of the past),[81] the ideological component ends up strongly conditioning the direction of the scientific work, suggesting that 'system' and 'dogmatics' are the only possible forms in which to include *scientia iuris*. Orestano called this an "insulting illusion",[82] and the reason for this drastic judgement was the rejection of each holistic abstraction.[83] He warned that to speak of *scientia iuris* in absolute terms and in the sense of a unitary whole is a fiction of our mind,[84] and it becomes a very dangerous notion if one fails to consider that it is, in fact, a fiction: in every science, we always proceed through individual experiences, and that generated by the Roman juridical experience is no exception.

The same approach was followed by Raggi, even though the title with which his last lessons were published – *Il metodo* (the method, not the methods!) *della giurisprudenza romana* – might lead to a misunderstanding, seeming to propose a global image of the jurisprudence.[85] Yet, that the question ended up being purely nominalistic is demonstrated by the fact that it was probably Orestano himself who suggested that title for the publication of Raggi's lessons in the *Scritti*.[86] Some hypotheses to explain the apparent inconsistency were advanced,[87] but in

---

[80] R. Orestano, 'Ideologia, parola da non far più paura', now in *Edificazione del giuridico* (n. 12) 287. On the current value of Orestano's statement, see now, with lucid observations, E. Stolfi, 'Ancora su Vittorio Scialoja (ed Emilio Betti)', in I. Piro (ed.), *Scritti per Alessandro Corbino*, 7 (Tricase 2016) 66.

[81] Orestano, 'Ideologia' (n. 80) now in *Edificazione del giuridico* (n. 12) 287.

[82] Orestano, 'Ideologia' (n. 80) now in *Edificazione del giuridico* (n. 12) 288.

[83] Also in that sense the master's teaching appeared to G. Tarello, 'Quattro buoni giuristi per una cattiva azione', in Materiali per una storia della cultura giuridica 7 (1977) 165 ff., as a 'liberation', given the threefold rejection of metaphysics, linguistic ontology and the general theory of law understood in the universal sense.

[84] Orestano, *Introduzione* (n. 1) 364.

[85] Cf. Campolunghi, Fusco, 'Prefazione' to Luigi Raggi, *Il metodo della giurisprudenza romana* (n. 32) 16.

[86] Cf. Campolunghi, Fusco, 'Prefazione' to L. Raggi, *Il metodo della giurisprudenza romana* (n. 32) 16.

[87] Cf. Campolunghi, Fusco, 'Prefazione' to L. Raggi, *Il metodo della giurisprudenza romana* (n. 32) 17: perhaps to point out that Raggi's work tended toward a unifying perspective, or to recall a phrase from the first lesson (cf. L. Raggi, *Il metodo della giurisprudenza romana* [n. 32] 31), which spoke precisely of 'discourse on the method' of the Roman jurists.

any case the student's viewpoint did not deviate, also in this regard, from that of the teacher: in the last years of his life, Raggi had worked on an archive of jurisprudence, jurist by jurist,[88] and among his authors of reference was Kunkel, whose studies (not only prosopographical ones) on jurists, on their social background and on the specific economic and political contexts in which they lived are known. The only acceptable unitary image of the Roman jurists was given by the (certainly not negligible) circumstance of being an expression of the highest strata of society, "linked to the dominant class by very strong interests".[89]

Raggi's last lesson, almost his spiritual testament, ended by underlining the risks inherent in a historiographical process that interprets the sources by erasing the central characteristic of the Roman juridical discourse, the case law tendency, thereby intending to eliminate the contradictions. I sense a similarity (or something more) with another shrewd conclusion formulated, about 20 years earlier, by Schwarz in his work on contentious law: the positivistic mentality of the nineteenth century, with its convictions about the completeness of codified norms or of law itself – the author wrote – has sent the concept of *ius controversum* into oblivion, which today sounds rather strange; from this, the intention to once again approach the viewpoints of the classical jurists, which does not find space within historical-juridical research.[90] To the contrary – Schwarz concluded – "here is one of the fundamental problems not only of Roman law and of its history but also of the law of all times and thus also of the present".[91]

Beyond possible direct ancestries, this statement could ideally be considered a starting point for the fight undertaken by Orestano and Raggi against every dogmatic-systematic pyramid. For this reason, the concept of 'juridical experience', borrowed from Capograssi's thought, was particularly useful to understand how the same 'model' generated by dogmatic constructions was, in turn, not an absolute value but rather the product of precise historical conceptions of law, to be definitively demolished so as to eliminate also the barriers between the study of positive law and legal historiography.[92] In this regard, Raggi's think-

---

[88] Cf. Orestano, *Prefazione* to L. Raggi, *Scritti* (n. 20) XIX.

[89] Raggi, *Il metodo della giurisprudenza romana* (n. 32) 44.

[90] Schwarz, 'Das strittige Recht' (n. 16) 225 = 'Il diritto controverso' (n. 16) 197.

[91] Schwarz, *loc. ult. cit.*

[92] Thus A. Mantello, 'Orestano 'par lui-même'', in *Atti dell'Accademia Nazionale dei Lincei. Rendiconti della classe di scienze morali, storiche e filologiche*, ser. IX, 20 (2010) 850 = *Variae* 2, ed. by F. Lamberti (Lecce 2014) 1456.

ing was particularly lucid: it did not escape his notice that the central question consisted of *Bewußtsein*, the awareness of one's intrinsic historicity; in this perspective, a common thread linked the ancient legal thought to the modern one. Here is the passage with which the scholar concluded his article on the external and internal history of law:

> In fact, the methodological refinement has highlighted that alongside, and I would almost say above, the problem of identifying the conceptualizations and logical schemata adopted by the Romans, there is the problem of identifying our conceptualizations, our ideological structure, our social conditioning as determining elements of the nature and results of the historiographical investigation. Once the study of the logical procedures (and the social condition) of the Romans is allowed to be included in the *content* of the Roman law studies, once the Pandectistic bulwark (with its illusion of arriving at the construction of a pure Roman law, a perfect systematization of juridicity itself, removed from the subjectivity of different historiographical angles) is breached, we cannot but classify as arbitrary the exclusion, from that *content*, of the study of the logical procedures, the ideological attitudes, the political concerns of the scholars in Roman law, since they are precisely these aspects, with their various influences on the historiographical analysis, that determine, from time to time, the concrete dimension and structure of the *content* itself. (transl.).[93]

Likewise, denial or even only minimization, by modern historiography, of the controversial nature of the law of the *prudentes* means to set itself outside historical reality. This is a concept so strongly rooted in the perspectives of the Roman jurists that it is not possible to make it the content of a particular juridical category. On this point, Schwarz's judgment was drastic.[94] He underlined that the ideas of *ius controversum* and *ius ambiguum* repulsed the *prudentes*, since to them law appeared objective and juridicity something stable: *ius* as such cannot be controversial, not *ambiguum*, not *dubium* and not even *incertum*.[95] It should be noted that this judgement was reported verbatim by Raggi in his lesson without mentioning its paternity;[96] and it might appear clear

---

[93] Raggi, 'Storia esterna e storia interna del diritto', in *Scritti* (n. 20) 100-101. The italics are those of the author.

[94] Cf. Schwarz, 'Das strittige Recht' (n. 16) 207 = 'Il diritto controverso' (n. 16) 179.

[95] Schwarz, 'Das strittige Recht' (n. 16) 209-210 = 'Il diritto controverso' (n. 16) 181-182.

[96] Raggi, *Il metodo* (n. 32) 127. The omission was probably due to the didactic purpose of the lessons.

why he spoke of 'method' and not of 'methods', wishing to highlight the identity element deeply rooted in the individual physiognomies of the jurists: to continuously aspire to *ius certum*, to a stable and applicable law, through an incessant dialectic, the result of a permanent controversiality and the continuous interweaving of the topical and axiomatic methods (according to the well-known distinction formulated by Esser). [97]

Raggi also mentioned the difference between divergences of opinion and conflictuality. The *prudentes* did not perceive their contrasting opinions as conflicts; [98] this was because, far from claiming to reach absolute truths, their discourse was dialectical, tending towards mediation between opposing positions, neither of which was accepted or rejected *a priori*; [99] it constantly involved dialogue; sometimes it appeared as a *weighing up of premises*, in the sense that it tended to verify their logical consistency, their ability to attain the desired result; [100] it often made use of analogy in order to ascertain the common characteristics and the divergent ones in the practical cases taken into consideration and compared. [101] None of this is in the reassessment of the jurisprudential 'material', according to a compact and homogeneous reconstruction, in which the *ius controversum* ended up being eliminated from the scene. Interpreted in this manner – Raggi concluded his course of lessons – Roman law could no longer be "that enormous gymnasium of opinions" that it had been for centuries. [102]

5. "An enormous gymnasium of opinions"

The idea of the 'vocation' of the jurisprudential constructions of the Romans to go beyond their time to be elevated to pure categories, in-

---

[97] Raggi, *Il metodo* (n. 32) 37. The work discussed by Raggi was that by J. Esser, *Grundsatz und Norm in der richterlichen Fortbildung des Privatrechts. Rechtsvergleichende Beiträge zur Rechtsquellen und Interpretationslehre* (Tübingen 1956, 1974^3).

[98] Schwarz, 'Das strittige Recht' (n. 16) 210 = 'Il diritto controverso' (n. 16) 182.

[99] Raggi, *Il metodo* (n. 32) 37.

[100] Raggi, *Il metodo* (n. 32) 36 (The italics are those of the author). On this point, see Campolunghi, Fusco, *Prefazione* to L. Raggi, *Il metodo della giurisprudenza romana* (n. 32) 22.

[101] Raggi, *Il metodo* (n. 32) 118.

[102] Raggi, *Il metodo* (n. 32) 162.

dependent of the social contexts in which they were generated and "fungible for the most diverse historical uses" (transl.),[103] was widespread – wrote Orestano – in the Roman law studies of the first half of the last century. Rooted in those 'continuistic' views was "a history without history: a linear and completely fictitious development".[104] The rhetorical question that followed the drastic affirmation once again targeted an illustrious name: "had Schulz perhaps not written that the origin of 'European jurisprudence' should be sought in the work of the jurist Quintus Mucius?"[105] The legal tradition of continental Europe, based on the study and re-elaboration of Roman law, had been accustomed to the isolation and impersonality of the *prudentes*; in that scenario, the link between the categories of modern private law and those of ancient legal thought were self-legitimized in the firm conviction of having to perpetuate the conceptual abstractions inherited from tradition, transmitting them to subsequent generations because they were considered eternal and 'founding', in the name of continuity between past and present assumed as a dogma of faith.

Nor could the legal tradition be considered an indistinct and unitary whole. With regard to the study of Roman law from the Middle Ages to the contemporary period, Orestano stated that the closer we get from the first medieval interpreters to Pandectism, the greater is the gap between the old and the new study of Roman law, to the point that only the ancient texts under study remain in common.[106] It may be that the master, in expressing this thought, had in mind an idea of De Francisci, to which he would explicitly refer in the *Introduzione*:[107] there is a time at which every discipline that has reached a certain degree of maturity feels the need to look back upon itself, to proceed with a critical review of the results, to a verification of the procedures by which it has amassed its patrimony of knowledge; in short, it feels the need for a deter-

---

[103] R. Orestano, 'Diritto romano, tradizione romanistica e studio storico del diritto', in RISG (1950) 245.

[104] Orestano, 'Diritto romano, tradizione' (n. 103) 245.

[105] Orestano, *loc. ult. cit.*

[106] The thought appears to have been formulated in a handwritten text that Orestano indicated, many years later, as the "very first nucleus of my writings" (dating from 1946 to 1948). A reproduction appears as an appendix to the work by Mantello, 'Orestano 'par lui-même'' (n. 92) 865-869 = *Variae* 2 (n. 92) 1471. The cited point is on p. 866 = 1472.

[107] Cf. Orestano, *Introduzione* (n. 1) 11-12.

mination of its method and the principles upon which it is based.[108] Therefore, Orestano was a Romanist who narrated and demonstrated the *loss of meaning* of the categories of Pandectism, in particular criticizing the idea of a scientific law made up of conceptual hypostases rather than concrete directives aimed at social action.[109]

The perspectives that tied this thought by a double thread to that of Raggi were animated by common inspirational motives, which I will now, proceeding toward the conclusions, attempt to list (despite the difficulty of summarizing an epochal labour of ideas and values in a few lines). In the first place, the incessant fight against abstract constructions and the identification of law with the preceptive-authoritative datum:[110] a viewpoint in which legal science could not be reduced to exercising dogmatics, to outlining systematic classifications or ordering schemata.[111] Secondly, a thinking alien to any *a priori* definition, developed on the basis of the concept of 'juridical experience' as an antidote to dogmatism, because of its suitability – I am referring to an observation by Mantello – to understand the historical relativity of every past and present legal phenomenon, and together, the relativity of every reflection on it.[112] Thirdly, the 'inhomogeneity' of Roman jurists, each with his own personality, and thus controversiality as a peculiar element of *scientia iuris*. Fourthly, the identification of heuristic schemata not subordinate to the law in effect, albeit in full awareness that, once freed from that form of dependence (as well as from the 'myth of the system'), things became more complicated, because it was necessary to place everything under discussion.[113]

Hence, the discovery of 'disorder': "to fight against dogmatism means liberation, but it also means bringing disorder where order reigned".[114] In this outlook, the 'crisis of Roman law', which had been discussed and

---

[108] Cf. P. De Francisci, *Storia del diritto romano* I (Roma 1926) 32 (Milano 1939², 38).

[109] Thus Brutti, *Antiformalismo* (n. 18) 679. The italics are those of the author.

[110] Cf. Mantello, 'Orestano 'par lui-même'' (n. 92) 848 = *Variae* 2 (n. 92) 1454.

[111] Cf. Mantello, 'Orestano 'par lui-même'' (n. 92) 849 = *Variae* 2 (n. 92) 1455.

[112] Mantello, 'Orestano 'par lui-même'' (n. 92) 850 = *Variae* 2 (n. 92) 1456. V. also *ibid.* 857 = 1463.

[113] Orestano, 'Lasciando la cattedra', in *Scritti*, 3 (n. 25) 1737 (= *'Diritto'. Incontri e scontri* [n. 10] 50).

[114] Orestano, 'Lasciando la cattedra', in *Scritti*, 3 (n. 25) 1737 (= *'Diritto'. Incontri e scontri* [n. 10] 49).

was discussed from Jhering onward, was in essence for the master (and his student was certainly in agreement) a 'crisis of the studies of Roman law': a spiritual crisis due to the awareness by some of them of the progressive and increasingly wider discrepancy between the studies of Roman law and those of modern law, with the effect of raising doubts about the purpose and usefulness of the work of scholars of ancient law.[115] However, this was a problem as delicate as it was misplaced: because, once the intrinsic unity of legal knowledge was recognized, it was logical to forcefully reject the idea of the dichotomy between historical and scientific study of law.[116]

The new methodological approach that slowly gained success, opening up new horizons for the Roman law studies of the time, was based on a simple and clear assumption: the study of Roman law does not need any specific justification. On this point, Orestano's assessment was drastic: "It and its necessity are justified like any other study based on a mature awareness of the historicity of all legal phenomena".[117]

I will conclude now. I am imagining the master vividly engaged in his teaching: cropping up in the 'draft' of his last lesson[118] are phrases such as "today's Roman law studies – enrichment through the multiplication of questions", or metaphorical images such as "weft and warp = our being",[119] and also "it is important not to take oneself too seriously", in addition to the (repeated) words that express the great themes of a life: "history – historicism – historicity".[120] The break with a certain academic tradition was inevitable. And it is perhaps for similar reasons that the master's student concluded his lessons, a few months before he died, saying that his discourse on the method of the jurists had been

[115] Orestano, 'Lasciando la cattedra', in *Scritti*, 3 (n. 25) 1737 (= *'Diritto'. Incontri e scontri* [n. 10] 49).

[116] Cf. Campolunghi, *s.v. Orestano* (n. 5) 1462.

[117] Orestano, 'Lasciando la cattedra', in *Scritti*, 3 (n. 25) 1737 (= *'Diritto'. Incontri e scontri* [n. 10] 49).

[118] Lesson held at La Sapienza on 19 May 1979. The teacher's handwritten draft was published at the end of Mantello's summary note that opens Orestano's *Scritti* edited by M. Campolunghi and C. Lanza, 1 (Napoli 1998) XVL-XXI, as well as in A. Mantello, *Nota di lettura per R. Orestano*, *Scritti*, in *Variae* 2 (n. 92) 1211-1270.

[119] Recalled by Grossi, 'Storia di esperienze giuridiche e tradizione romanistica' (n. 2) 546.

[120] Mantello, 'Nota di lettura', *Scritti* (n. 118) 1270.

animated by the spirit of proposing a series of problems starting from scratch, “from a ‘clean’ blackboard”.[121] Both scholars were convinced that law, with its personalities and its juridical forms, follows the facts and the life of men, in a process of constant metamorphosis, which does not exclude – rather necessarily implies – instability, contradiction, disorder.[122] Hence the vision of a Roman law understood in the sense of *ius controversum*, of “an enormous gymnasium of opinions”.[123] A *tranche d’histoire*, Orestano stated in the painful commemoration of Raggi, recalling his very astute thinking. Sometimes a teacher could take lessons from his student, and Orestano possessed the necessary humility to recognize it:

> Human history, beyond the unfathomable dawn, has no beginning and no end: the most we can expect is to understand pieces of it. For me this was a great lesson: the *tranches d’histoire*, as living parts of a continuous process, which does not permit isolation and schemata. (transl.)[124]

[121] Raggi, *Il metodo* (n. 32) 164.

[122] It is because of this, as maintained by Brutti, ‘Antiformalismo’ (n. 18) 727, that only a dynamic representation can truly help to understand the juridical events, accustoming the interpreter to description of the contradictory profiles and the instability of law.

[123] Thus Raggi, *Il metodo* (n. 32) 162. On the page, the metaphor generally refers to Roman law, but it is clear that the author was thinking here of the thought of the jurists.

[124] Orestano, *Prefazione* to L. Raggi, *Scritti* (n. 20) XI-XII. The italics are those of the author.

Chapter 5

ROMAN LAW AND ROMAN JURISTS IN AMERICAN LEGAL CULTURE

Clifford Ando

1. Introduction

The title of this chapter deliberately confounds two different ways of conceiving the history of Roman law in America.

On the one hand, one might study the citation and influence of Roman law and the Roman law tradition in the production of American law: its influence on public law in the writing of the American Constitution; the importation of specific content and frameworks of understanding from the civil law into the common law; the legacies of the civil law in Louisiana especially, but also California, not least as regards real property and succession; and the citation of Roman law in comparative terms in academic (and appellate) legal argument. On the other, one might write a history of the scientific study of Roman law as an academic project (whether dogmatic or socio-historical), among professors of law and history.

That said, although the two fields of study can be separated for analytic purposes, they are not fully divorced in reality: context shapes and impels academic interests, not least in the study of Roman law in the United States. In what follows, I devote some time to each type of history, concentrating on three topics, the last in two parts. After these introductory remarks, I turn to Roman law and civil law in the US, 1790-1850. In the third section, I will say a few words about Roman law in American legal theory and comparative law, 1900-1950, focusing on the figure of Roscoe Pound. The fourth section takes up the academic study of Roman law, among both ancient and medieval historians and professors in American law schools.

2. Roman law and civil law in the US, 1790-1850

Regarding the influence of Roman law (or what Pound calls "the modern Roman law") and the civil law in the US, there is a small but intelligent literature whose arguments converge on a number of points.[1] Most importantly, there was an historical window, stretching approximately from 1790 to 1850, during which the desirability of exploiting Roman and civil law sources was widely discussed and, in actual case law, the civil law was widely cited. The historical conditions that opened this window gradually diminished in their influence; the institutional contexts of knowledge production contributed to a rapid decline; and the doctrinal areas in which this influence was felt were limited and specific. I will sketch the contours of the scholarly consensus in a moment; I want, however, also to say a word about public law.

It would be very difficult to overstate the importance of republican ideology for the early history of American public law and constitutional thought. Some aspects of this history have been traced in John Pocock's classic work of 1975, *The Machiavellian Moment: Florentine Political Thought and the Atlantic Republican Tradition*;[2] similar questions are treated from a very different perspective in Mortimer Sellers, *American Republicanism: Roman ideology in the United States Constitution* (1994).[3] But it has been an object of study in American legal history for a very long time: Charles Howard McIlwain's *Constitutionalism Ancient and Modern* is one of most prominent books of American legal history in the 20th century.[4] (I observe that McIlwain trained and practiced as a lawyer, and also taught Latin, before becoming a professor of history and winning the Pulitzer Prize.) Roman public law has also been a topic of enduring interest in American political thought: Senator

---

[1] See R. Pound, 'The Influence of Civil Law in America', in Louisiana Law Review 1 (1938/39) 1-16; P. Stein, 'The Attraction of the Civil Law in Post-Revolutionary America', in Virginia Law Review 52 (1966) 403-434; R.H. Helmholz, 'Use of the Civil Law in post-revolutionary American jurisprudence', in Tulane Law Review 66 (1991/92) 1649-1684; M.H. Hoeflich, 'Roman law in American legal culture', in Tulane Law Review 66 (1991/92) 1723-1743; Id., *Roman and civil law and the development of Anglo-American jurisprudence in the nineteenth century* (Athens 1997).

[2] J.G.A. Pockock, *The Machiavellian Moment: Florentine Political Thought and the Atlantic Republican Tradition* (Princeton 1975).

[3] M.N.S. Sellers, *American Republicanism: Roman ideology in the United States Constitution* (New York 1994).

[4] C.H. Mcilwain, *Constitutionalism Ancient and Modern* (Ithaca 1947 [1940]).

Robert Byrd delivered a series of 14 lectures from the Senate floor on the history of the Senate of republican Rome.[5] But despite the interest accorded to Roman public law by scholars like these, as in other traditions of scholarship, so in the United States the study of Roman public law and its influence in history has been wholly separated from the study of the influence of Roman private law. This has occurred to the detriment of both.

Three historical factors contributed to create opportunities for the citation and use of Roman and civil law material in case law and legislative deliberation in the US. These were: (1) a prevailing sentiment against England and, not coincidentally, a fondness for France; (2) deep admiration for the Code Napoléon; and (3) the catalyst provided by the absorption of the Louisiana territory. (The influence of the Louisiana purchase in political life was of course enormous, adding some 2.15 million square kilometers to the United States. However, it encompassed perhaps 50-60,000 non-indigenous inhabitants, so its effect in social or private-law terms was in the medium term largely contained.).

What is more, the United States was undergoing massive social, demographic and economic changes in these decades, not least in consequence of a great expansion in trade. It is thus conventional to say – people at the time did in fact say – that the volume and range of activity that came before the courts in the years after the Revolution was very much greater than had been the case before; the legal system as a whole became vastly more differentiated and specialized; and the existence of a federal structure in America meant that problems of pluralism and conflict of laws and judicial review and so forth were all being worked out at enormous speed. In this context, there was both need and appetite for intellectual aid. In a famous speech delivered before the Suffolk County Bar in 1821 (but published only in 1829), Joseph Story, a justice of the Supreme Court from 1811-1845, reflected on this problem thus:

> Connected with this, and, as a mine abounding with the most precious materials, to adorn the edifice of our jurisprudence, is the study of the foreign maritime law, and above all of the civil law. ... Where shall we find the law of contracts so extensively, so philosophically, and so persuasively expounded, as in the pure, moral, and classical treatises of

[5] R.C. Byrd, *The Senate of the Roman Republic addresses on the history of Roman constitutionalism* (Washington 1995).

> Pothier? Where shall we find the general doctrines of commercial law so briefly, yet beautifully laid down, as in the modern commercial code of France? Where shall we find such ample general principles to guide us in new and difficult cases, as in that venerable deposit of the learning and labors of the jurists of the ancient world, the Institutes and Pandects of Justinian? The whole continental jurisprudence rests upon this broad foundation of Roman wisdom; and the English common law, churlish and harsh as was its feudal education, has condescended silently to borrow many of its best principles from this enlightened code. ... There is no country on earth, which has more to gain than ours, by the thorough study of foreign jurisprudence. We can have no difficulty in adopting in new cases such principles of the maritime and civil law as are adapted to our own wants, and commend themselves by their intrinsic convenience and equity. Let us not vainly imagine, that we have unlocked and exhausted all the stores of juridical wisdom and policy. Our jurisprudence is young and flexible, but it has withal a masculine character, which may be refined and exalted by the study of the best models of antiquity. [6]

Story provides an exhortation, but he also distills trends visible empirically in two domains, including both reports of cases (discussed in detail in Helmholz, "Roman law") and the book trade (discussed by Stein, "Attraction of the civil law," where much more might be done). [7]

That said, Story already had an intuition where aid was needed, and the view in historical perspective, whether that of Pound or Helmholz, largely bears him out: "the modern Roman law" was influential only in specific domains: bailment, contracts, commercial law, and maritime law being chief among these. One aspect of this list should stand out: these are the very domains wherein English law was already being influenced, and continued to absorb, structures and doctrines from continental jurists, not least through the influence of Mansfield. In other words, whatever the material and ideological forces that drove the process – including some notional desire to distinguish American from English law –, as a doctrinal matter, the history of Roman and civil law in the US in this period cannot be divorced from trends in England.

By mid-century, the force of these early, explicit overtures at borrowing had come to an end. In part this was because, as Story also fore-

---

[6] J. Story, 'An address delivered before the Members of the Suffolk Bar, at their anniversary, on the fourth of September, 1821, at Boston', in The American Jurist 1 (1829) 1-34.

[7] See R.H. Hoeflich, 'Roman law in American legal culture' (n. 1); P. Stein, 'The Attraction of the Civil Law' (n. 1).

saw, the fragmentation of jurisdiction in the US militated against the intellectualizing forces essential to borrowing and transfers from foreign law. Some measure of this is provided by a letter written by James Kent to the editors of the newly-founded (and soon to be ended) Louisiana Law Review. The editors had mailed the first issue to a number of famous jurists, including both Joseph Story and James Kent; the first issue contained an article about Savigny; the fourth contained "an outline of the history of Roman law." The editors printed letters from both Story and Kent at the end of the second issue. I quote that of Kent:

> Your first article on the History of Jurisprudence in Louisiana, with the admirable analysis of the *Coutume de Paris*, and *Savigny's* Treatise of Possession arrested and fixed my thorough attention. I admire the Roman law, but I am too old (by the way I am 78 this day), or too dull, or too much disciplined in the English common law, to relish greatly the metaphysical theories and philological minutiae of the German Philosophers and Jurists. What you say in limitation of the details of even Mr. Savigny concurs with my impressions. I am tired of everlasting Commentaries on Roman law and Roman early History. Life is too short, and we have too much to learn and put in practice this side of the Atlantic to enter deeply into such kind of researches. As far as concerns my own private study and amusement, I would not give one cent for any new, laborious, profound and prolix German Commentator on Virgil, Horace, Juvenal, Livy or Tacitus, because my relish for them is sufficiently strong, glowing and accurate for all the useful purposes for which I study them. So I find sufficient in the texts of the Institutes and the Pandects for all the illustration of the principles of the Roman Jurisprudence, that I care for, without troubling myself a great deal even with the critical labors of the masters of the old school, such as Bynkershoek, Heineccius, &c., and much less with those of the new German School, of which Thibaut is the leader of the codifiers and Savigny of the historical school, though of the two, I am altogether with Savigny. [8]

Kent's response is altogether more interesting because he was among the most learned, astute and assiduous readers of foreign law in the United States in his time. [9]

Up to a point, the growing insularity or, perhaps, self-sufficiency of American private law in the second half of the nineteenth century, may be attributed to the reversion of American legal education and legal

---

[8] James Kent, 'Chancellor Kent', in Louisiania Law Journal 2 (1841) 159.

[9] J.H. Langbein, 'Chancellor Kent and the History of Legal Literature', in Columbia Law Review 93 (1993) 547-594.

training to the English model. Training to be lawyer remained largely an apprenticeship in the United States. It was thus learned via handbooks and reports. With some caveats, it may be asserted that professional schools of law became dominant features of the landscape only at the turn of the nineteenth to the twentieth century; and only in their train do we see widespread engagement with the intellectualizing and rationalizing trends implicated in contemporaneous forms of comparison, legal theory and legal philosophy. To these I now turn.

3. Roman law in American legal theory and comparative law, 1900-1950

Where Roman law is concerned, the boundary between historical and comparative study might seem slight, particularly in the 19th century, before the emergence of a self-reflective practice of comparative law, whose great champion in English was of course Maine, and which was institutionalized at the 1900 Paris *Congrés international de droit comparé*.

In a contribution of this scope, I must write with radical brevity about a fascinating period in the history of American legal thought.[10] Even a sketch of the influence of Maine would be the work of many pages.[11] What I want to highlight is the very complex reception that European comparative law had in the American legal academy. Nineteenth-century projects of comparison often took for granted some version of natural law theory, according to which any given code or articulation of positive law was merely declaratory, within one or another degree of imperfection, of some ideal.[12] [The theory of course flattered itself that its ambition was the assimilation of the legal to the moral.] Comparison was thus an effort to identify which aspects of any given positive law better approximated the ideal, thus to justify the replacing of the worse with the better. One outcome of such projects of assimilation to a single standard would be the unification of all national laws to a single model, as indeed was stressed by Henri Lévy-Ullman in his in-

---

[10] D.S. Clarck, 'Development of Comparative Law in the United States', in M. Reimann – R. Zimmerman (curators), *The Oxford Handbook of Comparative Law* (Oxford 2012 [2006]).

[11] See R.A. Cosgrove, *Scholars of the Law: English Jurisprudence from Blackstone to Hart* (New York 1996) 119-147.

[12] R. Pound, 'Comparative Law in the Formation of American Common Law', in Acta Academiae Universalis Iurisprudentiae Comparativae 1 (1928) 183-197; Id., 'The Influence of Civil Law in America', in Louisiana Law Review 1 (1938/39) 1-16.

troduction of the French society of comparative legislation to the United States, via remarks published in the *Harvard Law Review*:

> Its main object is, by putting the knowledge of the laws of all countries within the reach of everybody, gradually to bring about uniformity in legislation through the development of the science of law; this is pre-eminently a work of civilization and of progress, which, as such, commends itself to the attention of the whole world. [13]

Of course, scientific epistemologies in law are not necessarily associated with the metaphysical claims of natural law, nor need natural law arguments rely on comparison as a heuristic. [14] Their unification at this moment in the discipline is both contingent and remarkable.

I cite this background for two reasons. First, the dawn of the twentieth century marked the emergence of comparative law as an institutionalized practice in the United States. Very rapidly, the United States came to contribute the largest number of delegates to international congresses of comparative law, and the first years of the 20th century, like the first years of the 19th, witnessed a remarkable number of translation projects of both foreign legislation and foreign scholarship. Indeed, in 1911 the United States Congress ordered the Library of Congress "to collect the essential materials necessary for an accurate knowledge of the legal institutions of every civilized country." [15]

The second reason that I aver to the history of comparative law is that Roman law, and scholars of Roman law, played an important role in the transformation of the French/European project of comparison, which was the pursuit of unification around an ideal, into an American project of comparison, based in a sociology of law. Perhaps the seminal figure in this transformation was Roscoe Pound, though Oliver Wendell Holmes would be a close second, alongside John Wigmore. Pound himself taught Roman law in the Latin Department of the University of Nebraska, and continued to do so even after his appointment as a professor of law. Materials that he assembled there were published in 1906 by mimeograph under the title "Readings in Roman law." From Nebraska, Pound moved to Northwestern, then Chicago, and to Harvard,

---

[13] H. Lévy-Ullman, 'Account of the French Society of Comparative Legislation', in Harvard Law Review 10 (1896) 161-167.

[14] R.H. Helmholz, *Natural Law in Court: A History of Legal Theory in Practice* (Cambridge 2015).

[15] Quoted in Clark, 'Development of Comparative Law' (n. 10) at n. 23.

where he served as professor and Dean for many decades. In 1914 he published an expanded version of his earlier coursebook under the more programmatic title, *Readings in Roman Law and the Civil Law and Modern Codes as Developments thereof. An Introduction to Comparative Law*. For those who have not studied this text, it is a document of remarkable learning and organization. [16]

I focus here solely on the assimilation of historical to comparative study. This trajectory finds its fruition in Pound's essays on comparative law. There he asserted an emphatic relationship between the achievements of historical jurisprudence in the 19th century with sociological jurisprudence in his day: legal precepts cannot be studied historically "outside their historical and social setting," nor can contemporary precepts be judged "apart from their social psychological setting" and "without regard to how they function in action." [17] Or, in the words of John Wigmore: "Modern scientific thought has made it generally understood that a legal institution can be fully comprehen[d]ed only in the light of the social, economic, religious, political, racial, and climatic circumstances which surround it." [18] In this way, the project of comparison was transformed from a Platonic one, which aimed to reveal the transcendent, to a Socratic one, which aspired only to expose the normative as contingent. Thanks largely to the remarkable influence achieved by Roscoe Pound, and in spite of its own prestige, Roman law played a role in this transformation.

4. The academic study of Roman law, 1900-1980

The use of Roman law in the work of prominent American legal theorists of the twentieth century – perhaps especially Roscoe Pound, Max Radin, and Lon Fuller – is a topic deserving extended investigation in its own right. I close this chapter, however, by discussing the scientific study of Roman law by professors in American law schools and among ancient historians and philologists in the first decades of the 20th century.

---

[16] R. Pound, *Readings in Roman Law and the Civil Law and Modern Codes as Developments thereof. An Introduction to Comparative Law, compiled, edited and translated by Roscoe Pound* (Cambridge 1914 [1906]).

[17] R. Pound, 'The Revival of Comparative Law', in Tulane Law Review 5 (1930/31) 1-16.

[18] J.H. Wigmore, 'Jottings on comparative legal ideas and institutions', in Tulane Law Review 6 (1931/32) 51.

(a) American law schools, 1925-c. 1980

Earlier I discounted the importance of legal education in university schools of law in the 19th century. One index of their importance is their number: only 25 law schools participated in the foundation of the AALS. (Today there are 179 members, plus 22 fee-paying non-member institutions.) I do not want to dismiss the 19th century law schools out of hand: several professors published translations of Justinian's *Institutes*, as well as introductions to the study of Roman law.[19] Also, Yale Law School retained a professor of Roman law throughout its early history.[20] But the number of positions was always small. For example, during the refugee crisis of the 1930s, efforts to place emigrés professors of law in positions in American law schools failed in part because there were only 10 professorships of Roman or comparative law in the entire US. Today that number is smaller still. Indeed, I believe there is only one permanent chair of the Roman law tradition in the US, namely, the Robbins Professor at Boalt Hall School of Law.

In the years between 1925-1980, the historical study of Roman law in the United States in American law schools was dominated by two figures, A. Arthur Schiller, who arrived at Columbia University Law School in 1926 and remained there for 45 years, and David Daube, who came to Boalt as Robbins Professor in 1970, at age 61. One notable feature of their careers, as of Alan Watson, who arrived in the US in 1979, is that by virtue of working in law schools, I believe none had a single PhD student in legal history in the American phase of their careers. What is more, as Schiller himself makes clear in his selected studies (and Peter Stein emphasizes in his obituary), he was the only American law scholar of his generation to make a career in Roman law. It was his hope that the publication of a collection of his 'American' papers might "dispel the type of folk-lore which has come into

---

[19] T. Cooper, *The Institutes of Justinian* (New York 1841 [1812]); L.S. Cushing, *An Introduction to the Study of the Roman Law* (Boston 1854); W. Grapel, *Sources of the Roman civil law an introduction to the Institutes of Justinian* (Philadelphia 1857); see also J.M. Walker, *An inquiry into the Use and Authority of Roman Jurisprudence in the Law concerning Real Estate* (Charleston 1850); J. Hadley, *Introduction to Roman law, in twelve academical lectures* (New York 1873); and G. Hoadly, *A lecture upon Roman law procedure* (Cincinnati 1877).

[20] The sequence includes such figures as James Hadley, Simeon Baldwin, Albert Wheeler, and Charles Sherman.

vogue in Europe respecting the interest in Roman law in the United States."[21]

Against this optimistic claim, advanced very nearly on his behalf alone, one might cite the anecdotal evidence provided by the list of translators recruited by Alan Watson for the Pennsylvania translation of Justinian's Digest.[22] On my count, of the thirty translators recruited in 1979-1980, only one was an American, to wit, Bruce Frier.

I should like to emphasize three things about Schiller's scholarship; these facts are well known but deserve repetition. First, he also wrote many, many books and articles on African law, military law and Indonesian law, not as a sideline but as preeminent expert in the Americas. The preface by Roger Bagnall and William Harris to his Festschrift makes no acknowledgment of this.[23] Memorials to Schiller in African law journals make no mention of his Roman law scholarship, either. Second, despite this immense learning across many bodies of law, I do not know of any essay of his that is avowedly comparative. Third, Schiller commenced his career working on legal papyrology, notably in Coptic, and this work continued throughout his life. Coptic legal papyri were not an obvious field of study for a young lawyer in the 1920s, yet these were the object of his first publications and his JD thesis of 1932. His work remains in many ways foundational to that field.

(b) Ancient and medieval historians, 1900-1960

In the first 60 years of the twentieth century, a small number of professional historians in the US produced a handful of notable works on Roman law. I have located obituaries for a number of these persons, but not all. The godfather of the movement appears to have been Frank Frost Abbott, who was professor of Latin at Chicago before moving to Princeton in 1907. Abbott's most popular book was a history of Roman political institutions, but his greatest achievement was the collection of legal documents on Roman municipal administration that he published with Allan Chester Johnson in 1926.[24] *Municipal Administration in the*

---

[21] A.A. Schiller, *An American Experience in Roman Law. Writings from publications in the United States* (Göttingen 1971).

[22] A. Watson, *The Digest of Justinian* (Philadelphia 1985).

[23] R.S. Bagnall, V.H. William, *Studies in Roman Law in Memory of A. Arthur Schiller* (Leiden 1986).

[24] F.F. Abbot, *A history and description of Roman political institutions* (Boston

Roman Empire remains, in my view, the single most comprehensive and consistently fascinating work in its field. It would be a huge service to Roman history to update it and translate all the Greek and Latin texts contained in it.

Together with Paul Robinson Coleman-Norton and Frank Card Bourne, Johnson also published a volume of translations of laws and legal instruments of every kind, *Ancient Roman Statutes.*[25] The notes are in some respects out of date, and of course further texts have since been discovered. But this remains the most comprehensive collection of its kind known to me, and a significant number of the documents must have received their first modern translation in it. It is a phenomenal achievement and deserves to be more widely known. It should surely be updated.

Finally, everyone here will know the translation of the Theodosian Code published by Clyde Pharr, Theresa Sherer Davidson and Mary Brown Pharr, in 1952.[26] Although frequently cited as Pharr's translation, investigative work by Linda Jones Hall has revealed the very great use made by Clyde Pharr of translations produced by women in his department, as well as his exploitation of the generosity of Fred Blume, who between 1920 and 1952 translated the Latin text of both Justinian's Code and the Novellae.[27] The later history of Blume's translation is for Bruce Frier to tell. Returning to Pharr, for present purposes, however much Clyde Pharr may have appropriated the work of others for his own credit, the lasting influence of the translation is evident to all historians of law and late antiquity.

These individuals did not produce interpretive historical works of any note, at least so far as I know. But commencing at least from the collection of inscribed statutes made by Antonio Augustín, the study of Roman law has relied upon corpora of epigraphic and papyrological texts, and also on translations. In my view, *Municipal administration in the Roman Empire, Ancient Roman Statutes,* and *The Theodosian Code*

1902); F.F. Abbot, A.C. Johnson, *Municipal Administration in the Roman Empire* (Princeton 1926).

[25] A.C. Johnson, P.R. Coleman-Norton, F.C. Bourne, *Ancient Roman Statutes. A translation, with introduction, commentary, glossary, and index* (Austin 1961).

[26] C. Pharr, T.S. Davidson, M.B. Pharr, *The Theodosian Code and Novels, and the Sirmondian Constitutions. A translation with commentary, glossary, and bibliography* (Princeton 1952).

[27] L.J. Hall, 'Clyde Pharr, the Women of Vanderbilt, and the Wyoming Judge: The story behind the translation of the Theodosian Code in mid-century America', in RLT 8 (2012) 1-42.

deserve mention alongside FIRA, Bruns, the *Fontes*, Girard-Senn, and so forth, as major contributions to our shared endeavor.

I should like to close by mentioning one student of the lawyer-historian Charles McIlwain, namely Myron Piper Gilmore, who trained at Harvard and remained there throughout his career, but for a period of civilian service during the Second World War. Gilmore's dissertation is a lovely, elegant and economical work, *Argument from Roman Law in Political Thought, 1200-1600.*[28] He is one of a handful of American legal historians who have focused on late medieval thought. More recently, this tradition has produced a few excellent historians of recognizable type: canonists, delvers in the archives of particular jurisdictions, codicologists. Gilmore is one of a tiny number who read creatively and responsibly in the scholarly tradition from the twelfth century to the Humanists. So far as I can tell, nearly all of them have been autodidacts. In that sense, their number should not be called a tradition at all. But Gilmore is certainly worth reading.

[28] M.P. Gilmore, *Argument from Roman Law in Political Thought, 1200-1600* (Cambridge 1941).

Part II

STORIES OF JURISTS AND OF JURISPRUDENCE

Chapter 6

LAW AND LITERATURE. THE CASE OF ROMAN JURISPRUDENCE IN LATIN LITERARY WORKS

Oliviero Diliberto

SUMMARY: 1. Introduction. – 2. Law and literature. State of matter. – 3. Law teaching in Rome. – 4. The authors and their audience. – 5. Latin writers and law. – 6. Jurists in the mirror of literary works. – 7. Legal fragments in literary works. – 8. Jurists quotations in legal works and in literary texts. – 9. Law and grammar. – 10. A first conclusion. – 11. Horace, the *Satires* and law: problems of method.

1. Introduction

The topic that I will address is obviously vast[1] and inherently very complex: it is sufficient to mention, already at the beginning, the mere circumstance that the sources to be analysed are often very different from each other and, more often than not, well known and studied for centuries.

What is perhaps missing, instead, is an analysis of them as a whole. Therefore, I will try to outline a few proposals of methods to deal with the subject, risking summariness and limiting myself to subjecting to the attention of our scientific community only some examples – I believe paradigmatic ones – of non-legal sources dealing with Roman jurisprudence.

I will start with an observation, which I consider of interest for our purposes, by an Italian scholar of processual-civil law, Bruno Cavallone: "there repeatedly emerges [...] the observation that historians and critics of literature and art often fail to see or understand 'in their own field' things that are obvious for the intruder (the jurist)".[2] With great simplicity,

[1] The bibliography cited from time to time – with respect to a literally boundless production – will truly be reduced to the essential. I warmly thank my student, Dr. Gaia Di Trolio, whose contribution to the preparation of this work was invaluable.

[2] B. Cavallone, *La borsa di miss Flite. Storie e immagini del processo* (Milano 2016) 14 f.

Cavallone pointed out that scholars of literature (even Latinists), perhaps very authoritative ones, often do not appreciate the legal nuances of the texts they are examining: they just *do not see* certain things.

Naturally we, legal historians, read literary texts with a different eye. And thus many new elements emerge in the interpretation of such texts.

Now, the cultured, amusing and very refined book by Cavallone, with which I began, is included in that very particular branch of knowledge – initially very widespread in Anglo-Saxon circles but now well established everywhere – called *Law and Literature*. The date of birth of this movement commonly coincides with the publication of James Boyd White's *The Legal Imagination: Studies in the Nature of Legal Thought and Expression.*[3]

Since then, as part of an increasingly rich and fruitful scientific debate, research has been developing along two different, albeit intertwined, lines: *Law in Literature* and *Law as Literature*. Here we are obviously interested in the former.

Such research has also been conducted intensely in Italy,[4] a forerunner perhaps being a volume by Mario A. Cattaneo dedicated to Goldoni and Manzoni.[5]

The literary authors dealt with are now innumerable, with each country favouring the analysis of its own classics.[6]

Hence, this particular legal-literary science has scrutinized authors

---

[3] (University Press, Chicago 1973).

[4] Only by way of example, cf.: D. Carpi (ed.), *Shakespeare and Law* (Ravenna 2003); A. Malinconico, *Diritto e letteratura, Manzoni e Pirandello* (Roma 2008); C. Faralli, M.P. Mittica (eds.), *Diritto e letteratura, prospettive di ricerca* (Roma 2010); C. Di Fonzo, *Dante tra diritto teologia ed esegesi antica* (Napoli 2012) (on Alighieri and law, we cannot fail to mention the fundamental contribution of S. Menzinger, *Dante e i confini del diritto* [2014], Italian translation, Roma 2016); V. Vitale, *Diritto e letteratura. La giustizia narrata* (Milano 2012); G. Labriola, F. Romeo (eds.), *Niccolò Machiavelli e la tradizione giuridica europea* (Napoli 2016); L. Melosi, *Ius Leopardi. Legge, natura, civiltà* (Firenze 2016); L. Moscati, *Alessandro Manzoni avvocato. La causa contro Le Monnier e le origini del diritto d'autore in Italia* (Bologna 2017). On all this, see lastly L. Peppe, 'Gli eterni ritorni: l'incontro tra antropologia e diritto romano. Intorno a *Giuristi nati. Antropologia e diritto romano*', in Legal Roots 6 (2017) esp. 511 ff.

[5] M.A. Cattaneo, *Carlo Goldoni e Alessandro Manzoni. Illuminismo e diritto penale* (Milano 1987). In less recent times, it is worth mentioning the authoritative, albeit isolated precedent of P. Rossi, *Guicciardini criminalista* (Milano 1943).

[6] For example, many dense works on Balzac and law have recently appeared in France, among which it is worth recalling: N. Dissaux (ed.), *Balzac, romancier du droit*, Proceedings of a study day in June 2011 at the *Maison Balzac* (Paris 2012); M. Lichtlé, *Balzac, le texte et la loi* (this is the collection of articles published by the author, one of the great Balzac specialists, chief editor of *Anneé balzacienne*) (Paris 2012).

from almost all periods and parts of the world, up to and including contemporary writers. Here I will mention only one example, in my opinion an eloquent one: M. Logaldo's article on Truman Capote.[7] And we could go on and on.

2. Law and literature. State of matter

We come then to the topic of Roman jurisprudence in literary works written in Latin. The subject of Roman law in the works of Latin literature is certainly not new in our field of study. Indeed, we can say that it was broadly discussed by scholars from the mid-nineteenth century through the first half of the twentieth century. Eugène Henriot, counsellor at the French Court of Cassation, published *Les poètes juristes*[8] in 1858 and then in 1865 the three very dense volumes dedicated to *Moeurs juridiques et judiciaires de l'ancienne Rome*,[9] with an impressive catalogue of Latin literary sources.

In Italy, Emilio Costa published his volume on Roman law in works by Plautus[10] in 1890 and then in 1893 the volume on Terence,[11] but above all, a few decades later (1927), the well-known *Cicerone giureconsulto*.[12]

In the 1930s, Filippo Stella Maranca wrote on literary authors such as Ennius, Plautus, Varro, Horace, Ovid, Virgil, Seneca, Isidore, but also Homer and Dante Alighieri.[13]

Fabio Lanfranchi also dealt (1938) with law in Roman rhetorical works.[14]

---

[7] M. Logaldo, 'Crime Sublime: Literary Mercy and the Law in Truman Capote's In Cold Blood', in D. Carpi (ed.), *Practising Equity, Addressing Law* (Heidelberg 2008) 355 ff.

[8] *Les poètes juristes, ou Remarques des poetes latins sur les lois, le droit civil, le droit criminel, la justice distributive et le barreau* (Paris 1858; facsimile reprint Aalen 1970).

[9] (Paris 1865; facsimile reprint Aalen 1973).

[10] E. Costa, *Il diritto privato romano nelle commedie di Plauto* (Torino 1890; facsimile reprint Roma 1968).

[11] E. Costa, *Il diritto privato nelle commedie di Terenzio* (Bologna 1893; facsimile reprint Roma 1973).

[12] E. Costa, *Cicerone giureconsulto* (Bologna 1927; facsimile reprint Roma 1964).

[13] Complete literature in R. Hassan, *La poesia e il diritto in Orazio. Tra autore e pubblico* (Napoli 2014) 3 nt. 7, 67 nt. 10.

[14] F. Lanfranchi, *Il diritto nei retori romani: contributo alla storia dello sviluppo del diritto romano* (Milano 1938).

Yet, these were almost always works with a – how to say it? – erudite-encyclopaedic flavour or mere lists of citations referring to law or legal institutions. Instead, the texts of Latin literature were rarely studied so that jurists could obtain from them ideas able to provide different interpretations of these literary texts or suggestions which, based on these texts, would yield novelties in the purely legal-historical field.

As known, the attitude of scholars has markedly changed in the last few decades: I will limit myself to two examples. The Plautine sources have been the subject of new and incessant reviews,[15] as occurred for the literature of the Augustan period.[16] Conversely, and perhaps a symmetrical phenomenon, there has been a different sensitivity to legal issues among historians of the Latin literature.[17]

More specifically regarding Roman jurisprudence in literary works, it is needless to underline the endless quantity, in the study of Roman law, of quotations, exegeses, comments on literary passages in which jurists and/or their works are mentioned. Important studies on single literary authors have also appeared (particularly, as is obvious, on Cicero,[18] even though he was a 'literary' author *sui generis*), although a systematic and overall approach to the subject is lacking thus far.

Let us get closer by degrees.

3. Law teaching in Rome

In the meantime, we can consider an objective fact: the knowledge of law in Rome was widespread among broad intellectual classes and not only among jurists. Quotations of laws, of very technical institutions, of

---

[15] Recent literature in D. Di Ottavio, *Uti legassit … ita ius esto. Alle radici della successione testamentaria in diritto romano* (Napoli 2016) 43 f., note 29. Now also see Peppe, 'Gli eterni ritorni' (n. 4) 531 ff.

[16] R. Hassan, 'Tradizione giuridica romana antica e ideologia augustea. Il catalogo dei dannati del Tartaro virgiliano (Aen. 6.608-614)', in B. Santalucia (ed.), *Repressione criminale nella Roma repubblicana fra norma e persuasione* (Pavia 2009) 493 ff.; U.C.J. Gebhardt, *Sermo Iuris. Rechtssprache und Recht in der augusteischen Dichtung* (Leiden-Boston 2009).

[17] A particular sensitivity to our topics is found above all in Elisa Romano, 'Echi e riuso della legge nella letteratura latina', in J.-L. Ferrary (ed.), *Leges publicae. La legge nell'esperienza giuridica romana* (Pavia 2012) 177 ff.

[18] For all, see lastly D. Mantovani, 'Cicerone storico del diritto', in Ciceroniana ns. 13 (2009) 297 ff.; F. Tamburi, *Il ruolo del giurista nelle testimonianze della letteratura latina. I. Cicerone* (Napoli 2013).

verba taken directly from the legal lexicon are too extensive to be considered a coincidence.

A first explanation of this phenomenon, almost a kind of prerequisite, is found in Roman pedagogy. The education of the classes that could afford to study, moreover with a rather homogeneous pedagogical path, was characterized by the study of law. This is well known for the Twelve Tables (and the consequences of the mnemonic learning of them are, in my opinion, of great interest).[19] The ancient law ("the national grammar of the Romans", as Norden[20] called it) was learned by the *pueri* in early school age, as a sort of abecedarium for mere linguistic learning. Then, in the third educational level (15-20 years), rhetoric, literature and true law were studied.

Henry Marrou, in his important history of pedagogy of the ancient world, maintained that the originality of the Roman school with respect to the Greek one lay precisely in the study of law.[21]

Very clear traces of all this are found in the literary sources. All the archaic literature is permeated by references to the legal institutions and lexicon: Plautus is a resounding (I knowingly use this term after a careful and systematic examination of his works)[22] demonstration of this.

Later, in the first century BCE, Ovid complained that he never again wanted to study (*amor.* 1.15.5) *leges verbosas*;[23] Horace (to whom we will return later) declared (and demonstrated) several times how much he had studied law, being moreover a fierce opponent of that type of study;[24] Virgil studied law, pleaded a case (not very well) in *tribunal*, and then dedicated himself solely to literature: although he demonstrated his mastery of legal language.[25]

---

[19] O. Diliberto, 'Ut carmen necessarium (Cic. leg. 2,23,59). Apprendimento e conoscenza della legge delle XII Tavole nel I sec. a.C.', in M. Citroni (ed.), *Letteratura e civitas. Transizioni dalla Repubblica all'Impero. In ricordo di E. Narducci* (Pisa 2012) 141 ff. Now see also Peppe, 'Gli eterni ritorni' (n. 4) 531 ff.

[20] E. Norden, *La letteratura romana* (Berlin 1905¹; Italian translation Bari 1958) 10.

[21] H.-I. Marrou, *Histoire de l'éducation dans l'Antiquité*, 2. *Le monde romain* (1948¹; Paris 1981) 93 ff. for the study of law.

[22] O. Diliberto, M.V. Sanna (ed.), *Le parole del diritto. L'età arcaica* (Cagliari 2016) 63 ff.

[23] Diliberto, 'Ut carmen' (n. 19) 144, note 13.

[24] Diliberto, 'Ut carmen' (n. 19) esp. 150, but *passim*.

[25] Hassan, 'Tradizione' (n. 16) 493 f.; Ead., *La poesia e il diritto* (n. 13) *passim*.

4. The authors and their audience

However, there is a second point which, in my opinion, is very important, indeed decisive, for our analysis. In literary works, references to law often appear as mere allusions, more or less veiled, implicit.

Therefore, the key point is not only the author's expertise (as thus far, more or less, we have tried to investigate in the study of Roman law) but also the *ability of that author's audience* to understand (or not) such allusions. Hence, the point is the author/reader relationship.

To entertain or interest, a text (and even more so an allusive phrase concerning law) had to be understood. As a perspicacious scholar of popular and mass literature, Stefano Bartezzaghi, wrote "to play with words they must be known by all the interlocutors: a clever quip, a witty allusion, a satirical deformation" will be effective only if understood "by a number of people infinitely larger than that of the specialists".[26] After all, "each action of reading is a [...] transaction between the ability of the reader [...] and the type of ability that a given text requires to be read".[27]

Naturally, the understanding of legal allusions must be related to the different cultural levels of the audience. However, in the case of Plautus, for example, the audience for comedies and the theatre was vast and not necessarily cultured: and Plautus, as mentioned, constantly included references to law in his texts.

I propose a first, provisional working hypothesis. The ability to understand law in Rome was substantial and certainly much more so than that of the recipients of modern and contemporary literature. We will return to this point.

5. Latin writers and law

Let us come to the Latin texts, but first a preliminary consideration. The non-juridical sources are – it is obvious, but it must be restated – very different from each other (epic, elegy, comedy, satire, history, erudition, comments and biographies of previous authors, grammar, rhetoric, philosophy, treatises on agriculture, medicine, natural history, etc.).

---

[26] See the recent S. Bartezzaghi, *Scrittori giocatori* (Torino 2010) 13.

[27] U. Eco, *Interpretation and Overinterpretation* (Cambridge 1992[1]); Ital. trans. Milano 1995), 82.

Each kind of source has *its own* language and it is within each of those different languages that the passages concerning jurisprudence should be examined.

Indeed, it is clear that the author of a grammatical treatise or of a commentary on a previous work (e.g. Verrius Flaccus, Nonius Marcellus, Macrobius, Servius) is more attentive to the controlled use of words than is a poet. But even this rather obvious consideration must be balanced with another one. The knowledge (and curiosity) with respect to law varies, even quite markedly, within the same categories, from author to author. In fact, what counts are the individual biographies, the intellectual training of each one, and (possibly) the public offices held.

An example. At a certain point in his life, Gellius was asked to hold the office of *iudex privatus* and he read up on and studied jurisprudential texts.[28] He also tells us which law books he examined: we will return to this. And we will see how important this is: Gellius's expertise in the field of law was far from trivial.[29]

However, *personal interest* in law also counts: if references to law are strewn throughout the works of Ovid and Horace, in Catullus, for example, more or less in the same period, there are hardly any traces of them.

6. Jurists in the mirror of literary works

It is time to examine the texts, obviously only *per exempla*. Let us proceed in order, approaching the subject always by orienting the analysis toward the relationship between the author and his audience.

In the first place, we know of poets (not scholars or grammarians) who mentioned illustrious jurists, assuming as given that the audience knew or recognized them.

Ennius, in a very famous verse of the *Annales* (10.329 Sk.) mentioned Sextus Aelius:[30] *homo catus Aelius Sextus*.

---

[28] I allow myself to refer to what, at the time, I had maintained in *Materiali per la palingenesi delle XII Tavole*, I (Cagliari 1992) 129 ff.

[29] In addition to my work mentioned in the preceding note, I refer to some recent studies on the matter: I. Mastrorosa, 'Aulo Gellio e la legislazione di Roma arcaica: tra etica e diritto', in *Costruzione e uso del passato storico nella cultura antica* (Atti Convegno Firenze 2003) (Alessandria 2007) 339 ff.; R. D'Alessio, 'Note su Gellio, diritto e giurisprudenza', in SCDR 27 (2014) 447 ff.; J. Spruit, 'Aulus Gellius als Richter. Eine Beitrachtung zu Gellius, Noctes Atticae XIV, 2', in RIDA 63 (2016) 263 ff.

[30] In the context of a boundless and fragmented literature, I will refer only to: F.M. d'Ippolito, *Forme giuridiche di Roma arcaica*^{2} (Napoli 1997) 208 ff.,

This occurrence had an impact on Pomponius, who recalled Ennius's praise of Sextus Aelius in the *Enchiridion* (D. 1.2.2.38). This is also very well known.

As the context of the citation is unknown, at the moment we can only note the singularity of the mention of the jurist by Ennius who, on the other hand, made multiple references to law in his works.[31]

And more. Horace made Trebatius Testa a protagonist of his *Satires* (we will return to the point in the concluding remarks). The jurist is, by one count, made fun of good-naturedly (he is consulted by the poet for the recipe of a medicine against insomnia, which Trebatius reads out as if it were a decemviral verse);[32] elsewhere, the jurist pronounces a *responsum* on the same Horatian satires, in the sense of whether or not they are *mala carmina*;[33] finally, at the end of this article, we will observe a possible further example of the role of Trebatius in the writing of Horace's *Satires*.[34]

These are very well-known texts. Therefore, the fame of the jurist Trebatius must have been widespread among Horace's readers.

However, I wish to bring to the attention of scholars a lesser-known text, albeit obviously not unknown in our field of study, which I believe may represent a paradigmatic example of what I am arguing:

> Pers. *sat.* 5.88-90:
> *Vindicta postquam meus a praetore recessi,*
> *cur mihi non liceat, iussit quodcumque voluntas,*
> *excepto siquid Masuri rubrica vetavit?*

In a book certainly not dedicated (or addressed) to jurists, Persius explicitly mentions Masurius Sabinus. The subject is manumission. "Once away from the praetor and having become my own man [that is, free] thanks to the *vindicta*, for what reason have I not been allowed to do what my will commands, except what is prohibited by the rubric of Masurius?"

---

later republished in Id., *Problemi storico-esegetici delle XII Tavole* (Napoli 2003) 77 ff.; Diliberto, Sanna, *Le parole del diritto* (n. 22) 43; lastly see A. Schiavone, *The Invention of Law in the West* (Cambridge [Mass.]-London 2012) 118 ff.

[31] Diliberto, Sanna, *Le parole del diritto* (n. 22) 41 ff.

[32] For all, with previous literature, see Hassan, *La poesia e il diritto* (n. 13) 27.

[33] Cf. again Hassan, *La poesia e il diritto* (n. 13) 27 f.

[34] Cf. *infra* §§ 13-14.

The satires of Persius are imbued with Stoic doctrine (only the wise man is truly a free man), but in this case we should note the linguistic precision with which the legal institutions are mentioned (*vindicta* and *rubrica*).

Nevertheless, the reference to Masurius (Sabinus) is striking. Persius absolutely takes for granted that his readers know the person he is mentioning:[35] his audience had to 'recognize him', at least to know the name, as a jurist. Otherwise, the meaning of the verses in question would not have been understood.

Hence, the Roman jurists were also known to an audience of readers who were not experts in law.

Moreover, the non-legal sources provide not only the simple mention of the name but also biographical information on the jurists, their education, their frequentations. Naturally, Cicero emerges over everyone else. However, again Horace, in addition to making Trebatius Testa a protagonist, also mentioned Alfenus Varus, Galba, Aulus Cascellius, Valerius Messalla Corvinus and others.[36]

Very different sources underlined the very upright character and great juridical science of Nerva, Tacitus and Frontinus.[37]

Aulus Gellius (13.10.1-2), in describing the boundless culture of Labeo, underlined that he was particularly versed in grammatical studies and an excellent connoisseur of archaic Latin.[38]

We could go on and on.

7. Legal fragments in literary works

Again. The literary sources provide citations of works that would otherwise be unknown to us. Aulus Gellius alone, for example, preserved three passages of Labeo's commentary on the Twelve Tables,[39] as well as the mention of Neratius's *De nuptiis* (*Noct. Att.*

---

[35] F. Schulz, *History of Roman Legal Science* (Oxford 1946; 1953²) 156 nt. 7, had taken from this text of Persius the idea that Sabinus's *Libri iuris civilis* were 'known to the laymen', i.e. to non-jurists.

[36] Hassan, *La poesia e il diritto* (n. 13) 25 ff.

[37] F.P. Bremer, *Iurisprudentiae antehadrianeae quae supersunt*, II (Lipsiae 1898) 300 f.

[38] M. Pavese, *Scire leges est verba tenere. Ricerche sulle competenze grammaticali dei giuristi romani* (Torino 2013) 63.

[39] Diliberto, *Materiali* (n. 28) 29 ff.

4.4.4) and Sabinus's *de furtis*, to which I will return shortly. [40]

Several passages from Trebatius's *de religionibus*, unknown to the Digest, have come down to us through numerous texts by Macrobius, Gellius, Servius, even Arnobius, and other minor authors. [41]

Again, we could go on and on: but it should be emphasized that a systematic investigation of this sort must still be carried out.

In the literary texts, we also find citations of Roman jurisprudence not conserved in the Digest or in other jurisprudential works, and they are often comparable with those known to us through the juridical sources.

These are often very valuable texts. It is hardly necessary to recall what we know from Cicero's works and correspondence of the jurisprudence of his time. Just as is very famous the dialogue on the Law of the Twelve Tables between the jurist Sextus Caecilius (Africanus?) and the philosopher Favorinus, as narrated by Gellius (*noct. Att.* 20.1): from it we obtain many very important pieces of information. [42]

However, as mentioned previously, these citations of jurisprudential works taken from literary texts occasionally allow us to reconstruct relations between the jurists themselves. One example, among many, concerns Masurius Sabinus. There are numerous citations of lexical interpretations of this jurist (who showed a marked interest in words, etymology, etc.) preserved in Pliny, Gellius and Macrobius. [43]

In the comparison between Gellius and Macrobius (in the examination of the lemma *religiosus*), we learn – in another famous text – that Sabinus reported almost to the letter a definition by Servius Sulpicius.

> Macr. *sat.* 3.3.8: *Servius Sulpicius religionem esse dictam tradidit, quae propter sanctitatem aliquam remota ac seposita a nobis sit, quam a reliquendo dicta, ut a carendo.*

> Gell. 4.9.8: *Masurius ... Sabinus ... 'Religiosum', inquit 'est quod propter sanctitatem aliquam remotum ac sepositum a nobis est verbum a reliquendo dictum, tamquam caerimoniae a carendo.*

These two texts are almost identical.

---

[40] Cf. *infra* § 9.

[41] Bremer, *Iurisprudentiae antehadrianeae* (n. 37) I, 404 ff.

[42] Diliberto, *Materiali* (n. 28) 173 ff., 271 ff.

[43] Bremer, *Iurisprudentiae antehadrianeae* (n. 37) II, 313 ff.

Bremer believed that Macrobius was in error.[44] Yet, more simply there could have been a dependency between the two authors (and this certainly would not be surprising) or a common source.

8. Jurists quotations in legal works and in literary texts

In this regard, let us examine the treatises on the *genera furtorum* of respectively Gellius[45] and Gaius.[46]

---

[44] Bremer, *Iurisprudentiae antehadrianeae* (n. 37) II, 323.

[45] Gell. 11.18.6: *Decemviri autem nostri (…) neque pari severitate in poeniendis omnium ge-nerum furibus neque remissa nimis lenitate usi sunt.* (7) *Nam furem, qui manifesto furto prensus esset, tum demum occidi permiserunt, si aut, cum faceret furtum, nox esset, aut interdiu telo se, cum prenderetur defenderet.* (8) *Ex ceteris autem manifestis furibus liberos verberari addicique iusserunt ei, cui furtum factum esse, si modo id luci fecissent neque se telo defendissent; servos item furti manifesti prensos verberibus adfici et e saxo praecipitari, sed pueros impuberes praetoris arbitratu verberari voluerunt noxiamque ab his factam sarciri.* (9) *Ea quoque furta, quae per lancem liciumque concepta essent, proinde ac si manifesta forent, vindicaverunt.* (10) *Sed nunc a lege illa decemvirali dicessum est. Nam si qui super manifesto furto iure et ordine experiri velit, actio in quadruplum datur.* (11) *Manifestum autem furtum est, ut ait Masurius, quod oblatum; Labeo duo, manifestum et nec et oblatum species potius actionis esse furto cohaerentes quam genera verius videtur, sicut inferius apparebit.* (12) *Furti concepti, item oblati, tripli poena est. Sed quod sit 'oblatum', quod 'conceptum' et pleraque alia ad eam rem ex egregiis veterum moribus accepta neque inutilia cognitu neque iniucunda, qui legere volet, inveniet Sabini librum, cui titulus est de furtis.* (13) *In quo id quoque scriptum est, quod volgo inopinatum est, non hominum tantumneque rerum moventium, quae auferri occulte et subripi possunt, sed fundi quoque et aedium fieri furtum; condemnatum quoque furti colonum, qui fundo, quem conduxerant vendito possessione eius dominum intervertisset.* (14) *Atque id etiam, quod magis inopinabile est, Sabinus dicit furem esse hominis iudicatum, qui cum fugitivus praeter oculos forte domini iret, obtentu togae tamquam se amiciens, ne videtur a domino, obstitisset.* (15) *Aliis deinde furtis omnibus, quae 'nec manifesta' appellantur poenam imposuerunt dupli.* (…) (19) *Quam caste autem ac religiose a prudentissimis viris, quid esset 'furtum', definitum sit, praetereundum non puto, ne quis eum solum esse furem putet, qui occulte tollit aut clam subripit.* (20) *Verba sunt Sabini ex libro iuris civilis secundo: Qui alienam rem adtrectavit, cum id se invito domino facere iudicare deberet, furti tenetur.* (21) *Item alio capite: Qui alienum iacens lucri faciendi causa sustulit, furti obstringitur, sive scit.* (22) *Haec quidem sic in eo, quo nunc dixi, Sabunus scripsit de rebus furti faciendi causa adtrectatis.* (23) *Sed meminisse debemus secundum ea, quae supra scripsi, furtum sine ulla quoque adtrectatione fieri possa sola mente atque animo, ut furtum fiat, adnitente.* (24) *Quocirca ne id quidem Sabinus dubitare se ait, quin dominus furti sit condemnandus, qui servo suo, uti furtum faceret, imperavit.*

[46] Gai. 3.182: *Transeamus nunc ad obligationes quae ex delicto nascuntur, veluti*

For many years now, I have dealt *ex professo* with these texts, the obvious relationship between them and the probable sources:[47] thus, I refer the reader to those pages for a more thorough analysis, limiting myself here to recalling the fundamental points of interest to us.

The coincidences between the two passages are clear and very well known in our milieu. Nevertheless, a brief premise is necessary. Gellius stated that when he was called to hold the office of *iudex privatus* (*noct. Att.* 14.2.1) he had acquired and studied the *libri iuris civilis* of Masurius Sabinus (the only jurist explicitly cited on this point), as well as other works by unidentified jurists and the *lex Iulia iudiciorum*.

Hence, Gellius knew Sabinus well.

Now, Gaius initially affirmed (3.183) that there was a jurisprudential discussion on the subject of the different *genera furtorum*. Servius Sulpicius and Masurius Sabinus (once again the coincidence of opinions, already found on *religiosus*) identified four types (including among the *genera* also *oblatum* and *conceptum*). Labeo, instead, proposed only two types (*manifestum* and *nec manifestum*). Gaius (even though a Sabinian) followed the opinion of Labeo.

Therefore, Gaius based the treatise on the two identified *genera furtorum*. In fact, *oblatum* and *conceptum* were examined in terms of their respective actions.

For Gellius, instead, there were four types of *furta*. That is, Gellius followed Sabinus: he had studied him and did not diverge from him. In

si quis furtum fecerit, bona rapuerit, damnum dederit, iniuram commiserit; quarum omniun rerum uno genere consistit obligatio, cum ex contractu obligationes in IIII genera diducantur, sicut supra exposuimus. (183) *Furtorum autem genera Ser. Sulpicius et Masurius Sabinus IIII esse dixerunt, manifestum et nec manifestum, conceptum et oblatum; Labeo duo, manifestum et nec manifestum; nam conceptum et oblatum species potius actionis esse furto cohaerentes quam genera verius videtur, sicut inferius apparebit.* (184) *Manifestum furtum quidam id esse dixerunt, quod dum fit deprehenditur.* (…). (189) *Poena manifesti furti ex lege XII tabularum capitalis erat. Nam liber verberatus addicebatur ei cui furtum facerat; utrum servus efficertur ex addictio ne, an adiudicati loco constitueretur, veteres quaerebant. In servum aeque verberatum animaduertebatur. Sed postea inprobata est asperitas poenae et tam ex servi persona quam ex liberi quadrupli actio praetori edicto constituta est.* (190) *Nec manifesti furti poena per legem XII tabularum dupli inrogatur, eamque etiam praetor conservat.* (191) *Concepti et oblati poena ex lege XII tabularum tripli est, eaque similiter a praetore servatur.* (192) (…) *Hoc solum praecipit (scil.: lex) ut qui quaerere velit nudus quaerat licio cinctus, lancem habens qui si quid invenerit iubet id lex furtum manifestum esse.* (…). (195) *Furtum autem fit non solum cum quis intercipiendi causa rem alianam amovet, sed generaliter cum quis rem alienam intuito domino contrectat.*

47 Diliberto, *Materiali* (n. 28) 230 ff.

the passage in question, Gellius mentioned the jurist six times, and he also indicated that the subject of *furtum* was dealt with in the second *iuris civilis* book (§ 20), as well as in the otherwise unknown *liber de furtis* (§§ 12 -13).

Gellius followed this expository order:

1. Qualified hypotheses of *fur manifestus* (*nocturnus* and *diurnus qui se telo defendit*). 2. *Fur manifestus* free man, punished with *verberatio* and *addictio*. 3. *Fur manifestus* slave, *verberatio* and being hurled from the cliff. 4. *Quaestio lance licioque*. 5. Subsequent interventions by the praetor and quadruple punishment for *fur manifestus*. 6. Sabinian definition of *fur manifestus*. 7. *Conceptum* and *oblatum* (punishment *in triplum*). 8. *Nec manifestus* punished *duplum*. 9. Final considerations with a reflection, again, of Sabinus.
   Instead, let us see Gaius:

1. *Fur manifestus* free man, *verberatio* and *addictio*. 2. *Fur manifestus* slave, death. 3. Subsequent modifications and punishment *in quadruplum*. 4. *Nec manifestus* (almost with the same expressions as Gellius: this would be a residual category). 5. *Conceptum* and *oblatum*, punishment *in triplum*. 6. *Lance licioque*. 7. Final general discussion on *furtum*.

Of the two authors, one chose two types of *furta* (Gaius, following Labeo's opinion) and the other four (Gellius, following Sabinus): but the treatment was entirely similar.

Some passages are almost identical (*fur manifestus*, *furta oblata* and *concepta*, final reflections on *furtum*: taken directly from Sabinus as Gellius stated, but identical or almost in Gaius).

However, Gellius, as we know, followed Sabinus's exposition. He explicitly stated this. That is, Gellius preferred the jurist whom he had expressly wished to study, instead of Labeo, whose opinions on *furtum* he nonetheless knew very well[48] Gellius's teacher of law was Sabinus.

Yet, through Gellius and the coincidence with the examined passages of the Gaian institutions, we can hypothesize, without much hesitation, that the Antonine jurist, while choosing to follow Labeo in the case of the *genera furtorum*, then in the concrete treatment of *fur-*

[48] Diliberto, *Materiali* (n. 28) 39 ff.

tum (as on countless other occasions: naturally, the circumstance is very well known), once again remained a Sabinian. Thus, Gaius's main source on the topic of *furtum* was Sabinus, but we learn this from Gellius's texts.

Allow me to make a further remark, interesting also in regard to Gellius's working method. Indeed, in the text in question, the author also mentioned Aristo in a curious, interesting comparative digression,[49] but he spoke explicitly of one of his recollections (§ 16). Sabinus had it in front of him. Aristo evidently read it and remembered his opinion. Yet, correctly, he distinguished between direct quotation and mnemonic exercise.

A further example can be given in relation to Gellius and Sabinus.

> Gell. 11.18.21: *Item [Sabinus l.2 iuris civilis] alio capite: Qui alienum iacens lucre faciendi causa sustulit, furti obstringitur, sive scit cuius sit, sive nescit.*

> Ulp. 41 *ad Sab.*, D. 47.2.43.4: *Qui alienum quid iacens lucri faciendi causa sustulit, furti obstringitur, sive scit cuius sit sive ignoravit.*

We are still on the topic of *furtum*, dealing with the subject of someone who embezzles, *lucri faciendi causa*, a *res iacens*.

The comparison between the two passages has been disputed among scholars since the classic work of Huvelin,[50] but Lenel himself wondered, on a palingenetic level, how much of Ulpian's passage was taken verbatim from Sabinus.[51]

What interests us is that (once again) thanks to Gellius we can place with certainty the Sabinian-Ulpianean fragment within the work (in the second book, consistently with the overall treatment of *furtum*); just as, again from Gellius, we learn that Ulpian, commenting on Sabinus, reported the latter's passages directly and slavishly.

We could consider many examples. Once again, in Ulpian's commentary *ad Sabinum* (D. 33.9.3.9, 22 *ad Sab.*), in this case regarding

---

[49] That interesting digression has not escaped the attention of the astute work of C. Pelloso, *Studi sul furto nell'antichità mediterranea* (Padova 2008) esp. 26 f.

[50] P. Huvelin, *Études sur le furtum dans le très ancien droit romain*, I. *Les sources* (Lyon-Paris 1915; facsimile reprint Roma 1968) 703.

[51] O. Lenel, *Palingenesia Iuris Civilis*, II (Leipzig 1889) 1166.

penus,[52] the jurist proposed a definition of *ligna et carbones*: well, the comparison between Gellius (*noct. Att.* 4.1.21-23) and Ulpian let us to understand that the definition we find in Ulpian literally coincides with Sabinus's writing in the second *iuris civilis* book.[53]

Again, we could go on and on.

However, some other observations must be made. Indeed, Gellius offered 'additional' (so to speak) material concerning institutions and jurisprudential opinions known to us *aliunde*.

> Gell. 4.2.9-10: *De sterila autem muliere, si nativa sterilitate sit, Trebatium contra Labeonem respondisse dicunt. Nam cum redhiberi eam Labeo quasi minus sanam putasset, negasse aiunt Trebatium ex edicto agi posse, si ea mulier a principio genitali sterilitate esset. At si valetudo eius offendisset exque ea vitium factum esset, ut concipere fetus non posset, tum sanam non videri et esse in causa redhibitionis.*

> Ulp. 1 *ad ed. aed. cur.*, D. 21.1.14.3: *De sterili Caelius distinguere Trebatium dicit, ut, si natura sterilis sit, sana sit, vitio corporis contra.*

In the text in question,[54] Gellius was dealing with a problem concerning hidden defects. Did the sterility of the female slave fall into this category or not?

The author states that it was said by some (*dicunt*) that Trebatius had replied to Labeo. The latter (on the basis of the *edictum* of the curule aediles) believed that an *actio redhibitoria* was available. Trebatius excluded it if the slave were sterile from birth, while he considered it possible if the sterility depended on *vitium* after the birth itself.

Now, almost the entire second chapter of book IV of the Attic Nights deals with the difference between *morbus* and *vitium*.

---

[52] On *penus*, lastly and with previous literature, M. Genovese, 'Quarta Falcidia e penus legata in D. 35.2.1.8 (Paul. l. s. ad leg. Falc.)', in *Studi in on. di A. Metro*, III (Milano 2010) 43 ff.

[53] On all this, cf. Diliberto, *Materiali* (n. 28) 238.

[54] The two texts, taken individually and in their obvious connection, have been the subject of innumerable analyses: for a first bibliographical survey, I refer the reader simply to R. Ortu, *'Aiunt aediles ...'. Dichiarazioni del venditore e vizi della cosa venduta nell'editto de mancipiis emundis vendundis* (Torino 2008) 120 ff.; N. Donadio, 'Garanzia per i vizi della cosa e responsabilità contrattuale', in E. Jakab, W. Ernst (eds.), *Kaufen nach römischen Recht* (Berlin-Heidelberg 2008) 61 ff. (lit. in notes 27-29).

Well, at a place slightly before (4, 2, 3 and 5), Gellius mentions Caelius Sabinus's *liber de edicto aedilium curulium* in which – says Gellius – the jurist talked about Labeo's opinions on the matter. Therefore, in all probability, Gellius read about the contrast between Trebatius and Labeo in Caelius Sabinus (as Talamanca pointed out in his well-known study on Trebatius).[55]

However, the information is confirmed by Ulpian's text (D. 21.1.14.3) reported subsequently. It is not by chance that Ulpian, in his commentary on the edict of the aediles, mentioned Caelius and reported Trebatius's opinion already known to us.

Thus, Ulpian was reading the commentary on the edict of the aediles by Caelius Sabinus, like Gellius, but the latter was infinitely more detailed (so much so that, in reporting the passages by Caelius, in addition to Labeo and Trebatius, he also noted the opinions of Balbus and Servius Sulpicius on specific points).

It is superfluous, at this point, to mention once again how valuable are these materials deriving from non-legal texts.

9. Law and grammar

Again (and moving toward the conclusion).

At times, non-legal texts help us to understand the same sources of the jurists. Gellius (*noct. Att.* 1.18.3-6) dealt with the topic of etymology of the word *furtum*, stating that Varro would have obtained *furtum a furvo, id est nigro*. Gellius criticized the great scholar good-naturedly, almost ashamed of himself ("but who am I to contradict a man of Varro's stature?"). In fact, for Gellius, *furtum* derived instead from the Greek *for*.

Well, in Paul. 39 *ad ed.*, D. 47.2.1pr., the etymology *furtum a furvo, id est nigro*, was attributed to Labeo, once again in contrast to the opinion of Sabinus (*furtum a fraude*). However, Paulus concluded in the sense (already observed in Gellius) of derivation from the Greek *for*.

Hence, Labeo followed Varro, or perhaps they both had a common source, unknown to us: once again, this is information learned from Gellius.

Conversely, Paulus followed an opinion that Gellius had already

---

[55] M. Talamanca, 'Trebazio Testa fra retorica e diritto', in G.G. Archi (ed.), *Questioni di giurisprudenza tardo-repubblicana* (Milano 1985) 60 ff.

supported, most probably on the basis of common readings. In this case, it cannot have been Sabinus, whose etymology (*furtum a fraude*) was explicitly criticized by Paulus himself.

10. A first conclusion

I will begin to conclude.

I believe that, even from these summary considerations, there clearly emerges the pervasiveness of law in Roman literary works. Knowledge of law was considered a sign of prestige and authority by Roman society as a whole.

Obviously, this does not mean that there were no specialisms and specialists. Quite the contrary. But the relations among literary creation, its use and diffusion, and juridical and especially jurisprudential specialisms was much stronger than in other ancient societies and, even more so, than in modern and contemporary ones.

In short, the authors of the different scientific and cultural circles read each other. Clearly not all to the same extent and with the same interest. However, the phenomenon seems quite clear to me.

There emerges once again the need for systematic work. Only such comprehensive research could demonstrate the greater or lesser diffusion (and relative knowledge) of the works of the single Roman jurists in the broadest intellectual circles, in different periods and in different cultural milieus.

11. Horace, the *Satires* and law: problems of method

We started with the considerations of Cavallone, according to whom scholars of Latin literature, with few very important exceptions, often do not notice (*do not see*) the legal references contained in the literary texts they are examining.

Well, having checked almost all the main comments on Horace's *Satires*, I was able to ascertain that none of them discussed – as instead it deserves – a very interesting text studied by Hassan,[56] whose convincing interpretation I tried to develop further in one of my recent works.[57]

---

[56] Hassan, *La poesia e il diritto* (n. 13) 103 ff.

[57] O. Diliberto, 'La satira e il diritto. Una nuova lettura di Horat. sat. 1.3.115-117', in AUPA 55 (2012) 385 ff.

I will summarize its conclusions here for the sole aim of proposing a rather new method of investigation of the literary sources.

Let us observe:

Horat. *sat.* 1.3.115-117:
Nec vincet ratio hoc, tantundem ut peccet idemque, qui teneros caules alieni fregerit horti et qui nocturnus sacra divum legerit.

Horace is criticizing the Stoic doctrine: not all faults must be placed on the same level, nor punished with the same severity. In this regard, he mentions two macroscopic examples from which to understand the obvious disparity between the faults of men: the picking of tender cabbages on someone else's land and sacrilege (theft of *res sacrae*).

The difference in severity of the two cases must have been clear to any reader, demonstrating – according to Horace – the senselessness of the Stoic doctrine.

However, hidden behind these cases lie two precise legal situations. The picking of vegetables on someone else's land (which could give rise to *actio ex lege XII tabularum* or to *actio ex lege Aquilia*) and, indeed, sacrilege.

Meanwhile, Horace, as effectively underlined,[58] carried out serious juridical studies and belonged to an intellectual circle that included contemporary jurists, among whom the aforementioned Trebatius Testa, of whom he was a friend and companion.[59] The poet moved with ease in the field of law.

But the reader of the *Satires*?

At this point and on the basis of the text in question, I propose several possible levels of understanding of this passage by Horace's audience.

1. All the readers understood that the two faults mentioned cannot be placed on the same level and thus must not be punished in the same way.
2. Those who had studied law would easily see that these are two precise legal situations.
3. Finally, there could have been a further and more particular level of

[58] Hassan, *La poesia e il diritto* (n. 13) 11 ff.

[59] Cf. *supra* § 7.

understanding: that of a much more restricted and select audience. The jurists.

Indeed, let us compare Horace's text (*qui teneros caules alieni fregerit horti*) with the third *caput* (very famous, as is obvious) of the *lex Aquilia*:

> Ulp. 18 *ad ed.*, D. 9.2.27.5: *Tertio autem capite ait eadem lex Aquilia: 'Ceterarum rerum praeter nomine et pecudem occisos si quis alteri damnum faxit, quod usserit fregerit ruperit iniuria, quanti ea res erit in diebus triginta proximis, tantum aes domino dare damnas esto.*

Horace appears singularly precise: *qui* ... *fregerit*. He may have *wished* to underline a correspondence with the words of law.

Yet, we can try to go further in the analysis (entering, I realize, a minefield).

The many discussions of the Roman jurists – dating to the late Republic – on the notion of *arbor* were very detailed: it was a matter of understanding which plants could be included. The jurisprudential texts list, not infrequently with minute distinctions, the plants that could be considered trees and the related jurisprudential debates.

However, the conclusion was quite clear. To be considered *arbores*, and thus be included in the protection of *actio arborum furtim caesarum* or *actio de arboribus succisis* (on which the discussions of the jurists were endless: let us limit ourselves here to indicating the action *ex lege duodecim tabularum*), the plants had to present characteristics of firmness in the ground: that is, those with roots. Otherwise, the *actio ex lege Aquilia* applied.

In this regard, Gaius offers us a valuable annotation (precisely, and not by chance, in the commentary on the Twelve Tables):

> Gai. *ad leg. XII tab.*, D. 47.7.4: *Certe non dubitabur, si adhuc adeo tenerum sit, ut herbae loco sit, non debere arbores numero haberi.*

Therefore, herbs could not be considered trees, because they were too ... *tenera.*

Once again, although we certainly cannot exclude chance, Horace's text seems almost juridically perfect in its reference to *tender* cabbages: an adjective that would otherwise seem redundant. Indeed, cabbages are tender regardless. Hence, they cannot be included in the notion of *arbores* and thus one could act, in the case of their picking, with the *ac-*

tio ex lege Aquilia: the one whose *verba* seem to be echoed in the text of Horace under examination.

Nevertheless, the final suggestion is another one. Horace mentioned the picking of vegetables and sacrilege.

Well, we have already underlined how much Horace was linked to Trebatius (as you will remember, he even made him a character of his satires). Now, we know with certainty that Trebatius had dealt on several occasions with *res religiosae*, with sacred law and related matters,[60] and thus perhaps (but this is mere conjecture) even with sacrilege.

Yet, we also know, in this case with certainty, that Trebatius had dealt with the cutting of other people's plants and the related competition between the two actions *ex lege XII Tabularum* and *ex lege Aquilia*.

We observe, in fact:

> Paul. 9 *ad Sab.*, D. 47.7.1: *Si furtim arbores caesae sint, ex lege Aquilia et ex duodecim tabularum dandam actionem Labeo ait: sed Trebatius ita utramque dandam, ut iudex in posteriore deducat id quod ex prima consecutus sit et reliquo condemnet.*

Labeo and Trebatius – according to Paulus – had two different opinions on the matter. But what is relevant here is that Trebatius had actively participated in the jurisprudential discussion on the cutting of other people's plants and related actions.

To sum up, Horace proposed a situation (*qui teneros caules alieni fregerit horti*) that seems to follow to the letter the hypothesis of the third *caput* of the *lex Aquilia*, highlighting the tenderness of the picked cabbages, as if to underline that the reference to that law is juridically exact (otherwise it would have been possible to resort to actions *ex lege XII Tabularum*).

But who would have been able to understand such subtleties, such nuances? Only jurists, of whom Horace himself was a friend.

If we add to this that Trebatius, with whom the poet was intimate, was interested in the subject, I cannot avoid the suggestion of that third level of writing addressed to the (few) people able to understand it: precisely the contemporary jurists and especially Trebatius Testa.

---

[60] Texts reported in Diliberto, 'La satira' (n. 57) 396.

This would have been a more profound level of writing, addressed to those readers – legal specialists – who would also have been able to smile at the irony implicitly addressed to them. This would confirm – in other ways – what has already been demonstrated by Mario Citroni, in relation to the "duplicity or plurality of the levels of destination" of Horace's work. [61]

[61] M. Citroni, *Poesia e lettori in Roma antica. Forme della comunicazione letteraria* (Roma-Bari 1995) 280 ff., 290 f., but also 343 and *passim*.

Chapter 7

GREEK THOUGHT AND ROMAN JURISTS: A PRELIMINARY SURVEY ON POMPONIUS'S *ENCHIRIDION*

Fara Nasti

SUMMARY: 1. *Omnia manu a regibus gubernabantur*: Pomponius a reader of Polybius? – 2. Pomponius and Aristotle.

Studies on the relationship between Greek thought and Roman jurisprudence – more precisely we should say: the influence of Greek philosophy on Roman jurisprudence – have favoured some subjects, leaving many others in the shadows. For this reason, we must admit that this research field has still to be exhaustively investigated. Suffice it to think, for example, that attention has been given almost exclusively to the period of Roman expansionism, while far fewer investigations have addressed the first centuries of our era.

Likewise, we can ask if the influence of Greek philosophy on the writing of Roman jurists should receive greater attention than, at first sight, it has been afforded: certainly, we are faced with the difficulties arising from our only partial knowledge of Roman jurisprudence, but perhaps it is also necessary to deal with a scarce interest in the clues of history emerging from such works. Therefore, in this context, it is not surprising that the question of the relationship between Greek historical thought and Roman jurisprudence has never been raised.

And it is exactly within the framework just described that an analytical commentary[1] on Pomponius's *Enchiridion*, which inevitably subjects the work to a thorough new investigation, would provide new per-

[1] However, the need had long been felt. I am thinking, for all, of D. Nörr, 'Pomponius oder Zum Geschichtsverständnis der römischen Juristen', in ANRW, II.15 (Berlin-New York 1976) 497 ff. = 'Pomponio o 'della intelligenza storica dei giuristi romani'', Italian translation by M.A. Fino, E. Stolfi, in RDR 2 (2002) 167 ff. = D. Nörr, *Schriften 2001-2010* (ed. T.J. Chiusi, H.-D Spengler, J. Paricio) (Madrid-Barcelona-Buenos Aires 2012) [from which the citations are drawn] 175 ff., esp. 204.

spectives: here I will report some initial results of the work in progress for the *Scriptores iuris Romani* project.

1. *Omnia manu a regibus gubernabantur*: Pomponius a reader of Polybius?

The schema of the *Enchiridion*, judging from what remains of it, is substantially clear: Pomponius dealt first with *origo atque processus iuris*; then, in the second section, with the *nomina* and the *origo* of the magistratures; in the third, he reported the *successio auctorum*. Yet, the main questions concerning this work, long since raised in our field of study, remain fundamentally unresolved: I am referring to those regarding its formation (the models, the sources and the independence of the jurist with respect to them), and also, thinking about a more general framework, on the destination of the *Enchiridion* and the identification of the literary type to which it belonged (also taking into account the consolidated hypothesis that places it within the context of works intended for elementary teaching, as the title would seem to suggest). Or, again, the questions about its problematical position amongst Pomponius's works and thought, and the possibility of attributing to it, as has been done, a deeper meaning than what appears to emerge: a sense and a political context that seem to be required and implicit in the choice and originality of the subject.

As for the models followed by Pomponius, there is no doubt concerning the content of the third section, on the *successio auctorum*, for which a link with the Hellenistic genre of *diadochai* is indisputable.[2]

---

[2] Rightly recalled by F. Schulz, *History of Roman Legal Science* (Oxford 1953²) 169, who mentioned also some Roman comparisons: Cicero's *Brutus* and Suetonius's *de grammaticis et rhetoribus*. Much has been written on the *Enchiridion*, its tripartite division, the problem of transmission and the state of the work, and the ideology underlying its composition, and I make no claim to mentions all the contributions here. However, I assume knowledge of some fundamental works on Pomponius and, in particular, on his Manual, referring the reader to the literature and the critical discussion contained in them: apart from the well-known bibliographical appendix on Sextus Pomponius edited by G. De Cristofaro, in F.P. Casavola, *Giuristi adrianei* (Napoli 1980) 314 ff., I am thinking – in addition to the above-mentioned works by Schulz and by Nörr, 'Pomponio' (n. 1) esp., for the overall structure of the work, p. 203 –, of M. Bretone, 'L'Enchiridion di Pomponio', in *Tecniche e ideologie dei giuristi romani* (Napoli 1982²) 209 ff.; L. Lantella, *Le opere della giurisprudenza romana nella storiografia* (Torino 1979) 7 ff.; E. Stolfi, *Studi sui libri ad edictum di Pomponio. I. Trasmissione e fonti* (Napoli 2002) esp. 261 ff., 295

Instead, it remains unclear whether Pomponius followed one or more exemplars for the first two parts of the *Enchiridion*, as well as for the creation of the work's overall structure.

More generally, the use of Varro – whose *libri iuris civilis* would have been a precedent of the *Enchiridion* – has been hypothesized,[3] as has Capito's *Coniectanea*. However, in both cases, the state of the texts or, for Varro, our complete lack of knowledge of the work, prevent us from adding further considerations to those that must remain hypotheses, albeit reasonable ones. Instead, there is evidence for a possible connection with Sextus Aelius's Tripertita.[4] Regarding the use of Cicero, I do not believe it has ever been questioned that he might have been a source for some passages of Pomponius's work; however, if I am not mistaken, no hypothesis has ever been advanced about the possibility that Cicero's works may have been a model for the jurist.[5]

It seems to me that the conclusions reached so far, the sources examined and the possible archetypes proposed can be supplemented by others.

It is appropriate to read what is for us the *incipit* of the first section, where Pomponius deals with the *origo iuris* and its *processus*.

> Pomp. *l.s. ench.*, D. 1.2.2.1: *Et quidem initio civitatis nostrae populus sine lege certa, sine iure certo primum agere instituit omniaque manu a regibus gubernabantur.* 2. *Postea aucta ad aliquem modum civitate ipsum Romulum traditur populum in triginta partes divisisse, quas partes curias appellavit propterea quod tunc rei publicae curam per sententias partium*

---

ff.; 305 ff. with previous literature; A. Schiavone, *The Invention of Law in the West* (Cambridge [Mass.]-London) 156 ff., esp. 383 ff. on the tripartite division of the work.

[3] Again according to Schulz, *History* (n. 2) 168 f., esp. 169; these are hypotheses critically discussed by Nörr, 'Pomponio' (n. 1) 193 ff.

[4] Bretone, in *Tecniche e ideologie* (n. 2) 224 ff.; Schiavone, *The Invention of Law* (n. 2) 383 f.

[5] According to Schulz, *History* (n. 2) 169, Pomponius used as a source, directly or indirectly, Cicero's *Brutus*, *De oratore* and *De re publica*, along with Varro's *De iure civili*. On the relationship between Cicero and Pomponius, I refer to M. Bretone, *Pomponio lettore di Cicerone*, Labeo 16 (1970) 174 ff. = *Tecniche e ideologie* (n. 2) 274 ff. from which I draw, paraphrasing, the title of this section: moreover, in his opinion, Pomponius would have known Cicero's *de iure civili in artem redigendo*; Nörr, 'Pomponio' (n. 1) 197 f.; D. Nörr, 'Cicero-Zitate bei den klassischen Juristen', in *Ciceroniana III, Atti III Colloquium Tullianum 1976* (Roma 1978) 111 ff. = D. Nörr, *Historiae iuris antiqui. Gesammelte Schriften*, eds. T.J. Chiusi, W. Kaiser, H.-D. Spengler, vol. II (Goldbach 2003) 1187 ff.; Stolfi, *Studi* (n. 2) 287 ff. with previous bibliography.

> *earum expediebat. Et ita leges quasdam et ipse curiatas ad populum tulit: tulerunt et sequentes reges.*
>
> 1. And, indeed, at the beginning of our community the people first began to live without certain statute law, without certain rights, and everything was governed by the hand of the kings. 2. Then, when the community grew to reach a certain size, it is passed down that Romulus himself divided the people into thirty parts, which he called *curiae*, since at that time he took care of the community by means of their deliberations. Thus, he himself presented to the people some curiate laws: and the subsequent kings also presented them.

The jurist's description has some important elements of absolute originality: in particular, the description the pre-Romulean phase. I believe that Pomponius drew on the thought of Polybius for this description; that is, he wished to apply to the narration of the origins of Rome at least a segment of the well-known constitutional theory expounded in the *Histories*. And in my mind this observation can provide a new perspective on the works that might have inspired Pomponius in composing the *Enchiridion*.

Certainly, it is necessary to consider the formation of an ideology connected with the history of the originations of cities, and thus also with that of Rome; and it is true that, in referring to the founding moment of the Urbs, it would have highlighted, according to some traditions, the humility of its creators and the absolute simplicity of what would later become the civic body of Rome, established after a progressive acceptance of a crowd of humble strangers.[6] However, this description – which refers to the establishment of the Roman people, and to its living without certain statute law, without certain rights – cannot be compared with that of Pomponius. If I am not mistaken, only the jurist mentioned a Roman monarchy prior to that of Romulus, and he did so referring explicitly to the initial moment of the *civitas* (*et quidem initio civitatis nostrae...*). What is more, it is quite evident that this description makes clear his desire to become an interpreter of that historiographical tradition, well represented by Livy and by Dionysius of Halicarnassus, who highlighted the continuity between Romulus and

[6] This point was dealt with by L. Peppe, 'Riflessioni intorno all'esecuzione personale', in AUPA 53 (2009) 115 ff., esp. 127 ff., with the evaluation of some sources. The article was partly reused in L. Peppe, 'Fra corpo e patrimonio. Obligatus, addictus, ductus, persona in causa mancipi', in A. Corbino, M. Humbert, G. Negri (eds.), *Homo, caput, persona. La costruzione giuridica dell'identità nell'esperienza romana* (Pavia 2010) 435 ff.

the kings of Alba Longa and thus, more or less indirectly, between the destruction of Troy and the foundation of Rome.[7] Therefore, if the kings to whom Pomponius alluded were, as is likely, the Latin kings, it becomes even more significant that only Pomponius emphasized the contrast between a form of pre-Romulean monarchy and the rule of Romulus. Albeit in the context of a genetic (and only indirectly identifiable) continuity between the first king of Rome and the kings of Alba, the break, the discontinuity represented by Romulus at the beginning of the Roman *civitas*, was striking for Pomponius.

And it is exactly this explicit and strong contrast which, in my opinion, constitutes the originality of the passage of the *Enchiridion*. In other words, we must bear in mind Polybius's thinking in order to explain the meaning and peculiarity of Pomponius's expression *omnia manu a regibus gubernabantur*.

The constitutional theory of the historian is well known and yet it is

[7] As is known, the topic is complex and has been the subject of important studies characterized by very different orientations – I am thinking, for example, of A. Momigliano, 'An Interim Report on the Origins of Rome', in JRS 53 (1963) 95 ff. = A. Momigliano, *Le origini di Roma*, in *Roma arcaica*, Firenze 1989, 5 ff. esp. 11 ff., to which I refer the reader – which have dealt both with the gradual constitution, with partly Greek, partly Etruscan, partly indigenous materials, of the myth of the foundation of Rome as a synthesis of the legend of Romulus with that of Aeneas, and with the meaning of the legend of Romulus. And on the relationship between the foundation of Rome and the Hellenistic world, which is clearly visible also in the story of the arrival of Aeneas in Latium and of the Trojan ancestry of Rome, see L. Canfora, 'Roma "città greca"', in QS 39 (1994) 5 ff. esp. 34 ff.: Rome had ended up a "common product of the Trojans and the Greeks". In this sense, the importance given by Dionysius of Halicarnassus to the theory of the Greek origin of Rome is well explained. Nor should there be any doubt that "The founder of the nascent city of Rome was Romulus, the only person to whom the Etruscan rite of the primigenial furrow was unanimously attributed": thus, according to the perspective of A. Carandini, *La nascita di Roma. Dèi, Lari, eroi e uomini all'alba di una civiltà* (Torino 1997) 54, who deals, esp. 109 ff., also with the composition of a myth of the foundation of Rome as a fusion between the "Alban-Roman indigenous saga and Trojan-Lavinian heroic saga". Naturally, this does not mean denying the reasonableness of the reconstructions which, on the basis of some historical testimonies (Polybius and Cicero, for example), thought of a "continuous constitutional creation, thus a centuries-old process"; because in this "phased generation of the settlement and of the community, the Romans recognized the Romulean foundation – not the subsequent ones – as an essential discriminant because it was the first to be based on a 'mixed' constitution": A. Carandini, *Remo e Romolo. Dai rioni dei Quiriti alla città dei Romani* (Torino 2006) 83. And on the contribution of law as an element of progress in the history of civilization in the perspective of Cicero, but also of Pomponius, see D. Mantovani, 'Cicerone storico del diritto', in Ciceroniana 13 (2009) 297 ff., esp. 308 ff.; but also Mantovani and Nörr cit. *infra* in notes 17-18.

useful to recall some passages. In particular those in which Polybius describes the types of constitutions in order to narrate the extraordinary history of Rome, which had led it to gain control of almost all the inhabited world in only 53 years. He stated that he wished to distinguish himself from those who had maintained that there were three forms of government; and in fact, after indicating royalty, aristocracy and democracy,[8] he proceeded to describe three others, different in some respects from the first three: monarchy, oligarchy, ochlocracy.[9]

Hence, without avoiding a hint of polemic, Polybius entered into the complex discussion on constitutional forms;[10] there are no explicit

---

[8] Pol. 6.3.5 συμβαίνει δὴ τοὺς πλείστους τῶν βουλομένων διδασκαλικῶς ἡμῖν ὑποδεικνύειν περὶ τῶν τοιούτων τρία γένη λέγειν πολιτειῶν, ὧν τὸ μὲν καλοῦσι βασιλείαν, τὸ δ'ἀριστοκρατίαν, τὸ δὲ τρίτον δημοκρατίαν. 6. δοκεῖ δέ μοι πάνυ τις εἰκότως ἂν ἐπαπορῆσαι πρὸς αὐτούς, πότερον ὡς μόνας ταύτας ἢ καὶ νὴ Δί' ὡς ἀρίστας ἡμῖν εἰσηγοῦνται τῶν πολιτειῶν. 7. κατ' ἀμφότερα γὰρ ἀγνοεῖν μοι δοκοῦσι. (Well, most of those who wish to didactically inform us on these topics cite three kinds of constitutions: they call the first of them kingship, the second aristocracy, the third democracy. 6. It seems to me, in truth, that one could correctly reply by asking them if they are presenting us with these constitutions as the only ones or, rather, as the best ones. 7. In effect, it seems to me that in both cases they are in error).

[9] Pol. 6.4.1 ὅτι δ'ἀληθές ἐστι τὸ λεγόμενον ἐκ τούτων συμφανές. 2. οὔτε γὰρ πᾶσαν δήπου μοναρχίαν εὐθέως βασιλείαν ῥητέον, ἀλλὰ μόνην τὴν ἐξ ἑκόντων συγχωρουμένην καὶ τῇ γνώμῃ τὸ πλεῖον φόβῳ καὶ βίᾳ κυβερνωμένην: 3. οὐδὲ μὴν πᾶσαν ὀλιγαρχίαν ἀριστοκρατίαν νομιστέον, ἀλλὰ ταύτην, ἥτις ἂν κατ' ἐκλογὴν ὑπὸ τῶν δικαιοτάτων καὶ φρονιμωτάτων ἀνδρῶν βραβεύηται. 4. παραπλησίως οὐδὲ δημοκρατίαν, ἐν ᾗ πᾶν πλῆθος κύριόν ἐστι ποιεῖν ὅ, 5. τι ποτ' ἂν αὐτὸ βουληθῇ καὶ πρόθηται παρὰ δ' ᾧ πάτριόν ἐστι καὶ σύνηθες θεοὺς σέβεσθαι, γονεῖς θεραπεύειν, πρεσβυτέρους αἰδεῖσθαι, νόμοις πείθεσθαι, παρὰ τοῖς τοιούτοις συστήμασιν ὅταν τὸ τοῖς πλείοσι δόξαν νικᾷ, τοῦτο καλεῖν δεῖ δημοκρατίαν. 6. διὸ καὶ γένη μὲν ἓξ εἶναι ῥητέον πολιτειῶν, τρία μὲν ἃ πάντες θρυλοῦσι καὶ νῦν προείρηται, τρία δὲ τὰ τούτοις συμφυῆ, λέγω δὲ μοναρχίαν, ὀλιγαρχίαν, ὀχλοκρατίαν. (That my statements are true is evident from the following: 2. not every monarchy must be defined as kingship, but only the one spontaneously accepted and guided by wisdom rather than by fear and force; 3. nor, certainly, should each oligarchy be considered aristocracy, but only that which is governed by men chosen as the most just and sensible. 4. Similarly, one should not call democracy that system in which the mass is free to do whatever it desires and has in mind to do; 5. the one instead in which the tradition and the custom of worshiping the gods, caring for one's parents, respecting the elderly, obeying the laws, when in these communities the opinion of the majority prevails, must be called democracy. 6. Therefore it must be said that there are six kinds of constitutions, the three of which everyone speaks and which have just now been named and the three naturally related to them, namely monarchy, oligarchy, ochlocracy).

[10] As is well known, there is a very rich literature on the topic of the constitutional forms and their examination by Herodotus, Plato, Aristotle, Polybius. In ad-

mentions in this passage, but the allusion to the political theories of Plato and Aristotle is rather patent. And if it is true that, as has been argued, the political lexicon referring to constitutional regimes was enriched thanks to Polybius,[11] we must not underestimate the complexity of the previous thinking on the subject, especially as it has come down to us from the pages of Aristotle's *Politics*. Indeed, it was Aristotle, in turn polemicizing with those who had preceded him, who subjected the theory of the three forms of government to a thorough critical analysis. In that treatise, he rejected the idea of trying to determine the best constitution in an absolute sense: for Aristotle, this search required the evaluation of the context, of the way to identify the best constitution with respect to the different conditions. Moreover, for each of the three forms of righteous rule – rule of one, of a few, of many, which he called monarchy, aristocracy, *politeia* – one must consider the degenerate forms (tyranny, oligarchy and democracy) and the existence of different types of the same form of government.[12] Finally, the philosopher distinguished between the denomination of a constitution and its true structure. He had made it clear that a series of elements, mostly economic-social ones, contributed to the establishment of a certain constitutional form: the economic strength of each of the parts making up its framework, their number, class differences and so on.[13]

---

dition to the works to which reference will be made in the following pages (all with references to earlier literature), of use to what is being discussed in these pages is the article by L. Canfora, 'La tipologia costituzionale', in QS 37 (1993) 19 ff. An important note on the thread linking Herodotus to Machiavelli is in A. Schiavone, *The End of the Past* (Cambridge 2000) 266 f. with previous literature.

[11] R. Weil, *Polybe, Histoires*, Livre VI (Paris 1977) 16 f.

[12] For example, with regard to the government of many, he identified four types of democracy (the one characterized by tribes; the one organized as an assembly of citizens; the one with the drawing of lots of the magistratures; and finally the one in which the assembly has decisional power over the entire city – the last one would have been the worst) and he called *politeia* the correct form in which the majority governs in the interests of all, distinguishing it from the deviant form, democracy, in which the majority governs in its own interest.

[13] Studies on Aristotle's political thought and on the text of his *Politics* seem to have been particularly intense in recent years also in Italy; it is sufficient to consider the translation and commentary on the work that appeared very recently, to which reference will be made from time to time. Apart from works dedicated to the forms of government described by Aristotle, see the reflections contained in the introductory note by L. Bertelli and M. Moggi in book IV of the Erma di Bretschneider edi-

Therefore, according to Polybius, it is necessary to distinguish – from the substantive and terminological point of view – between kingship (βασιλεία) and monarchy (μοναρχία); only the former has positive value and is characterized by spontaneous acceptance by the associates and by the enlightened guidance of the monarch (Pol. 6, 4, 2). Instead, not every monarchy is so.[14]

In effect, Polybius proceeded by degrees in his narration, following the historical course of the forms of government. And, having indicated the instinctive principle which, in humans as in animals, causes the aggregation of individuals, he discussed in the sixth chapter of book VI the reasons for the association of humans: they must be identified as the feelings of gratitude for those who defend the community and, together, the force of reasoning and intellect.

These are the points of Polybius's story from which I think the parallel with Pomponius is possible:

> Pol. 6.4.7: πρώτη μὲν οὖν ἀκατασκεύως καὶ φυσικῶς συνίσταται μοναρχία, ταύτῃ δ'ἕπεται καὶ ἐκ ταύτης γεννᾶται μετὰ κατασκευῆς καὶ διορθώσεως βασιλεία. 8. μεταβαλλούσης δὲ ταύτης εἰς τὰ συμφυῆ κακά, λέγω δ'εἰς τυραννίδ', αὖθις ἐκ τῆς τούτων καταλύσεως ἀριστοκρατία φύεται.
>
> The first to form, through a spontaneous and natural process, is monarchy; it is followed by kingship, which emerges from the previous one following a process of elaboration and improvement. 8. Kingship is modified into the degenerate form, connected to it by nature, which is tyranny; and the fall of this regime in turn generates aristocracy.

A monarchy – it can be defined as a spontaneous, natural monarchy – is the first constitutional form. Yet, we must make a distinction. In a literal sense, monarchy is the first recognition of government by one; as mentioned, it arises from recognition of the supremacy of one person

---

tion (Roma 2014) 7 ff.; as well as the essays by L. Canfora, 'La democrazia nella Grecia antica', XII ff., and by R. Kraut, *La democrazia greca*, XXXIII ff. and 'Introduzione alla 'Politica' di Aristotele', LXXXIX ff. in *Aristotele, Politica*, vol. I (Milano 2016) cit. *infra*, note 23, all with indication of previous literature.

[14] Pol. 6.4.1: ὅτι δ' ἀληθές ἐστι τὸ λεγόμενον ἐκ τούτων συμφανές. 2. οὔτε γὰρ πᾶσαν δήπου μοναρχίαν εὐθέως βασιλείαν ῥητέον, ἀλλὰ μόνην τὴν ἐξ ἑκόντων συγχωρουμένην καὶ τῇ γνώμῃ τὸ πλεῖον ἢ φόβῳ καὶ βίᾳ κυβερνωμένην. (That my statements are true is evident from the following: 2. not every monarchy must be defined as kingship, but only the one spontaneously accepted and guided by wisdom rather than by fear and force).

over all others. However, it is a constitutional form destined to change, and the change is an improvement and allows the transition to kingship, to *basileia*:

> Pol. 6.6.10: ἐν οἷς ὅταν ὁ προεστὼς καὶ τὴν μεγίστην δύναμιν ἔχων ἀεὶ συνεπισχύῃ τοῖς προειρημένοις κατὰ τὰς τῶν πολλῶν διαλήψεις, καὶ δόξῃ τοῖς ὑποταττομένοις διανεμητικὸς εἶναι τοῦ κατ᾽ ἀξίαν ἑκάστοις, 11. οὐκέτι τὴν βίαν δεδιότες, τῇ δὲ γνώμῃ τὸ πλεῖον εὐδοκοῦντες, ὑποτάττονται καὶ συσσῴζουσι τὴν ἀρχὴν αὐτοῦ, κἂν ὅλως ᾖ γηραιός, ὁμοθυμαδὸν ἐπαμύνοντες καὶ διαγωνιζόμενοι πρὸς τοὺς ἐπιβουλεύοντας αὐτοῦ τῇ δυναστείᾳ. 12. καὶ δὴ τῷ τοιούτῳ τρόπῳ βασιλεὺς ἐκ μονάρχου λανθάνει γενόμενος, ὅταν παρὰ τοῦ θυμοῦ καὶ τῆς ἰσχύος μεταλάβῃ τὴν ἡγεμονίαν ὁ λογισμός.
>
> In these circumstances, if the head, the one who has greatest power, always contributes to supporting what has been said, according to the general judgment, and seems to his subordinates capable of giving to each according to merit, 11. they, no longer fearing his strength, but rather approving his good judgement, submit to him and help to conserve his power, even when he is very old, united in defending him and in opposing those who undermine his dominant position. 12. And in this way a king (βασιλεὺς) is inadvertently born from a monarch (ἐκ μονάρου), when reasoning replaces violence and force (καὶ δὴ τῷ τοιούτῳ τρόπῳ βασιλεὺς ἐκ μονάρχου λανθάνει γενόμενος).

Characteristic of kingship is recognition of the wisdom of the monarch, of his good governance; the perception of fairness is what determines the passage from one constitutional form to another. This, according to the historian, is how a king is born from a monarch.[15]

Let us return to Pomponius's initial passage, D. 1.2.2.1, reported previously. The contrast between the pre-Romulean phase and that of the government of the famous founder is very clear. As has been correctly observed, for Pomponius the birth of *ius* occurred only with Romulus.[16]

---

[15] Polybius is probably inspired here by Aristotle: the one he is describing is the monarchy which, for Aristotle, is of a regal and constitutional type and which, for the philosopher, is in contrast to a tyrannical monarchy; on this point see C. Zizza, *Aristotele, La politica, Introduzione* (Roma 2016) libri V-VI, 13, on the difference between the two types of monarchy, which consists not so much in the manner in which the *archon* has attained power, but in the manner in which he exercises it.

[16] I refer to D. Mantovani, 'Mores, leges, potentia. La storia della legislazione romana secondo Tacito (Annales, III 25-28)', in M. Citroni (ed.), *Letteratura e civitas. Transizioni dalla Repubblica all'Impero. In ricordo di Emanuele Narducci* (Pisa 2012) 353-404, esp. 396 ff. "The beginnings of Rome are lost in a perhaps even pre-

With the division of the people into thirty *curiae*, and through the government of them, Romulus took care of the city; in contrast, originally, without certain law, without certain rights, everything was in the hands of the kings.[17] In Pomponius's text, it is at this point that we must place the clear contrast between the two different types of monarchical government: one negative, the natural monarchy (in this case the allusion is probably to the Latin monarchy), which characterizes the very first form of the government and in which there was no trace of law and rights; the other positive, *basileia*, a constitutional regime based on law, on equilibrium, on wisdom; and, significantly, it was Romulus who initiated it.

I believe that what Polybius had described can be found in that very original Pomponian *incipit*: not all monarchies can be defined as kingship; kingship, that is *basileia*, occurs only as a consequence of improvement of the first form of government. Prior to kingship and thus before Romulus, there was a phase in which everything was entrusted to a monarchical government, but which must be kept distinct from *basileia*.

Hence, in Pomponius's account, Romulus represents *origo iuris* – which is the subject of Pomponius's treatise – but also the birth of *basileia*.

That Pomponius had Polybius in mind, that he was using the Polybian schema centred on the contrast between monarchy and kingship, seems to me beyond any doubt; and a further consideration can be added in support of what has been maintained thus far.

Polybius had described the transition from monarchy to *basileia*, and he had also described the next transformation: the degeneration into tyranny. And then, the transition to an oligarchic constitution and, later, to a democratic constitution. But democracy also degenerates, and the decline must occur in the second generation of democratic regimes:

> Pol. 6.9.6-9: λοιπὸν ὅταν ὁρμήσωσιν ἐπὶ τὸ φιλαρχεῖν καὶ μὴ δύνωνται δι' αὑτῶν καὶ διὰ τῆς ἰδίας ἀρετῆς τυγχάνειν τούτων, διαφθείρουσι τὰς οὐσίας, δελεάζοντες καὶ λυμαινόμενοι τὰ πλήθη κατὰ πάντα τρόπον. 7. ἐξ ὧν ὅταν ἅπαξ δωροδόκους καὶ δωροφάγους κατασκευάσωσι τοὺς πολλοὺς διὰ τὴν ἄφρονα δοξοφαγίαν, τότ' ἤδη πάλιν τὸ μὲν τῆς δημοκρατίας καταλύεται, μεθίσταται δ' εἰς βίαν καὶ χειροκρατίαν ἡ δημοκρατία. 8. Συνειθισμένον γὰρ τὸ πλῆθος ἐσθίειν τὰ ἀλλότρια καὶ τὰς ἐλπίδας ἔχειν

Romulean phase in which everything was in the hands of the kings, *sine lege certa sine iure certo*. This preamble, rather than stating a simple fact, already offers the interpretative key (...)" (p. 397) (transl.).

[17] Mantovani, 'Mores, leges, potentia' (n. 16) 396 ff. And on the values recalled by Pomponius, including certainty of law, see Nörr, 'Pomponio' (n. 1) 1057 = 222, recalled also by Mantovani, 'Mores, leges, potentia' (n. 16) 397 note 157.

τοῦ ζῆν ἐπὶ τοῖς τῶν πέλας, ὅταν λάβῃ προστάτην μεγαλόφρονα καὶ τολμηρόν, ἐκκλειόμενον δὲ διὰ πενίαν τῶν ἐν τῇ πολιτείᾳ τιμίων, τότε δὴ χειροκρατίαν ἀποτελεῖ. 9. καὶ τότε συναθροιζόμενον ποιεῖ σφαγάς, φυγάς, γῆς ἀναδασμούς, ἕως ἀνάποτεθηριωμένον πάλιν εὕρῃ δεσπότην καὶ μόναρχον.

Therefore, if they yield to the thirst for power and do not manage to acquire it on their own and by their own merit, they squander their patrimonies, doing anything to attract and corrupt the masses, 7. as a result of this, when they have rendered the majority venal and avid for gifts through their mad greed for glory, then democracy dissolves in turn and transforms into violence and forceful domination (μεθίσταται δ' εἰς βίαν καὶ χειροκρατίαν ἡ δημοκρατία). 8. In fact, the mass, now accustomed to devouring the property of others and to placing the hopes of life in the wealth of others, if it finds a leader that is generous and audacious but excluded by poverty from political offices, 9. then creates domination by force (τότε δὴ χειροκρατίαν ἀποτελεῖ) and, gathering together, carries out massacres, proscriptions, redistributions of land, until, reduced to a beastly state, it again finds a despot and a monarch.

The cycle of constitutional regimes is concluded:

Pol. 6.9.10: Αὕτη πολιτειῶν ἀνακύκλωσις, αὕτη φύσεως οἰκονομία, καθ' ἣν μεταβάλλει καὶ μεθίσταται καὶ πάλιν εἰς αὑτὰ καταντᾷ τὰ κατὰ τὰς πολιτείας.

This is the cyclical evolution of the constitutions, this is the direction given to things by nature, following which the state of the constitutions is transformed, alters and returns again equal to itself.

I do not think there can be any doubt that the moment of constitutional transformation described by Polybius with the term χειροκρατία (6.9.7; 6.9.9) finds full correspondence in the expression of the *Enchiridion 'omnia manu a regibus gubernabantur'*. Χείρ is *manus*; hence, χειροκρατία literally assumes the meaning of government exercised by *manus*: this obviously alludes to government by force, by violence, to government without rules of law. [18]

---

[18] In Polybius, according to D. Musti, 'Introduzione', in *Polibio, Storie* (Milano 2002) 38, in addition to being domination by brute force, *cheirokratia* is "also, perhaps, domination by the 'worst' – *cheir* is the root of both the comparative *cheirones* and the superlative *cheiristoi* – with an ambivalence desired, or at least not avoided, to double the negative value of the term and the effect of establishing a literal antithesis to aristocracy".

There is more. In Polybius's account, *cheirokratia*, as we have seen, is not related to the degenerate form of *basileia* or of government of one person alone. For the historian of Megalopolis, government by force follows the degeneration of democracy, but together constitutes the moment of transition from the degenerate form of democracy to a new cycle of constitutions with government of one person alone; it becomes the point zero of the constitutional cycle. Therefore, the dissolution of every constitutional form, government by force, closes the circle of constitutions, but it also establishes the beginning of a new cycle. Evidently, for Pomponius, in thinking similar to that of Polybius, the primigenial condition of Rome was to be understood as dissolution of the previous constitutional form and the beginning of a new cycle.

The fact that the jurist used a calque to fully render the meaning of χειροκρατία = *omnia a manu gubernabantur* seems to me particularly significant; that is, it is indicative of his dependence on the historian of Megalopolis and it is also an explicit reference, a citation, of Polybius's work, or, at least, a testimony of a Polybian trace in his own narration.

Indeed, the term χειροκρατία has a weighty meaning and is used in very few occurrences in the context of Greek literary production.[19] In almost all the few cases, it more generally alludes to a period of chaos and violence, but it is not placed in relation to the theory of constitutional regimes. A single passage, by Appian, presents a context similar to that

---

[19] Although the textual state of Polybius's work has to be taken into account, this term must be a *hapax* in his *Histories*; it was used very few times afterwards, by Diodorus 36.6 (36.8), Dionysius of Halicarnassus (6.65; 8.72), Plutarch (*Mor., De Alexandri Magni fortuna aut virtute* 332 c). And it is hardly necessary to mention that at least Diodorus and Plutarch availed themselves directly or not – I am thinking of the role played by Posidonius – of Polybius (see, for example, the introduction by P. Pedech, BL 2003, XVIII-XIX on the gaps that can be filled only to a limited extent thanks to the fact that Diodorus used Polybius for books 28-31 of his historical library; and then Livy, who used it for the IV and V decades and a bit less also for the III. And again, Plutarch used Polybius for some lives [Aratus, Philopoemen, Flamininus, Aemilius Paulus]). Another later author to use the term was Appian, *bell. civ.* 1, 2, 17. Diodorus dealt with the events of 104 BCE and, more precisely, of the second slave revolt in Sicily led by Salvius and Athenion, which threw the island into turmoil from Lilibeus to Morgantina (104-101 BCE); it is worth remembering that Diodorus's source, for books 33-39, would have been predominantly Posidonius, who continued of Polybius's *Histories*.

of Polybius (and of Pomponius). Appian, in *bell. civ.* 1.2.17, wrote of the death of Tiberius Gracchus on the Capitol:

> App. *bell. civ.* 1.2.17: ἡ δὲ πόλις ἐπὶ τῷ Γράκχου φόνῳ διῄρητο ἐς λύπην καὶ ἡδονήν, οἱ μὲν οἰκτείροντες αὑτούς τε κἀκεῖνον καὶ τὰ παρόντα ὡς οὐκέτι πολιτείαν, ἀλλὰ χειροκρατίαν καὶ βίαν, οἱ δ᾽ ἐξειργάσθαι σφίσιν ἡγούμενοι πᾶν, ὅσον ἐβούλοντο.
>
> For the death of Gracchus, the city was divided between pain and joy; some mourned themselves, the man [Gracchus] and the current situation, believing that the community (*politeia*) would no longer exist, but that there would be only domination by force (*cheirokratia*) and violence; others thought they had obtained everything they wanted.

The reference to *cheirokratia* was accompanied by a consideration on the hypothetical (and feared) decline of constitutional order ("Some mourned ... believing that the *politeia* would no longer exist, but that there would be only domination by force [*cheirokratia*] and violence ..."), similar to what we read in Polybius.

However, in Polybius, as mentioned, *cheirokratia* was a precise moment in the cycle of constitutions, of an ending and a new beginning, just as it was a moment of prelude to a new beginning (Romulus) for Pomponius.

It seems to me, then, that there are sufficient grounds to maintain that Pomponius had read Polybius and that, probably, he wished to demonstrate in his writing the existence of a relationship between his account and the work of the historian of Megalopolis: Pomponius showed that he knew both the terminology used by Polybius and his thinking on constitutional regimes, which he applied, with some differences, to the description of *origo iuris*.

Although it is true that the historian's work has come to us only in part, as the result of a selection that was drastic and unfavourable especially starting from the sixth century CE, there must instead have been no problem in the previous centuries, since Polybius's *Histories* were an important point of reference and were adopted by Posidonius, Cicero, Strabo, and later by Sempronius Asellio, Diodorus Siculus and, again, by Pliny and Plutarch through to Appian, Pausanias, Athenaeus, Aulus Gellius in the second century CE.[20]

---

[20] Moreover, the use of the historian would be greater during the fourth and

Therefore, if Polybius can be included among the models used by Pomponius for his description of the Romulean monarchy, it will also be necessary to examine the meaning of the choice and the influence that Polybius's work might have had on the jurist's historical perspective.[21]

Firstly, the reference to *cheirokratia* and to what it represents in the theory of constitutional cycles – if interpreted in terms of Polybius, as proposed here – suggests that Pomponius may have wished to include Rome and its history in a universal temporal continuum. We should wonder, though, if the conception of time and the cyclical nature of the constitutional forms, present and well known in Polybius's work, were not the subject of a revival and a new reflection by the jurist. In the same way, there arises the question – very difficult to answer given the textual state of the *Enchiridion* – whether Pomponius may have shared Polybius's idea of a mixed constitution which, as is well known, would have represented for the historian the fortune of Rome, and possibly with what moment it may have coincided: with the Republic or with the enlightened Principate of the central decades of the second century CE? And this is not to mention other less visible but equally relevant aspects, such as the concept of Tyche.

Was then Pomponius a reader of Polybius? I consider this likely. And I would not exclude that the jurist may have also known some of the models followed by the historian.

---

fifth centuries. The lack of an organic study of the fortune of Polybius's *Histories* was mentioned by M.L. Arduini, *Trattato di metodologia della ricerca storica, Dall'età greca classica agli inizi di roma imperiale* (Milano 2000) esp. 167 ff. on Polybius; 246 ff. A reading of the critical essays by A. Momigliano, in particular regarding Polybius, is always important, 'Polibio, Posidonio e l'imperialismo romano', in Atti Acc. Scienze Torino 1972-3 = Momigliano, *La storiografia greca* (Torino 1982) 258 ff.; A. Momigliano, 'Polibio fra gli Inglesi e i Turchi', in *La storiografia greca* (Torino 1982) 273 ff.

[21] For example, we would expect to find in the *Enchiridion* also the description of the further phase of the constitutional monarchical regime, the degeneration of *basileia*, i.e. tyranny. Judging by what has come down to us, there are no explicit references to this constitutional form, although the description of the expulsion of the Tarquins, unarguably recognized as tyrants by the entire historiographical tradition, may be significant in this regard. However, on this point, I refer the reader to the monographic work in progress.

2. Pomponius and Aristotle

I believe that Pomponius could have been inspired by Aristotle, the author of the *Politics*[22] but also of the *Constitution of the Athenians*.[23]

Indeed, a knowledge of these two works, of their argumentative and expository schemata, permeates all the long fragment of the *Enchiridion*. This is not the place to demonstrate this: in this regard, I refer the reader to the work to which I called attention at the beginning of this chapter. Nevertheless, it seems to me useful, for the ideas I am proposing, to consider a well-known passage in the fourth book of *Politics*, 1297b-1298a, where Aristotle, after having described why there are several constitutions, what the respective differences are and, again, which is the best constitution, proceeds to examine a different topic, addressing an important aspect in constitutional theory:

> Arist. *Pol.* IV.14.1297b-1298a[24] [1297b] πάλιν δὲ καὶ κοινῇ καὶ χωρὶς περὶ ἑκάστης λέγωμεν περὶ τῶν ἐφεξῆς, λαβόντες ἀρχὴν τὴν προσήκουσαν αὐτῶν. ἔστι δὴ τρία μόρια τῶν πολιτειῶν πασῶν, περὶ ὧν δεῖ θεωρεῖν τὸν σπουδαῖον νομοθέτην ἑκάστῃ τὸ συμφέρον: ὧν ἐχόντων καλῶς ἀνάγκη τὴν πολιτείαν ἔχειν καλῶς, καὶ τὰς πολιτείας ἀλλήλων διαφέρειν ἐν τῷ διαφέρειν ἕκαστον τούτων. ἔστι δὲ τῶν τριῶν τούτων ἓν μὲν τί τὸ βουλευόμενον περὶ τῶν κοινῶν, [1298α] δεύτερον δὲ τὸ περὶ

[22] In this article, I have used and refer in different ways to the recent editions of Aristotle's *Politics* and the related translations, to which I add some modifications: the one edited by C.A. Viano, *Aristotele, Politica* (Milano 2002); the one published for the Lorenzo Valla series, with introduction by L. Canfora and R. Kraut, translation R. Radice, T. Gargiulo, commentary by T.J. Saunders, R. Robinson (Milano 2014) vol. I (libri I-IV); edition in several volumes, edited by L. Bertelli and M. Moggi (dir.), L'Erma di Bretschneider, Roma 2011-16 (thus far books I-VI). In this regard, for the passages used here, see vol. IV of this last edition, with Greek text edited by L. Curnis, translation B. Guagliumi, introduction P. Accattino, commentary by F. Pezzoli, G. Besso, M. Canevaro (Roma 2014).

[23] That the *Constitution of the Athenians* is a work, if not by Aristotle, at least by his school, is now an undisputed fact. For the reading of the text, its transmission and the main problems connected with it, I have used above all the recent edition, with introduction, translation and extensive commentary by P.J. Rhodes, translation A. Zambrini, T. Gargiulo, P.J. Rhodes (Milano 2016). But also the one by G. Mathieu, B. Haussouillier, *Aristote, Constitution d'Athènes* (Paris 2003[10]) and the edition by G. Lozza (Milano 1991).

[24] For this and the other passages mentioned below, I compared my translation with those reported in note 23, as well as with that of R. Laurenti, *Aristotele, Opere*, vol. IV (Roma-Bari 1973).

τὰς ἀρχάς, τοῦτο δ' ἐστὶ τίνας δεῖ καὶ τίνων εἶναι κυρίας, καὶ ποίαν τινὰ δεῖ γίνεσθαι τὴν αἵρεσιν αὐτῶν, τρίτον δέ τί τὸ δικάζον.

Now let us speak again, in order, of constitutions, both in a general sense and with reference to each of them, using as a starting point the one conforming to them. There are three parts in all constitutions, concerning which the good legislator must see what is useful to each one: when these are well ordered, by necessity the constitution is also well ordered, and the constitutions differ from one another in so far as each of these three parts differs. Of these three parts, the first deals with the deliberations on common affairs, the second concerns the magistratures (that is, what they must be and in which sovereign fields and which one is the preferred system), the third is the part that renders justice.

The subject is well known: it is the consideration of the three parts which, according to Aristotle, make up every constitution.[25] That, in Aristotle's *Politics*, the study of each constitution derives from the examination and the structure of each of these three parts (on the deliberations, the magistratures, the courts) is explicitly stated in other passages of the same work. In the overall structure of the *Politics*, as it has come down to us, this passage constitutes a central point also for the following chapters.

In a less clear manner, the examination of the same elements also returns in the *Constitution of the Athenians*. In the first part of the work, from the initial chapter to chapter 41, the historical path, the events surrounding the constitution of Athens from the trial of the Alcmaeonidae (but the beginning is lost)[26] to 403 is dealt with in brief. Examination of the structure of government begins in chapter 42; more precisely, the exposition follows some thematic sections on the ways to gain citizenship (§ 42), on the magistratures (§§ 43-62) and finally on the courts (§§ 63-69).

The very close connection between the theoretical treatment of the *Politics* and that of the *Constitution of the Athenians* is evident and no longer debated. Moreover, it is hardly necessary to recall Aristotle's method, based not only on theoretical reflection but also on historical research: the collection of the 158 constitutions – one of which is the

[25] There is no need to recall that only within certain limits can a comparison be made with the three modern legislative, executive and jurisdictional functions: it would not be appropriate to dwell on this point.

[26] Also the initial fragments of the work are reported in the recent edition by P.J. Rhodes mentioned in note 23.

Constitution of the Athenians – is the factual basis of the philosopher's thought on political theory.

I believe that Pomponius had this schema in mind and utilized it in the *Enchiridion* as a model of the tripartite division of his work. This is a hypothesis that requires a thorough analysis, which I cannot put forth now. Instead, it would be appropriate to return to the general plan of the *Enchiridion* and, in particular, to an important passage which begins the description of the magistratures.

Just as for Aristotle, for Pomponius the magistratures were the essential element in a community to ensure the realization of law. The jurist wrote this explicitly in a passage that is certainly one of the most significant and the most suitable to provide an interpretation of the *Enchiridion*:[27]

> D. 1.2.2.13 *Post originem iuris et processum cognitum consequens est, ut de magistratuum nominibus et origine cognoscamus, quia, ut exposuimus, per eos qui iuri dicundo praesunt effectus rei accipitur: quantum est enim ius in civitate esse, nisi sint, qui iura regere possint? Post hoc dein de auctorum successione di-cemus, quod constare non potest ius, nisi sit aliquis iuris peritus, per quem possit cottidie in melius produci.*

> After having explained the origin and development of law, it follows that we should know the names and the origins of the magistratures, because, as we have said, the result of the action is obtained through those in charge of the jurisdiction: indeed, what does it matter that there is law in a city if there are not also those who rule the law?[28] After

[27] Also in this case, I will limit myself, in this article, to providing the essential elements of the interpretative line that I intend to present and I will not make reference to textual problems: I am thinking, in particular, of the different interpretive proposal *in melius* or *in medium produci*, on which see, in addition to Bretone, *Tecniche e ideologie* (n. 2) esp. 239, more recently, M. Talamanca, 'Pomp. sing. ench. D. 1.2.2.13: 'in melius' od 'in medium' produci?', in *Liber amicorum J. Miquel. Estudios romanísticos con motivo de su emeritazgo* (Barcelona 2006) 965 ff. I refer the reader instead to another contribution on the description of the magistratures in the *Enchiridion*, as well as the commentary being prepared for the edition of the *SIR* project. On the tone of the passage, its connection with the third part of the *Enchiridion*, the role reserved for jurists in Pomponius's description, see Schiavone, *The Invention of Law* (n. 2) 384 f., but also A. Schiavone, 'Immagini del ius in Gaio e Pomponio', *Ius controversum e auctoritas principis. Giuristi principe e diritto nel primo impero, Atti Copanello 1998* (Napoli 2003) 117 ff.

[28] I translate the expression "(...) *qui iura regere possint*" as reported in the text, rather than, for example, "those who can apply the law", to clearly render the

that, we will deal with the succession of authors, since law cannot exist if there are not experts who can improve it day by day.

This passage, more than any other of those that have come down to us, demonstrates the connection between the first and third sections of the *Enchiridion*. Pomponius, while recalling the content of the treatise up to that point (*origo iuris*), introduces the topic about to be discussed (*nomina et origo magistratuum*) and anticipates the exposition of the third part, *successio auctorum*.

Quite rightly, much has been written about these lines, especially on the essential role that Pomponius reserves for jurists and for *scientia iuris*. It does not seem to me, however, that any hypothesis has been advanced concerning the model or source that Pomponius might have followed. Yet, we can make a couple of comparisons. First with Cicero, although to me this comparison is only relatively convincing. I am referring to a passage from the *de legibus*:

> Cic. *de leg.* 3.2.5: *Magistratibus igitur opus est, sine quorum prudentia ac diligentia esse civitas non potest, quorumque discriptione omnis rei publicae moderatio continetur. Neque solum iis praescribendus est imperandi, sed etiam civibus obtemperandi modus. Nam et qui bene imperat, paruerit aliquando necesse est, et qui modeste paret, videtur qui aliquando imperet dignus esse.*

> Therefore, it is necessary that magistrates exist, without whose wise care there can be no community, and the entire government of the republic is founded on their diffusion. And one must not only prescribe to the magistrates how they should exercise their power of command but also to the citizens how they should obey. In fact, also those who wish to command wisely must have obeyed at another time; and those who meekly obey will in turn be worthy of commanding.

Cicero's acceptance of Plato's theory of laws permeates the *de legibus*: laws are not only, and not so much, the product of convention but rather the expression of natural law; however, in the general context of the Platonic ancestry of the work, this passage demonstrates instead a

meaning, in my opinion significant, of the expression *regere iura*, which has no counterpart in the jurisprudential tradition – as already noted by F. Grelle, 'Le categorie dell'amministrazione tardoantica: officia, munera, honores', in A. Giardina (ed.), *Società romana e impero tardoantico 1, Istituzioni, ceti, economie* (Roma-Bari 1986) 37 ff. – in which the use of the verb *regere* together with the plural of *ius* is certainly not by chance.

strong Aristotelian spirit, if one considers the well-known theory of *archein* and of *archestai* expounded here with so much evidence.[29]

The initial expression is especially worthy of attention, with the explicit reference to the necessary role of the magistratures, without whose care the community could not exist. Hence, we must consider the possibility that this passage also constitutes further confirmation of the use of Cicero by Pomponius.

Another comparison, between Pomponius and Aristotle, is more compelling and significant. At the beginning of the sixth book of the *Politics*, Aristotle dealt with the different constitutional forms, and more precisely with oligarchy. The discussion closed with passage 1321b, immediately followed by the thoughts on magistratures:[30]

> Arist. *Pol.* VI.7.1321b, 43 ss.: πῶς μὲν οὖν χρὴ καθιστάναι τὰς δημοκρατίας καὶ τὰς ὀλιγαρχίας, διωρίσθω τὸν τρόπον τοῦτον.
> ἀκόλουθον δὲ τοῖς εἰρημένοις ἐστὶ τὸ διῃρῆσθαι καλῶς [5] τὰ περὶ τὰς ἀρχάς, πόσαι καὶ τίνες καὶ τίνων, καθάπερ εἴρηται καὶ πρότερον. τῶν μὲν γὰρ ἀναγκαίων ἀρχῶν χωρὶς ἀδύνατον εἶναι πόλιν, τῶν δὲ πρὸς εὐταξίαν καὶ κόσμον ἀδύνατον οἰκεῖσθαι καλῶς. ἔτι δ' ἀναγκαῖον ἐν μὲν ταῖς μικραῖς ἐλάττους εἶναι τὰς ἀρχάς, ἐν δὲ ταῖς μεγάλαις [10] πλείους, ὥσπερ τυγχάνει πρότερον εἰρημένον (...)

> VI.7.1321b, 43 sgg.: And that is enough on the constitution of democracies and oligarchies.
> 8. After what has preceded, it is now necessary to carefully determine certain things about the magistratures, that is their number, their kinds, their abilities, as mentioned above. Without the necessary magistratures,[31] it is impossible for a city to exist; without those who safeguard

[29] On Cicero's *de legibus*, especially with respect to the description of the Roman constitution, and on Cicero's political thinking in the work, see F. Fontanella, 'Introduzione al de legibus di Cicerone I e II', in Athenaeum 85 (1997) 487 ff.; 86 (1998) 179 ff. (especially on the magistratures); F. Cancelli, *Introduzione a Le leggi* (Roma 2003), and more recently J.W. Atkins, *Cicero on Politics and the Limits of Reason. The Republics and Laws* (Cambridge UP 2013) with previous literature; useful for framing Cicero's thought with respect to Plato and Polybius is the work of J.-L. Ferrary, 'L'archéologie du re publica (2.2.4-37, 63): Cicéron entre Polybe et Platon', in JRS 74 (1984) 87 ff.

[30] Aristotle had already dealt with the magistratures in *Pol.* 4.14.1298a, 1 sgg.; 15.1299a, 3 sg., but on the "labyrinth of the text", as correctly written by Viano, see the pages dedicated by the scholar to the complex structure of the *Politics*, in *Aristotele*, cit., 9 ff., and, recently, a new reflection by T. Pangle, *Aristotle's Teaching in the Politics* (London-Chicago 2013).

[31] For this passage, I have followed the translation by Viano, *Aristotele*, cit., ex-

> good order and correct behaviour, the city cannot live well. Moreover, it is necessary that in the small cities the magistratures are in smaller numbers, in the large cities in greater numbers, as we have already had occasion to say.

The magistratures were essential also for Aristotle; more precisely, he distinguished necessary magistratures, without which the city could not exist, from magistratures that could be defined as useful and important.

Firstly, it should be noted that, both for Aristotle and for Pomponius, this was a turning point in the articulation of the discourse. The philosopher had just concluded (at least for this part of the work) the discussion on constitutions ("And that is enough ...") and was moving on to a new subject, the importance of the magistratures. Pomponius had concluded the first section, on the origin of *ius*, and was introducing, as we have said, the two parts of the work: on magistratures and *successio auctorum*.

It is remarkable that the words, the same words, that Aristotle reserved for magistratures – i.e. that they were essential to the life of the city – were used by Pomponius, in the just-cited passage, to refer to *scientia iuris*.

In effect, in his discourse, the jurist did not analyse the distinction between necessary magistratures and useful magistratures, but indicated their nonetheless essential role. And if for Aristotle the survival of the city was linked to the magistratures, for Pomponius the survival of law was related to *scientia iuris*.

In the tripartite division of powers and functions, Pomponius shifted the weight, we might say, to the third component. The words that both Aristotle and Pomponius used are practically the same, albeit referring to two different elements of the constitutions and in the context of a non-identical but related discussion.

Can we hypothesize that Pomponius had Aristotle in mind when writing this passage of the *Enchiridion*? It seems to me that the strong similarity of the context, the identity of the transmitted concept (but which we find, as mentioned above, in a more concise form in Cicero) and the use of expressions favour this idea. Nevertheless, we cannot ignore the complex problem of the knowledge of Aristotle's works in Rome in the second century CE and, more precisely, of their circula-

---

cept for the expression τῶν μὲν γὰρ ἀναγκαίων ἀρχῶν χωρὶς (...) which I translated as 'necessary magistratures', not 'essential' ones. It should be recalled that for Aristotle, in addition to a group of necessary magistrates described below, there was another group of magistratures "no less necessary, but higher, because they require much experience and loyalty" (1322 a).

tion, i.e. direct and integral or instead indirect and partial through repertories, anthologies, intermediate sources.[32] It is not possible to thoroughly discuss this subject here, but the question, despite the undeniable difficulties and controversial opinions, must not necessarily be resolved in a negative manner. Especially if we consider the circulation of intermediate authors and the existence of commentaries on Aristotle's works,[33] or even some, albeit sporadic, direct attestations,[34] as well as the great notoriety and rediscovery of Aristotle's works shortly after the period in which Pomponius was writing, certainly from the end of the

---

[32] This is a topic on which the opinions of scholars vary between strong scepticism and a more or less explicitly confident attitude. In this context, investigation of Cicero's knowledge of Aristotle – also because of the role played by him with respect to Pomponius – as well as of the other intermediate sources is obviously of great importance. On this point see, among others, E. Bréguet, *Introduction*, in *Cicéron, La République*, I (Paris 2012) 118 ff., who certainly considers possible Cicero's use of Aristotle's works; of a different opinion was P. Moraux, 'Cicéron et les ouvrages scolaires d'Aristote', in Ciceroniana 2 (1975) 81 ff. Lastly, on the diffusion of Aristotle's works, the situation is discussed by A. Falcon, *Aristotelismo* (Torino 2017) 28 ff., esp. 30 on the rediscovery of Aristotle's writings, the work of Apellicon of Teos and the editorial activity of Andronicus of Rhodes during the first century BCE.

[33] The earliest Peripatetic commentary on the *Nichomachean Ethics* is from the second century CE; it was done by Aspasius, who lived in the first half of the second century: see A. Falcon, *Aristotelismo* (n. 32) 45.

[34] It is worth mentioning what appears to be the most recent attestation of the *Politics*: two papyrus fragments (of Ann Arbor and Brussels), first published separately, dated to the first/second century CE, which contain a few lines of the work (*Pol.* 4.4.1292a.30-1292b and 1293a.15-18). The papyrus was rightly discussed by G. Besso and M. Curnis, in *Aristotele, La politica* I (Roma 2011) 9 f.; see the edition by G. Menci, 'P. Mich. inv. 6643 + P. Brux inv. E 8073', in *Corpus dei papiri filosofici greci e latini (CPF). Testi e lessico nei papiri di cultura greca e latina*, I.1 (Firenze 1989) 265 ff., which states that the two texts belong to the same papyrus scroll, even though the parts of the columns of writing are not contiguous. The incomplete state of the papyrus scroll renders uncertain whether we are dealing with the transmission of columns of an integral version of Aristotle's work or whether some parts of the *Politics* were passed down together with other works. In favour of the more felicitous hypothesis are the fact that the passage is not known from another context of indirect tradition and the presence of a *diple obelismene* marking the end of chapter 4, which is known from the later manuscript tradition. This suggests the antiquity of the division of the work into chapters, but also the correctness of the later codex transcription. Regarding the relationship between Aristotle and Polybius (indeed, the latter seems to use an Aristotelian terminology in some places of the sixth book), I refer the reader to the updated *status quaestionis* by Besso and Curnis in the introductory section dedicated to the history of the text, from p. 3 ff.

second century CE, thanks to the activity of Alexander of Aphrodisias.[35]

At this a point, we can try to pull together the threads of what has been discussed.

There is a good reason to add both Aristotle – the Aristotle of the *Politics* and the *Constitution of the Athenians* – and Polybius to the authors who might have inspired Pomponius in the composition of his work. Yet, this should not be surprising, also judging by what is known about the cultural milieu of the second century and, specifically, the education of Pomponius: indeed, it may constitute a further starting point for a better understanding of the jurist's thought and the originality of his work.[36]

In the light of these considerations, at least two structural data of the *Enchiridion* have gained weight and merit further reflection: the model chosen by Pomponius for the writing of the *successio auctorum* and the title of the work. We have already mentioned some characteristics of the literary genre of *diadochai* – followed in the Manual for the *successio auctorum* – not necessarily of Aristotelian ancestry but certainly much used in Peripatetic circles: there is no doubt that Pomponius followed this schema, well known during the second century CE and which could be considered consolidated also in Rome.

And the Greek title of *Enchiridion* is certainly not by chance: to me, the choice shows the desire to let the reader understand the more remote origin of his work, the model, or perhaps the models, followed by Pomponius, but also the desire to transmit those archetypes to Rome and to render them immediately recognizable.

I believe that what has been advanced thus far, together with other elements that seem to emerge from the reading of the work, constitutes evidence of the complex and sophisticated nature of the *Enchiridion*[37] and leads to new assessments. The work of re-editing and commentary, as I mentioned at the beginning, is in progress, but I think that we can now anticipate the need for a general reconsideration of the purpose of the work.

---

[35] On which see in summary, lastly Falcon, *Aristotelismo* (n. 32) 45 ff.

[36] On the 'outline of an intellectual education, of Pomponius, there is a series of useful reflections in Stolfi, *Studi* (n. 2) 261 ff.

[37] Therefore, not an elementary work, which would have given "a sketch, necessarily summary and elementary, of private law", as maintained, for example, by Schulz, *History* (n. 2) 168.

Chapter 8

CONCERNING PAUL. 29 *AD ED.*, D. 13.6.17.3: *OFFICIUM, BENEFICIUM, COMMODARE*. (WITH AN APPENDIX ON THE ALTERITY BETWEEN MORALITY AND LAW) *

Giuseppe Falcone

SUMMARY: 1. Introduction. – 2. Textual analysis of the source. – 3. '*Officium*' in D. 13.6.17.3 as an abstract category: moral duty in opposition to 'legal' obligation. – 4. Different meaning of '*officium*' as a specific contractual task, which appears in some other texts. – 5. *Officium* and *beneficium* in Paulus's analysis of the *commodatum* and of the related instruments of protection. – *Appendix*.

1. Introduction

In connection with his comment on the edict concerning the *actio commodati contraria* and in order to clarify and justify the scope of application of this processual instrument,[1] Paulus made an interesting theoretical consideration in which, with reference to the contract of commodatum, the perspective of legal transaction (*commodare*; *obligatio*; *negotium*) intersects that of ethical dimension (*officium*; *beneficium*):

> Paul. 29 *ad ed.*, D. 13.6.17.3: *Sicut autem voluntatis et officii magis quam necessitatis est commodare, ita modum commodati finemque praescribere eius est qui beneficium tribuit. Cum autem id fecit, id est postquam com-*

---

[1] O. Lenel, *Palingenesia iuris civilis* (Lepizig 1889) 1022, refers Paulus's text (no. 446) considered in the present study to the commentary on the edictal title *'Commodati vel contra' (EP* 98). In particular, the *actio commodati contraria*, explicitly mentioned at the end of D. 16.3.17.3 (but also see, within it, the mentions *'invicem propositae sunt actiones'* and *'mutuas... actionesque civiles'*), already appears in D. 16.3.17.1 '*Contraria commodati actio etiam sine principali moveri potest, sicut et ceterae quae dicuntur contrariae*'.

modavit, tunc finem praescribere et retro agere atque intempestive usum commodatae rei auferre non officium tantum impedit, sed et suscepta obligatio inter dandum accipiendumque. Geritur enim negotium invicem et ideo invicem propositae sunt actiones, ut appareat, quod principio beneficii ac nudae voluntatis fuerat, converti in mutuas praestationes actionesque civiles. ut accidit in eo, qui absentis negotia gerere incohavit: neque enim impune peritura deseret: suscepisset enim fortassis alius, si is non coepisset: voluntatis est enim suscipere mandatum, necessitatis consummare. Igitur si pugillares mihi commodasti, ut debitor mihi caveret, non recte facies importune repetendo: nam si negasses, vel emissem, vel testes adhibuissem. Idemque est, si ad fulciendam insulam tigna commodasti, deinde protraxisti, aut etiam sciens vitiosa commodaveris: adiuvari quippe nos, non decipi beneficio oportet. Ex quibus causis etiam contrarium iudicium utile dicendum est.

The passage was studied in a fundamental work by Dieter Nörr in specific regard to the relationship between ethics and law.[2] And it has been considered from the same point of view in other studies in the last few decades.[3] Notwithstanding the attention repeatedly dedicated to it, I believe that the double reference to *officium* contained therein deserves to be examined once again, together with the reference to *beneficium* and with the relationship established by the jurist with the juridical-*commodatum* operation.

2. Textual analysis of the source

The source, once adjudged to be heavily altered and sometimes almost entirely of post-classical or Justinian creation,[4] is now generally consid-

[2] D. Nörr, 'Ethik und Recht in Widerstreit? Bemerkungen zu Paul. (29 ad ed.) D. 13.6.17.3', in *Ars boni et aequi. Fest. f. W. Waldstein zum 65. Geburtstag* (Stuttgart 1993) 267 ff.

[3] A. Mantello, 'Un'etica per il giurista? Profili d'interpretazione giurisprudenziale nel primo Principato', in *Per la storia del pensiero giuridico romano. Da Augusto agli Antonini (Atti del seminario di San Marino, 1214 gennaio 1995)* (Torino 1996) 163 f.; G. Falcone, *'Obligatio est iuris vinculum'* (Torino 2003) 177 ff.; T. Rundel, *Mandatum zwischen utilitas und amicitia. Perspektiven zur Mandatarhaftung im klassischen römischen Recht*, Münster 2005, 189 ff.; G. Finazzi, 'Amicitia e doveri giuridici', in A. Corbino, M. Humbert, G. Negri (eds.), *Homo, caput, persona. La costruzione giuridica dell'identità nell'esperienza romana* (Pavia 2010) 738 ff.

[4] In addition to the usual *Index Interpolationum*, the reader can consult the critical report of various diagnoses of alteration made, in recent times, by G. Finazzi,

ered largely reliable as far as the substance is concerned,[5] even though here and there individual objections are still made, above all on the formal level. An independent critical evaluation of the textual data should be conducted.[6]

In my opinion, there is no reason to replace the words '*inter dandum accipiendumque*' with '*inter dantem accipientemque*'.[7] These words can be maintained, the construction '*inter*' + gerund expressing a temporal perspective and precisely the sense of 'during', 'the moment in which'. This is consistent with two other passages of the discourse, also arranged in a temporal manner: '*cum id fecit, id est postquam commodavit...*' and '*ut appareat, quod principio beneficii ac voluntatis fuerat ...*'. However, in this perspective, they should be understood not as "between the moment of giving and the moment of receiving back"[8] (in this case, one would have encountered '*recipiendumque*'), but rather as indicating the moment of the encounter between the *dare* by the commodans and the *accipere* by the commodatarius, which completes the contract. In substance, Paulus indicates the obligatory relationship that the commodans assumes (*suscepta obligatio*) when, after he has decided to *commodare*, there occurs the fusion of the two elements of *dare* and *accipere* between the parts of an *obligatio re contracta*.

Ricerche in tema di negotiorum gestio. II.2. Obbligazioni gravanti sul gestore e sul gerito e responsabilità (Cassino 2006) 41 ff. and notes within.

[5] With the exception of J. Paricio, 'La pretendida formula «in ius» del comodato en el Edicto pretorio', in RIDA 29 (1982) 241, who considers the entire text very incoherent and unreliable. Also I. Cremades Ugarte, *El officium en el derecho privado romano. Notas para su estudio* (Salamanca 1988) 106, considers the text "muy interpolado" (within the framework, moreover, of a rather offhand analysis of it).

[6] Without, however, it being necessary to dwell specifically on categorical and apodictic condemnations of the parts of the text in which *officium* and *beneficium* are mentioned as "useless", "verbose", "pretentious" (thus, G. Segrè, 'Studi sul concetto del negozio giuridico nel diritto romano e nel nuovo diritto germanico', in RISG 28 (1899) 214 note 104 = *Scritti giuridici*, I (Cortona 1930) 258 note 1; S. Perozzi, *Istituzioni di diritto romano*, 2 (Firenze 1908) 17 note 2; E. Betti, 'Sul valore dogmatico della categoria "contrahere" in giuristi proculiani e sabiniani', in BIDR 28 (1915) 18 note 3). On the contrary, as we will see, it is the notations that involve *officium* and *beneficium* in constituting the cornerstones of Paulus's overall reasoning.

[7] '*Inter dantem accipientemque*' is read in the *vulgata*; and it is a solution accepted by Fr. Eisele, 'Weitere Studien zum Texte der Digesten', in ZSS 30 (1909) 113 and note 1, and by E. Betti, 'Sul valore dogmatico' (n. 6) 18, and adjudged "möglicherweise richtige" by Nörr, 'Ethik' (n. 2) 269 note 3.

[8] Thus J. Michel, *Gratuité en droit romain* (Bruxelles 1962) 595 note 7.

Likewise, I believe that we can assume the integral genuineness of the motivation *'Geritur enim – praestationes actionesque civiles'.*[9] Indeed, if the reference to bilaterality in the carrying out of the juridical operation (*geritur negotium invicem*) is opposed to the unilaterality of the *voluntas* of granting (or not) a *beneficium*, the emphasis on bilaterality at the level of obligatory effects (*invicem propositae sunt actiones; converti in mutuas praestationes actionesque civiles*) is well justified by the fact that the discourse is part of a commentary on the *iudicium contrarium* due to the commodatarius against the commodans.[10] Similarly, the very use of the terms *'praestationes'* and *'actiones civiles'* can be attributed to Paulus,[11] as it is very well linked to the peculiar overall approach of the discourse, directed – as will be expressly seen – at coordinating the ethical perspective (*officium*, *beneficium*) and the legal dimension: on the one hand, *'praestationes'* helps to underline the now obligatory relationship bearing with it true legal duties (i.e. *praestationes*);[12] on the other hand, the mention of *actiones civiles* must have been meant to signal the existence of protective instruments of positive law (of the *civitas*) in addition to the

[9] In this passage, instead, the references to the bilaterality of effects are considered reworked by P. Cerami, 'Il comodato', in *Derecho romano de obligaciones. Homenaje al prof. J.L. Murga Gener* (Madrid 1994) 327 (= Id., 'Ricerche romanistiche e prospettive storico-comparatistiche', in AUPA 43 [1995] 317).

[10] Moreover, also from a general point of view, it is unnecessary to commit oneself to justifying an alleged "mistake" made by Paulus in presenting commodatum (as well as mandate) as an operation from which are derived obligatory effects for both parties, thinking, as a possible justification, to the fact that, just as for selling and renting, also for commodatum there existed a formula *in ius ex fide bona* (utilizable as *iudicium contrarium*): in this sense, G. Scherillo, s.v. 'Comodato (dir. rom.)', in ED VII (1960) 992 (recalled by Finazzi, *Ricerche* (n. 4) 42 note 54). In reality, the traditional characterization of commodatum and mandate as 'imperfect bilateral' contracts, with the caution that they only possibly may originate obligations also for the comodans and the mandator, is more a need of modern interpreters: it is sufficient to consider the naturalness, so to speak, with which Gai. 3.155 expresses himself '... *contrahitur mandati obligatio, et invicem alter alteri tenebimur in id, quod vel me tibi vel te mihi bona fide praestare oportet*'.

[11] In contrast, the words '*actiones civiles*' are considered to be the work of compilers by (in addition to Betti, *loc. cit.* [n. 6]) A. d'Ors, 'Observaciones sobre el 'edictum de rebus creditis'', in SDHI 19 (1953) 189; F. Pastori, *Il commodato nel diritto romano* (Milano 1954) 90 and note 63; M. Kaser, 'Oportere und ius civile', in ZSS 83 (1966) 32 note 149. Lastly, P. Zannini, 'Comodato, precario, comodato-precario: maneggiare con cura', in Φιλία. *Studi per G. Franciosi*, IV (Napoli 2007) 2869 f., states that the reference to *actiones civiles* can arouse "some suspicions".

[12] Other confirmations of '*praestationes*' from the *libri ad edictum* of Paulus are in D. 10.3.1 and in 19.4.1.

"impediment" (against an untimely request) deriving from *officium* (*infra*, § 5).[13]

As for the mention, in the central part, of *mandatum* – *'voluntatis est enim suscipere mandantum, necessitatis consummare'* – I believe we must exclude the possibility, even if authoritatively proposed,[14] that this is in continuity with the immediately preceding phrases on *absentis negotia gerere* (*'ut accidit – coepisset'*), which would refer, according to this interpretation, to the operation conducted after a specific mandate.[15] Indeed, while the *suscipere mandatum* is determined, notoriously, by simple consent, the jurist expressly insists, in the preceding notations, on an effective initiation of activity: *'negotia gerere incohavit'*, *'si is non coepisset'*. That is, these notations were not made in relation to the *mandatum*, but rather in relation to the spontaneously undertaken *negotiorum gestio*. Therefore, the reference to *mandatum* is a novelty with respect to the discourse carried out thus far. There are two possible solutions to justify the presence of this novelty. Either we accept the recent hypothesis that the original text was *'voluntatis est [enim] <etiam> suscipere mandatum, necessitatis consummare'*[16] or we imagine

---

[13] Long ago, B. Biondi, 'Iudicia bonae fidei', in AUPA 7 (1918) 94, sensed that the qualifier *'civiles'* alluded to the fact that this was an instrument of positive law in opposition to the non-juridical dimension of *officium*; however, he attributed this meaning to the qualifier (as, for that matter, the entire phrase *'Cum autem id fecit – consummare'*!) to the Justinian compilers. It does not seem to me that the different explanation (of maintenance) of the designation *'civiles'* proposed by Finazzi, *Ricerche* (n. 4) 43 and note 59, can be accepted because of the fact that the only *formula commodati contraria* was probably the one in *ius*, so that the qualifier would have been used to specify that this was not *actiones honorariae*: indeed, it is difficult to imagine that Paulus, in specifying that commodans and commodatarius are exposed to reciprocal actions, did not keep in mind that the former had available also an *actio commodati in factum*. On the other hand, the explanation in question is based explicitly (cf. note 59 *in fine*) on the assumption that the phrase *'actiones civiles'* referred to the *formulae*; however, in their direct and specific contrast to *beneficium* and *nuda voluntas*, the *actiones* were probably referenced by Paulus as processual instruments considered as a whole and from the outside, not in relation to the specific profile of their *conceptio verborum*.

[14] By Nörr, *Ethik* (n. 2) 269 note 6.

[15] The German scholar mentions, in this regard, Gaius in D. 44.7.5pr. *'Si quis absentis negotia gesserit, si quidem ex mandatu, palam est ex contractu nasci inter eos actiones mandati …'*.

[16] This is proposed by Finazzi, *Ricerche* (n. 4) 41 and 44, referring to the version Bas. 71621 'καὶ τὴν ἐντολὴν ἑκουσίως μὲν ὑποδέχεταί τις, ἐξ ἀνάγκης δὲ πληροῖ' (transl. Heimbach: *Etiam mandatum sponte quis suscipit, necessario autem implet*). However, it should be pointed out that the version of the Basilika is, on the whole,

that, in the transmission of the text, a passage, even a very short one, in which the comparison was extended to the figure of *mandatum* was lost:[17] to me, the latter solution has the advantage of preparing an indication which, even with the aforesaid amendment [*enim*] <*etiam*>, would remain somewhat too abrupt and isolated.

The genuineness of the phrase "*aut etiam sciens vitiosa commodaveris*" is not certain. Its origin as an insertion was argued long ago,[18] because of the substance, since this is not, unlike the other two examples to which it is compared (... *si pugillares commodasti, ... importune repetendo*; *si ... tigna commodasti, deinde protraxisti*), a case of early request for restitution, as we would have expected given the framework of the entire Pauline elaboration ('*Cum autem id fecit, id est postquam commodavit, tunc finem praescribere et retro agere atque intempestive usum commodatae rei auferre ...*'), and because of the form, due to the tense '*commodaveris*', different from the '*commodasti*' used in relation to the two examples to which it is compared. While the salience of the form can easily be overcome, since the use of '*commodaveris*' can be justified as expressing the fact that the *vitiosa* nature of the beams would have emerged only much later than the effective *commodare*, the autonomy of the case effectively raises some perplexities. That is unless one thinks of a purposeful expansion of the content scope by Paulus himself, aimed at grouping together hypotheses in which the commodatarius suffers a tort and thus has the right to obtain compensation by means of *iudicium* contrarium.[19]

---

very different from that of the Digest, being the result of a radical paring down of Paulus's discourse: cf. *infra*, § 5 on note 56 (in which the entire text is transcribed).

[17] It could be thought of – just as an example – as a short and essential passage of the type "the same must be said *si quis mandatum suscepisset*" (perhaps lost by a mistake induced by the preceding homeoteleuton '*coepisset*').

[18] By K. Heldrich, *Das Verschulden beim Vertragsabschluss* (Leipzig 1924) 37 f.; F. Schwarz, 'Die Konträrklagen', in ZSS 71 (1954) 130; G. Provera, *Contributi alla teoria dei iudicia contraria* (Torino 1951) 105 f.

[19] Thus, explicitly, Pastori, *Il commodato* (n. 11) 388; however, this reasoning must be considered implicit among the majority of scholars, who in the last few decades have not made any further comments on this part of the text. Moreover, it should be specified that, when an insertion of the proposal of this case is accepted, there would not derive from it a spurious character also of the phrase '*adiuvari quippe nos, non decipi beneficio oportet*'. In fact, the verb '*decipi*' can very well indicate – in addition to being defrauded by virtue of the comodans having purposely delivered defective beams – also being defrauded by the fact that the comodans has firstly, by giving in commodatum, shown willingness to allow the use of the thing and then, instead, requests the premature restitution of the thing. On the other

Finally, it seems to me that F. Schwarz[20] – to my knowledge, the only scholar to have noticed and tried to solve the problem – was correct in considering the *'etiam'* of the concluding sentence '*Ex quibus causis etiam contrarium iudicium utile dicendum est*' an indication that, in the original text,[21] there appeared, just before this, the reference to another processual decision sanctioning the behaviour of the commodans, a response with respect to which the *iudicium contrarium* could be indicated as an additional instrument: "for these hypotheses, it should be said that the *iudicium contrarium* can also be used". The German scholar was especially thinking about the mention of a *denegatio actionis* in view of the premature processual request of the commodans. Perhaps we could, as a not necessarily alternative conjecture, imagine a reference to *retentio* (cf. Pomponius in D. 13.7.8pr. '... *non tantum retentionem, sed etiam contrariam pigneraticiam actionem habebo* ...'). In any case, the omission might have been caused, more than by an oversight of an amanuensis, by a deliberate simplification, by the Compilers, of a discourse that had as its main subject the presence of '*actiones*' (... *invicem propositae sunt actiones* ...; ... *converti in mutuas praestationes actionesque civiles*).

3. '*Officium*' in D. 13.6.17.3 as an abstract category: moral duty in opposition to 'legal' obligation

In Paulus's overall reasoning, the *officium*-element, which I specifically intend to consider on this occasion, appears twice: in the initial sentence, where it is stated that giving in commodatum is a question of *voluntas* and *officium*, instead of necessitas;[22] and in the remark that the untimely request for restitution of the thing given in commodatum is prevented not only by *officium* but also by *obligatio*.

We are dealing with a use of the term '*officium*' with the highest

hand, the image of a *beneficium* which (instead of helping) "leads to deceit" is used on another occasion by the same Paulus: D. Pap. 5 *quaest.* 46.5.8pr.: *PAULUS notat: qui sub condicione institutus est, adgnita bonorum possessione, cogitur substituto in diem cavere longiorem: praetor enim beneficium suum nemini vult esse captiosum et potest videri calumniose satis petere, quem alius antecedit.*

[20] Schwarz, 'Die Konträrklagen' (n. 18) 130.

[21] A text which, however, Schwarz (*loc. cit.*) considered "ein nachklassischer Traktat".

[22] Glossa previously noted that the relation '*magis* ... *quam*' is adopted here as "*elective, non comparative*".

possible degree of conceptual abstraction. Here it is assumed, like '*voluntas*' and '*necessitas*', as an abstract category, and it alludes to the very idea of moral duty in opposition to 'legal' obligation.

In this regard, I will state once and for all that, in relation to *officium*, I am speaking in terms of 'moral' duty,[23] adopting the adjective (protected from the mutability that may have marked the notion of morality through history) in adherence to the meaning given by the same Roman sources, and precisely in adherence to the qualification, from Cicero onwards (*de fato* 1),[24] as *'moralis'* of the *philosophia* that deals with *mores*, that is to say of behaviours as external objectivizations of *virtutes*, that is of predispositions and internal solicitations.[25] **[A.]** And I also point out that, with regard to the scope of *officium*, awareness of an opposition between the moral sphere and the legal sphere in relation to two different types of dutifulness **[A.]** – already attested, in the Roman culture, by Seneca's thinking on the subject of *beneficia*[26] – also belonged, at the

---

[23] According to an adjectivization traditionally used *sic et simpliciter* in our field of study: from F. Schulz, *Prinzipien des römischen Rechts* (München 1934) 14 ff., to Nörr, 'Ethik' (n. 2) *passim*, to G. Finazzi, 'Amicitia' (n. 3) *passim*.

[24] '... *quia pertinet ad mores, quos ethos illi vocant, nos eam partem philosophiae de moribus appellare solemus, sed decet augescentem linguam latinam nominare moralem*'.

[25] Cf., for example, Cic. *acad.* 1.34: '*pars philosophiae, quae posita est in virtute et in moribus*'; *de orat.* 1.10.42 '... *nihil te de bonis rebus in vita, nihil de malis, nihil de animi permotionibus, nihil de hominum moribus, nihil de ratione vitae didicisse*' (the reference to moral philosophy is revealed by the immediately preceding mention of Socrates); *de orat.* 1.19.85: '*de dis immortalibus, de disciplina iuventutis, de iustitia, de patientia, de temperantia, de modo rerum omnium, ceteraque, sine quibus civitates aut esse aut bene moratae esse non possent*'; 1, 19, 86: '*de aequitate, de iustitia, de fide, de frangendis cupiditatibus, de conformandis hominum moribus*'. As for Seneca – some of whose positions I will consider in the following note – it will suffice to recall *epist.* 71.47, in which the mention of *philosophia* concerning *mores* is coordinated with *virtutes* and *honestum*.

[26] Indeed, a motif that recurs in *de beneficiis* is the contrast between *beneficium* and juridical operation (*creditum*, mostly) from the point of view of dutifulness that is inherent, from the passive side, in the two figures. There is a duty of restitution of the *beneficia*, for which it is a matter of '*officium reddendi*' (*ben.* 1.3.8; 1.4.6; 2.32.1; 4.21.3; 5.22.1; 5.25.6; 7.22.1; 7.26.3; 7.28.1; see *epist.* 81.6 and 25) and for which Seneca (like Cicero, Sallust, Caesar, Livy) adopts the same terminology of obligatory relations: '*debere*', '*obligare/i*', '*obstringere*'. However, this is a dutifulness which, although perceived as pressing, Seneca clearly represents as different and opposed to legal dutifulness, of *creditum*: the observance of the latter is attributed to the existence of processual mechanisms (cf. *ben.* 3.7.13, transcribed *infra*, in note 50; 3.14.2; 7.23.3), and thus is a '*res necessaria*' and not voluntary (*infra*, note 50 *in fine*); the observance of *officium reddendi* is, instead, referred to the *ar-*

bitrium of the beneficiaries (3.7.1) as it is directed and solicited by internal impulses such as *fides* and *pudor* (1.2.4; 3.1.4; 3.14.2; 5.23.1; 7.28.3; 7.29.2; see *epist.* 81, 12 *in fine*). On the very summary data reported here, I refer the reader to the specific examination by Falcone, *'Obligatio'* (n. 3) 75 ff. I consider unjustified the underestimation of the two profiles that emerge from the aforesaid Senecan elaboration – that is: the opposition 'processual coercibility – non-coercibility' in relation to the two types of dutifulness and the importance of interiority and the individual choice directed by *virtutes* – recently made by R. Fiori, *Vir bonus. Politica diritto filosofia nel de officiis di Cicerone* (Napoli 2011) 180 ff. (which, in this way, firmly excludes the possibility of discerning, still in relation to the first Principate, merely an awareness of the separation between law and morality: see p. 141 ff.).

Regarding the first profile, Fiori (*Vir bonus* [n. 26] 188 f.) writes: "the distinction between *beneficium* and *creditum* - better: between *officium* and *debitum* – is not so much in *cogere* as a coercive instrument predisposed by the positive system as in being the former addressed to the establishment of a lasting relationship between the parties, even beyond the *referre gratiam*, and the latter aimed instead at mere fulfilment of an economic need. In other words, *cogere* becomes relevant not in the sense that coercion is the characteristic of 'juridicity' and thus of *creditum*, but in the sense that in the credit relationship [...] there is not established that relationship of reciprocal *amicitia* which instead the *beneficium* aims to constitute". However, the pursuit, through the practice of *beneficia*, of a "relationship value" (p. 188) is considered by Seneca to be an aspect not already prevalent and characterizing the dichotomy between the two figures, but rather further with respect to the matter of the type of dutifulness deriving from having received (as *beneficium* or as *creditum*) and as pertaining to a distinct and particular part (*'altera pars'*) of his theorizing, indicated with the words '*quomodo se gerere homines in accipiendis beneficiis de-beant*' (*ben.* 2.18.1): it is in this context that Seneca, having introduced the rule (§ 2) '*non ab omnibus accipiendum*' and warning that, rather '*eligendum est, a quo beneficium accipiam; et quidem diligentius quaerendus beneficii quam pecuniae creditor*' (§ 5), explains the need for greater care in the choice of the person from whom to request a *beneficium* with the circumstance that the exchange of *beneficia* determines the onset of a lasting relationship and *amicitia*.

As for the second profile, Fiori, *Vir bonus* (n. 26) 189, states that the virtue which specifically governs the observance of *officium*, that is *pudor*, is not an "internal impulse" (as I had considered it in *'Obligatio'* [n. 3] 81), but "a completely heteronomous mechanism, in the sense that it indicates [...] an attitude of the spirit formed in relation to the system of values expressed by the ethics of the group". Now, there is no doubt that, as this scholar has pointed out, "*beneficia* [...] belong to a code of behaviour on which all of Roman society was based" (p. 187). For my part, I would add that it is equally certain that the practice of *officia* is indissolubly linked to that widespread and totalizing phenomenon consisting in the collective control of the behaviours of individuals as reflections of internal quality and attitudes (I refer the reader to G. Falcone, 'L'attribuzione della qualifica 'vir bonus' nella prassi giudiziaria d'età repubblicana', in AUPA 54 [2010-2011] esp. 90 f.), control perceived as very conditioning (this was previously pointed out by Schulz, *Prinzipien* (n. 23) 15). Moreover, within this same context is the very fact that *pudor* is the specific virtue ensuring the observance of *officium*: indeed, it is the feeling of restraint, the inner predisposition to feel the weight of social control and the collec-

time of Paulus, to jurisprudential reflection, as shown by the following

---

tive judgement of disapproval for the failure to comply with *officium*. However – and this is the point that separates me from the Roman scholar – restraint is, in itself, a feeling or attitude of the spirit and thus its intervention for observance of *officium* should be considered an internal incentive and solicitation to effectuate, by means of behaviours, the values shared and 'codified' by the social body. In other words, social control and the judgment of approval/disapproval are external factors with respect to the individual's action, but the consideration or not of this control, the worrying or not about this judgment (and thus the orientation or not of one's behaviour in the sense of observance of *officium*) depends on the possession or not of *pudor* by the individual and on the degree to which this virtue solicits and directs the will. So much so that it is Seneca himself who speaks in this regard, on several occasions, about *'conscientia'*: *'bona'*, if one has decided for the observance of the *officium* of *reddere gratiam*, *'mala'* in the opposite case. For example, in *ben*. 3.1.4, he states that an unreturned *beneficium* remained a prisoner *'in mala conscientia'*, *'in malis pectoribus'*. And in a structured unitary context (*ben*. 4.21.3 ff.), he repeatedly uses, for the opposite case of restitution of the *beneficium*, as equivalent and exchangable the syntagmas *'bona conscientia'*, *'voluntas bona'* and *'bona fides'* (the reference is to virtue-*fides* which explained its capacity to induce compliance). It is worthwhile discussing this second comparison. In *ben*. 4.21.3, Seneca states that, as for any virtue, also in the case of '*gratum esse*' (cf. 4.19 in fine: '*Quid est autem honestius, quam gratum esse? Huius virtutis materia tam late patet quam vita*'), each evaluation concerns the soul ('*Nam ut omnium aliarum virtutum, ita huius ad animum tota aestimatio redit*'). Therefore (§ 4), just as the eloquent man remains so even if he is silent, just as the strong man remains so even if he keeps his hands in his belt, a person is grateful (simply) if he wishes to be so and has no other witness to his desire except himself ('*ita gratus est etiam qui vult tantum nec habet voluntatis suae ullum alium quam se testem*'). Moreover (§ 5), sometimes a person is grateful even if to common opinion he seems ungrateful: then, what else does this person follow but his conscience? ('*Hic quid aliud sequitur quam ipsam conscientiam?*'). And he (§ 6), even if subjected to torture, will never come to say: "What have I desired? What good to me now is *bona voluntas*? "('*Quid mihi volui? Quid nunc mihi prodest bona voluntas?*'). This rhetorical question leads, immediately afterward, to a consideration in which an equivalence is established between *'bona voluntas-bona conscientia-bona fides'*, which demonstrates how the *fides* that presides, like *pudor*, over the fulfilment of *officium*, is considered to be activated and implemented by *conscientia*. I recall the entire passage: "If also *bona fides* sees torture applied to itself, it does not descend from its summit and stand above the penalty. [...] The subject will not hear this voice: "what benefit to me now is *bona voluntas*?" It also benefits him in torture, even in fire: even if the fire approaches the individual limbs and gradually surrounds the living body and the heart full of *bona conscientia* dissolves drop by drop: fire will please him who makes *bona fides* shine". In the same order of ideas, cf. also *ben*. 5.25.5 '*Paucis animus sui rector optimus; proximi sunt, qui admoniti in viam redeunt*'; 6 '*Inest interim animis voluntas bona, sed torpet modo deliciis ac situ, modo officii inscitia*'.

Therefore, the weighty existence of the two profiles in Seneca's model having been reaffirmed, the opposition between the dutifulness of *officium* and the dutifulness deriving from *creditum* is interpreted as an expression of the awareness of a separateness between 'law' and 'morality' (in the sense specified in the text). [**A.**]

passage on the subject of *fideicommissa*, accepted by the compilers of the Institutes of Justinian:

> I. 2.23.1: *Sciendum itaque est omnia fideicommissa primis temporibus infirma esse, quia nemo invitus cogebatur praestare id de quo rogatus erat: quibus enim non poterant hereditates vel legata relinquere, si relinquebant, fidei committebant eorum, qui capere ex testamento poterant: et ideo fideicommissa appellata sunt, quia nullo vinculo iuris, sed tantum pudore eorum qui rogabantur continebantur. Postea primus divus Augustus semel iterumque gratia personarum motus, vel quia per ipsius salutem rogatus quis diceretur, aut ob insignem quorundam perfidiam iussit consulibus auctoritatem suam interponere. Quod quia iustum videbatur et populare erat, paulatim conversum est in adsiduam iurisdictionem: tantusque favor eorum factus est, ut etiam praetor proprius crearetur, qui <de> fideicommissis ius diceret, quem fideicommissarium [appellabant] <appellamus>.*

The jurist, author of the excerpted text,[27] illustrates a historical development: from an initial phase, in which *fideicommissa* were *'infirma'* because they were based not on a *vinculum iuris* but exclusively on the *pudor* of the *rogati* subjects ('... *nullo vinculo iuris, sed tantum pudore eorum qui rogabantur continebantur*') – who thus could not have been forced to fulfil their obligation if they had not wanted to do so –, to an increasingly progressive excogitation of ever more stable and specific forms of processual protection of the will of the settlor. In other words, the jurist establishes a contrast between the mere importance of *pudor* and "a situation that is binding in terms of law" (I would translate "*vinculum iuris*" thusly)[28] since it is creating a constraint to fulfilment on the basis of processual instruments. That *officium* is contrasted with the legal dimension (*vinculum iuris*)[29] can be considered certain due to the reference to *pudor*. In this regard, in addition to a statement such as that of Plautus (*trin.* 697) that "recalling one's own *officium* constitutes the *honos* of the *homo pudicus*", the conceptual couple *'pudens et officiosus'* of some Ciceronian passages[30] and the repeated Senecan juxta-

---

[27] In my opinion, Gaius in the *Res cottidianae*: cf. Falcone, *'Obligatio'* (n. 3) 50 ff. and esp. 60 ff. (also see 100 ff.). *Ivi*, 50 note 133, the reasons for the proposed slight modifications.

[28] For this interpretation, cf. Falcone, *'Obligatio'* (n. 3) 101 note 283.

[29] As was well seen by G. Negri, *La clausola codicillare nel testamento inofficioso* (Milano 1974) 215.

[30] Cic. *fam.* 13.21.2; *pro Roscio com.* 6.18.

positions of *pudor* and *officium* of restitution of the *beneficium*[31] can be advanced; but above all, a passage from *De finibus bonorum et malorum* (2.18.58-59)[32] in which Cicero, precisely with reference to the fulfilment of a fideicommissal *rogatio*, speaks explicitly of *'officium sequi'*, referred to the solicitation of *virtutes* (*humanitas*, *probitas*, *aequitas*, *fides*, *iustitia*), and puts forth such *officium sequi* as an example of conduct that cannot be coerced by the positive legal system (§ 2.17.57).[33] However, in the light of this conceptual tradition, it is remarkable that, while proposing to explain the term *'fideicommissum'* (*'et ideo fideicommissa appellata sunt, quia ...'*), the jurist had not mentioned *fides*, as we would have expected in an etymological perspective, but instead *pudor*.

Returning to Paulus's discourse, it can be observed that the very general and so to say 'categorical' scope of the term *officium* is the same that this jurist adopted when, in order to justify the gratuitousness of the *mandatum*, he indicated the foundation, historical and dogmatic at the same time,[34] of this contract:

> Paul. 32 *ad ed.*, D. 17.1.1.4: *Mandatum nisi gratuitum nullum est: nam originem ex officio atque amicitia trahit, contrarium vero est officio*

---

[31] *Supra*, note 25.

[32] Cic. *fin.* 2.18.58: *Si te amicus tuus moriens rogaverit, ut hereditatem reddas suae filiae, nec usquam id scripserit* [...] *nec cuiquam dixerit, quid facies? Tu quidem reddes; ipse Epicurus fortasse redderet, ut Sex. Peducaeus, Sex. F., is qui hunc nostrum reliquit effigiem et humanitatis et probitatis suae filium, cum doctus, tum omnium vir optimus et iustissimus, cum sciret nemo eum rogatum a C. Plotio, equite Romano splendido, Nursino, ultro ad mulierem venit eique nihil opinanti viri mandatum exposuit hereditatemque reddidit. Sed ego ex te quaero, quoniam idem tu certe fecisses, nonne intellegas eo maiorem vim esse naturae, quod ipsi vos, qui omnia ad vestrum commodum et, ut ipsi dicitis, ad voluptatem referatis, tamen ea faciatis e quibus appareat non voluptatem vos, sed officium sequi, plusque rectam naturam quam rationem pravam valere.* 59. [...] *Perspicuum est* [...], *nisi aequitas, fides, iustitia proficiscantur a natura, et si omnia haec ad utilitatem referantur, vir bonus non posse reperiri; deque his rebus satis multa in nostris de re publica libris sunt dicta a Laelio.*

[33] In fact, the discourse in *fin.* 2.18.58-59, is the paradigmatic explanation of the affirmations that Cicero makes immediately before, at the end of § 57, concerning the impossibility of sanctioning certain behaviours. In particular, in the concluding lines of § 57, he praises the correct conduct of the powerful Pompey, who, if he had wished, '*esse ... iniquus poterat inpune*', and he exclaims: '*Quam multa vero iniuste fieri possunt, quae nemo possit reprendere!*'. On Cicero's commentary, cf. Falcone, *'Obligatio'* (n. 3) 93 ff.

[34] The coexistence of both purposes is dealt with by Negri, *La clausola codicillare* (n. 29) 244.

merces: interueniente enim pecunia res ad locationem et conductionem potius respicit.

In this text, we can note the dual recourse to the idea of *officium* as such: a first time, paired with and on the same level as the figure and the value of *amicitia* ('*originem ex officio atque amicitia trahit*'); a second time, when the jurist observes that the *merces*-element is contrary to the figure of *officium* ('*contrarium vero est officio merces*'). These two Pauline passages are the attestations of "*officium*" possessing a higher level of abstraction in the jurisprudential documentation that has come down to us: higher abstraction not only, as is obvious, with respect to the uses of the term in the concrete sense of task, office, service, single specific duty or group of duties, role, but also with respect to wide-ranging uses such as '*ex officio amicitiae gerere*' (the same Paulus, D. 42.5.23, on the subject of impuberal *negotium*) or '*ex officio pietatis facere*' (Marcianus, in D. 5.2.2, on the subject of testaments), '*ex officio pietatis dare*' (Ulpian, in D. 25.3.5.17, on the subject of foodstuffs): uses that are, instead, characterized by the indication of a precise referent (*amicitia*, *pietas*).[35]

In the text on *iudicium contrarium commodati*, "*officium*" essentially expresses ethical dutifulness tout court. A significant correspondence – without the suggestion of the comparison being translated into hypotheses of cultural ancestry or even a specific loan – is shown by the use of the term in two important passages of Cicero's *De officiis*:

Cic. *off.* 1.10.31: *Sed incidunt saepe tempora, cum ea, quae maxime videntur digna esse iusto homine, eoque quem virum bonum dicimus, commutantur fiuntque contraria, ut reddere depositum, facere promissum quaeque pertinent ad veritatem et ad fidem, ea migrare interdum et non servare fit iustum. Referri enim decet ad ea, quae posui principio fundamenta iustitiae, primum ut ne cui noceatur, deinde ut communi utilitati serviatur.* 32. *Potest enim accidere promissum aliquod et conventum, ut id effici sit inutile vel ei, cui promissum sit, vel ei, qui promiserit … Nec*

[35] On an even more general level is the '*officio pietatis fungi*' of Papinianus, in D. 10.2.57pr. ('*Arbitro quoque accepto fratres communem hereditatem consensu dividentes pietatis officio funguntur …*') and Celsus's '*officium fidei praestandae*' mentioned by Ulpian in D. 24.1.5.15 ('*Si quis rogatus sit praecepta certa quantitate uxori suae hereditatem restituere et is sine deductione restituerit, Celsus libro decimo digestorum scripsit magis pleniore officio fidei praestandae functummaritum quam donasse uideri …*'), which alludes to the fulfilment of a specific duty or task (*officio fungi*), that of '*praestare fidem*' by performing a fideicommissum. Differently, for the same case of fulfilment of a fideicommissum *rogatio*, Cicero (*fin.* 2.18.58-59) spoke, in an abstract perspective, of '*officium sequi*' tout court: cf. *supra*, note 31.

promissa igitur servanda sunt ea, quae sint iis, quibus promiseris, inutilia, nec si plus tibi noceant, quam illi prosint cui promiseris, contra officium est maius anteponi minori, ut, si constitueris cui piam te advocatum in rem praesentem esse venturum atque interim graviter aegrotare filius coeperit, non sit contra officium non facere quod dixeris, magisque ille, cui promissum sit, ab officio discedat, si se destitutum queratur. Iam illis promissis standum non esse quis non videt, quae coactus quis metu, quae deceptus dolo promiserit? Quae quidem pleraque iure praetorio liberantur, nonnulla legibus;

Cic., *off.* 3.25.95. … *Ergo et promissa non facienda non numquam neque semper deposita reddenda. Si gladium quis apud te sana mente deposuerit, repetat insaniens, reddere peccatum sit, officium non reddere. Quid? Si is, qui apud te pecuniam deposuerit, bellum inferat patriae, reddasne depositum? Non credo: facies enim contra rem publicam, quae debet esse carissima. Sic multa, quae honesta natura videntur esse, temporibus fiunt non honesta: facere promissa, stare conventis, reddere deposita commutata utilitate fiunt non honesta.*

The meaning and the particular perspective are similar: both in Cicero and in Paulus, *officium* is the abstract dutifulness to which the adoption (and evaluation) of behaviours is to be related. Cicero says of a certain behaviour that "it is *contra officium*" or that its author "*ab officio discedit*",[36] and of another behaviour, instead, that "it is *officium*"; the Severan jurist states that *officium* "prevents" the untimely claim by the commodans for restitution.

It should be specified that the two texts by Paulus, the one on *iudicium commodati contrarium* and the one on the gratuitousness of the *mandatum*, are the only ones in which the term *'officium'* is used in relation to duty as such.[37] It must also be pointed out that a use of the

[36] A similar conceptualization is found in *off.* 1.14.43 '… *id autem tantum abest ab officio, ut nihil magis officio possit esse contrarium*'.

[37] In fact, I do not believe that D. 21.1.31.14 (Pedius-Ulpian) can be put forward as further confirmation of a general value of '*officium*', '*Quod in procuratore diximus, idem et in tutore et curatore dicendum erit ceterisque, qui ex officio pro aliis interveniunt: et ita Pedius ait*'. Negri, *La clausola codicillare* (n. 29) 246 interprets the text in the sense that Pedius "resorts to the concept of *officium* to justify the *ratio* of each spontaneous intervention (my spacing) in the care of others' interests. However – apart from the fact that the texts evoked in support (D. 3.1.1.5; 4.5.5.2; 4.5.6; 5.1.12.2; 16.1.1.1; 16.1.2.1; 50.17.2pr.) are, in reality, not helpful, because they speak of *officia* or *officium* in the more concrete sense of 'tasks', 'assignments' –, reservations are raised by the fact that, instead of words such as, for example, *'eisque, qui ex officio … interveniunt'*, the jurist writes *'ceterisque qui ex officio … interveniunt'*. In truth, this

adverbial form *'officiose'* is documented only in a text by Paulus himself.[38] These two facts can certainly be a coincidence, attributable to mere chance in the surviving documentation. Yet, it is thought-provoking that Paulus is once again the jurist who, facing the *interdictum 'De homine libero exhibendo'*, accomplishable by *quivis de populo* for the case of a free man held by someone *dolo malo* and thus indicated by Ulpian as a proposal by the praetor *tuendae libertatis causa*, instead devised the framework as an instrument *'officii tuendi* causa',[39] having considered, that is, *officium* as an interest to be protected, and precisely the duty of solidarity in human coexistence.[40] Albeit with the aforesaid awareness of a possible chance occurrence of the first two data, there emerges the hypothesis that we are dealing with a series of indications of a primary attention and appreciation by Paulus, perhaps more accentuated than in other jurists, of the ethical perspective of *officium* as such.

---

makes preferable an interpretation according to which Pedius alluded "to the remaining subjects" who also intervene, such as the *procurator* and the *curator*, not spontaneously but on the basis of a role, or assignment, entrusted to them (*'ex officio'*): I would think, for example, of the *cognitor*, but also of the figures of the *curator prodigi* and the *curator furiosi* (that is, Pedius and Ulpian, by explicitly mentioning the *curator* next to the *tutor*, could have been thinking primarily of the most important figure, that of the *curator* of people aged under 25 years).

[38] Paul. 5 *sent.*, D. 34.9.21: *'Portiones quoque eorum fisco vindicantur, qui mortem libertorum suspecto decedentium non defenderunt: omnes enim heredes vel eos qui loco heredis sunt officio se agere circa defuncti vindictam convenit'*.

[39] Paul. 63 *ad ed.*, D. 43.1.2.1: *'Interdicta autem competunt uel hominum causa uel diuini iuris aut de religione, sicut est 'ne quid in loco sacro fiat' uel 'quod factum est restituatur' et de mortuo inferendo uel sepulchro aedificando. hominum causa competunt uel ad publicam utilitatem pertinentia uel sui iuris tuendi causa uel officii tuendi causa uel rei familiaris. publicae utilitatis causa competit interdictum 'ut uia publica uti liceat' et 'flumine publico' et 'ne quid fiat in uia publica': iuris sui tuendi causa de liberis exhibendis, item de liberto exhibendo: officii causa de homine libero exhibendo: reliqua interdicta rei familiaris causa dantur'*. At the time, the general classification of interdicts conserved in this fragment was considered of postclassical origin by A. Berger, 'Miszellen aus der Interdiktenlehre', in ZSS 36 (1915) 160; instead, the text has been implicitly considered classical by G. Santucci, *Operis novi nuntiatio iuris publici tuendi gratia* (Padova 2001) 49 ff. and by R. Scevola, *'Utilitas publica'*. II. *Elaborazione della giurisprudenza severiana* (Padova 2012) 159 ff.

[40] C. Bertolini, *Appunti didattici di diritto romano. Il processo civile*, III (Torino 1915) 52: prohibitions "implored not for an individual interest *sensu stricto*, but rather for an interest of humanity"; E. Costa, *Profilo storico del processo civile romano* (Roma 1918) 108: the prohibitions *officii tuendi gratia* "have their basis in a pure sense of human and civil solidarity"; more recently, F. Cancelli, *s.v.* 'Ufficio (dir. rom.)', in ED XLV (Milano 1992) 608: "human solidarity".

4. Different meaning of '*officium*' as a specific contractual task, which appears in some other texts

It has been authoritatively maintained[41] that, in view of Paulus's determination of a dichotomy between *officium* and legal duties, a different line of thought, perhaps Sabinian, would also attribute legal obligations to *officium*. This would be demonstrated by the following passages (the first and third on the subject of mandate, the second on mandate and deposit):

> Iav. 7 *ex Cass.*, D. 17.1.36.2: … *propius est, ut cum huiusmodi incommodis mandatum suscipi possit praestarique officium et in partibus emendis perinde atque in toto debeat ab eo, qui tale mandatum sua sponte suscepit;*

> Afric. 8 *quaest.*, D. 47.2.62(61).5: … *multo tamen aequius esse nemini officium suum, quod eius, cum quo contraxerit, non etiam sui commodi causa susceperit, damnosum esse;*

> Gai. 9 *ad ed. prov.*, D. 17.1.27.2: *Qui mandatum suscepit, si potest id explere, deserere promissum officium non debet, alioquin quanti mandatoris intersit damnabitur: si vero intellegit explere se id officium non posse, id ipsum cum primum poterit debet mandatori nuntiare, ut is si velit, alterius opera utatur* …[42]

Along this interpretative line, it has been said that for Javolenus, Africanus and Gaius, in contrast to the Severan jurist, "*officium* is not extraneous to legal duties and opposed to them, but coincides with legal obligation".[43]

In reality, a comparison in these terms and the consequent identification of different lines of thought cannot be proposed. Indeed, Paulus, on the one hand, the other three jurists, on the other, reason with different meanings of the term *officium*. As we have just underlined, the Severan jurist is thinking of the concept of moral duty as such, the others of the more concrete value of task, office, specific duty undertaken. This is demonstrated by the context of the statements and

---

[41] Nörr, 'Ethik' (n. 2) 275.

[42] On the same level, by the same jurist, is the text of Gai. 4.83: … *nec interest, praesens an absens cognitor detur. sed si absens datus fuerit, cognitor ita erit, si cognoverit et susceperit officium cognitoris.*

[43] Finazzi, 'Amicitia' (n. 3) 739 f.

the use of the adjectivizations *'officium suum', 'id officium', 'promissum* officium'.[44] Secondly, the perspectives and purposes of the discourses are completely distinct: for Paulus, unlike for the three jurists, it is not a matter of indicating behaviours, services, duties to which an *'obligatus'* subject is called upon on the basis of a contract, but a matter of indicating the correspondence of the decision to *commodare* with a general ethical dutifulness and, in the continuation of the discourse, of stigmatizing a behaviour of the commodans as contrary to this dutifulness. So much so that Paulus himself, when he refers, like the three jurists, to the content of a contractual duty, does not hesitate to use, from the same concrete point of view, the same terminology *'officium praestare'* used by Javolenus on the subject of *mandatum*:

> Paul. 5 *quaest.*, D. 19.5.5.4: … *si pacti sumus, ut tu a meo debitore Carthagine exigas, ego a tuo Romae, uel ut tu in meo, ego in tuo solo aedificem, et ego aedificaui et tu cessas, in priorem speciem mandatum quodammodo interuenisse uidetur, sine quo exigi pecunia alieno nomine non potest: quamuis enim et impendia sequantur, tamen mutuum officium praestamus et potest mandatum ex pacto etiam naturam suam excedere (possum enim tibi mandare, ut et custodiam mihi praestes et non plus impendas in exigendo quam decem)* …

[44] In substance, in the passages of the three jurists, *'officium'* is placed in the more concrete perspective in which, for example, there is also the well-known passage of Cicero's oration *pro Roscio amer.* (§ 111) which constitutes the testimony-principle of the relation among *mandatum*, *fides* and *amicitia* and which speaks of *'mutua officia'* (an expression which Finazzi, 'Amicitia' (n. 3) 762, recently interpreted in the concrete sense of "reciprocal services"): '*In privatis rebus, si qui rem mandatam non modo malitiosius gessisset, sui quaestus aut commodi causa, verum etiam neglegentius, eum maiores summum admisisse dedecus existimabant. Itaque mandati constitutum est iudicium non minus turpe quam furti, credo, propterea quod quibus in rebus ipsi interesse non possumus, in iis operae nostrae vicaria fides amicorum supponitur; quam qui laedit, oppugnat omnium commune praesidium et, quantum in ipso est, disturbat vitae societatem. Non enim possumus omnia per nos agere; alius in alia est re magis utilis. Idcirco amicitiae comparantur, ut commune commodum mutuis officiis gubernetur.* 112. *Quid recipis mandatum, si aut neglecturus aut ad tuum commodum conversurus es? Cur mihi te offers ac meis commodis officio simulato officis et obstas? Recede de medio; per alium transigam. Suscipi sonus offici quod te putas sustinere posse; quod maxime videtur grave iis qui minime ipis leves sunt. Ergo idcirco turpis haec culpa est, quod duas res sanctissimas violat, amicitiam et fidem. Nam neque mandat quisquam fere, nisi amico; neque credit, nisi ei quem fidelem putat. Perditissimi est igitur hominis simul et amicitiam dissolvere et fallere eum qui laesus non esset, nisi credidisset*'.

5. *Officium* and *beneficium* in Paulus's analysis of the *commodatum* and of the related instruments of protection

Officium as a moral duty is expressed, in the concrete case considered by Paulus, by providing help to others through the granting of a *beneficium*.[45] This term appears three times in the discourse, and at three key points. A first time to specify that, in the phase of formation of the agreement, the determination of limits and duration of the use of the *res* lies with the one who *"beneficium tribuit"*, i.e. the commodans; a second time when the jurist explains that what at the beginning of the negotiation had been a matter of *beneficium* and of simple will, following the formation of the obligatory commitment, is transformed (*converti*) into a relationship of reciprocal services and actions; a third time in the moralizing notation *'adiuvari quippe nos, non decipi beneficio oportet'*. However, the idea of *beneficium* must also be read between the lines of the discourse in the central part of the text, where Paulus makes a comparison with the position of the manager of the affairs of an absentee: the words *'ut accidit in eo ...'* summarize the previous notation concerning the conversion of a beneficial voluntary initiative into a relationship of reciprocal services and actions, with the consequence that the manager cannot abandon *impune* the business undertaken. And the same must be said of the further reference[46] to *mandatum*, the acceptance of which (*suscipere*) is evidently considered a *beneficium* by Paulus.

Paulus relates both *officium* and *beneficium* to the *voluntas*-element. Considered in this regard are the *incipit* of the text *'Sicut autem voluntatis et officii magis quam necessitatis est commodare, ita modum commodati finemque praescribere eius est qui beneficium tribuit'* and the formulation '*... quod principio beneficii ac nudae voluntatis fuerat ...*'.. The meaning of this connection consists in this: that giving in commodatum is the fruit of a voluntary determination, responding to a feeling of dutiful solidarity, not forced by a *necessitas*, by a (pre-existing) obligation; and it is *beneficium* since it is a beneficial voluntary action, an emanation of that duty, characterized by the gratuitousness of the concession.[47] Only once the commodans *'beneficium tribuit'*, that is having made the decision to

---

[45] Cf. G. Negri, 'La gestione d'affari nel diritto romano', in *Derecho romano de obligaciones* (n. 9) 671: "merely ethical sense of solidarity".

[46] Cf., in fact, *supra* § 2 in notes 14-17.

[47] Moreover, we should recall the connection between gratuitousness and *officium* (of which *beneficium-commodare* is a manifestation) inscribed by Paulus himself in D. 17.1.1.4 (*supra*, § 3).

commodare he concludes the contract, does there occur *necessitas*, i.e. the obligatoriness of the legal services, pursuant to the existence of actions to sanction the non-fulfilment of such services: with regard to the commodans, there occurs especially the obligation to allow the commodatarius the enjoyment of the thing in the times and in the ways established (abstaining, in particular, from an early request for restitution of the thing). This also applies to the relation between the voluntariness of the management of an absentee's affairs with respect to the *necessitas* to carry them to fruition once (freely) undertaken and for the voluntariness of the acceptance of an assignment (*suscipere mandatum*), i.e. the conclusion of a contract of *mandatum*, with respect to the *necessitas* of fulfilment of the *mandatum* itself.

It has been appropriately observed[48] that this type of reasoning well lends itself to being evaluated as a purely technical-juridical reflection, analogous to others carried out by *prudentes* – including Paulus 32 *ad ed.* D. 17.1.22.11: '*sicut autem liberum est mandatum non suscipere, ita susceptum consummari oportet*'[49] -, without it having to rely on cultural loans of any kind and, in particular, of a presumed connection with the contrast fixed by Seneca in *De beneficiis* between voluntary fulfilment of the *beneficia* and fulfilment induced by the existence of a processual instrument, which renders the fulfilment itself a *'res necessaria'* (*ben.* 3.7.1-3).[50] I would add that also the fact that Paulus projects obligato-

[48] By Finazzi, 'Amicitia' (n. 3) 739 f.

[49] The notation constitutes the framework of a discourse on the possibility of *renuntiare* by the agent. To this text Finazzi, 'Amicitia' (n. 3) 739 adds the notation of Javolenus, 7 *ex Cass.*, D. 17.1.36.2: '*... propius est, ut cum huiusmodi incommodis mandatum suscipi possit praestarique officium et in partibus emendis perinde atque in toto debeat ab eo, qui tale mandatum sua sponte suscepit*'. However, the notation of Gaius in D. 34.5.7.1 (Gai. 1 *fideicomm.*) can also be cited: 'Cum quidam pluribus heredibus institutis unius fidei commisisset, ut, cum moreretur, uni ex coheredibus, cui ipse vellet, restitueret eam partem hereditatis, quae ad eum pervenisset: verissimum est utile esse fideicommissum: nec enim in arbitrio eius qui rogatus est positum est, an omnino velit restituere, sed cui potius restituat: plurimum enim interest, utrum in potestate eius, quem testator obligari cogitat, faciat, si velit dare, an post necessitatem dandi solius distribuendi liberum arbitrium concedat' (on this passage, cf. Falcone, *'Obligatio'* [n. 3] 103 note 286). The following statement by Labeo, reported by Paulus himself in D. 3.5.18.2 (Paul. 9 *ad ed.*), is placed instead in a different perspective, and thus I do not believe (unlike Nörr, 'Ethik' [n. 2] 273 f.) that it can be included among possible precedents ('Vorbildern') of the Pauline opposition *'voluntas – necessitas'*: '*Si libero homini, qui bona fide mihi serviebat, mandem, ut aliquid agat, non fore cum eo mandati actionem Labeo ait, quia non libera voluntate exsequitur rem sibi mandatam, sed quasi ex necessitate servili ...*'.

[50] Sen. *ben.* 3.7.1: *... pars optima beneficii periit, si actio sicut certae pecuniae aut*

riness-*necessitas* into the accomplishment of *actiones* (‘*invicem propositae sunt actiones*’; ‘*praestationes actionesque civiles*’) is justified in the same purely technical-juridical perspective: rather than appearing as an echo of Seneca’s ‘*res necessaria*’, this is explained most naturally in the circumstance that the specific object of the jurist’s comment is precisely the scope of application of an action, the *iudicium commodati contrarium*. Moreover, the depiction of *commodare* in terms of *beneficium* was rooted within the same jurisprudential environment, as demonstrated by a passage of the commentary on the provincial edict of Gaius that assumed the commodatarius *sic et simpliciter* as ‘*beneficii debitor*’.[51]

---

ex conducto et locato datur. Hoc enim in illo speciosissimum est, quod dedimus vel perdituri, quod totum permisimus accipientium arbitrio; si appello, si ad iudicem voco, incipit non beneficium esse, sed creditum. 2. *Deinde cum res honestissima sit referre gratiam, desinit esse honesta, si necessaria est; non magis enim laudabit quis quam* g r a t u m h o m i n e m *quam eum, qui depositum reddidit aut, quod debebat, citra iudicem solvit.* 3. *Ita duas res, quibus in vita humana nihil pulchrius est, corrumpimus, gratum hominem et beneficium; quid enim aut in hoc magnificum est, si beneficium non dat, sed commodat, aut in illo, qui reddit, non quia vult, sed quia nec esse est? Non est gloriosa res gratum esse, nisi tutum est ingratum fuisse.*

To fully appreciate this testimony, it is appropriate, on the one hand, to consider the fact that *‘referre gratiam’* is qualified as *‘res honestissima’* in conformity with the consideration of *gratum esse* as *virtus* with respect to which “nothing is more *honestum*” “(*ben*. 4.19.4 in fine: *‘Quid est autem honestius, quam gratum esse? Huius virtutis matter tam late patet quam vita’*; see also *ben*. 1.4.4: *‘honestissima contentio’* in relation to *se grate gerere*; and *ben*. 4.6.3: the coincidence between *gratum esse* and *honestum* is most striking and unanimously perceived), and, on the other hand, that the affirmation that this *res* ‘*desinit esse honesta, si necessaria est*’ is matched with an assumption such as that clearly expressed by Seneca in *epistula* 66, and especially in § 16 ‘*nihil honestum est quod ab invito, quod a coacto fit; omne honestum voluntarium est. Non potest honestum esse quod non est liberum; nam quod timet servit*’ e nel § 17 ‘… *Omne honestum iniussum incoactumque est*’.

The connection between the structure of Paulus’s discourse and Seneca’s elaboration was argued, for the first time, by Nörr, ‘Ethik’ (n. 2) 270 ff., followed by Mantello, ‘Un’etica’ (n. 3) 163 and by me (*‘Obligatio’* [n. 3] 177 ff.).

[51] Gai. 13 *ad ed. prov*., D. 47.2.55.1: ‘*Eum, qui quod utendum accepit ipse alii commodaverit, furti obligari responsum est. ex quo satis apparet furtum fieri et si quis usum alienae rei in suum lucrum convertat. nec movere quem debet, quasi nihil lucri sui gratia faciat: species enim lucri est ex alieno largiri et beneficii debitorem sibi adquirere. unde et is furti tenetur, qui ideo rem amovet, ut eam alii donet*’. Gaius gives news of a judgement, according to which a person who has given in *commodatum* something belonging to someone else from whom he had received it in *commodatum* is culpable of theft; and after having noted that, in the light of the aforesaid judgement someone also commits theft if he converts the *usus* of someone else’s thing into his own profit, Gaius overcomes the hypothetical objection (evidently related to the gratuitousness of the *commodatum*) that, in this case, there would not be a *facere sui lucri causa*, observing that a type of *lucrum* consists in making donations with other people’s goods and in acquiring for

Although the key element of Paulus's reasoning is the contrast between the free formation of the will to *commodare* and the necessariness of behaviours once the contract is concluded (*'suscepta obligatio'*; *'geritur negotium'*) and although, in this light, the jurist forcefully underlines the emergence of the commitment and coercibility of the obligatory relationship (*'quod principio beneficii ac nudae voluntatis fuerat converti in praestationes actionesque civiles'*), it is noteworthy that *officium* with its moral duty continues to be perceived as present and as playing a role: now no longer a solicitor of a behaviour (*commodare*) but an impediment to conduct contrary to the spirit of solidarity and *beneficentia* (the premature request for restitution of the loaned thing): *'non officium tantum impedit, sed et suscepta obligatio'*. Indeed, the internal structure of this statement reveals that the persistent presence and operation of *officium* is taken for granted, as a certain basis with respect to which the obstructive scope of the intervened *obligatio* constitutes the addition of a further perspective. In other words, for Paulus, the moral dimension of *officium* is not replaced by the conclusion of the legal operation: in its representation of the regime of commodatum, the legal dimension coexists with an underlying moral dimension.

The final part of the text also gives an account of this coexistence. After the comparison with *negotiorum gestio* and *mandatum*[52] is finished, concrete examples of the behaviour of the commodans are presented under the conceptual framework *'non recte facies'*, whose mean-

---

oneself a *beneficii debitor*. The fact that Gaius adopts this last expression without any explanation reveals that there were widespread and rooted in Roman society and culture both the representation of *comodatum* as *beneficium* and the fact that the recipient of a *beneficium* was *adstrictus* by a duty to reciprocate, a duty so compelling as to qualify the recipient as *'debitor'* (cf., moreover, Petron. *satyr.* 126 *'Sive ergo nobis vendis quod peto, mercator paratus est, sive* [...] *commodas, effice ut beneficium debeam'*). On Gaius's text, I refer the reader to Falcone, *'Obligatio'* (n. 3) 133.

On this occasion, it is worth noting that, if giving in *commodatum* is intended as *largiri* due to its gratuitous nature, the representation of this *largiri* as a *beneficium* helps Gaius, rather than to emphasize this gratuitousness, to justify instead the idea that giving in commodatum is to be considered a source of *lucrum*, precisely because of the duty to reciprocate. To this latter proposal can be added a passage by Ulpian (15 *ad ed.*, D. 5.3.25.11), in which the donor (and Gaius, in closing, compared donation with *commodatum*) is presented, by the very fact of giving, as the author of a *'sibi aliquem naturaliter obligare'* (albeit denying, with respect to the specific matter addressed, that this constitutes an enrichment for the donor): *'Consuluit senatus bonae fidei possessoribus, ne in toto damnum adficiantur, sed in id dumtaxat teneantur, in quo locupletiores facti sunt ... Nec si donaverint, locupletiores facti videbuntur, quamvis ad remunerandum sibi aliquem naturaliter obligaverunt ...'*. [**A.**]

[52] Cf. *supra*, § 2 in notes 14-17.

ing is "you will not behave correctly" from a moral point of view. The sense is the same one recognizable in other jurisprudential texts, e.g. that in which Ulpian qualifies as *'non recte facere'* and, shortly afterward, as *'facinus'* the conduct of the concubine who, after having been such with the patron, began to be such also with his son or grandson (25.7.1.3).[53] Indeed, Paulus attributes the diagnosis *'non recte facies'* directly to the paraenetic notation[54] '*adiuvari quippe nos, non decipi beneficio oportet*'. In substance, with perfect correspondence with the initial correlation *'non officium tantum, sed et suscepta obligatio'* (where the *obligatio* is made explicit in terms of *negotium* and this, in turn, in terms of reciprocal *praestationes* and *actiones*), also the concluding part contains an indication of the contrariness to *officium* (*'non recte facies'*) and the coexisting processual reaction of positive law: '*contrarium iudicium utile dicendum est*'.[55]

I do not know if the comparison to the figures of *negotiorum gestio* and *mandatum* implies that also with regard to these operations Paulus represented a coexistence between ethical moment and legal perspective (that is, if for the jurist *"officium impedit"* also the abandonment of the agreement undertaken or of the task assumed) or if this comparison had been thought by Paulus as limited to the distinction between *nuda voluntas* and subsequent *necessitas*. In any case, the overall discourse on commodatum shows an emphasis on the ethical profile in the focalization – take note – not of the (simple) dogmatic configuration of a contract but of its concrete juridical regime and of the related instruments of protection proposed in the praetorian edict. When we consider that in the corresponding version of the Basilika (Bas. 13.1.17), alt-

---

[53] D. 25.7.1.3: *Si qua in patroni fuit concubinatu, deinde filii esse coepit vel in nepotis, vel contra, non puto eam recte facere, quia prope nefaria est huiusmodi coniunctio, et ideo huiusmodi facinus prohibendum est.* For other uses in the same perspective, cf. Ulp. 18 *ad Sab.*, D. 7.1.13.8: '… *si balineum sit in domo usibus dominicis solitum vacare in intima parte domus vel inter diaetas amoenas, non recte nec ex boni viri arbitratu facturum, si id locare coeperit, ut publice lavet*'; Ulp. 80 *ad ed.*, D. 50.16.73: '*Haec verba in stipulatione posita 'eam rem recte restitui' fructus continent: 'recte' enim verbum pro viri boni arbitrio est*'; Ulp. 1 *de off. procons.*, D. 1.16.4.4: '*Recte et ordine faciet, si edictum decessori suo miserit significetque, qua die fines sit ingressurus*'; nonché Gai. 2 *fideicomm.*, D. 36.1.65.10: '*Si vero nominis ferendi condicio est, quam praetor exigit, recte quidem facturus videtur, si eam expleverit: nihil enim male est, honesti hominis nomen adsumere* …'.

[54] "The finale is a tribute to the almost paraenetic morality": thus Cancelli, *s.v.* 'Ufficio', (n. 40) 613.

[55] The reference to *iudicium contrarium*, as stated above (§ 2), in the classical original had to be preceded, with all likelihood, by the mention of a further legal reaction to the reprehensible behaviour of the mandator.

hough completely lacking reference to *officium* (and to *beneficium*), the discourse maintains an incisive clarity on the technical-juridical level,[56] what stands out even more is the peculiar argumentative option and the entire direction assumed by Paulus, i.e. to have placed the illustration of the functioning of *iudicium contrarium commodati* in the perspective of the coexistence of the legal dimension and the moral dimension. Together with the elements mentioned above (§ 3), i.e. the use of *'officium'* in a 'categorial' function (in this passage as in D. 17.1.1.4), the *hapax legomenon* of the finding of *'officiose'* and the consideration of *officium* as an interest protected by the *interdictum De homine libero exhibendum*, this could be a further suggestion of this jurist's primary attention[57] to the scope of the moral dutifulness of *officium* in the analysis of the legal institutions.

My intervention – programmatically limited to the presence of *officium* in the development of D. 13.6.17.3 – ends here, albeit with the hope of being able in a future study to broaden the field of investigation by verifying the existence of further signs and profiles of Paulus's sensibility and attention to the ethical perspectives related (or relatable) to the legal process.[58]

---

[56] Bas. 71615 'Ο κιχρῶν ὀφείλει, εἴτι βούλεται, συμφωνεῖν ἐν ἀρχῇ· μεθὸ γὰρ χρήσει, οὐ δύναται πρὸ καιροῦ ἀφαιρεῖσθαι τὸ χρησθέν. Ἴσως γὰρ ἔχρησάς μοι πτυχτὴν εἰς τὸ ἐν αὐτῇ προσγράψαι μοι τὸν χρεώστην μου, ἢ ξύλαι εἰς ὑπόρθωσιν. Εἰ δὲ καὶ ἐν εἰδήσει αὐτὰ ἐπίψογα παράσχῃς, ἐνέχῃ τῇ κατὰ τῶν ἐν χρήσει λαμβανόντων ἀγωγῇ. Καὶ ὁ ἀρξάμενος γὰρ τὰ τοῦ ἀπόντος διοικεῖν οὐκ ἀζημίως αὐτὰ καταλιμπάνει· εἰ μὴ γὰρ αὐτὸς διῴκησεν, ἴσως ἂν ἕτερος διῴκησε. καὶ τὴν ἐντολὴν ἑκουσίως μὲν ὑποδέχεταί τις, ἐξ ἀνάγκης δὲ πληροῖ' (transl. by Heimbach: *Qui commodat, ab initio, si velit, pacisci debet: postquam enim commodavit, ante tempus definitum auferre rem commodatam non potest: fortasse enim pugillares mihi commodasti, ut in eis debitor meus mihi caveret, vel tigna ad fulcimentum. Nam et si sciens ea vitiosa commodaveris, commodati actione teneris. Nam et qui absentis negotia gerere incohavit, impune ea non deserit: nisi enim ille gessisset, alius fortasse gesturus erat. Etiam mandatum sponte quis suscipit, necessario autem implet*). The striking defleshing of Paul's text is due to the fact that, according to the normal provenance of the Greek versions of the Digest fragments collected in the Basilika, this text also had to derive from the *summa* of the Anonymus (cf., for all, J.H.A. Lokin, Van der Wal, *Historiae iuris graeciromani delineatio* [Groningen 1985] 82).

[57] As for the classical jurist – in my opinion, Gaius, as I have mentioned – author of the text preserved in I. 2.23.1 on the legal recognition of *fideicommissa* (*supra*, § 3), the fact that he has set his discourse in terms of the contrast between two historical phases does not allow us to know if '*tantum pudore … continebantur*' implies that, with regard to the more mature regime of the institution, now accompanied by processual protection, he too, like Paulus regarding commodatum, represented a coexistence between the two dimensions, that of *pudor/officium* and the legal one.

[58] Cf. for now, some remarks on the point, Mantello, 'Un'etica' (n. 3) 162 ff.

APPENDIX*

[p. 189] Said in a less elliptical way, *mores* are the customs or overall behaviours that characterize an individual (therefore, external and objectively observable data), but understood as external reflections or results of inner predispositions, solicitations, evaluations of the individual, which, in turn, may or may not conform to meta-positive values developed by the culture to which the person belongs as *virtutes* (*iustitia, aequitas, fides, pudor, pietas, humanitas*, etc.).

A clear example of the consideration of *mores* as objectivizations of *virtutes* is the full overlap between the two elements found in a passage of *De officiis* (1.45-46): after having said that the examination of *mores* is one of the elements contributing to the choice of the recipients of a *beneficium*, Cicero, in order to specify what this element consists of, exclusively discusses the *virtutes* of the benefactor, to then conclude the discourse with the words: '*Atque haec in moribus*'. Here is the entire passage: *off.* 1.45. *Tertium est propositum, uti in beneficentia dilectus esset dignitatis; in quo et mores eius erunt spectandi, in quem beneficium conferetur, et animus erga nos et communitas ac societas vitae et ad nostras utilitates officia ante collata.* 46. *Quoniam autem vivitur non cum perfectis hominibus planeque sapientibus, sed cum iis, in quibus praeclare agitur, si sunt simulacra virtutis, etiam hoc intellegendum puto, neminem omnino esse neglegendum, in quo aliqua significatio virtutis appareat, colendum autem esse ita quemque maxime, ut quisque maxime virtutibus his lenioribus erit ornatus, modestia, temperantia, hac ipsa, de qua multa iam dicta sunt, iustitia. Nam fortis animus et magnus in homine non perfecto nec sapiente ferventior plerumque est, illae virtutes bonum virum videntur potius attingere. Atque haec in moribus*'.

It is in the light of this overlap between behaviours (*mores*) and virtues, of which the behaviours are an expression, that, for example, the same Cicero (*Lael.* 19) finds it natural to define who the '*boni viri*' are from the point of view of observation of the conduct in which the possession of the virtues is manifested: '*Qui ita segerunt, ita vivunt, ut eorum probetur fides, integritas, aequitas, liberalitas, nec sit in eis ulla*

---

* On various points dealt with in this Appendix, cf., more extensively, G. Falcone, *La definizione di obligatio, tra diritto e morale. Appunti didattici* (Torino 2017) *passim*.

cupiditas, libido, audacia, sintque magna constantia, [...] *hos viros bonos* [...], *ut habiti sunt, sic etiam appellandos putemus* ...'.

Regarding the fact that *virtutes* determine the individual's behaviours (*mores*) since they have been accommodated by his inner *habitus* and thus direct his will, it is sufficient to refer to a notation such as that of Sen. *epist.* 95.57 '*Actio recta non erit nisi recta fuerit voluntas; ab hac enim est actio. Rursus voluntas non erit recta nisi habitus animi rectus fuerit; ab hoc enim est voluntas. Habitus porro animi non erit in optimo nisi totius vitae leges perceperit* ...' (that the syntagm '*leges vitae*' alludes to virtues is clear from the preceding statements in §§ 55-56), or to the exchange between virtue-*fides* and *voluntas* in two passages of *De beneficiis* pertaining to the *officium* of restitution of the *beneficium*: if in *ben.* 5.23.1 Seneca states that "the *fides* of some people weakens in view of the restitution of the *beneficium*", in *ben.* 5.25.6, he expresses the same concept with the words '*Inest interim animis voluntas bona, sed torpet* ...'.

[p. 189] As well as in relation to the profile of processual coercibility, the awareness of a clear alterity between the legal sphere and the moral sphere of *officia* is explicitly attested from the point of view of the "source" of the dutifulness. Cf. Sen. *de ira* 2.28.1: *Si uolumus aequi rerum omnium iudices esse, hoc primum nobis persuadeamus, neminem nostrum esse sine culpa; hinc enim maxima indignatio oritur: 'nihil peccaui' et 'nihil feci'. Immo nihil fateris. Indignamur aliqua admonitione aut coercitione nos castigatos, cum illo ipso tempore peccemus, quod adicimus malefactis adrogantiam et contumaciam.* 2. *Quis est iste qui se profitetur omnibus legibus innocentem? Vt hoc ita sit, quam angusta innocentia est ad l e g e m bonum esse! Quanto latius officiorum patet quam iuris regula! Quam multa pietas humanitas liberalitas iustitia fides exigunt, quae omnia extra publicas tabulas sunt!* '

Seneca contrasts '*regula officiorum*' and '*regula iuris*', at the same time assuming '*regula*' as a prescriptive indication and as a criterion on the basis of which to evaluate and judge the action of the individual (for other examples of Seneca's use of the term '*regula*', see the following passages: *ben.* 3.11.3: '... *legem dicimus iusti iniustique regulam esse* ...'; *ben.* 7.2.1-2: '... *sine ulla mora veniat illa turpis honestique distinctio. Sciat nec malum esse ullum nisi turpe nec bonum nisi honestum; hac regula vitae opera distribuat; ad hanc legem et agat cuncta et exigat miserrimosque mortalium iudicet*'; *epist.* 95.39: '*Putemus aliquem facere quod oportet: non faciet adsidue, non faciet aequaliter; nesciet enim qure faciat. Aliqua vel casu vel exercitatione exibunt recta, sed non erit in manu regula ad quam exigantur, cui credat recta esse quae fecit. Non promittet se talem in perpetuum qui bonus casu est*'). In particular, Seneca maintains that, if we evaluate things according to the criterion of *officia*, we cannot necessarily say that we are innocent in the same way in which we can say it with respect to *ius*: in fact, the criterion of evaluation of *officia* is more rigorous than the criterion of *ius*, since values such as *pietas*, *humanitas*, *liberalitas*, *iustitia* and *fides* require behaviours that remain outside the prescriptions of positive laws. Hence, this source clearly assumes the scope of *officia* (and the above-mentioned values) as 'non-juridical', as 'other' than *ius* and as opposed to it. Moreover, the fact that Seneca exposits these concepts and this contrast between *regula officiorum* and *regula iuris* with absolute naturalness, taking them for granted and as immediately recognizable by readers, demonstrates that this must have been a widespread concept: since *De ira* was written in the 40s of the first century CE, it follows that, with regard at least to the source of dutifulness-*officium* (meta-positive values, and not prescriptions of a particular legal system: *leges*, *publicae tabulae*), awareness of the opposition between *officium* and *ius* had to be rooted in Roman society as late as the first century BCE.

Evaluation of the passage as clear testimony of a contrast between the moral sphere and the legal sphere is not affected by the circumstance, reported by Mantello, *Un'etica* (n. 3) 161, that Seneca seems to juxtapose, rather than counterpose, positive decrees and the sphere of *officium*, affirming that '*leges a scelere deterrent, praecepta in officio adhortantur*' (*epist*. 94.37), nor by the circumstance that Seneca alludes (in the wake of the rest of a long tradition of Platonic ancestry) to an educational function of *leges* (*ibid*.: '*leges quoque proficiunt ad bonos mores*'). The same can be said for the fact that "in Seneca's thought *regula* tends to be synonymous with *lex*" (Mantello cites, as an example, the words of *ben*. 3.11.3 ['*… legem dicimus iusti iniustique regulam esse …*']); in fact, in the passage of *De ira*, '*regula*' explicitly refers to both *officia* and *ius*. I agree instead with this scholar in excluding a representation, for this contrast, in terms of separation between "normative systems".

[Note 26] With specific reference to *pudor*, we can add to the general considerations the concrete textual data offered by Caes. *bell. civ*. 3.60.2 '*… idque ita esse cum ex aliorum obiectationibus tum etiam ex domestico iudicio atque animi conscientia intellegebant. quo pudore adducti …*'. I think that it is not too risky to talk about "internal forum" in regard to this text. However, it is a text that warns us to broaden our gaze beyond the production of Cicero and Seneca when we wish to reconstruct the effective perception that, in Roman republican and high imperial society, there were mechanisms and values related to the scope of dutifulness.

In the same way, with regard to the tradition of the modern age (dealt with by Fiori, *Vir bonus* (n. 26) 141 ss., in a chapter which – consistently with the idea that in Roman thought the preconditions for the establishment of a distinction between law and morality would be lacking – is entitled "Ethics and law: the interpreter's lenses" and which, in the same order of ideas, opens with a section entitled "Today we are all Kantians"), we must not lose sight that, alongside specific jusnaturalist theoretical-systematic constructions such as those of Heinecke's *Elementa iuris naturae et gentium*, according to which "legal dutifulness [...] is not characterized by coercibility but by the external provenance of obligations, whose *auctor* is primarily God" or of Wolff's *Ius naturae methodo scientifica pertractatum*, according to which "the *obligatio interna* concerns the conscience and the *externa* the interpersonal relationships, and the distinction between coercible and non-coercible obligation is set within the latter" (so Fiori, *Vir bonus* (n. 26) 177 note 135, who quotes both theories to argue that not even with the jusnaturalists subsequent to Thomasius would there be a true distinction between law and morality), a notation such as, for example, that expressed by Vinnen (moreover, prior to the construction of the two above-mentioned authors) in the commentary on the Institutes of Justinian provides a very different indication. The Dutch jurist, in the introductory section of the commentary on the Title concerning obligations (*In quattuor libros Institutionum imperialium commentarius*, Venetiis 1783, t. II, p. 80), after having enunciated the traditional tripartition between *'obligationes naturales'*, *'obligationes civiles'* and *'obligationes mixtae'*, illustrates the figure of *'obligatio naturalis'* with the help of Paulus's words (D. 50.17.84.1) *'Is natura debet, quem iure gentium dare oportet'*, specifying: "Haec obligatio conscientias quidem hominis d e v i n c i t , cum sit vinculum naturae et aequitatis, *dict. leg.* 95. § 3 [in reality, § 4: this is D. 46.3.95.4] *de solut. cit. leg.* 84. § 1. *de regul. jur.* quo loco verbo *oportere* quaedam *necessitas moralis* significatur: in foro tamen exteriori & iure civili eam efficaciam non habet, ut actionem aut exactionem producat". Regardless of the reliability or not of the attribution of Paulus's words to the sphere of non-coercible natural obligations, what he observes here is the reference to *conscientia* and the use of the qualification *'moralis'* in relation to the fact that the natural obligation "*devincit conscientias*" without being relevant to the "external forum" and to the law, not producing processual coercibility. These affirmations, already significant per se, are all the more so since the coordination between processual coercibility and the sphere of 'law' were expressed by Vinnen also in the commentary on the words '*necessitate adstringimur*' of the definition of *obligatio* (p. 82): "*quae necessitas in eo consistit, ut nisi obligatus praestet id, quod debetur, jure judicioque experiri cum eo hoc nomine liceat, invitumque ad solutionem compellere*". On the other hand, Vinnen had introduced (p. 80) the above-mentioned tripartite division of the *oo.* with a statement that, to include all three categories, eliminated the *necessitas*-element ("*Omnis obligatio vinculum quodam juris est, quo adstringimur ad aliquid praestandum*"): now, the fact that this last element returns instead (albeit mitigated by '*quaedam*') in the description of *obligatio naturalis* makes even more evident the author's intention to establish a clear contrast between a compulsion binding only by means of *conscientia* and processually incoercible, and thus '*moralis*', and a coercible compulsion, characteristic of law. Well, the fact that Vinnen expresses himself naturally in those terms, without lingering on further clarifications, suggests that a connection such as the one between *conscientia* and '*moralis*' conceptualization and an opposition between the 'moral' dimension and 'ius' as an opposition between non-coercibility and processual coercibility must have formed part of the conceptual armamentary of the jurists of the time.

[Note 51] At the end of D. 47.2.55.1 ('*unde et is furti tenetur, qui ideo rem amovet, ut eam alii donet*'), Gaius compares the hypothesis of commodatum with the case of subtraction of someone else's thing, which someone has performed for the purpose of making a donation, acquiring the donee – it is the implied common denominator – as a *debitor* who has the duty to reciprocate. The naturalness with which Gaius represents the fulfilment of an act of liberality as a source of a moral duty to reciprocate on the part of the accipient (who then, explicitly with regard to the commodatum, is *sic et simpliciter* qualified as *debitor*) indicates that it must have been an obvious point of view well present in the interpretative procedure of the jurists. In my opinion, this allows us to interpret with more confidence the testimony of Ulpian preserved in Ulp. 15 *ad ed.* D. 5.3.25.11: *Consuluit senatus bonae fidei possessoribus, ne in totum damno adficiantur, sed in id dumtaxat teneantur, in quo locupletiores facti sunt. quemcumque igitur sumptum fece-*

rint ex hereditate, si quid dilapidauerunt perdiderunt, dum re sua se abuti putant, non praestabunt. nec si donauerint locupletiores facti uidebuntur, quam uis ad remunerandum sibi aliquem naturaliter obligauerunt. plane si ἀντίδωρα acceperunt, dicendum est eatenus locupletiores factos, quatenus acceperunt: uelut genus quoddam hoc esset permutationis'. Indeed, the text has been considered spurious (of postclassical or Justinian production) precisely in the part that interests us here, i.e. in the passage in which it is stated that those who have made donations "*ad remunerandum sibi aliquem naturaliter obligaverunt*" (I refer the reader, for historiographical indications in this sense, to the recent work by L. Di Cintio, *Natura debere. Sull'elaborazione giurisprudenziale romana in tema di obbligazione naturale* (Catania 2009) 163 ss.; for her part, the author maintains the genuineness of the text, albeit with arguments and a perspective not coinciding with the interpretation I am proposing here). However, the fact that the passage in question evidently falls within the same order of ideas manifested – above all with dry determination – by Gaius, according to whom the donation determines in favour of the donor an *'adquirere sibi debitorem'*, seems to me to permit a direct attribution to Ulpian. As for the recourse to the conceptual guise "*naturaliter obligare*" to express the idea of making it obligatory to reciprocate – in accordance with an *officium reddendae gratiae* – it could derive from the implementation of a traditional representation, elaborated since Cicero, which attributed to nature the *officium* itself and the *virtutes* that govern its observance (cf., for example, *inv.* 2.161: from *naturae ius* derives *gratia*, in which are contained the *memoria officiorum* and the *remunerandi voluntas*; *fin.* 2.58-59: the virtues that lead to *'officium sequi'* derive from *natura*; *fin.* 3.22; 23; 4.18: the *officia* originate from *principia naturae*; *fin.* 5, 66: life corresponding to *honestum* and virtues can be considered *recta et honesta et constans et naturae congruens; rep.* 3.33: *vera lex* is the *recta ratio naturae congruens ..., quae vocet ad officium iubendo; leg.* 1.43: *voluntas referendae gratiae* is related to *natura; Lael.* 49-50: *benevolentia*, that is the sentiment underlying the reciprocal exchange of *officia*, comes from *natura*; *off.* 1.146: a reprehensible attitude is indicated as discrepant *'ab officio naturaque'*; on these and other sources of similar scope, see Falcone, *'Obligatio'* (n. 3) 148 ss. note 402): an implementation which also tends to confirm the genuineness of the passage, when one thinks, for example, of the well-known presence in the Ulpianean documentation of the subject of *aequitas naturalis*, also rich in cultural derivations dating back to Cicero. If its genuineness is assumed, the text in question would reveal the presence also in Ulpian's reasoning of the non-juridical element of the dutifulness of *reddere gratiam* in the perspective of a dialectic between *officium* and 'juridical', but in the opposite perspective with respect to Gaius. In fact, the latter justifies a 'juridical' solution, the sanction of an act as a *furtum*, arguing not from the juridical construction of the act (which would not have involved the recognizability of *lucrum* given the nature of liberality of the act itself), but from the 'non-juridical' configuration of the act itself as *beneficium*, obligatory in relation to the *officium reddendi gratiae*. On the other hand, Ulpian's standpoint in excluding that the *naturaliter obligare* to reciprocate the *beneficium*-donation involves an enrichment in favour of the possessors of good faith of *hereditas*, with consequent patrimonial responsibility, expresses a split between a significance, on the moral level of *officium*, of the duty to reciprocate and its insignificance on the level of law.

Chapter 9

ROMAN JURISTS AND THE EMPIRE: HISTORY AND INTERPRETATION

Valerio Marotta

SUMMARY: 1. The legal lexicon of dominion. – 2. The territorial dimension of power. – 3. *Communis patria*. – 4. Fictions of ubiquity and *ius publicum* of Late Antiquity.

1. The legal lexicon of dominion

It is difficult to reconcile the two different perspectives mentioned in the subtitle of this contribution. There is no doubt that history and interpretation are always related to each other; however, historical reality and the reality of historical representation – as it has been defined by many generations of scholars based on different criteria over time – cannot be completely framed by my camera lens. Beyond the metaphor, herein I will be limited to proposing some examples, without any pretence of a rational connection. However, I will avoid using the term Empire as a sort of container in which to place different political institutions, exclusively united by the same name.

Scholars of Roman law have not given this subject the attention which, despite the sources, it would have deserved. In a short article, it is not possible to consider most, if not almost all, of the historiography. However, I must mention one work that is, at least in my opinion, more important than the others: *Stipendium vel tributum* [1] by Francesco Grelle, a model, perhaps insuperable, of research on legal-political thought of the Imperial period.

Grelle underlined that the nature and meaning of taxation were at the centre of a debate between the Antonines and the Severans, in which the jurists – unlike many of their contemporaries, who saw in the fulfilment of tax obligations a typical aspect of active participation in the Roman imperial community – continued constantly to relate it

[1] *Stipendium vel tributum. L'imposizione fondiaria nelle dottrine giuridiche del II e del III secolo* (Napoli 1963).

to the authority of the people and the prince over the provinces [2] and thus to victory and to subjugation of the defeated. [3] Yet, the negative connotations of the provincial territory go far beyond the mere tax regime. [4] The *praedia stipendiaria* [5] and – it must be assumed – those of *civitates liberae*, which could perhaps be called *iuris peregrini*, [6] were unsuitable for most of the sacred activities, [7] they were not alienable by means of *mancipatio*, [8] they were not subject to

---

[2] Grelle, *Stipendium* (n. 1) 65 ff.

[3] Authentic regularity can also be appreciated in the thinking of ancient grammarians on the term *provincia*: the unbreakable connection between victory, defeat and subjugation. Cf. Fest., 253 Lindsay *provinciae appellantur quod populus Romanus eas prouicit, id est ante uicit*. See F. Grelle, 'Provinciali e sudditi fra Augusto e Vespasiano: le dottrine giuridiche' (1990), now in Id., *Diritto e società nel mondo romano* (L. Fanizza ed.) (Roma 2004) part. 333 f.

[4] F. Grelle, 'L'appartenenza del suolo provinciale nell'analisi di Gaio 2.7 e 2.21' (1990) now in Id., *Diritto e società* (n. 3) part. 310.

[5] As well as those subjected to *tributum*. On this distinction (*stipendium / tributum*) see F. De Martino, *Storia della costituzione romana*[2], IV.2 (Napoli 1975) 868 ff., esp. 877 ff. F. Mercogliano, T. Spagnuolo Vigorita, *s.v. Tributi (storia) a. Diritto romano*, in ED. XLV (Milano 1992) 85-104, esp. 98 f., with other references; E. Lo Cascio, 'La struttura fiscale dell'Impero romano', in Id., *Il princeps e il suo impero. Studi di storia amministrativa e finanziaria romana* (Bari 2000) 177-203; J. France, ' "Tributum" et "stipendium". La politique fiscale de l'empereur romain', in RHD-FE 84 (2006) 1-17.

[6] A.H.M. Jones, 'In eo solo dominium Populi Romani est vel Caesaris' (1941), in Id., *Studies in Roman Government and Law* (Oxford 1960) part. 148. Cf., in this regard, also Plin. min. *ep*. 10.50 *Potes, mi Secunde carissime, sine sollicitudine religionis, si loci positio uidetur hoc desiderare, aedem Matris Deum transferre in eam quae est accommodatior; nec te moueat, quod lex dedicationis nulla reperitur, cum solum peregrinae ciuitatis capax non sit dedicationis, quae fit nostro iure*. However, I consider to be valid the arguments against this solution presented by F. De Martino, *Storia della costituzione romana*[2], II (Napoli 1973) 353 ff.

[7] Gai. *inst*. 2.7 *Sed in prouinciali solo placet plerisque solum religiosum non fieri, quia in eo solo dominium populi Romani est uel Caesaris, nos autem possessionem tantum et usumfructum habere uidemur; utique tamen, etiamsi non sit religiosum, pro religioso habetur: item quod in prouinciis non ex auctoritate populi Romani consecratum est, proprie sacrum non est, tamen pro sacro habetur.*

[8] Gai. *inst*. 2.46. This does not mean that *mancipatio* was not used, at times also by *peregrini* (it is sufficient to recall the famous *emptio domus*, mentioned in *Fontes Iuris Romani Antejustiniani*[2], III *Negotia*, n. 90, as well as the others referred to in nos. 87, 88, 89). In these negotiational documents (dated to around the middle of the second century CE), the formulary *emit mancipioque accepit* ("he bought and he acquired"), the signing by at least five witnesses (at times Romans, at times all foreigners, at times *cives* and *peregrini*), and other elements that recall *mancipatio*, are used in deeds of purchase of slaves between Romans and foreigners and be-

usucaption.[9] Furthermore, as Cicero pointed out in *Pro Flacco*,[10] they,

tween foreigners. In the document containing the deed of purchase of a house (*emptio domus*), a *peregrina* and a Roman used the formulary of donation for the alienation of half of a house, not susceptible, in principle, either to prescription or to transfer by means of *mancipatio*, because it was located in a region (*Alburnus Maior* in the *vicus Pirustarum*) subject, like the other provincial *fundi*, to land tax. It is extremely unlikely that the *ius Italicum* was attributed to *Alburnius Maior*, as conjectured by M.R. Cataudella, 'Società e diritto nell'Africa romana. 'Ius italicum': aspetti e riflessioni', in A. Mastino (ed.), *L'Africa romana. Atti del IV convegno di studio* (Sassari, 12-14 dicembre 1986) (Sassari 1987) 131 f. In this waxed tablet (*Fontes Iuris Romani Antejustiniani*², III Negotia, n. 90) from Transylvania, the *mancipio dans* was a *peregrina*: so that, in any case, by means of the *mancipatio*, nothing could have been transferred to the purchaser that was more than was owned by the alienor: cf., in this regard, Ulp. 29 *ad Sab.*, D. 41.1.20pr. *Traditio <Mancipatio> nihil amplius transferre debet uel potest ad eum qui accipit, quam est apud eum qui tradit <mancipio dat>*. In this text, in place of the term *mancipatio*, the compilers interpolated the word *traditio*. Through the *mancipatio*, the person who gives by mancipium cannot and must not alienate more than he possesses to the purchaser. Moreover, it should be borne in mind that there never existed (nor could ever have existed) an ownership *iuris gentium*, i.e. an ownership that could be considered common to Romans and *peregrini*. And this sufficiently explains – allow me this trivial observation – why the seller's obligations did not include also that of alienating the ownership of the thing sold to the buyer.

[9] Gai. *inst.* 2.21.

[10] Cic. *pro Flacc.* 79-80 *mitto quod aliena, mitto quod possessa per uim, mitto quod conuicta ab Apollonidensibus, mitto quod a Pergamenis repudiata, mitto etiam quod a nostris magistratibus in integrum restituta, mitto quod nullo iure neque re neque possessione tua; illud quaero, sint ne ista praedia censui censendo, habeant ius ciuile, sint necne sint mancipi, subsignari apud aerarium aut apud censorem possint.* See also Fest. 50 Lindsay *censui censendo agri proprie appellantur, qui emi et venire iure ciuili possunt.* Interesting for other aspects, Liv. 43.14.5-6 *censores ut eam rem adiuuarent, ita in contione edixerunt: legem censui censendo dicturos esse ut praeter commune omnium ciuium ius iurandum haec adiurarent: 'tu minor annis sex et quadraginta es, tu que ex edicto C. Claudi Ti. Semproni censorum ad dilectum prodisti, et quotienscumque dilectus erit + qua + hi censores magistratum habebunt, si miles factus non eris, in dilectum prodibis?'*. See, first of all, M. Kaser, *Eigentum und Besitz im älteren römischen Recht*² (Köln-Graz 1956) 174-180, esp. 179 f. Here, I will merely mention that the interpretation by P. Bonfante, 'Forme primitive ed evoluzione della proprietà romana (*res mancipi* e *res nec mancipi*)', (published in 1888-89 with the title *Res mancipi e nec mancipi*, Roma) in Id., *Scritti giuridici varii*, vol. II (Torino 1918) 60 and note 2 of Cic., *Pro Flacc.* 80 is certainly unfounded: in fact, in this context, Cicero – unlike what Bonfante wrote – does not at all contrast the *agri mancipi* with the *agri provinciales* or *vectigales*, since the land situated in the city of Apollonis, the subject of the orator's specific mention, did not fall within any of the above-mentioned three categories. In truth, this city was *libera*, i.e. not subject to provincial regulations. Hence, what is relevant, from Cicero's perspective, is the fact that the property claimed by Decianus from Apollonis was not a *res mancipi*: consequently, at least implicitly, Cicero – unlike what Bonfante wrote –

at least in principle, were not registered by the censors and their collaborators, so as to appear uninfluential, as *res nec mancipi*, for the purpose of determining the class and tribe of each member of the community. In short, their extraneousness to the city's organization explains why the *veteres* perhaps found that *[soli Italici nexum] esse, prouincialis soli nexum non e[sse]*. If we accept a hypothesis of reconstruction of Gaius's text (shared by many scholars) that would seem to coincide with the legal content of Cicero's *Pro Flacco*,[11] in the Imperial period this same dichotomy was advanced using a nomenclature different from the one in use around the middle of the second century BCE: while 'the Italic land' was to be considered '*màncipi*', the 'provincial' territory was to be considered '*non màncipi*'.[12]

Precisely because, according to Cicero (*Pro Flacco*, 80), for the purposes of assigning each *civis* to one of the five classes, only *res mancipi* could be taken into consideration in the census operations,[13] I consider

---

wished to contrast, looking at *ius civile* (an expression that should be interpreted here in the broader sense of *ius civitatis*), the things given by mancipium with all the others, i.e. those not given by mancipium: and only the former are, properly speaking, *res censui censendo*. Also falling into the same misunderstanding as Bonfante is F. Gallo, *Studi sulla distinzione tra 'res mancipi' e 'nec mancipi'* (Torino 1958) now in (with a *nota di lettura* by F. Zuccotti) in RDR 4 (2004) 14 note 10. But see De Martino, *Storia della costituzione romana*² (n. 6) 353 f., who appropriately recalls that Cicero's text concerned a free city in the *provincia* of *Asia* and thus a community that had preserved its law and its legal system.

[11] And in particular (*supra*, note 10), in Cic. *pro Flacc.* 80 the words (…) *sint necne sint mancipi*, (…).

[12] The caution, which I adopted in the text, is amply justified by the fact that Gaius's passage, as it was presented, is the result of a conjecture of modern interpreters, since the Verona palimpsest, in these lines, has a large gap: Gai. *inst.* 2.27 *Praeterea admonendi sumus, quod ueteres dicebant soli Italici nexum esse, provincialis soli nexum non esse, eandem habere significationem: solum Italicum mancipi est, prouinciale nec mancipi est. aliter enim ueteri lingua actus appellari solebat, qui nostra est mancipatio.* See the commentary by M. David, H.L.W. Nelson, *Gai institutionum Commentarii* IV. *Mit philologischen Kommentar herausgegeben. Kommentar* (Leiden 1960) 251-253, in part. 252, where other interpretational conjectures are advanced: *Praeterea admonendi sumus, quod ueteres dicebant soli Italici nexum esse, prouincialis soli nexum non esse, hanc habere significationem: solum Italicum mancipi esse, prouinciale nec mancipi esse. Aliter enim ueteri lingua actus uocatur, et quod illis nexus, idem nobis est mancipatio* (Beseler, Bonfante, Kübler, Bizoukides, De Zulueta) oppure *admonendi sumus secundum priscam linguam Italici soli nexum esse, prouincialis soli nexum non esse. Secundum nostram autem significationem solum Italicum mancipi est, prouinciale nec mancipi* (...) (Kniep).

[13] Cf. Cic. *pro Flacc.* 79-80 and Fest. 50 Lindsay (*supra*, n. 10): a summary in C. Nicolet, *Il mestiere di cittadino in Roma antica* (Ital. transl. Roma 1980) 64 ff., in

it plausible that this is why Gaius called them *pretiosiores* in a brief mention outside of the *sedes materiae.*[14] In my opinion, there is not, in the use of this adjective, any vague reminiscence of Rome's pre-civic past, when things of particular economic usefulness for the *gens* and its leaders would have been considered such.[15] In reality, there is here the

---

part. 89 f., 91 f.; L.P. Eberle, '*Law, Empire and the Making of Roman Estates in the Provinces During tha Late Republic*', in Critical Analysis of Law, 3.1 (2016) 50-69, 54 ss.On the *census*, see E. Lo Cascio, '*Il 'census' a Roma e la sua evoluzione dall'età 'serviana' alla prima età imperiale*', in Mefra 113.2 (2001) 565-603, in part. 598; as well as by the same author, 'Roman Census Figures in the Second Century BC and the Property Qualification of the Fifth Class', in L. De Ligt, S.J. Northwood (eds.), *People, Land and Politics: demographic developments and the Transformation of Roman Italy 300 BC-AD 14* (Leiden 2008) 239-256. On the *census* in the provinces, see by the same author 'Census provinciali, imposizione fiscale e amministrazioni cittadine nel Principato', Id. (n. 5) 205-219.

[14] Gai. *inst.* 1.192 *Sane patronorum et parentum legitimae tutelae uim aliquam habere intelleguntur eo, quod hi neque ad testamentum faciendum neque ad res mancipi alienandas neque ad obligationes suscipiendas auctores fieri coguntur, praeterquam si magna causa alienandarum rerum mancipi obligationisque suscipiendae interueniat. Eaque omnia ipsorum causa constituta sunt, ut quia ad eos intestatarum mortuarum hereditates pertinent, neque per testamentum excludantur ab hereditate, neque alienatis pretiosioribus rebus susceptoque aere alieno minus locuples ad eos hereditas perveniat.* Cf. anche Pap. 12 *resp.* Vat. Frg. 259 *Item. Mulier sine tutoris auctoritate praedium stipendiarium instructum non mortis causa Latino donauerat. Perfectam in praedio ceterisque rebus nec mancipii donationem esse apparuit, seruos autem et pecora, quae collo uel dorso domarentur, usu non capta. Si tamen voluntatem mulier non mutasset, Latino quoque doli profuturam duplicationem respondi; non enim mortis causa capitur quod aliter donatum est, quoniam morte Cincia remouetur.* For a thorough examination of this passage by Papinian and the complex counterpoint *intentio, exceptio, replicatio, duplicatio* which it presupposes, see G. Papa, *La 'replicatio'. Profili processuali e diritto sostanziale* (Napoli 2009) in part. 217 ff., with other references.

[15] Or also for the *pater* and his *familia*: thus Gallo (n. 10) 1-121, in part. 17-21. It is not important in this context to take a position in this regard, although I think that some preference should be given to the hypothesis of F. De Visscher, "Mancipium' e 'res mancipi'", in Id., *Nouvelles Études de droit romain* (Paris 1949) 193 ff., who criticized the theory of Bonfante, 'Forme primitive' (n. 10) 1-326. For the Belgian scholar, the *res mancipi* were those typical of the dominion of the situation of the *paterfamilias*, called *mancipium* (hence, dominion connected not only to the needs of agriculture, but also to those, for example, of war). For my part, I will merely state that Gaius's observation (*inst.* 1.192), characterizing *res mancipi* as *pretiosiores*, cannot be taken exclusively in its literal meaning (the most valuable things, for example), nor can a vague, uncertain historical reminiscence be understood in it. In other words, in this regard I think that reference must necessarily be made to a more precise institutional and political context. As for the distinction between *res mancipi* and *res nec mancipi*, the perspective now introduced by G. Nicosia, 'La nascita postdecemvirale della 'mancipatio' e quella ancora posteriore

allusion – perhaps through an implicit reference to the mythical Servian constitution of Rome [16] and to the timocratic traditions of the *urbs* – to those *res* with which, precisely because they were the object of *mancipium* (or, in Gaius's lexicon, [17] of *dominium*), the *dignitas* of all the

della distinzione tra 'res mancipi' e 'res nec mancipi'', in AUPA 59 (2016) 303-316, in part. 314 ff., seems to me particularly fertile.

[16] In this way, as is obvious, I certainly do not subscribe to the famous reconstruction of the otherwise excellent PH.E. Huschke, *Die Verfassung des Konigs Servius Tullius* (Heidelberg 1938) the object, at the time, of the harsh sarcasm of R. von Jhering, *Serio e faceto nella giurisprudenza* (It. transl. Firenze 1954) in part. 211 f., nor to the hypothesis formulated by R. von Mayr, *Römische Rechtsgeschichte*. I.2. *Das Privatrecht* (Berlin-Leipzig 1912) 39-40, which attributes the creation of this category exclusively to the needs of the census and thus to the Servian constitution. In Bonfante, 'Forme primitive' (n. 10) 55-62, there is a complete review of those theories that wished to find "a reason for the origin of *res mancipi* in their relationship with the 'State' regarding the establishment of the census, taxes and military service". Scholars adhering to this line of thinking include Th. Mommsen, *Römisches Staatsrecht*³, II (Leipzig 1887) 388 ff. It is also essential to underline that Bonfante himself (p. 60) wrote that "against all the authors who derive the distinction (*scil*: between *res mancipi* and *nec mancipi*) from the relationship of *res mancipi* with the State and with the census, the only objection is that the theory truly lacks positive arguments, since the two passages of Cicero and Festus (Cic. *pro Flacc.* 79-80; Fest. 50 Lindsay) are worth very little". However, as mentioned above (note 10), Bonfante's interpretation of these two fundamental testimonies and their consequent reappraisal is based on an incorrect definition of the legal status of the *pólis* of Apollonis in Asia.

[17] Gaius – unlike what occurs in the case of *habere in bonis*, with respect to which he speaks of *duplex dominium* to define the latter's relations with the *dominium ex iure Quiritium* – does not use this term for the *praedia stipendiaria*. This is largely attributable to the fact that, in the perspective of the Antoninian jurist, these *praedia* are *dominium populi Romani vel Caesaris*: *inst.* 2, 7. G.I. Luzzatto, 'La riscossione tributaria in Roma e l'ipotesi della proprietà-sovranità' (1953), in Id., *Scritti minori epigraficie papirologici* (Bologna 1984) 205-241; F. Grelle, 'La signoria del suolo nella Parafrasi di Teofilo' (1966), now in Id., *Diritto e società* (n. 3) 101-112; G. Grosso, 'La condizione del suolo provinciale negli schemi giuridici della giurisprudenza del principato' (1974), now in Id., *Scritti storico-giuridici*. II. *Diritto privato cose e diritti reali* (Torino 2001) 755-766; G.I. Luzzatto, 'Sul regime del suolo nelle province romane. Spunti critici e problematica' (1974), in Id., *Scritti minori* (n. 17) 525-569, in part. 527 ff.; Grelle, 'L'appartenenza del suolo provinciale' (n. 4) 293-312. Without dealing again with the *vexata quaestio* of the distinction between *praedia tributaria* and *stipendiaria* (Gai. *inst.* 2.21), I should underline that for Grelle there is absolute irreducibility of the *dominium populi Romani* to the patrimonialistic schema of public and private property, given that the dominion over the provinces was considered above all as power of extraction and management of economic riches. For Luzzatto, vice versa, this hypothesis, according to which Gaius reasoned in terms of sovereignty outside of privatistic schema, is to be roundly rejected. Giuseppe Grosso reached similar conclusions when he pointed out that,

members of the community was related to the magnitude of their riches, thus assigning to each *civis* the place it was due within a whole perceived as organic and unitary.[18] In this regard, the comparison with two of Tertullian passages, coincident and parallel, presents a further element in support of this conclusion. In effect, the apologist uses an argumentative schema that is not identical but certainly similar to the one used by the Antonine master:

> *ad Nat.* 1.10.23 *Sed enim <agri tri>buto onusti uiliores, hominum capita stipendio censa ign<obiliora> (nam hae sunt captiuitati notae, <poenae>): dei uero, qui magis tr<ibutarii>, magis sancti; immo, qui magis sancti, magis tributarii.*

> *apol.* 13.6 *Sed enim agri tributo onusti uiliores, hominum capita stipendio*

---

rather than to *in bonis habere* (for which Gaius does not hesitate to use the term *dominium*, albeit in a broader sense), in the face of the qualification of *dominium populi vel Caesaris* used by the Antoninian master for the *solum provinciale*, private law generically refers to the concept of *possessio vel usus fructus*. And, in effect, the categories used by Gaius, although *abusive* (when, as in this case, the use of the so-called κατάχρησις is required), undoubtedly refer to the sphere of *ius privatorum*.

[18] See F. Marco Simón, 'Ritual participation and collective identity in the Roman Republic', in F. Marco Simón, F. Pina Polo, J. Remesal Rodríguez (eds.), *Répúblicas y ciudadanos: modelos de partecipación cívica en el Mundo Antiguo* (Barcelona 2006) 153-166. In *pro Flacco*, Cicero, albeit ironically, emphasizes this aspect and reproaches Decianus for wishing to do something grand (*gloriosus*), censusing a vast area of land (that within the boundaries of the *pólis* of Apollonis) together with 130,000 sesterces in cash and the slaves of a certain Amyntas, without doing him – observes the orator – any harm in this way, since the latter continued to possess such slaves. However, at first Amyntas was very afraid in learning that Decianus had registered his slaves as his own. Therefore, he turned to the *iuris consulti*. Their response was to agree with him: if it were sufficient for Decianus to carry out a census of the goods of others in order to make them his own, he would have become extraordinarily rich: Cic. *pro Flacc.* 80 *Uerum esto, gloriosus fuisti, uoluisti magnum agri censeri, et eius agri qui diuidi plebi Romanae non potest. Census es praeterea numeratae pecuniae CXXX. Eam opinor tibi numeratam non esse abs te. Sed hoc omitto. Census es mancipia Amyntae neque huic ullam in eo fecisti iniuriam. Possidet enim ea mancipia Amyntas. Ac primo quidem pertimuit, cum te audisset seruos suos esse censum; rettulit ad iuris consultos. Constabat inter omnis, si aliena censendo Decianus sua facere posset, eum maxima habiturum esse.* It can also be observed that, in the late Republican period, a practice had been imposed – deplored by Cicero – by virtue of which also *res nec mancipi* were sometimes declared to the census: thus Mommsen, *Römisches Staatsrecht*^{3}, II (n. 16) 393. Finally, looking at the period of the Principate, there is no valid reason to conclude that, starting from the censorship of Vespasian and Titus, there would no longer have been a census of the Roman citizens: see F. De Martino, *Storia della costituzione romana*^{2}, IV.1 (Napoli 1974) 481; *Storia della costituzione romana*^{2}, IV.2 (n. 6) 920 f.

censa ignobiliora, nam hae sunt notae captiuitatis; dei uero, qui magis tributarii, magis sancti; immo qui magis sancti, magis tributarii.

Like the fields for which tax is paid – which have less value than those not taxed – the men subject to taxation live in a shoddier condition than Roman citizens[19] (*capita ... ignobiliora*)[20]. Indeed, this is the stigma of the defeated, the *nota* that attests to their subjugation. Vice versa, the higher the tax imposed on the gods, the more they are sacred; or better, the more they are sacred, the more they are subject to taxation.

The discussion presented by Tertullian can assume appreciably different meanings depending on whether the provincial land of the *agri tributo onusti* – subject to appropriation that was private but based on a legal title radically different[21] from the *dominium ex iure Quiritium* – is compared with land of a completely different nature: that is to say, either with lands similar to the *agri Romani* after the concession of *ius Italicum*[22] or more likely – since Carthage (the city of the apologist)

---

[19] The shoddier condition of those subject to the poll tax clearly emerges from a testimony taken from the *Acta martyrum Alexandrinorum*. During the Principate of Claudius, an Alexandrian nobleman, Isidore, referring to the Jews in order to underline their inferiority and at the same time support his claim to exclude them from the exercise of rights inherent in the πολιτεία of Alexandria, expressed himself in this manner: *Acta Isidori <et Lamponis>* C27 (Musurillo) "they do not have the same temperament as the Alexandrians (Ἀλ [εξανδρεύσι] ν ὁμοιοπαθείς), but instead live in the manner of the Egyptians (τρόποι δε Αἰγθπτί[ων ὁμοίοι]). Are they not perhaps on the same level as those who pay the tax (ἴσοι τοῖς φόρον τελούσι)?". See A. Magnani, *Il processo di Isidoro. Roma e Alessandria nel primo secolo* (Bologna-Napoli 2009) 20-22, 41-58, 79-110, with a broad literature. Cf. also, *infra*, note 31.

[20] *Ignobiliores* (*ignobiliora*) indicates the opposite of *nobiliores (nosco). Ignobiliores* are those men who lose or who have never enjoyed any esteem or social dignity. See J.-P. Waltzing, *Commentaire analytique, grammatical et historique de l'Apologétique* (Paris 1984²) 100.

[21] Agennius Urbicus ex Frontino speaks, in this regard, of *alia condicione*: *Grom.*, ed. Lachmann, I, 35, 13 and ff. = Thulin 23, 5 *et stipendiarios <agros> qui nexum non habent, neque possidendo ab alio quaeri possunt; possidentur tamen a priuatis, sed alia condicione; et veneunt, sed nec mancipatio eorum legitima potest esse*. In the expression *nexum habere*, the word *nexum* means the status of the land subjected to the *ius Quiritium* fixed by the XII Tables. These lands were – we could say – fully private property. For a thorough examination of the problem, see O. Behrends, 'Les rapports entre la terminologie gromatique et celle de la jurisprudence classique, leur points de contact et leur indépendence fondamentale: l'exemple de l'oeuvre de Frontin: structure, méthode, vocabulaire', in D. Conso, A. Gonzalez, J.-Y. Guillaumin (eds.), *Les vocabulaires techniques des arpenteurs romains* (Besançon 2005) 210.

[22] However, it is unlikely that, at the time of the composition of the *Ad Nationes*

was, even before the granting of this benefit (almost certainly after 198),[23] a *colonia immunis*,[24] and, since Octavian's new tax deduction of

and the *Apologeticum*, Carthage had already obtained this coveted privilege. In effect, the *Ad nationes* (as emerges from 1.17.4, a passage alluding to the military campaigns conducted by Septimius Severus against Pescennius Niger and Clodius Albinus, with a precise reference to the battle of Lugdunum fought on 19 February 197) was written in the early months of 197. And also the *Apologeticum* is certainly only slightly later than this date. On this point, see C. Moreschini, *Introduzione. Apologeticum*, in Tertulliano, *Opere Apologetiche. Ai Martiri – Apologetico – Ai Pagani – La testimonianza dell'anima – Polemica con gli Ebrei – A Scapula*, ed. by C. Moreschini, P. Podolak (Roma 2006) 159-169, in part. 165 ff.; Id., *Introduzione. Ad Nationes*, in Tertulliano, *Opere Apologetiche*, cit., 341 f.; as well as by the same author, *Introduzione a Tertulliano* (Brescia 2007). If one accepts this hypothesis (contested, on the basis of some conjectures of M. Sordi, by C. Minelli, 'La data dell'Apologeticum di Tertulliano', in Aevum 74.1 [2000] 187-189, oriented – but for the *Apologeticum* alone – toward 199-201), the conclusions of Cataudella, *Società e diritto* (n. 8) in part. 125, appear to be refuted *in limine*. He based his entire reconstruction on the assumption that the *Apologeticum* was composed after 202. Yet, the author of this work, nonetheless valuable, does not even question the relationship between *ad Nationes* and *Apologeticum*, nor does he consider it appropriate to cite the first of these two writings by Tertullian. But see also, *infra*, note 23, concerning the hypothesis of X. Dupuis, who, with excellent arguments, maintains that an attribution of the *ius Italicum* to Carthage prior to 211 is unlikely. On the *ius Italicum*, an expression used for the first time by Pliny the Elder, see T.H. Watkins, 'Coloniae and ius Italicum in the Early Empire', in Classical Journal 78 (1983) 219-336; M. Malavolta, *s.v. ius Italicum*, in DizEp. fasc. 73 e 74 (Roma 1985) 2305-2336, 2337-2336; T.M. Watkins, 'Vespasian and the Italic Right', in Classical Journal 84 (1988-1989) 117-136; E. Hermon, 'L'origine du ius Italicum, in P.G. Michelotto (ed.), *Λόγιος ἀνήρ. Studi di Antichità in Memoria di Mario Attilio Levi* (Milano 2002) 209-241; other considerations in M. Vitelli Casella, 'Qualche considerazione sull'attribuzione dello 'ius Italicum' alle comunità ispaniche e dalmate secondo la testimonianza di Plinio il Vecchio', in P. Ruggeri (ed.), *L'Africa romana. Momenti di continuità e rottura: bilancio di trent'anni di convegni "L'Africa romana"*, vol. II (Roma 2015) 1673-1680. F. Jacques, J. Scheid, *Roma e il suo impero. Istituzioni, economia, religione* (It. transl. Roma-Bari 1992) 311-313.

[23] Paul. 2 *de cens*., D. 50.15.8.11 *In Africa Carthago, Utica, Leptis Magna a diuis Severo et Antonino iuris Italici factae sunt*. However, this testimony cannot be taken as proof of the fact that the concession of the *ius Italicum* to Carthage must be attributed to the period of the co-rule of Septimius Severus with his sons Caracalla and Geta. Thus X. Dupuis, 'La concession du 'ius Italicum' à Carthage, Utique et Lepcis Magna: mesure d'ensemble ou decision ponctuelles?', in A. Chastagnol, S. Demougin, C. Lepelley (eds.), *Splendidissima civitas. Études d'Histoire Romaine en Hommage à François Jacques* (Paris 1996) 57-65.

[24] Cf. 'Année Épigrafique' (1963) 94, 20-21, which would attest to the existence of a *[de]fensor immunitatis perticae Carthaginiensium*. The word *pertica* – which refers to the land surveyor's instrument of the same name – represents the centuriated or assigned part of a *colonia* and, by extension, its territory. The extent of the benefit of *immunitas* was perhaps further expanded by Septimius Severus before

29 BCE, the fields of his vast *pertica* granted to Roman colonists coming from the peninsula were *immunes*[25] – with the *fundi* of this long[26] but sometimes narrow strip which, extending inland for more than one hundred kilometres,[27] intersected the territories of a large number of communities, originally all *peregrinae* like most of their populations. In time, there were established *pagi* of *cives Romani* colonists,[28] embedded as *énclaves* in the pre-existing Punic and Numidian *civitates*. Thus (and in this way one truly understands the meaning of Tertullian's

---

202-205: the coins bearing the legend *Indulgentia Augg. in Carthaginem* would seem to allude to this initiative. The extension of this privilege – which involved total exemption from taxes – was perhaps granted to compensate the city for the territorial reduction of its *pertica* and the consequent contraction of the *vectigalia* after the institutionalization of the new *municipia* created to unite into a single community the ancient *civitates peregrinorum* with the *pagi civium Romanorum* located in the ancient *pertica* of the Carthaginian colony. See Jacques, Scheid, *Roma e il suo impero* (n. 22) 312; as well as, *infra*, note 30.

[25] T.R.S. Broughton, 'The Territory of Carthage', in RÉL 47 bis (1969) 265-275; C. Poinssot, 'Immunitas perticae Carthaginensium, avec une observation de A. Piganiol', in Comptes rendus des Séances de l'Académie des Inscriptions (1962) 55-76; J. Gascou, 'Y avaitil un pagus carthaginois à Thuburbo Maius?', in AntAfr 24 (1988) 67-80; M. Christol, 'Uchi Maius et Carthage. 1, C(aius) Marius C(ai) f(ilius) Arn(ensi tribu) Extricatus', in AntAfr 40-41 (2005) 85-98.

[26] A. Mastino, V. Porcheddu, 'L''Horologium' offerto al 'pagus civium Romanorum' e alla 'civitas Numluli'', in *Misurare il tempo, misurare lo spazio. Atti del Colloquio AIEGL-Borghesi 2005* (Bertinoro, 20-23 ottobre 2005) (Faenza 2006) 144 f.

[27] Therefore, well beyond the *Fossa Regia*, a structure composed of an ancient moat and a military road, which stretching from the mouth of the Oued el-Kebir at *Thabraca* (Tabarka) then descended southward, passing north of *Thugga* (Dougga) and finally, after having bypassed Djebel Zaghouan, reaching the coast of the Lesser Syrtis (Gulf of Gabès) at *Thaenae* (Henchir Tina): Cf. Broughton, *The Territory of Carthage* (n. 25) 265 ff. *Thugga,* where a *pagus* of *cives Romani* was established (well after the middle of the second century CE), is more than 120 kilometres from Carthage.

[28] On the *pagi Romani* of the *pertica Carthaginiensis* and the nearby *civitates peregrinae*, see G.I. Luzzatto, 'Nota minima sulla struttura dei 'pagi' nell'Africa romana' (1973), in Id., *Scritti minori* (n. 17) 489-508, with previous literature. Also see L. Capogrossi Colognesi, *Persistenza e innovazione nelle strutture territoriali dell'Italia romana. L'ambiguità di una interpretazione storiografica e dei suoi modelli* (Napoli 2002) 64 f. and note 60; S. Aounallah, *'Pagus', 'castellum' et 'ciuitas': études d'épigraphie et d'histoire sur le village et la cité en Afrique romaine* (Bordeaux 2010) part. 59-118; L. Gagliardi, 'Fondazione di colonie romane ed espropriazioni di terre a danno degli indigeni', in MEFRA 127.2 (2015) 353-370, part. 360-364. Some other considerations are in S. Aounallah, L. Maurin, 'Remarques sur la topographie rurale et urbaine du 'pagus' et de la 'ciuitas' de Thugga (Dougga, Tunisie)', in I. Pimouguet-Pedarros, M. Clavel-Lévêque, F. Ouachour (eds.), *Hommes, cultures et paysages de l'Antiquitè à la période moderne* (Rennes 2013) 27-55. In any case, I generally accept the conclusions of Jacques, Scheid, *Roma e il suo impero* (n. 22) 319 f.

comment), there lived, side by side, natives – subject in full to payment of the land tax, as well as, as (most of the time) *peregrini*, to the *tributum capitis*[29] – and Roman *coloni* of the *pertica Carthaginiensis*, largely favoured with respect to their neighbours.[30]

If the apologist had considered nothing else but the relationship between foreign and Roman communities belonging to the same territory, the example he gave would undoubtedly have aroused even more the imagination of his readers. They would have immediately understood the meaning of his allusion to lands of equal agricultural value (because at times contiguous to one another) but clearly different because of their respective legal conditions.

The political-legal status of the *tributarii* appears worse if it is compared with the condition of the *Romani*[31] and of the citizens of the *liberae et immunes* communities.[32] The position of the *agri tributo onusti, res viliores* is equally so in comparison with the *agri immunes* and, even more so, with the *fundi in solo Italico*. Tertullian emphasizes the link between payment of tax and subjugation, emphasizing a widespread point of view in the *Africa proconsularis* of that time.[33]

---

[29] However, it is possible that Tertullian wished to refer to the lands not *immunes*, at least prior to the concession of the *ius Italicum*, of Carthage itself, i.e. those originally belonging to those who, although they had not come from *Italia*, had been integrated into the community during the establishment of the colony.

[30] Moreover, Tertullian describes an institutional and social reality destined, shortly thereafter, to be radically subverted (as already observed: *supra*, notes 24 and 29) by some decisive Severan provisions. In this regard, F. Jacques, "Municipia libera' de l'Afrique proconsulaire', in *Epigrafia. Actes du colloque international d'epigraphie latine en mémoire de Attilio Degrassi pour le centenaire de sa naissance*. Actes de colloque de Rome (27-28 mai 1988) (Rome 1991) 583-606; reconsidering the phases of the municipalization of proconsular Africa at the time of Septimius Severus, he concluded that the title of *municipium liberum* – as is the case with Thugga – borne by some of the towns included, before its dismantling, in the ancient *pertica Carthaginiensis*, was not intended to emphasize a presumed liberation from subjugation of this prestigious Roman colony. In his opinion, the term *liberus* referred instead to the extension to the new *municipia* of the privileges – above all fiscal immunity – hitherto enjoyed only by Carthage and its colonists living in the *pagi* established in the territory of the *pertica*. On this subject, also Aounallah, *'Pagus', 'castellum' et 'ciuitas'* (n. 28) 142-155.

[31] For a convincing discussion, see Petron. *sat*. 57.4 *Ridet! Quid habet quod rideat? Numquid pater fetum emit lamna? Eques Romanus es? Et ego regis filius. Quare ergo seruiuisti? Quia ipse me dedi in seruitutem et malui ciuis Romanus esse quam tributarius.*

[32] V. Marotta, *Ulpiano e l'Impero. II. Studi sui libri de officio proconsulis e la loro fortuna tardoantica* (Napoli 2004) 54.

[33] Thus Grelle, *'Stipendium'* (n. 1) 76.

Nevertheless, this is not the crucial point of his observations. The *res mancipi*, and especially the *fundi in solo Italico*, were perhaps for Gaius *pretiosiores* because the *cives* had to benefit from them in order to define their position and that of their family in the *census*,[34] and, if the possessors of a large patrimony, in order to aspire to a co-optation as senator or equestrian.[35] In contrast, according to the apologist the *agri tributo onusti* were characterized as *viliores*,[36] because by statute

---

[34] Which, still in the middle of the second century, had strong legal-social importance for those who aspired to preserve or obtain the privileged condition of *equites* or of senators.

[35] As is well known, there were minimum census requirements: see De Martino, *Storia della costituzione romana*², IV.1 (n. 18) 359; 554-558; C. Nicolet, 'Le cens sénatorial sous la république et sous Auguste', in JRS 66 (1976) 20-38, part. 37 f. Interesting in this regard are the testimonies of Plin. min. *ep*. 6.19.3-4 *Homullus deinde noster, uigilanter usus hoc consensu senatus, sententiae loco postulauit, ut consules desiderium uniuersorum notum principi facerent, peterentque, sicut aliis uitiis, huic quoque prouidentia sua occurreret. Occurrit, nam sumptus candidatorum, foedos illos et infames, ambitus lege restrinxit. Eosdem patrimonii tertiam partem conferre iussit in ea, quae solo continerentur, deforme arbitratus (et erat), honorem petituros Urbem Italiamque non pro patria, sed pro hospitio aut stabulo quasi peregrinantes habere*; as well as of H.A., *Marc. Ant.* 11.8 *leges etiam addidit de uicensima hereditatum, de tutelis libertorum, de bonis maternis et item de filiorum successionibus pro parte materna, ut qu[a]e senatores peregrini quartam partem in Italia possiderent.* The obligation, for senators of non-Italic origin, to invest first one third (with Trajan) and then one quarter (with Marcus Aurelius) of their assets in land of the peninsula can perhaps be explained not only by economic reasons (enhancing the demand for real estate and thus increasing the liquidity and assets of the Italian senators) but also by legal-institutional reasons: to ensure that senators of provincial origin declared, in their *professio*, a large part of *agri in solo Italico* among their properties. However, this is – obviously – only a conjecture, at the moment without any proof. In any case, see A.N. Sherwin-White, *The Letters of Pliny. A Historical and Social Commentary* (Oxford 1985³) 377. Moreover, as observed by S. Demougin, 'Le bureau palatin 'a censibus'', in MEFRA 113.2 (2001) part. 628-629, the secretary *a censibus*, among others, was, as coadjutor of the *princeps*, normally responsible for the *census equitum Romanorum*.

[36] In the sources, the opposition *res pretiosiores / res viliores* occurs only once, but in a completely different context from that regarding the distinction between *res mancipi* and *res nec mancipi*: Paul. 1 *ad ed*., D. 39.2.5.1 *Si plures sint domini, qui cauere debent, et aliquis non caueat, in portionem eius mittetur. Et contra si aliquot sint, qui caueri sibi desiderant, et alius pretiosiores, alius uiliores habeat aedes, sive unius domus plures habeant dispares partes: tamen non magnitudine dominii quisque, sed aequaliter mittentur omnes in possessionem.* In Menander 1 *de re militari*, D. 49.16.4.8 the word *pretiosior* (*pretiosiorem*, corrected by Salmasius in *gratiosiorem*: Momm. *Ad l.*) refers to the dignity or social position of an individual.

the land taxation was related to a *nota captivitatis*, diminishing the dignity of a *res* with respect to all others exempt from it.[37]

In short, the legal lexicon of the Empire and, consequently, the political thought of the jurists appeared to be so integrated into the institutional mechanisms of the *civitas*[38] as to reflect – implicitly but constantly – their presence, as in the case, for example, of the *res mancipi* and their role in defining the identity of each *civis* within the framework of citizenship. Hence, we must wonder how it was possible to transform this *ius* (*ius civile*) into a mechanism of integration of legally, ethnically and linguistically heterogeneous populations, and thus into an effective instrument of imperial domination.

Clifford Ando attempted to answer this question in a recent book.[39] The juridical operations devised by the jurists to transform *ius*, a right accessible in principle only to citizens, into an efficient mechanism of

---

[37] On tribute as a productive phenomenon of *status*, see V. Marotta, *La cittadinanza romana in età imperiale (secoli I-III d.C.). Una sintesi* (Torino 2009) 127 ff., as well as by the same author, 'Doppia cittadinanza e pluralità degli ordinamenti. La tabula Banasitana e le linee 7-9 del Papiro di Giessen 40 col. I', in AG 236 fasc. 3-4 (2016) 461-491, part. 465.

[38] In this regard, little or nothing is obtained from the reading of J. Harries, 'Lawyers and Citizens from Republic to Empire: Gaius on the Twelve Tables and Antonine Rome', in C. Rapp, H.A. Drake (eds.), *The City in the Classical and Post-classical World. Changing Contexts of Power and Identity* (Cambridge 2014) 62-80, part. 64 and 79. In effect, if it is undoubtedly a triviality to write (p. 64) that "the language of lawyers was traditional, even archaic, emphasizing continuity with the past", it seems ridiculous to contrast Pomponius and the other jurists of the Hadrianic-Antonine period with Ulpian, claiming that (p. 79) "with the advent of Septimius Severus would come a new brand of jurist, who wrote not about "Q. Mucius" or the Twelve Tables but about the (Praetorian) Edict and Masurius Sabinus's commentary on the *ius civile*", as if Pomponius had not written, among other things, also commentaries on *ad Sabinum* and *ad edictum*, following, at least in the latter case, a path already followed prior to him by many others (Servius, Labeo or Sextus Pedius, to mention only some of the most important names). In short, never more than in this circumstance is an extremely incomplete final bibliography (nothing really relevant was examined [except for a famous article by D. Nörr], not even the fundamental works of M. Bretone) the best indicator of the fact that too often judgments are made and adventurous hypotheses formulated without even bothering to acquire the necessary basic information.

[39] C. Ando, *Law, Language, and Empire in the Roman Tradition* (Philadelphia 2011) 1-36, 133-139, part. 22-27 = French translation *L'Empire et le droit. Invention juridique et réalités historiques Rome* (Paris 2013) 17-85, part. 60-68; as well as by the same author, ''Exemplum', Analogy, and Precedent in Roman Law', in M. Lowrie, S. Lüdemann (eds.), *Exemplarity and Singularity. Thinking through Particulars in Philosophy, Literature, and Law* (London-New York 2015) 111-122.

imperial integration included *fictio* – first in order of time and importance. I will follow this same itinerary, paying attention, if necessary, both to the ideas provided by the reading of their works and to the elaborations of the Imperial chancellery.[40] However, I am aware, on the basis of the lesson of Yan Thomas,[41] that, in considering the nature of this legal device, it is necessary to bear in mind that there is no mysterious union of being and non-being concealed within it but only a pragmatic synthesis. The *come se* is the only way to overcome, without aberrations, the principle of non-contradiction. In other words, in dealing with this phenomenon, we must avoid any 'substantialization' of it, guarding especially against the power of the illusory. This is a fascination that has misled even undisputed protagonists of twentieth-century historiography, foremost among them Ernst Kantorowicz,[42] although the latter especially must be recognized as having focused the debate on a broad topic of legal science: the role of *fictio* and of its applications in the genesis and development of political-legal institutions.[43]

2. The territorial dimension of power

Before discussing its uses in the construction of the imperial synthesis, it should be underlined that – on the basis of the materials collected about 40 years ago by Mario Talamanca[44] in a dossier to which very little can be added[45] – it would not seem that the jurists, between the first

---

[40] Cf., *infra*, 245.

[41] Y. Thomas, ''Fictio legis'. L'empire de la fiction romaine et ses limites médiévales' (1995), now in Id., *Les opérations du droit* (Paris 2011) 133 ff., 154, 305 and note 66 (as well as 162, 307 and note 86) = Italian translation Y. Thomas,*'Fictio legis'. La finzione romana e i suoi limiti medievali* (Macerata 2016) 58 s and note 66.

[42] It is the main limitation of a great and authentic masterpiece such as *I due corpi del Re. L'idea di regalità nella teologia politica medievale* (It. transl. Torino 1989).

[43] V. Marotta, *Esercizio e trasmissione del potere imperiale (secoli I-IV d.C.). Studi di diritto pubblico romano* (Torino 2016) 139 ff.

[44] M. Talamanca, 'Gli ordinamenti provinciali nella prospettiva dei giuristi tardoclassici', in G.G. Archi (ed.), *Istituzioni giuridiche e realtà politiche nel Tardo Impero (III-V sec. d.C.). Atti di un incontro tra storici e giuristi. Firenze, 2-4 maggio 1974* (Milano 1976) 95-246.

[45] First of all Frg. Dositheanum 12 *Peregrinus manumissor seruum non potest ad Latinitatem perducere, quia lex Iunia, quae Latinorum genus introduxit, non pertinet ad peregrinos manumissores, sicut et Octauenus probat. At praetor non permittet manumissum seruire, nisi aliter lege peregrina caueatur.* Therefore, a Roman magis-

and third centuries, paid persistent interest to the provincial situations in their literary works. Therefore, the perspective of Fritz Schulz – that jurisprudence was mainly the science of private law in force in the city of Rome and in Italy[46] – would be confirmed by the analytical examination of the sources. In effect, also the well-known Ulpianean testimony on the *constitutio Antoniniana*[47] (whose palingenetic position is strongly debated)[48] unequivocally indicates that this precise reference – without other confirmation in the *Institutiones Iustiniani*, in the Digest and in the *Codex repetitae praelectionis* – to a momentous decision, according to modern historiography, did not propose any connection with subjects for which the consideration of *status* and thus of *civitas* was foremost. To the contrary, it appeared in a completely marginal context.[49] The compilers – who, using this fragment, certainly showed

trate could, albeit in exceptional cases, apply the law of a foreign people in his court. A few thoughts on this subject are in W.P. Sullivan, 'Consent in Roman Choice of Law', in Critical Analysis of Law 3.1 (2016) 157-174, part. 162 f.

[46] F. Schulz, *I principii del diritto romano*, ed. by V. Arangio-Ruiz, (It. transl. Firenze 1946) 28. Somewhat different is the position of M. Lauria, *Corso di Diritto Romano. I. Diritto pubblico* (Napoli s.d. but 1949) 77, a page that perhaps inspired many investigations by his most eminent students in the 1960s (F. Casavola, M. Bretone, F. Grelle).

[47] Ulp. 22 *ad ed.* D. 1.5.17 *In orbe Romano qui sunt ex constitutione imperatoris Antonini ciues Romani effecti sunt.*

[48] However, instead of Lenel's two hypotheses, I continue to prefer another, also supported by the succession of subjects in the commentary on *Rubrica* / XV [§§ 83-88 *de adpromissoribus* "The co-promissori". In effect, according to Gaius (3.25), the *lex Iulia de vicesima hereditatium* excluded applicability of the *lex Cornelia* "*ad eas satisdationes, quae ex ea lege proponuntur*", i.e. to those guarantees introduced and provided for by it. In short, Ulpian, not unlike Cassius Dio, would have mentioned the general extension of Roman citizenship to the inhabitants of the Empire, in regard to the inheritance tax. In *Palingenesia iuris civilis*, vol. II, col. 542, Otto Lenel maintained that the jurist was examining the *lex Furia*, based on the hypothesis that the latter applied to Roman citizens alone. In the second edition of *Das Edictum Perpetuum. Ein Versuch zu einer Wiederherstellung* (Leipzig 1907) 298, and in the third (Leipzig 1927) 215, he concluded instead that the mention was due to the circumstance "das infolge jener Verallgeneinnerung die *sponsio* ihren nationale Charakter praktisch verloren ‹hat›". E. Schönbauer, 'Wortlaut und Sinn der Constitutio Antoniniana', in *Atti del Congresso Internazionale di Diritto Romano e di Storia del Diritto*, IV (Milano 1951) 131, hypothesized the rubric *de iure iurando*. P. Krüger, 'Additamenta III, Libri ad edictum', in Th. Mommsen, P. Krüger (eds.), *Corpus iuris civilis*[16], vol. I, *Institutiones, Digesta* (Berlin 1954) 952, merely mentioned that this passage regarded the rubric *ad epistulam divi Hadriani.*

[49] Marginal, but nonetheless significant, as Marotta, *La cittadinanza* (n. 37) 103-105, attempted to clarify, naturally accepting the palingenetic conjecture proposed here.

some interest[50] in the *constitutio Antoniniana*, enough to place it *in sede materiae* in the title *de statu hominum* (D. 1.5) – beyond the Ulpianean *libri ad edictum* were unable to identify anything more significant or more pertinent, not even in the *libri institutionum*, in which observations on the *condicio hominum* should have been found.

Is the latter perhaps evidence to conclude that Ulpian, Paulus and the younger Macro and Marcian showed a substantial lack of interest in the provincial legal systems and in the extension of citizenship considered in and of itself?

This has been authoritatively maintained.[51] I would be more cautious, at least in principle. Therefore, a reconsideration of the problem is necessary in the light of criteria of study not limited to mere recognition of empirical data.[52] In other words, the traces of jurisprudential thinking on the institutional forms of the Empire, on the Edict of Caracalla and on its effects cannot be identified in a case series that either never existed or, following the deletions to the texts by the Justinian commissioners,[53] has not existed for some time. Whoever wishes to avoid formulaic conclusions[54] or does not intend to limit himself to presuming the existence, unfortunately unverifiable in the light of the sources, of certain scenarios and of certain relationships[55] has the duty to tackle questions that can truly be rooted in what remains of these writings, thoroughly examining the doctrines that they develop.

---

[50] As emerges, despite the incorrect attribution of this provision to Antoninus Pius, also from a novella of 539: *Nov*. 78, 5. In this regard, see the valuable contribution of F. Goria, 'Romani, cittadinanza ed estensione della legislazione imperiale nelle costituzioni di Giustiniano', in *Da Roma alla terza Roma*. II. *La nozione di 'Romano' tra cittadinanza e universalità* (Roma 1984) 277-342.

[51] Talamanca, 'Gli ordinamenti provinciali' (n. 44) 198.

[52] It is, in effect, the only limitation of this fundamental study by Talamanca.

[53] However, improbable based on the considerations made by Talamanca, 'Gli ordinamenti provinciali' (n. 44) 197 f.

[54] It is a concrete risk, avoided only in part by the important contributions of L. De Giovanni, 'La giurisprudenza severiana tra storia e diritto: le 'Institutiones' di Elio Marciano', in Athenaeum 94.2 (2006) 487-505, part. 498; Id., *Istituzioni scienza giuridica codici nel mondo tardoantico. Alle radici di una nuova storia* (Roma 2007) part. 90-93 and of C. Corbo, *'Constitutio Antoniniana'. 'Ius Philosophia Religio'* (Napoli 2013) 79 ff. Finally, on Marcian and the effects of the *constitutio Antoniniana* on his *Institutiones*, some considerations in D. Dursi, *'Res communes omnium'. Dalle necessità economiche alla disciplina giuridica* (Napoli 2017) 13-16.

[55] As undoubtedly occurs in the fascinating pages of the lovely book by T. Honoré, *Ulpian. Pioneer of Human Rights. Second Edition* (Oxford 2002) 84 ff.

However, here I must deal exclusively with a preliminary problem, wondering whether, in the Severan period, the jurists attempted to define the Empire as a legal dimension. I would say no. Nevertheless, I believe that it is necessary to proceed further, proposing another subject which I would define by means of this specific question: from the fragments of their works, does there emerge some element that allows the conclusion that the Empire had incorporated *civitas*, that is, wishing to use contemporary nomenclatures and terms, that the Roman dominion constituted by now a territorial state?

No doubt it would be misleading to use even more explicit formulations which strain, already at first glance, the rules of a correct history of the institutions.[56] In effect, it makes no sense to wonder if it was by now a State that had had an Empire rather than a State that had an Empire.[57]

Let it be clear that I will not be able to deal, in the light of the testimonies of pre-Justian and Justinian compilations, with all the questions that theoretically should be considered in the study of the transition from an exclusively or predominantly civic identity to a completely different political synthesis such as the new ecumenical reality of the Empire. Yet, I at least have the duty to wonder if, between the first and third centuries CE, the *iurisconsulti* ever truly transcended the institutions of *civitas* in their legal-political reflections.

In reality, nobody can or wishes to deny the territorial dimension of the Roman dominion. In that regard, it would be sufficient to recall the so-called *lex provinciae* and the rules that governed the political and

---

[56] It can be mentioned that this term – State – if used in reference to premodern political syntheses, cannot assume any legal and institutional importance – unless we are satisfied with merely descriptive formulations.

[57] Cf. C. Maier, *Among Empires. American Ascendancy and its Predecessors* (Cambridge 2006) 5, as well as C. Ando, *Religion et Gouvernement dans l'Empire romaine* (Turnhout 2016) 18. B. Ward-Perkins, 'A most Unusual Empire: Rome in the Fourth Century', in Rapp, Drake (ed.), *The City* (n. 38) 109-129, in part. 127, wonders if "the Roman Empire was perhaps also a 'nation', for which the simplest definition is 'a state with which its subjects identify'?". I believe that this question, although formulated in a suggestive manner, can only lead to misleading conclusions. Another thing – and we will see it shortly (*infra*, pp. 240 ff.) – is to note, also on the basis of a valuable monograph by C. Ando, *Imperial Ideology and Provincial Loyalty in the Roman Empire* (Berkeley 2000) XI, the weight of the notion of *patria* and in particular the idea of *communis patria* in that decisive change of mentality that transformed "the Empire from an *imperium*, a collection of conquered provinces, to a *patria*, a focus for the patriotic loyalty of its subjects".

administrative life and private law of the cities and of the ἔθνη subject to provincial regulations, subjected, that is, to what the Greeks called ἐπαρχεία τῶν Ῥωμαίων.[58] Trajan very clearly distinguished the communities which, by treaty, *suis legibus ut<ebantur>*[59] from those that were *nostro iure obstrictae*.[60] These words clearly refer to the *lex provinciae* and to the other rules imposed, over time, by the imperial authority on the cities and on the *gentes* included in the *forma provinciae*; an institute – the *lex provinciae* – that profoundly marked, also from the perspective of the Hellenophone intellectuals between the second and third centuries CE, the domination of Rome over the Greek world. Aelius Aristides did not conceal from the public listening to his *Encomium* of the Urbs in 144[61] the new political and legal dimension in which peoples and *póleis* lived after the establishment of the ecumenical Empire of the Romans:

> ούδέ γε δεῖ νῦν περιήγησιν γῆς γράφειν ούδ' οἷς ἕκαστοι χρῶνται νόμοις ἀπαριθμεῖν, ἀλλ' ὑμεῖς ἅπασιν περιηγηταὶ κοινοὶ γεγόνατε, ἀναπετάσαντες ἁπάσας τῆς οἰκουμένης τὰς πύλας καὶ παρασχόντες ἐξουσίαν αὐτόπτας πάντων τοὺς θέλοντας γίγνεσθαι, νόμους τε κοινοὺς ἅπασι τάξαντες (…).[62]

No wonder, then, if in the Diocletian period the so-called Menander Rhetor, in his treatise of epideictic oratory, attempted, using the same *tópos* prepared or adopted by Aelius Aristides, to dissuade readers and

---

58 On the use of this expression in the Greek sources, see J. Richardson, *The Language of Empire. Rome and the Idea of Empire from the Third Century BC to the Second Century AD* (Cambridge 2009) in part. 45-49, 105 and note 188, with references to Republican period testimonies.

59 Cf. Plin. min. *ep*. 10.92.1: however, in this case, it is Pliny who uses these words.

60 Plin. min. *ep*. 10.93 (…) *In ceteris ciuitatibus, quae nostro iure obstrictae sunt, res huius modi prohibenda est*. See F. Grelle, 'Città e trattati nel sistema imperiale romano' (1990), now in Id., *Diritto e società* (n. 3) 324.

61 See P. Desideri, 'Introduzione', in F. Fontanella (ed.), *Elio Aristide, A Roma. Traduzione e commento* (Pisa 2007) 3-22, part. 4, with other information.

62 Ael. Aristid. *εἰς Ῥώμην* (*or*. 26 Keil) § 102: "And there is no longer any need to write guides describing the earth, or to enumerate the νόμοι that single peoples use, because you yourself have become the guides common to all men: you have opened all the doors of the oecumene and provided anyone who wishes with the opportunity to see everything directly; you have imposed common νόμοι (κοινοί) on everyone (…)". But reflections in this sense are, in my opinion, already in Dio Chrys. *or*. 41, 9.

students from exalting, in the panegyrics of the cities, their original and most characteristic laws:

> ἀλλὰ τὸ τῶν νόμων ἐν τοῖς νῦν χρόνοις ἄχρηστον· κατὰ γὰρ τοὺς κοινοὺς τῶν Ῥωμαίων νόμους πολιτευόμεθα, ἔθεσι δ' ἄλλη πόλις ἄλλοις χρῆται, ἐξ ὧν προσῆκον ἐγκωμιάζειν. [63]

Menander admitted that it would be interesting to cite, at least in the case of some *póleis*, the laws concerning inheritance, but that in such circumstances an orator could not and should not have taken them into account because they had by now been supplanted by the Roman νόμοι (διά τὸ τοῖς κοινοῖς χρῆσθαι τῶν Ῥωμαίων νόμοις). For the same reason, it seemed equally inappropriate, in such a political context, to mention the constitutions of the different cities, to celebrate their wisdom, since the *póleis* were governed by a single νόμος. [64] In its

[63] *Rh. Gr.* III, 363.10-14 = (*De demonstrativis dicendi generibus* [Russel, Wilson 1981] I, *lib.* III, pp. 66-67) Nowadays, however, the topic of laws is of no use, since we conduct public affairs by the common laws of the Romans. Customs however vary from city to city, and form an appropriate basis of encomium. (by Russel, Wilson 1981).

[64] *Rh. Gr.* III, 364.10-14 = (*De demonstrativis dicendi generibus* [Russel, Wilson 1981] I, *lib.* III, 68-69): Engl. transl. "In public affairs, we consider whether the city accurately lays down customs and the subjects of laws – inheritances by heirs (κλῆρον ἐπικλήρων) and other legal topics (καὶ ὅσα ἄλλα μέρη νόμων). This theme, however, is also pointless, because we use the common laws of the Romans (διά τὸ τοῖς κοινοῖς χρῆσθαι τῶν Ῥωμαίων νόμοις ἄχρηστον)". *Rh. Gr.* III, 360.13-16 = (*De demonstrativis dicendi generibus* [Russel, Wilson 1981] I, *lib.* III, pp. 60-61) "This last section of praise, however, is virtually useless today, since all Roman cities are governed by one (?) (ὑπὸ γὰρ μιᾶς αἱ Ῥωμαικαὶ ἅπασαι νῦν διοκοῦνται [...]). It was necessary however to mention it for the sake of completeness" (by Russel, Wilson 1981) For those who defend the essential content of the hypothesis of L. Mitteis, *Reichsrecht und Volksrecht in den östlichen Provinzen des romischen Kaiserreichs: mit Beiträgen zur Kenntniss des griechischen Rechts und der spätrömischen Rechtsentwicklung* (Leipzig 1891) the responsibility for these difficulties, recorded in the treatise of epidectic oratory attributed to Menander, lies with the emperor Caracalla and his edict. The rhetorician, speaking in the present (νῦν), in a text written ca. 80 years after 212 (D.A. Russel, N.G. Wilson, *Menander Rhetor*, Edited with Translation and Commentary, Oxford 1981, 'Introduction', p. XXXIX), would attest to the effects of the generalized granting of citizenship on the relations between Roman law and the legal traditions of the Hellenized East. In other words, this part of Menander's work would prove the clear contrast between the current state of things and the previous one. However, in my opinion, this interpretation of Menander's texts is incorrect. Indeed, to truly evaluate their meaning, *in primis* the legal-institutional one, it is necessary to consider the relationship the Greek intellectuals had, between the first and third century CE, with the glorious past of Hellas.

perspective, the real present (ἐν τοῖς νῦν χρόνοις) begins exactly where the ideal time of the 'Glory of the Greeks' ends. Hence, the object of Menander's reference is not the Edict of Caracalla but the Roman domination of the Greek world *tout court*. And Roman νόμος, in this perspective, is also every Roman law, regardless of its first origin, recognized or ratified by the victor who established and organized, in legal and administrative terms,[65] his own ἐπαρχεία.[66]

An explicit reference to the *lex provinciae* appears in Ulpian,[67] where, among other things, one of Celsus's opinions is mentioned. In his time, Celsus had discussed, with not well identified *quidam*, the scope of the *beneficium* granted by Pompey to the cities in the *lex provinciae* of Pon-

---

[65] On this subject, with further references to the sources, see V. Marotta, 'Conflitti politici cittadini e governo provinciale', in F. Amarelli (ed.), *Politica e partecipazione nelle città dell'Impero romano* (Roma 2005) part. 137-139.

[66] See Marotta, *La cittadinanza romana* (n. 37) 133-138, 152-155. Menander's testimony has been examined in recent years in the light of two opposing interpretations: one by M. Talamanca, 'Su alcuni passi di Menandro di Laodicea relativi agli effetti della 'constitutio Antoniniana'', in *Studi in onore di E. Volterra*, V (Milano 1970) 433-560, the other by J. Mélèze-Modrzejewski, 'Ménandre de Laodicée et l'Édit de Caracalla', in Id., *Droit impérial et traditions locales dans l'Egypte romain* (Aldershot 1990) XII, 335-366. I agree with that of Modrzejewski: however, it is always necessary to take into account the fact that the new *cives*, in their negotiating activities, should have followed the rules of the *ius Romanorum* regarding the law of successions, matrimonial law and family law in general. C. Humfress, 'Law's Empire: Roman Universalism and Legal Practice', in Rapp, Drake (eds.), *The City* (n. 38) 81-108 (with other references), presents a plausible picture of the effects caused by the generalized granting of citizenship, appropriately contesting any improper use of interpretative categories which can at most be used in the study of modern state entities. But see also, with particular regard to the documentation of the Middle Euphrates, G.D. Merola, *Per la storia del processo provinciale romano. I papiri del Medio Eufrate* (Napoli 2012). Lastly, G. Kantor, 'Local Law in Asia Minor after the 'Constitutio Antoniniana'', in C. Ando (ed.), *Citizenship and Empire in Europe 200-1900. The Antonine Constitution after 1800 years* (Stuttagart 2016) part. 45-47.

[67] 2 *ad ed.*, D. 50.1.1.2 *Qui ex duobus igitur Campanis parentibus natus est, Campanus est. sed si ex patre Campano, matre Puteolana, aeque municeps Campanus est, nisi forte priuilegio aliquo materna origo censeatur: tunc enim maternae originis erit municeps. Ut puta Iliensibus concessum est, ut qui matre Iliensi est, sit eorum municeps. Etiam Delphis hoc idem tributum et conseruatum est. Celsus etiam refert Ponticis ex beneficio Pompeii Magni competere, ut qui Pontica matre natus esset, Ponticus esset. Quod beneficium ad uolgo quaesitos solos pertinere quidam putant. Quorum sententiam Celsus non probat: neque enim debuisse caueri, ut uolgo quaesitus matris condicionem sequeretur (quam enim aliam originem hic habet?): sed ad eos, qui ex diuersarum ciuitatium parentibus orerentur.* In Pap. 1 *resp.*, D. 50.8.3, the words (...) *quae and lege fiunt recusare* (...) could perhaps refer to the *lex provinciae*, although other conjectures appear to be equally likely.

tus, understanding it correctly as an interpretative canon that took as its starting point the conservation of a meaning for the prescription whose normative value was to be fixed. Yet, it is not unlikely, as demonstrated by the situation of the family of Dio Chrysostom,[68] that the normative content of the *lex provinciae* of Pontus-Bithynia came to the attention of the *prudentes* precisely because it could interfere with the rules governing the acquisition by birth of Roman *civitas*.

The jurists allude to the effectiveness of Roman power with expressions such as *homines qui sunt sub imperio populi Romani*[69] or *civitates*

[68] It should be borne in mind that, in the years in which the Hadrianic jurist lived, this *beneficium*, previously granted by Pompey, must have interfered ever more frequently with the problems of transmission by birth of Roman citizenship. If it is assumed that this *lex data* concerned, together with Pontus, also the cities of Bithynia, all this would seem to be confirmed, according to some scholars, by the circumstances described in first person by Dio Chrysostom (a citizen of Prusa and *civis Romanus*, as well as of the *colonia* of Apamea) in a speech given to the curia of the latter city: *or.* 41.5-6 "it is thanks to your benevolence and by virtue of a gift that I am a member here (*scil.* in the *colonia Romana* of Apamea) of your city. Now all those who only have themselves to credit for having been made citizens obtain this privilege thanks to the generosity of a gift and not due to a natural necessity. In my case there is both, because my grandfather and my mother obtained, at the same time from the then emperor – who was their friend – Roman citizenship and your citizenship (τῆς Ῥωμαίων πολιτείας καὶ ὑμετέρας), and my father your citizenship. Consequently, I am your fellow citizen by grace and by birth (καὶ χάριτι καὶ γένει πολίτης)". Dio, if it is admitted that by virtue of the *lex Pompeia* he followed the *origo* of his mother and maternal grandfather, would have been a *civis Romanus*, as well as a citizen of the *colonia* of Apamea, by grace and by birth (καὶ χάριτι καὶ γένει πολίτης): see E. De Ruggiero, *La patria nel diritto pubblico romano* (Roma 1921) 151-153 and above all Y. Thomas, *Origine et commune patrie. Étude de droit public romain (89 av. J.-C.-212 ap. J.-C.)* (Paris-Rome 1996) 95-97. Different is the position of A. Raggi, 'Cittadinanza coloniaria e cittadinanza romana', in G. Salmeri, A. Raggi, A. Baroni (eds.), *Colonie romane nel mondo greco* (Roma 2004) 55-68, in part. 61-66, according to which Dio was born *peregrinus* and obtained Roman citizenship, in the Flavian period, together with his father Pasicrates. However, it must be underlined that, before the Hadrianic period *senatus consultum*, mentioned in Gai. *inst.* 1.78 (*infra*, note 77), Dio, under the rules of law then in force, would not even have been considered a legitimate child (that is, he would not have been considered *iustus patris filius*). In truth, if it were taken for granted that the discipline provided for by the *lex Pompeia* concerned also Bithynia proper and not only Pontus, I would have no hesitation in accepting the conclusions of Yan Thomas, for whom Dio would have been a citizen of the *colonia* of Apamea from birth by virtue of his mother's situation. In any case, this would necessarily imply that the rhetorician's father – Pasicrates – had also obtained *civitas Romana* prior to his conception or birth.

[69] Gai. *inst.* 1.53.

quae sunt sub imperio populi Romani,[70] or *litora, in quae populus Romanus imperium habet, populi Romani esse arbitror.*[71] *Imperium Romanum*, in the sense, as we would say today, of imperial synthesis, appears only one time[72] in the first book *de censibus* by Ulpian,[73] where the jurist proudly underlines that the city – Tyre – from which he took his *origo* had obtained the *ius Italicum* because of its unfailing loyalty to the *res publica* and the *Imperium Romanum.*[74]

In Gaius[75] and in Paulus,[76] the senate and the emperor, as legisla-

---

[70] Paul. *l.s. sen. cons.*, D. 36.1.27.

[71] Cels. 39 *dig.*, D. 48.8.3pr.

[72] As underlined by Richardson, *The Language of Empire* (n. 58) 208 f.

[73] Ulp. 1 *de cens.*, D. 50.15.1pr. *Sciendum est esse quasdam colonias iuris Italici, ut est in Syria Phoenice splendidissima Tyriorum colonia, unde mihi origo est, nobilis regionibus, serie saeculorum antiquissima, armipotens, foederis quod cum Romanis percussit tenacissima: huic enim diuus Severus et imperator noster ob egregiam in rem publicam imperiumque Romanum insignem fidem ius Italicum dedit.*

[74] It is probable that Ulpian's considerations in the introduction of his *de censibus* were taken from a speech given by the *legati* of Tyre in Rome or perhaps also in their city at the time of a visit by Septimius Severus to the East. The words *nobilis regionibus* (a formula pertaining to praise of the territory of Tyre) underline the richness and variety of the territory of this city which brings it prosperity. The expression *serie saeculorum antiquissima* concerns praise of its history. Tyre is very ancient and its origins date to the dawn of time. *Armipotens* is a phrase concerning the remembrance of a series of battles, primarily the prolonged resistance to Alexander's army. However, this adjective does not refer only to a distant past. In the present, the contribution provided by the city to Septimius Severus during the civil war against Pescennius Niger must also have seemed important (see, for a discussion, Cass. Dio, 74 [75].6.4-6 regarding the conflict that divided Nicomedia and Nicaea, each supporting one of the two contenders in battle). *Foederis quod cum Romanis percussit tenacissima* is a formula praising Tyre's ancient loyalty to the Romans. This loyalty was assured by a *foedus* always respected with determination by the city. It can be underlined that, in the Severan period, the Republican age *foedera* fully retained their prestige (see, for a discussion, *CIL* 11, 5631 = *ILS* 432, where mention is made of the decision of Septimius Severus – in response to a delegation – to confirm, in 210, the *foedus aequum* of Rome with Amiternum in *Umbria*): see M. Christol, 'Entre la cité et l'empereur: Ulpien, Tyr et les empereurs de la dynastie sévérienne', in F. Chausson, E. Wolff (eds.), *Consuetudinis amor. Fragments d'histoire romaine (IIe-VIe siècles) offerts à Jean-Pierre Callu* (Roma 2003) 163-188, as well as A. Hostein, *La Cité et l'Empereur. Les Éduens dans l'Empire romain d'après les Panégyriques latins* (Paris 2012) 100 ff.

[75] Inst. 1.53.

[76] *Supra*, note 70.

tors, assume an – at least virtually – ecumenical dimension,[77] since their decisions can affect the legal order of each community subject to the dominion of the *populus Romanus*. This is certainly the case exposited by the Antonine master: in fact, the *constitutio principis*, which he reports, concerned all the *homines* subject to the *imperium populi Romani*, thus modifying not only the city's legal order but also those of the communities and of the *gentes* included in the Roman sphere:

> Gai. *inst.* 1.53 *Sed hoc tempore neque ciuibus Romanis nec ullis aliis hominibus, qui sub imperio populi Romani sunt, licet supra modum et sine causa in seruos suos saeuire: (...).*

Instead, the example taken from the reading of the following passage seems more controversial:

> Paul. *l.s. sen. cons.*, D. 36.1.27 *omnibus ciuitatibus, quae sub imperio populi Romani sunt, restitui debere et posse hereditatem fideicommissam Apronianum senatusconsultum iubet.*

---

[77] Even more interesting in this perspective is another Hadrianic provision reported by Gaius. To satisfy the needs of a universal empire, Hadrian was the first to define, by means of *senatus consultum*, the condition of those born from unions without *conubium* (F. Casavola, *Giuristi adrianei*, with a bibliographical and prosopographical note by G. De Cristofaro (Napoli 1980) 211 ff.; Marotta, *La cittadinanza romana* (n. 37) 63), who would not have been able to establish a legitimate family. The *lex Minicia* – from the Republican period – had affected the unions between Roman and foreign citizens, attributing to the offspring the citizenship of the foreign parent (i.e. *status* <*peregrini*> [in Gai. *inst.* 1.78 the editors of the *Fontes Iuris Romani Antejustiniani*^{2} [II *Auctores*, p. 24] include it in this manner, although the conjecture <*deterioris*>*]* *parentis* is just as likely). Instead, this *senatus consultum* established that the children born from the union of a Roman citizen with a foreigner were legitimate. Thus, Hadrian and the senate did not abolish the norm of the *lex Minicia* (which was in contrast with the "rule of the law of the peoples", according to which the person born should have followed, in cases like these, the condition of the mother *civis Romana*), but limited themselves to declaring the legitimacy of filiation, easing the punitive spirit of the Republican law. The ultimate purpose of this reform was to safeguard the family that the foreigner had intended to form by uniting with a Roman woman. In this way, the *princeps*, defining the son of the *peregrinus* as a "legitimate son of the father", consciously established a supranational norm, which affected, at the same time, the Roman legal order and that of the other political communities of the Empire.

In this case,[78] as in that set out in the *Tituli ex corpore Ulpiani*,[79] it would in principle be legitimate to suppose that the subjects of these legal provisions were exclusively the *civitates Romanae* (*municipia* and *coloniae*).[80] In effect, based on a passage of Gaius's *commentarii*,[81] we know that Hadrian reaffirmed the prohibition, previously established by Vespasian,[82] against leaving *fideicommissa* to *peregrini*.

However, a fragment from Marcian – a passage referring to a rescript issued between 198 and 211, hence prior to the *constitutio Antoniniana* – concerned Sardis[83] and thus without any doubt a *civitas peregrina*:

> Marcian. 8 *inst.*, D. 33.1.24 *Cum erat certa pecunia, id est centum, rei publicae Sardianorum relicta per quadriennium certaminis Chrysanthiani, diui Seuerus et Antoninus rescripserunt uideri perpetuam pensitationem reliquisse testatorem per quadriennium, non in primum quadriennium.*[84]

---

[78] Cf. Tit. Ulp. 22.5. This text, like Paul. *l.s. sen. cons.*, D. 36.1.27, refers to a section of the *senatusconsultum Apronianum*, probably from the Hadrianic period.

[79] Tit. Ulp. 24.28 *Ciuitatibus omnibus, quae sub imperio populi Romani sunt, legari potest: idque a diuo Nerva introductum est, postea a senatu auctore Hadriano diligentius constitutum est.* For a first bibliographical picture, see, *infra*, authors cited in note 90, to which *adde* M. Avenarius, *Der pseudo-ulpianische 'liber singularis regularum'. Entstehung, Eingenart und Überlieferung einer hochklassischen Juristenschrift* (Göttingen 2005) 402 ff.

[80] Thus Talamanca, 'Gli ordinamenti provinciali' (n. 44) 181-183.

[81] Gai., *inst.* 2.285 *Ut ecce peregrini poterant fideicommissa capere, et fere haec fuit origo fideicommissorum. Sed postea id prohibitum est, et nunc ex oratione diui Hadriani senatus consultum factum est, ut ea fideicommissa fisco uindicarentu*r.

[82] *Gnōmōn Idiologi* § 18 τὰ\ς/ κατὰ πίστιν γεινομένας κληρονομίας ὑπὸ Ἑλλήνῳν\εἰς/ [[ὑπὸ]] Ῥω|μαίους ἢ ὑπὸ Ῥωμαίων \εἰς/ Ἕλληνας ὁ θεὸς Οὐεσπασιανὸς[ἀ]νέλαβεν, | οἱ μέντοι τὰς πίστεις ἐξομολογησάμενοι τὸ ἥμισ[υ ε]ἰλήφασι. "Fideicommissum bequests, left both by Greeks to Romans and by Romans to Greeks, the divine Vespasian confiscated; however, those who declared these fideicommissa received half". The last part of *Gnōmōn Idiologi* § 18 raises some problems, albeit not relevant for the purposes of our discussion. It must be assumed that, if the honoured people themselves declared their name, they received half of the bequest. Cf. *Gnōmōn Idiologi* 27 (ὅσα Ῥωμαῖος ἑξηκονταετὴς ἄτεκνος ἀγύναιος ὢν κληρονο|μεῖ, ἀναλαμβάνεται. ἐὰν δὲ ἔχῃ γυναῖκα τέκνα δὲ μὴ καὶ ἑαυ|τὸν προσανγείλῃ, τὸ ἥμισυ αὐτῷ συνχωρεῖται "When a Roman sexagenarian, who has neither wife nor children, inherits, it is confiscated. But if he has a wife and has no children and he himself declares, he is granted half of it". Cf. Paul. 7 *ad l. Iul. et Pap.*, D. 49.14.13pr.-1.

[83] L. Bürchner, *s.v. Sardeis*, in PWRE, I A2 (Stuttgart 1920) col. 2477 f.

[84] The *principes* interpreted this testamentary disposition as if it had established

However, it seems completely unreasonable to hypothesize an imperial intervention in a matter of *ius peregrinum.*[85] In this case, instead, the testator was a *civis*, who had left by *fideicommissum* a certain sum of money in favour of a *pólis* – and one of the most illustrious of the Empire –, which nonetheless remained, even more so before 212, in its original condition of a non-Roman city. The latter must be considered an established fact, since the eighth book of Marcian's *institutiones* is dedicated specifically to *fideicommissa* and the terminology used here (*pecunia relicta*) appears to be the usual one for this type of bequest. The *fideicommissum* that the testator had made in his will, precisely because it was intended for the celebration of the *Chrysanthina* – one of the most prestigious games of the Empire, since *hieroí*, *eiselastikoí* and *oikoumenikoí* –, was meant to guarantee the perpetuity of a ritual of fundamental importance for the religious life of Sardis,[86] a metropolis[87] of the *provincia* of *Asia* and the site, between the second and third centuries, of two imperial neocorates.[88] Yet, we can presume that similar occasions appeared very often in the life of the Empire's richest and most populous provinces. In fact, there are numerous cases of games established by private bequests in the Greek epigraphic documentation between the second and third centuries.[89] Therefore, it must be recognized that the overall examination of the sources confirms the plausibility of the hypothesis formulated by Ludwig Mitteis[90]: the *civitates pere-*

a sort of perpetual 'foundation'. On this specific point and on the history of the *Chrysanthina*, see M.L. Caldelli, 'Considerazioni sulla cronologia dei 'Chrysanthina' di 'Sardis'', in ZPE 109 (1995) 62-70, part. 68 f.

[85] Thus, in this regard, also Talamanca, 'Gli ordinamenti provinciali (n. 44) 184, note 241.

[86] The celebration of the *Chrysanthina* was closely related to the cult of Korē (Persephonē), a divinity at the centre of the Sardisean *pantheon*.

[87] A title not to be confused with that of πρώτη τῆς Ἀσίας, which belonged only to Ephesus, Pergamon and Smyrna: Cf. R. Haensch, *'Capita provinciarum'. Statthaltersitze und Provinzialverwaltung in der römischen Kaiserzeit* (Mainz am Rhein 1997) 24 ff. As for the title of metropolis, in the context of the *provincia* of *Asia*, cf. Mod. 2 *excusat.*, D. 27.1.6.2.

[88] See B. Burrel, *"Neokoroi". Greek Cities and Roman Emperors* (Leiden 2004) 38-42, 317 ff.

[89] See L. Moretti, *Iscrizioni agonistiche greche* (Roma 1953) 176 n. 65; 227 n. 78; 255 n. 86; 267 n. 90. At least for Pergamon and for its *Attálēa* (*Ibid.*, 267 n. 90), there can be no doubt that it was a *civitas peregrina*.

[90] L. Mitteis, *Römische Privatrecht bis auf die Zeit Diokletians*, I. *Grundbegriffe und Lehre von den juristischen Personen* (Leipzig 1908) 377; P. Voci, *Diritto ereditario romano. I. Introduzione. Parte generale*[2] (Milano 1967) 421.

grinae could have been the beneficiaries of bequests and *fideicommissa* of *cives Romani*.

Moreover, other findings attest, starting from the years of Hadrian, to testamentary bequests by people of senatorial rank to cities not only *peregrinae* but also not subject to the provincial regulations. Atticus,[91] the father of Herodes (one of the main protagonists of the political and cultural scene of the Empire in the second century),[92] left, according to Philostratus,[93] one mina each year to each Athenian.[94] In short, on a concrete historical basis, it must be considered that many eminent persons, of senatorial or even consular rank (as in the case of Atticus and his son Herodes), in order to strengthen the bonds of loyalty that united their families to their *póleis* of origin must have inevitably[95] been authorized to use, also in these circumstances, the usual schemata of the *ius privatum Romanorum*.[96]

Regarding the territorial dimension of the *imperium Romanorum*, the cases collected in *D*. 49.15 *De captivis et de postliminio et redemptis ab hostibus* present almost all the jurists' reflections on its *fines*.[97] There is the use of categories that extend the effectiveness of Roman power well beyond the regions specifically *redactae in formam provinciae*. The relations of *amicitia* among peoples not only excluded reciprocal *postliminium* but constituted a common line of defence against the enemies.

---

[91] H. Halfmann, *Die Senatoren aus dem östlichen Teil des Imperium Romanum bis zum Ende des 2. Jahrhunderts n. Chr.* (Göttingen 1979) 120-123. For a general evaluation of the integration processes of the Greek *élites* in the senatorial order, *ibid*., 16-98.

[92] W. Ameling, *Herodes Atticus*, I. *Biographie* (Hildesheim 1983) 136-138.

[93] *Vitae Sophistarum* 2.1 (549): καὶ διαθῆκαι δέ, ἐν αἷς τῷ Ἀθηναίων δῆμον κατὰ φυλὰς κατέλειπε καθ' ἕκαστον ἔτος μνᾶν καθ' ἕνα, μεγαλοφρονσύνην κατηγοροῦσι τοῦ ἀνδρός, ᾗ καὶ ἐς τὰ ἀλλὰ ἐχρῆτο, (...). "and the testament, in which (<Attico>) bequeathed to the Athenian people one mina each per year, reveals the generosity that this person demonstrated on other occasions, (...)".

[94] Cf. also Fronto, *ad M. Caes*. 3.3 (Van den Hout^2).

[95] The entry into the equestrian and senatorial order of many aristocrats originally from the Greek provinces undoubtedly intensified this need.

[96] Here a problem of dual citizenship is not in question. A citizen, Athenian and Roman at the same time, could have made use of Attic law in the exercise of his political rights and of *ius sacrum* to protect, as a member of a certain aristocratic γένος, his claim to hold a certain priesthood; however, concerning marriage law and inheritance law, he would have always had to rely only on *ius Romanorum*: in this regard, see Marotta, 'Doppia cittadinanza' (n. 37) 470-485.

[97] Cf. Grelle, 'Città e trattati' (n. 60) 317 ff.

This is clarified in a text by Paulus:

> 17 *ad Sab.*, D. 49.15.19.3 *Postliminio redisse uidetur, cum in fines nostros intrauerit, sicuti amittitur, ubi fines nostros excessit. Sed et si in ciuitatem sociam amicamue aut ad regem socium uel amicum uenerit, statim postliminio redisse uidetur, quia ibi primum nomine publico tutus esse incipiat.*

Benefit of *ius postliminii* can be had not only by those *in fines nostros* but also by those who manage to reach an allied city or the dominions of a *rex socius et amicus populi Romani.*[98] Paulus implicitly identifies the 'Empire' with a territorial dimension broader than the areas included in the Roman provincial organization. In this regard, his point of view coincides perfectly with that previously expressed by Strabo,[99] for whom:

> Ταύτης δὲ τῆς συμπάσης χώρας τῆς ὑπὸ Ῥωμαίοις ἣ μὲν βασιλεύεται, ἣν δ΄ ἔχουσιν αὑτοὶ καλέσαντες ἐπαρχίαν, καὶ πέμπουσιν ἡγεμόνας καὶ φορολόγους. Εἰσὶ δέ τινες καὶ ἐλεύθεραι πόλεις, αἱ μὲν ἐξ ἀρχῆς κατὰ φιλίαν προσελθοῦσαι, τὰς δ΄ ἠλευθέρωσαν αὑτοὶ κατὰ τιμήν.[100]

According to the geographer, of all the regions subject to the Romans, some are governed by kings, while others are governed, as prov-

[98] M.R. Cimma, *Reges socii et amici populi Romani* (Milano 1976) 228 f. (Cf. also Ead., *'Reges socii et amici'*, in Diritto@Storia 3 (2004) [*http://www.dirittoestoria.it/3/Memorie/Organizzare-ordinamento/Cimma-Reges-socii-et-amici.htm*]); D. Braund, *Rome and the Friendly King: The Character of the Client Kingship* (London-New York 1984) part. 181-190; by the same author, *Client Kings*, in Id. (ed.), *The Administration of the Roman Empire (241 BC-AD 193)* (Exeter 1988) 69-96; E. Paltiel, *Vassals and Rebels in the Roman Empire. Julio-Claudian Policies in Judaea and the Kingdoms of the East* (Brüssel 1991); M. Sommer, *Roms orientalische Steppengrenze. Palmira – Edessa – Dura Europos – Hatra. Eine Kulturgeschichte von Pompeius bis Diocletian* (Stuttgart 2005) part. 58-66; A. Raggi, 'Amici populi Romani', in MedAnt 11 (2008) 97-113; T. Kaizer, M. Facella (eds.), *Kingdoms and Principalities in the Roman Near East* (Stuttgart 2010); E. Baltrusch, J. Wilker (eds.), *'Amici – socii – clientes'? Abhängige Herrschaft im Imperium Romanum* (Berlin 2015). On the relations with the *reges amici* of the Germanic tribes, see L.F. Pitts, 'Relations between Rome and the German "Kings" on the Middle Danube in the First to the Fourth Centuries AD', in JRS 79 (1989) 1945-1958. For *Britannia*, see D. Mattingly, *An Imperial Possession. Britain in the Roman Empire, 54 BC-AD 409* (London 2006) 68-84.

[99] Therefore, I would not see a contradiction with the prevailing thought of the jurists indicated at the time by Cimma, *'Reges socii et amici populi Romani'* (n. 98) 223 and 228.

[100] *Geogr.* 17.3.24.

inces, by the Romans themselves, sending governors and tax collectors to them. But there are also free cities: the ones associated from the beginning with the dominators in a close relationship of friendship, the others, vice versa, left free as a sign of honour, in homage to their glorious past.

In any case, in a free and allied city [101] or in the realm of a *rex socius et amicus*, there was, as in the provinces, the full protection of Roman power (*nomen publicum*). [102] Even in Late Antiquity, despite the new configuration assumed by the peripheral administration, the connection between *libertas civium* and the effectiveness of 'Roman provincial power' was always reaffirmed. When, during the fifth century, large parts of the Gallic and Danubian provinces were removed from the control of the *principes*, the condition of the Romans now subject to *ius hostium* [103] was conceived almost as a form of exile, like the singular position of one who becomes a foreigner in his own land. According to Salvian, [104] after taking advantage of free men and profiting from the

---

[101] *Supra*, note 65. The security and freedom of the *cives* must have been assured even in the free cities, i.e. not subject to provincial regulations, and in the domains of the allied kings. For this reason, the loyalty of a federated *pólis* was also assessed on the basis of the effort made to assure the safety of Roman citizens: see Marotta, *La cittadinanza romana* (n. 37) 38 f., with references to the sources.

[102] Paulus's text can be profitably compared with Fest. *s.v. postliminium receptum* 244 Lindsay; Lab. 8 Πιθανῶν *a Paulo epitom.*, D. 49.15.30; Procul. 8 *epistul.*, D. 49.15.7.1; Pomp. 37 *ad Q. Mucium*, D. 49.15.5: Cf. Grelle, 'Città e trattati' (n. 60) 330 f. Now see, on many of these texts, M.F. Cursi, "Amicitia' e 'societas' nei rapporti tra Roma e gli altri popoli del Mediterraneo', in Index 41 (2013) part. 217-223, with ample literature.

[103] Salv. *de guber. Dei* 4.54 *cur uinci a barbaris patimur? cur iuri hostium subiugari?* And here a motif is presented which should always be considered when analyzing, as in the case of Menander Rhetor (*Rh. Gr.* III, 363.7 = [*De demonstrativis dicendi generibus* (Russel-Wilson 1981)] I, *lib* III, 66-67: *supra*, p. 229 f.), sources of opposite indication, i.e. testimonies by virtue of which it would seem to be legitimate to conclude that the Roman legal order had completely replaced the pre-existing one. In the Roman view, as in that of many other peoples of Antiquity, victory and defeat, mutually integrated, constantly define the condition of the subjugated populations. Their ancestral laws can survive only as a mere concession by the victor. Which, from a certain perspective, means that also this law is no longer, in the proper sense, an expression of authentic freedom and true autonomy. For a discussion, see also Ps. Clemens, *Recognitiones* 9.27.4-7 and Bardesanes, *Liber legum regionum* 43 (Nau).

[104] *De guber. Dei* 5.47 *Miserti quippe exulum non sumus. Ecce ipsi exules sumus: peregrinos fraude cepimus, ecce ipsi peregrinamur; praeiudiciis temporum ingenui status homines circumuenimus, ecce ipsi nuper quidem in alieno solo uiuere coepimus, sed praeiudicia iam timemus.*

circumstances, they began to pay for their sins, forced to live at home – now that the Barbarians had become their masters – as *in alieno solo*. Thus, faced with the danger of being subjected to foreign domination, those who wished to preserve their *libertas* had no other choice – and this was Saint Severinus's exhortation [105] to the inhabitants of *Noricum* – but to migrate *in Romani soli provinciam*. Therefore, the freedom of the *civis Romanus* [106] was assured, primarily if not exclusively, by the constant presence of imperial power and its administrative and judicial system. Although Salvian denounced with indignant vehemence the clear contradictions inherent in this exaltation of Roman power and of its virtues, [107] he could not help but acknowledge a legal-political doctrine defined some centuries before by the jurists of the period of the Principate. [108]

---

[105] Eugippus, *vita Sancti Severini* 31.6 *Ipse uero Fauianis degens in antiquo suo monasterio nec admonere populos nec praedicere futura cessabat, asserens uniuersos in Romani soli prouinciam absque ullo libertatis migraturos incommodo*. The saint would have foreseen the occupation of the *provincia* by the Rugii, urging its inhabitants to take refuge beyond the Alps.

[106] Salvian insists, albeit in order to invert the usual stereotype of imperial propaganda, on the position of the *cives Romani*, as well as on their presumed *libertas*: *de gubern. Dei* 5.5.22 *Itaque nomen ciuium Romanorum aliquando non solum magno aestimatum sed magno emptum nunc ultro repudiatur ac fugitur, nec uile tantum sed etiam abominabile paene habetur*; 5.5.22 *Itaque passim uel ad Gothos uel ad Bacaudas uel ad alios ubique dominantes barbaros migrant, et commigrasse non paenitet; malunt enim sub specie captiuitatis uiuere liberi quam sub specie libertatis esse captiui*; 5.6.24 *De Bacaudis nunc mihi sermo est, qui per malos iudices et cruentos spoliati, afflicti, necati, postquam ius Romanae libertatis amiserant, etiam honorem Romani nominis perdiderunt*.

[107] It is a polemical attitude which, despite a more pervasive use of irony, or better "of what is said and not said", returns identical in the well-known *excursus* of Priscus of Panium on that Roman merchant who, having settled with great fortune among the Huns, no longer felt any nostalgia for the Empire and its judicial apparatus; however, an *excursus* which also ends with a renewed homage to the Empire and its laws: Frg. 8 (Müller, *Frg. Hist. Graec.*, IV, 77-95, part. 86-88 = *Prisci Panitae Fragmenta*, F. Bornmann (ed.) (Firenze 1979) 46-50 = P. Carolla (ed.) [*Priscus Panita, Excerpta* (Berolini et Novi Eboraci 2008) Bibliotheca Teubneriana 37, 114]): "(…) and he told me that the laws of the Romans were fine and the constitution good (νόμοι καλοὶ καὶ ἡ πολιτέια Ῥωμαίων ἀγαθὴ), but the rulers were corrupting it because they were not as wise as the ancients".

[108] Interesting considerations on this subject in C. Ando, *Roman Social Imaginaries. Language and Thought in Contexts of Empire* (Toronto-Buffalo-London 2015) 7-28.

3. *Communis patria*

Rome, although being (what better example of *pomerium*?) a city based on land,[109] did not possess a unified territory.[110] The *imperium* grew hand in hand with the expansion of conquests. However – despite the strong effect that some images of Aristides's *Encomium* have on legal historians – on an institutional level it never constituted an extension of the *urbs*, or, to use the same expression of the Mysian rhetorician, its χώρα.[111] In reality, it was proposed instead as a constellation of cities, where, in order to manifest its εὔνοια towards the dominant power, in each of them there were sacrifices to the *dea Roma*, to Augustus and to

---

[109] F. Dupont, *Rome, la ville sans origine. L'Énéide: un grand récit du métissage* (Paris 2011) 55 f.

[110] Observations in this regard in C. Nicolet, *L'inventario del mondo. Geografia e politica alle origini dell'Impero romano* (It. transl. Roma-Bari 1989) 227 ff. At present, the territory, within the framework of general public law, is considered an element of the State because it contributes to making it what it is, to giving it its individuality, together with the population inhabiting it, but without becoming confused with the population, thus assuming a position analogous to that of the body for the human person. Regarding the internal system, it can largely be disclaimed that the territory can become the object of a legal relationship. Instead, it is considered a simple limit of validity of the state system or a means of localizing the validity of the regulations, or a reflected object of state power over the people, or, finally, a simple prerequisite for the existence of the State. See C. Mortati, *Istituzioni di diritto pubblico*, I^9 (Padova 1975) 110-122. Today, there often occurs the irreversible crisis of the territorial national state. However, more correctly (to avoid misunderstandings and misleading generalizations), I think that it would be appropriate to discuss crises of some specific national states. The end of territories is discussed in a recent collection of essays, and in ways that arouse concern, by S. Cassese, *Territori e potere. Un nuovo ruolo per gli Stati?* (Bologna 2016) part. 36 f. In his opinion, 'Global Polity' – which is elaborated (it should be borne in mind) within the context of the concert of strategic decisions of the great actors of the world scene and of so-called globalization, such as the US Federal Government, NATO, the EU, the IMF, the World Bank, the WTO, the OECD, etc. – would be based primarily, through indirect rule, on the national implementation. Strangely, the use of this notion, defined by the political anthropology and sociology of British colonial domination, does not cause embarrassment to a distinguished jurist and former judge of the Constitutional Court. We can wonder then if, in certain circles, it is taken for granted – once indirect rule has been identified as a reference criterion – that the Italian State (as well as, from time to time, its government, its armed forces, its secret services, etc.) assumes, with respect to the true centres of world power, functions and roles only different in magnitude from those once assumed by the African tribal chiefs – 'blackbirds', as defined by our Giovanni Giolitti – subject to the power of the government of the British monarch between the nineteenth and twentieth centuries. Why we should then rejoice in all this remains a mystery.

[111] Ael. Aristid. *εἰς Ῥώμην* (*or*. 26 Keil) § 61.

the *genius* of each reigning *princeps*. Therefore, for the jurists, the Roman conquests did not lead to the creation of a territorial state.[112] However, although never defined in a comprehensive study, this is still today the *communis opinio* of legal historiography.

According to an authoritative interpreter of the sources,[113] in Modestinus, Rome, although maintaining its pre-eminent position as the capital of the Empire, was nevertheless considered a πατρίς in the same way as the other πατρίδες:

> 2 *excusat.*, D. 27.1.6.11 Τόν ἐν Ῥώμῃ σοφιστεύοντα ἢ σαλαρίῳ ἢ καὶ χωρὶς σαλαρίου ἄφεσιν ἔχειν νεμομοθέτηται ὑπὸ τῶν θειοτάτων Σεβήρου καὶ Ἀντωνίνου, οὕτως ὡς ἂν εἰ ἔττυχεν ἐν ἰδίᾳ πατρίδι διδάσκων. αἷς νομοθεσίαις δύναταταί τις ἐκεῖνον προσαγαγεῖν τὸν λόγον, ὅτι κοινῆς οὔσης τε καὶ νομιζομένης πατρίδος τῆς βασιλευούσης εἰκότως ἂν ὡς ἐν ἰδίᾳ πατρίδι χρήσιμον ἑαυτὸν παρασχὼν ἀλειτουργησίαν καρπώσεται.[114]

The tension between Rome as the territorial seat to which the *populus Romanus* could be attributed, as an expression of the structure of the city-state, and Rome as a concrete communal and civic organization, which, from this perspective, had to be placed on the same level as the other *civitates* of the Empire, tends, in the opinion of Talamanca, to diminish, because, in the eyes of the jurist, the *urbs* would now be a *civitas* equal to the others, being distinct only in relation to the fact that it was the capital of the Empire, now clearly considered a territorial state, beyond the ideology of the city-state.

We can draw elements to formulate similar conclusions also from examination of a famous passage by Callistratus:[115]

---

[112] For its modern origin, see C. Tilly, *La formazione dello Stato in Europa. Riflessioni introduttive*, in Id. (ed.), *La formazione degli Stati nazionali nell'Europa occidentale* (Bologna 1984) 30.

[113] Talamanca, 'Gli ordinamenti provinciali' (n. 44) 201-203.

[114] Lat. Trans. Momm.: *Eum qui Romae rhetor est siue salario constituto siue sine salario uacationem habere constitutum est a diuis Seuero et Antonino, tamquam si in sua ciuitate profiteretur. Quarum constitutionum possit quis eam rationem reddere, quod cum urbis aeterna communis patria et sit et habeatur, recte tamquam qui in propria patria eius utilitatibus inservit immunitate fruatur.*

[115] Latin retranslation of Bas. 60.54.17pr.: Ὁ ἐξόριστος οὐ δύναται διάγειν ἐν Ῥώμῃ, κἂν μὴ προστεθῇ τοῦτο τῇ ψήφῳ, ἐπειδὴ πάντων ἐστὶ πατρίς, ἀλλ' οὔτε ἐν τῇ πόλει, ἐν ᾗ διάγει ὁ βασιλεὺς ἢ δι' ἧς παρέρχεται· μόνοις γὰρ ἔξεστι τὸν βασιλέα βλέπειν τοῖς δυναμένοις εἰς Ῥώμην εἰσιέναι· πατὴρ γάρ ἐστι τῆς πατρίδος ὁ βασιλεύς. O. Lenel, *Palingenesia iuris civilis*, I, col. 93 f., note 53 and

Call.? D. 48.22.18pr. (.......) *relegatus morari non potest Romae, etsi id sententia comprehensum non est, quia communis patria est: neque in ea ciuitate, in qua moratur princeps uel per quam transit, iis enim solis permissum est principem intueri, qui Romam ingredi possunt, quia princeps pater patriae est.*

The exile cannot reside in Rome, even though the *sententia* does not explicitly specify it, since it is the *communis patria*; nor can he enter or settle in a city in which the *princeps* is staying or passing through. Hence, this can be contemplated only by those able to enter Rome: in fact, the prince is the father of the country.

Callistratus's conceptualization appears to be of extraordinary ideological density. Nevertheless, in my opinion, it is not true that the *princeps* – the holder of the highest office – would transform the city form of the State into that of a territorial Empire, because wherever he goes he would take the *communis patria* with him.[116] In other words, I would not identify here the extreme threshold of the political conception of the ancient world when, the model of the *pólis* by now exhausted, that of the territorial State is appearing on the horizon.[117]

The idea that, in Callistratus's perspective, the *princeps* embodies the *pater patriae communis* of that complex supranational organism that we identify as the *Imperium Romanorum* is undoubtedly a valid one.[118] However, we certainly cannot see in this image the sign of passage toward the construction of an authentic territorial state. Indeed, it must always be borne in mind that, here as elsewhere, the notion of

---

note 4. In *Littera Florentina* there is only a blank page. Mommsen, in reference to fragm. 10-18, wrote: *quae sequuntur usque ad finem tituli omissa in spatio vacuo paginarum quattuor in F supplentur secundum B.*

[116] F. Casavola, 'Il concetto di 'urbs Roma': giuristi e imperatori romani' (1992), now in Id., *'Sententia legum' tra antico e moderno*, with a *nota* by F. d'Ippolito and a *postfazione* by the author, I. *Diritto romano* (Napoli 2000) 355-364, part. 360 f. As well as by the same author, *Lo spazio nell'esperienza giuridica del mondo antico* (1999), now in Id., *'Sententia legum'*, I, 523-528, part. 527 f.

[117] Casavola, 'Il concetto di 'urbs Roma'' (n. 116) 26. However, this is a very widespread idea. See, for example, C. Rapp, H.A. Drake, 'Polis – Imperium – Oikoumenē: A World Reconfigured', in Rapp, Drake (eds.), *The City* (n. 38) 1-13.

[118] Casavola, 'Il concetto di 'urbs Roma'' (n. 116) 26. However, E. Voegelin, *La nuova scienza politica. Con un saggio di Augusto Del Noce su 'Eric Voegelin e la critica dell'idea di modernità'* (It. transl. Torino 1968) 141 ff., speaking of the *princeps*, of "existential representative of that vast agglomeration of territories and peoples under the dominion of Rome", used an essentially similar formulation.

Roma communis patria presents, first of all, a fiction: a fiction of ubiquity.[119]

In this perspective, consideration of the place or city where the *princeps* resides as equivalent to Rome is a legal artifice of fundamental importance, without which some decisive transformations of the institutions of the Principate and the Late Antiquity Empire would perhaps remain without a plausible explanation on the legal-constitutional level.

Callistratus's formulation is reflected in many other texts, primarily in a famous passage by Herodian, in which he reports that the brother-in-law of Commodus,[120] addressing the young prince – eager, a few months after the death of his father, to return to the city – exclaimed during a *consilium* "Rome is that place where the emperor is" ("ἐκεῖ τε ἡ Ῥώμη, ὅπου ποτ' ἂν ὁ βασιλεὺς ᾖ")[121]:

> Herod. 1.6.4–5 Τοιαῦτά τινα προφασιζομένου τοῦ μειρακίου οἱ μὲν ἄλλοι συνεστάλησάν τε τὴν ψυχήν, καὶ σκυθρωπαῖς ταῖς ὄψεσιν ἐς γῆν ἔνευσαν. Πομπηιανὸς δέ, ὃς πρεσβύτατός τε ἦν ἁπάντων καὶ κατ' ἐπιγαμίαν προσήκων αὐτῷ (συνῴκει γὰρ τῇ πρεσβυτάτῃ τῶν ἀδελφῶν τοῦ Κομόδου), "ποθεῖν μέν σε", ἔφη, "τέκνον καὶ δέσποτα, τὴν πατρίδα

[119] However, for *communis patria* see, in addition to Mod. 2 *excusat.*, D. 27.1.6.11, also *l.s. de manumiss.*, D. 50.1.33: on which, in particular, G. Viarengo, *Studi su Erennio Modestino. Profili biografici* (Torino 2009) 40 ff.; Macer 2 *de re militari*, D. 49.16.13.3, as well as CTh. 6.2.25 (a. 426). Also see *Tabula Heracleensis* l., 157 to be compared with Paul. 1 *resp.*, D. 50.5.9pr. More broadly, with bibliographical information, Marotta, *Esercizio e trasmissione* (n. 43) 103-119, with other references and other literature.

[120] Claudius Pompeianus, knight of Antioch, *adlectus inter praetorios*. He married Lucilla, sister of Commodus, after the death of Lucius Verus in 169. He had been *legatus* of *Pannonia inferior* during the Marcomannic Wars in 167, holding the consulate in 173, for the second time, as ordinary consul (*Prosopographia Imperii Romani*[2] C 973): see G. Alföldy, *Konsulat und Senatorenstand unter den Antoninen* (Bonn 1977) 187; P.M.M. Leunissen, *Konsuln und Konsulare in der Zeit von Commodus bis Severus Alexander (180-235 n. Chr.)* (Amsterdam 1989) 372.

[121] Herod. 1.6.5. Strangely, this formulation does not occur, in such explicit forms, in any other ancient testimony. However, it returns identical in the writings of medieval period jurists. Baldo degli Ubaldi, *Commentaria in primam Digesti veteris partem. Comm. ad* D. 5.1.2.3 *De iudiciis: ubi quisque agere vel conveniri debeat?* (Venetiis 1599) f. 258 v.: *Roma sit communis patria, et intelligo ubicumque est Papa vel Imperator*. Sinibaldo Fieschi (Innocence IV), *Apparatus in quinque libros decretalium, glossa a X*, 2, 4, Venetiis 1578, f. 117a, identified Rome with the pope's residence: *ubi papa est*. A few years later, Henricus de Segusio (Hostiensis), *In quintum decretalium librum commentaria*, commento a X, 5, 20, 4, 1, Venetiis 1581, f. 60 va., gave official guise to this doctrine, formalizing it in the axiom *ubi papa, ibi Roma*. On this subject, cf. M. Garcia Pelayo, *Miti e simboli politici* (It. transl. Torino 1970) 102 f.

εἰκός· καὶ γὰρ αὐτοὶ τῶν οἴκοι ὁμοίᾳ ἐπιθυμίᾳ ἑαλώκαμεν. Ἀλλὰ τὰ ἐνταῦθα προυργιαίτερα ὄντα καὶ μᾶλλον ἐπείγοντα ἐπέχει τὴν ἐπιθυμίαν. Τῶν μὲν γὰρ ἐκεῖσε καὶ ὕστερον ἐπὶ πλεῖστον αἰῶνα ἀπολαύσεις, ἐκεῖ τε ἡ Ῥώμη, ὅπου ποτ' ἂν ὁ βασιλεὺς ᾖ". [122]

And, in a context close to, but not fully identifiable with, that of the legal professions or legal knowledge, it is worth recalling a passage from the *Glossaria Latina*: [123]

nauicularii sunt qui transferebat frumenta in urbem aut ubicumque erat imperator.

In this case, the identification of the place where the *princeps* resides with Rome is only implicit but still immediately apparent.

In the writings of the jurists, the mechanism described by Callistratus is also used in:

Ulp. 6 *ad ed.*, D. 3.2.2.4 *Ignominia autem missis neque in urbe neque alibi, ubi imperator est, morari licet.*

Macer 2 *de re militari*, D. 49.16.13.3 *et is, qui ignominia missus est, neque Romae neque in sacro comitatu agere potest.*

[122] "As the young man advanced his aspirations, the onlookers felt their hearts tighten and, with sombre faces, glanced at the ground. Pompeianus, the eldest and linked to Commodus by ties of kinship (in fact, he had married the older of his sisters), spoke in the name of all. It is right – he said – my son, and my prince, that you feel nostalgia for the fatherland: in fact, we are also filled with the same longing for our homeland. Yet, the tasks that await us here are more serious and more pressing, and silence our sentiments. Later you will be able to enjoy the life of the capital for as long as you wish, and besides, Rome is that place where the emperor is". See J.-P. Coriat, *Le prince législateur. La technique législative des Sévères et les méthodes de création du droit impérial à la fin du principat* (Rome-Paris 1997) 183 f. Lastly on this text, C. Ando, 'Triumph in the decentralized empire', in J. Wienand, F. Goldbeck (eds.), *Der römische Triumph in Prinzipat und Spätantike* (Berlin-Boston 2017) 397-417. Also see G.W. Adams, *The Emperor Commodus. Gladiator, Hercules or Tyrant*, (Boca Raton [Florida] 2013) 144 ff.; A. Galimberti, *Erodiano e Commodo. Traduzione e commento storico al primo libro della Storia dell'Impero dopo Marco* (Göttingen 2014) 73 f. In political terms, Claudius Pompeianus's reflection can be compared with the speech by Lentulus in Luc. *Phars.* 5.15-37.

[123] *Corpus Glossariorum Latinorum*, rec. Goetz [*Glossae Codicis Leid. Voss. Lat.* 88] 5, 658, 7. For other aspects of this text, see L. De Salvo, *Economia privata e pubblici servizi nell'Impero romano. I 'corpora naviculariorum'* (Messina 1992) 232 note 38.

The *miles* discharged with a *missio ignominiosa* (a dishonourable discharge) [124] could not reside either in Rome or in the city or place where the emperor and his *comitatus* were quartered. The ruling, to which Ulpian and Macer refer, is undoubtedly the same as D. 48.22.18. Two interweaving fictions operate explicitly in this last text, implicitly in the other two. The first (a fiction of ubiquity) allows us to infer – such is the significance of the words *Roma communis patria* – that he who stays in the *urbs* is considered as if he had never abandoned his *patria*. The second coincides with the idea – clearly defined in its specific aspects by Herodian – that the *urbs* follows the *princeps* by means of *oikouménē* ("Rome is the place where the emperor is"). [125]

The search for the device explained by the formula *Roma communis patria* can be extended well back in time and, in the case of the *constitutiones principum*, at least to the Hadrianic period. This is what emerges from the *consultatio* of Egnatius Taurinus, proconsul of Baetica, to Trajan's successor:

> Ulp. 7 *de off. proc.* Coll. 1.1.11.2 *sed cupiditatis culpam coercendam credidi, ut ceteri eiusdem aetatis iuuenes emendarentur, ideoque Mario Euaristo urbe, Italia, prouincia Baetica in quinquennium interdixi* (…). [126]

---

[124] See S.E. Phang, *Roman Military Service. Ideologies of Discipline in the Late Republic and Early Principate* (Cambridge 2008) 145 f.

[125] This statement would seem to be contradicted by Septimius Severus' speech in Herod. 2. 10.9 (but also cf. Herod. 3.15.6; 5.2.3; 5.5.1): cf. Galimberti, *Erodiano e Commodo* (n. 122) 74. Also see the monograph of the archaeologist E. Mayer, *Rom ist dort, wo der Kaiser ist. Untersuchungen zu den Staatsdenkmälern des dezentralisierten Reiches von Diocletian bis zu Theodosius II* (Mainz-Bonn 2002) 1-27, part. 1, largely dedicated to the monumentalization of the new imperial residences between the third and fourth centuries. Appropriate in this perspective is the mention of Pan. Lat., 3(/11).12.1-2, in which the role of Milan, which for a few days enjoyed a *maiestas* similar to that of Rome, is exalted. In fact, it may have seemed that the *sedes imperii* was there where the two emperors (Diocletianus and Maximianus) had met: *Ipsa etiam gentium domina Roma immodico propinquitatis uestrae elata gaudio uosque e speculis suorum montium prospicere conata, quo se uultibus proprius expleret, ad intuendum cominus quantum potuit accessit. Lumina siquidem senatus sui misit beatissimae illi per eos dies Mediolanensium ciuitati similitudinem maiestatis suae libenter impartiens, ut ibi tunc esse sedes imperii uideretur quo uterque venerat imperator.* On this subject, but in a perspective very different from mine, also see S.-A. Fusco, '… "La dov'è l'imperatore" ovvero il decentramento della centralità', in AARC 13 (2001) 65-81.

[126] Cf. also Ulp. 8 *de off. proc.*, D. 47.18.2 (…) *sed enim diuus Marcus effractorem equitem Romanum, qui effracto perforatoque pariete pecuniam abstulerat, quinquennio abstinere iussit prouincia Africa, unde erat, et urbe et Italia.*

Here the term *urbs* encompasses both Rome and the *origo* of Marius Evaristus (a city of Baetica unknown to us).[127]

Therefore, it must be recognized that this device (*Roma communis patria*) was not established directly or indirectly by the *constitutio Antoniniana*. Its operation on a general scale, hence beyond the Roman *colonia* and *municipalia*, does not depend on the extension of citizenship to all the free inhabitants of the Empire.[128] Moreover, regarding its norma-

---

[127] If this *patria (origo) / communis patria* symmetry might seem merely implicit, that of *Italia / prouincia Baetica* is not. Also see, for a discussion, CI. 4.55.5 (a. 225) (…) *qui autem de prouincia certa, nec in Italia* (…).

[128] And this is demonstrated also by a fragment of Cervidius Scaevola 1 *dig*., D. 50.7.13 *Legatus creatus a patria sua suscepta legatione in urbem Romam venit et nondum perfecta legatione domum, quae erat in ipsius civitate Nicopoli, emit. Quaesitum est, an in senatus consultum inciderit, quo prohibetur legati ante perfectam legationem negotiis vel priuatis rebus obstringi. Respondit non uideri teneri*. Not subject to the prohibition, sanctioned by a *senatus consultum*, against conducting activities of private interest during a diplomatic mission was the *legatus* (ambassador) who, having arrived in Rome or, perhaps more likely, having stopped there during his journey, had arranged for, *nondum perfecta legatione*, the purchase of a *domus* in his *patria*. Indeed, the *legatus* did not violate the prohibition decreed by the *senatus consultum* precisely because of the principle of Rome's ubiquity: those who arrive in Rome are considered as if they had never left their *patria*. See M. Talamanca, 'I clienti di Cervidio Scevola', in BIDR 103/104 (2000/2001) 581 f., note 392 with bibliography, to which I would add F. Grelle, *L'autonomia cittadina fra Traiano e Adriano* (Napoli 1972) 22, 51 f. Other considerations are in Thomas, *"Origine" et "commune patrie"* (n. 68) 18 note 29, with other information; V. Marotta, 'I 'mandata' nei libri 'de officio proconsulis' di Ulpiano. Tecniche di governo e regole d'opportunità sociale', in E. Stolfi (ed.), *Giuristi e 'officium'. L'elaborazione giurisprudenziale di regole per l'esercizio del potere fra II e III secolo d.C.* (Napoli 2011) 170 ff. At first glance, it is not easy to understand to what the words *nondum perfecta legatione* allude. According to Talamanca, the spontaneous answer is that the purchase had occurred while the *legatus* was still in Rome. Nevertheless, he cannot understand how he could have proceeded with such a purchase in the *patria* so far away. Talamanca excludes that the *legatus* could have availed himself of a representative, because in doing so he would not have violated the prohibition against dealing with his affairs during the *legatio*. Hence, it can be assumed that the purchase had been made before leaving for Rome, after having taken on the assignment, a hypothesis, for Talamanca, preferable to the idea that the purchase had taken place after returning home but before having provided his report. In truth, this attempt at clarification conflicts with the content of the passage by Cervidius Scaevola: we should avoid adding, to the subject of our exegesis, factual details that do not emerge from it either implicitly or explicitly. Moreover, if the words *(...) quo prohibetur legate ante perfectam legationem negotiis vel priuatis rebus obstringi* are evaluated, it seems clear to me that conferring upon a representative, during the *legatio*, the task of purchasing a house in his *patria* could have given rise, at least in theory, to conduct prohibited by the *senatus consultum* (cf. the words [...] *vel priuatis rebus* [...]). Almost all the interpreters have wondered if this Nicopolis must be identified as a *civitas Romana*: Talamanca concluded thusly, but without providing evi-

tive content, the famous Edict of Caracalla can be compared to the acts of *adsignatio viritana* of citizenship and not to the promotion of a foreign city to the rank of Roman community. In other words, starting from 212, there was no process of municipalization of the Empire comparable with that of Italy after the social war. Consequently, by effect of the *constitutio Antoniniana*, the constitutional structures of the communities were not standardized to a single model. The foreign cities did not automatically become Roman *municipia*. To the contrary, they continued to ask and obtain – in the decades immediately following this provision – promotions of *status*.[129] Moreover, there is also another, chronologically certain, proof of the seriousness of the device explained by D. 48.22.18pr. and by the other texts parallel to the *constitutio Antoniniana*. It is a *quaestio* of Papinianus, put to death at the end of 211 or at the beginning of 212, in any case before the issuing of the Edict of Caracalla:[130]

> Pap. 10 *quaest.*, D. 18.7.5 *Cui pacto uenditoris pomerio cuiuslibet ciuitatis interdictum est, urbe etiam interdictum esse uidetur. Quod quidem alias cum principum mandatis praeciperetur, etiam naturalem habet intellectum, ne scilicet qui careret minoribus, fruatur maioribus.*

In this part of book X of his *quaestiones*, the jurist[131] examines negotiation clauses such as the *leges venditionis*, especially considering those applying to the sale of slaves. In fact, added to this type of contract – at times to help the alienated *servus*, at times (as in our case) to inflict a penalty on him (afflictive clauses) – were some special agreements, as emerges from

---

dence. For my part, I would recall that of the three (or at most four) cities with this name – still in existence at that time and mentioned by our literary and epigraphic sources – only *Nicopolis ad Nestum*, founded by Trajan in Thrace, was perhaps a *colonia*. Therefore, it is more likely, considering the generic formulation of this text, that Scaevola intended to refer to the *pólis* known quintessentially by that name at that time: the free and federated city founded via synoecism by Octavianus in Epirus to celebrate his victory in the Battle of Actium. It is impossible that Cervidius Scaevola was referring to Nikopolis upon Lykos in *Armenia minor*: ἡ μη/τρό[πολις] καὶ δὶς / [ν]εω[κόρος] Νικοπο/λιτῶν ['Ιτ]α[λ]ικὴ κολωνία: H. Gregoire, *Rapport sur un voyage d'exploration dans le Pont et en Cappadoce*, BCH 33 (1909) 35, n. 13.

[129] Cf. Marotta, *La cittadinanza romana* (n. 37) 154, with other information.

[130] For an overview, see A. Magioncalda, 'Un giurista al servizio dell'imperatore. La carriera di Emilio Papiniano', in Materiali 30.2 (2000) 454 ff.

[131] For a different interpretation, cf. J. Cujacius, *Opera. Ad Parisiensem Fabrotianam editionem diligentissime exacta auctiora atque emendatiora. Editio altera Pratensis. Tomus Quintus* (Prato 1861) 444.

examination of the cases passed down to us with the title 18.7 [132] of the Digest and from a passage of the *Vaticana Fragmenta.* [133] As in the example presented here by Papinianus, the sale of a slave proceeds on condition that he does not reside in Italy or in a certain *civitas*. In the *pactum* at the centre of this *quaestio*, it was established that a *servus* must not cross the *pomerium* of a certain city. To the jurist, it seems clear that the slave was forbidden to enter not only the city indicated by the seller (probably the latter's *origo*) but also the *urbs*, i.e. Rome. Papinianus uses the *argumentum a minori*: in fact – he observes – it is the same *naturalis intellectus* that demonstrates how more always includes, within itself, less. The reason for which those who lack minor goods certainly cannot enjoy greater ones, that is, those prohibited from entering a certain city [134] are at the same time prohibited from entering the city of Rome. In this simple but effective argumentative path, the jurist notes contextually how, with reference to other subjects (*alias*), the *mandata* [135] apply the same principle. Instead, the connection of the expression *pomerium* with *civitas*, as well as with *urbs*, raises some perplexity. Papinianus must have known that it indicated the furrow, the strip of land, traced by the plough [136] that defined the *urbs*, separating it from the *ager*. [137] However, in his examination of this problem, he does not refer the term *pomerium* exclusively to the border of those *civitates* – the *coloniae* – founded and inaugurated in the image of Rome. In this way, the jurist alludes, regardless of the specific legal status of each city, to any clear line of demarcation from the countryside. [138] After

---

[132] A. Sicari, *'Leges venditionis'. Uno studio sul pensiero giuridico di Papiniano* (Bari 1996) 43 ff.

[133] See Frg. Vat. 6: Sicari, *'Leges venditionis'* (n. 132) 301 ff.

[134] *Origo* and *domicilium* are terms which, for a slave, could not present any precise technical meaning.

[135] Cf. Ulp. 10 *de off. proc.*, D. 48.22.7.15-16: see Marotta, *I 'mandata'* (n. 128) 170-176.

[136] Cf., for example, Pomp. *l.s. ench.*, D. 50.16.239 *Urbs ab urbo appellata est: urbare est aratro definire. Et Varus ait urbum appellari curuaturam aratri, quod in urbe condenda adhiberi solet.*

[137] On the notion of *urbs Roma* in the thought of jurists, lastly see S. Querzoli, *Scienza giuridica e cultura retorica in Ulpio Marcello* (Napoli 2013) 103-117, with bibliography, to which *adde* that collection in Corbo, *'Constitutio Antoniniana'* (n. 54) 81-83. On the *inauguratio* and the delimitation of the *pomerium*, see G. De Sanctis, *La logica del confine. Per un'antropologia dello spazio nel mondo romano* (Roma 2015) 121 ff., in part. 132-135, with other bibliography; M. Bettini, *Dèi e uomini nella città. Antropologia, religione e cultura nella Roma antica* (Roma 2015) 27-34.

[138] At times, at least on some occasions, the walls: in effect – in Apul. *met.* 2.1

all, only at the cost of complete equation of the augural line of the *urbs* with those which, according to non-uniform rules, delimited the *ager* or the χώρα of *civitates* and *póleis* from their urban core, could the legal device considered in the Papinian *quaestio* be generally applied.[139]

This explicit reference to the *pomerium* and thus to the *urbs* makes it easy to understand when the device described by the jurist was developed. In effect, in the Republican period, both the *Tabula Heracleensis* l. 157[140] and the *lex de Gallia Cisalpina* – implicitly in c. XXI (ll. 10 s.), explicitly in c. XXII (ll. 40 ff.)[141] – used the same *fictio* underlying the expression *Roma communis patria*. According to the *lex Rubria*, the *iudicia* established in the *municipia* had to be the equivalent of the urban ones. Evidence to support this conclusion is found, in this law, concerning the *confessio in iure*, in a *fictio* defined by the words *atque utei esset essee oporteret, sei is (…) Romae apud praetorem (…) in iure confessus esset.*[142]

In the *lex Irnitana* [c. 91 {XB} ll. 3–4],[143] issued in the Flavian peri-

---

(…) et arbores quae pomerium ambirent similiter foliatas (…) crederem - pomerium provides almost a synonym of them.

[139] As in the cases referred to in the texts mentioned in note 119 and note 135.

[140] *Qui pluribus in municipieis colon<i>eis praefectureis domicilium habebit et is Romae census erit, quo magis in muncipio colonia praefectura h(ac) l(ege) censeatur, e(ius) h(ac) lege) n(ihilum) r(ogatur).*

[141] Thomas, *"Origine" et "commune patrie"* (n. 68) 20-22.

[142] C. XXII, ll. 40-43.

[143] <LXXXXI> || [42] *R(ubrica). Quo iure in tertium denuntietur, dies diffidatur diffi[43]<s>susue sit, res iudicetur, lis iudici((i)) damni sit, res iudi*[44]*cio esse desinat.* [45] *Quacumque de re priuata iudices arbitri in eo municipio da*[46]*ti subditi addictiue h(ac) l(ege) erunt, is iudicibus arbitris<ue> et is,* [47] *quos inter ii iudices arbitriue dati subditi addictiue* [48] *h(ac) l(ege) erunt, de ea re in tertium aduersario iudici arbitro*[49]*ue in biduo proximo denuntiandi, diem diffidendi, dies* [50] *diffis[sos] iurandi, antequam iudicent, iudicandi litem ae*[51]*stumandi, per quos dies et ubi ex h(ac) l(ege) licebit oportebit, et si* [52] *neque dies diffi<s>sus neque iudicatum fuerit, uti lis iudi*[53]*ci arbitroue damni sit, et si intra it tempus, quod legis Iuli*[54]*ae, quae de iudic<i>s priuatis proxime lata est, kapite (decimo secundo)* 10 B *senatusue consultis ((ad it kaput)) ad it kaput legis pertine*[2]*ntibus compr<e>hensum est, iudicatum non sit, uti res in iudi*[3]*cio non sit, siremps lex ((r)) i(us) [c](ausa)que esto adque((m)) uti esset si eam rem* [4] *in urbe Roma praetor p(opuli) R(omani) inter ciues Romanos iudicari iussisset* [5] *et de e(a) r(e), ex <quacumque> lege rogatione((m)) quocumque plebis scito iudicia pri*[6]*uata in urbe Roma fient, agi, fieri, denuntiari, diem diffin[[den]]*[7]*di, diem diffi<s>sum esse, iudicari, litem iudici damni esse, rem in* [8] *iudicio non esse oporteret, praeter quam quod per alios dies* [9] *et alio loco h(ac) l(ege) denuntiari, rem iudicari, diem diffindi opor*[10]*tebit.*

Itaque iis omnibus, de ea re et in eos dies in quos ex h(ac) l(ege) lice[11]*bit, de-*

od, we find the same device, although in this case, since the *municipes* of Irni in Baetica were mostly not *cives Romani* (but *Latini*), the fiction had to be reformulated with these words: "just as if a praetor of the Roman people had ordered, in the city of Rome and among Roman citizens, to judge that dispute".[144]

Callistratus's conceptualization and the other parallel texts, firstly the *lex Rubria* and the *lex Irnitana*, demonstrate that, when one reflects on the Roman Empire and on the doctrines formulated by its jurists, it is not possible to adopt the notion of territorial State in the modern and contemporary sense of homogeneous normative space.[145]

4. Fictions of ubiquity and *ius publicum* of Late Antiquity

The granting of Roman citizenship to all the inhabitants of the *orbis Romanus* did not lead, in 212, to the creation of a territorial state. Between 89 and 42 BCE, in the process of municipalization of Italy, the expedient of a fiction was used in the *leges de civitate* (without any doubt, in a different context, in the *lex Rubria <de Gallia cisalpina>*), by virtue of which everything was evaluated as if the *municeps* in Rome continued to reside in his own *patria* and, in his own *patria*, continued to be in Rome. Likewise, before and after the *constitutio Antoniniana*, in the place of the creation of an authentic territorial state the same legal artifice allowed perpetuation for centuries of the political fiction of the *civitas*,

nuntiandi intra it municipium et mille passus ab eo mu[12]*nicipio, aut ubi pacti erunt, diem diffi<n>dendi, iudicandi in foro* [13] *eius municipi aut ubi pacti erunt, dum infra fines eius munici*[14]*pi, utique ex [[h]]isdem causis dies diffinda((n))tur, diffi<s>sus sit,* [15] *utique, si neque diffi[s]sum e lege neque iudicatum sit per quos di*[16]*es quoque loco ex h(ac) l(ege) iudicari licebit oportebit, iudici arbitro<ue>* [17] *lis damni sit, utique, si intra it tempus quod supra compr<e>hensum* [18] *est iudicatum non sit, res in iudicio non sit, <siremps lex> ius <causaque> esto <atque> uti si <praetor populi Romani inter> ciues Ro*[19]*manos <iudicari> iussisse<t> ibique d(e) e(a) r(e) iudicium fieri oporteret ex ((lege roga*[20]*tione plebisue scitis)) quacumque lege rogatione quocumque* [21] *plebis scito iudicia <priuata> in urbe Roma fieri oporte[bi]t, praeterqum* [22] *quod per alios dies et alio loco ex hac lege denuntiari, rem*[23]*que iudicari, diemque diffindi oportebit.*

[144] *(…) siremps lex ((r)) i(us) [c](ausa)que esto adque((m)) uti esset si eam rem* [4] *in urbe Roma praetor p(opuli) R(omani) inter ciues Romanos iudica-ri iussisset.* On the *iudicia legitima* in the *municipia,* see I. Fargnoli, 'Si eam rem in urbe Roma … iudicari iussisset. Sulla legittimità dei giudizi nella lex Irnitana', in Iura 60 (2012) 246 ff.

[145] O. Beaud, 'Que peut apprendre un juriste de droit public en lisant Yan Thomas?', in P. Napoli (ed.), *Aux origines des cultures juridiques européennes. Yan Thomas entre droit et sciences sociales* (Rome 2013) 117-149, part. 123-133.

precisely because the *urbs* followed the *princeps* by means of the *oikouménē* ("Rome is that place where the emperor is"). In Callistratus, Ulpian and Macer, consideration of the place or city where the *princeps* resided as equivalent to Rome was a decisive fiction, [146] without which it would have been difficult to legitimize, on the juridical level, some of the most important institutional changes of Late Antiquity.

Therefore, the soil of Rome, at least virtually, was everywhere. [147] I will give a single but – I hope – illuminating example of the peculiar operation of this fiction between the fourth and fifth centuries. Some verses of Claudian, [148] taken from the *Panegyricus dictus Honorio Augusto consulati sexti*, certainly referable to 404, [149] can be compared with the *Gratiarum Actio* written by Ausonius in 379 on the occasion of his election to the consulate by the emperor Gratian.

To thank the prince on the occasion of his election to the consulate, the Gallo-Roman rhetorician wished first of all to celebrate the silent dialogue between the emperor and God and the special relationship that bound the former to the latter. [150] In contrast, the Alexandrian poet dealt with the voting procedures in the Campus Martius. According to Claudian, Honorius would have performed his sixth consulate respecting the rules established by an ancient tradition, once the comitia had assembled on the ancient *campus sollemnis* of Rome:

---

[146] It is not possible here to dwell on its most probable historical origin. Perhaps it was elaborated on the basis of an extensive interpretation of a tralaticial *caput* (relating to the *tribunicia potestas*) of the so-called *leges de imperio*; a *caput* in which, as in other cases (attested also by the *lex de imperio Vespasiani: capita* III and VIII), the *fictio* was used: see Marotta, *Esercizio e trasmissione* (n. 43) part. 110 ff.

[147] Dupont, *Rome, la ville sans origine* (n. 109) 56.

[148] M. Dewar, *Claudian, Panegyricus de sexto consulatu Honorii Augusti. Edited with Introduction, Translation, and Literary Commentary* (Oxford 1996) 5, 63-70. I was not able to consult J.TH.C. King, *Claudian's 'Panegyricus dictus Honorio Augusto sextum consuli': A Commentary*, Thesis (Ph. D.) (Queen's University of Belfast 2000). Other considerations in C. Castello, 'Una voce dissonante nella Roma cristiana di Onorio. Il panegirico di Claudiano del 404 d.C.', in AARC 3 (Perugia 1979) 153-196; M. Wheeler, 'The Emperor's Love of Rome in Claudian's Panegyric on the Sixth Consulate of Honorius', in S. Mcgill, J. Pucci (eds.), *Tradition and Innovation in the Latin Poetry of Late Antiquity* (Heidelberg 2016) 195-220; J.-L. Charlet, 'Analyse', in Claudien, *Oeuvres. Tome III. Poèmes politiques (399-404)*, Texte ètabli et traduit par J.L. Charlet (Paris 2017) 225 ff., part. 225-228 (other bibliography XLVI f.).

[149] Claudian. *Panegyr. dictus Honorio Aug. consulati sexti.*

[150] *Gratiarum Actio*, 9.42 *quae tu pontifex maximus Deo participatus habuisti*; 9.43 *consilium meum ad Deum re<t>tuli* (the last words taken from the same *epistula* of Gratian: cf., *infra*, p. 253 and note 155.

vv. 1–10 *Aurea Fortunae Reduci si templa priores Ob reditum uouere ducum, non dignius umquam Haec dea pro meritis amplas sibi posceret aedes Quam sua cum pariter trabeis reparatur et urbi Maiestas; neque enim campus sollemnis et urna Luditur in morem, species nec dissona coetu*

Aut peregrina nitet simulati iuris imago. Indigenas habitus natiua Palatia sumunt, Et, patriis plebem castris sociante Quirino, Mars Augusta sui renouat suffragia campi.

The ancients had offered golden temples to *Fortuna Redux* for the safe return of their commanders. Hence, it should not be surprising that this divinity should demand a larger temple in exchange for her services,[151] since the splendour of both of the consulate (*trabeae*) and of Rome had been restored at the same time. The annual elections in the *campus sollemnis*[152] (Campus Martius), according to the prescribed forms and the counting of votes, were not conducted merely for show, based on established custom, nor was this a mere appearance not in accordance with the dignity of that assembly nor was this the splendour of a foreign imitation or a simulated law. The native *Palatinus* donned indigenous clothes, and, just as *Quirinus* united the plebs and the army, *Mars* renewed the imperial elections of his *Campus*.

Certainly, it is impossible to believe that the *comitia*[153] had actually been convened according to the procedures still in use in the Republican period.[154] However, we must believe Claudian when he claims that,

---

[151] On the cult of *Fortuna Redux*, established by the senate at the time of Augustus on 12 October 19 BCE, see J. Champeaux, *'Fortuna'. Recherche sur le culte de la Fortune à Rome et dans le monde romain*, voll. I e II (Rome 1982). Other considerations are in J.-L. Charlet, 'Notes complémentaires. Panégyrique pour le sixième consulat', in *Claudien, Oeuvres. Tome III* (n. 148) 363 f.

[152] Cf. Luc. *Phars.* 5. 392-394 *fingit* (*scil.* Giulio Cesare) *sollemnia Campus / et non admissae dirimit suffragia plebis / decantatque tribus et uana uersat in urna.*

[153] See P. Veyne, *L'empire gréco-romain* (Paris 2005) 26 and note 52, for whom, in the fourth and early fifth centuries, the comitia of the Roman people still existed, albeit as mere simulacrum. In effect, Claudian underlines the fact that, with his initiative, Honorius had placed the Roman plebs on the same level as the soldiers.

[154] However, it is possible that those rituals, which according to Cassius Dio were still respected in the middle of the third century, were followed at least in part (*infra*, note 160): on this point, see Marotta, *Esercizio e trasmissione* (n. 43) 187 ff. Regarding Claudian's testimony, perhaps we might wonder how all this was reconciled (if it was reconciled) with the principles established by the new Christian *decorum*. In effect, despite the pronouncements of Theodosius, Arcadius and Honorius himself against pagan cults (cf. CTh. 16.10.12; 13; 14; 15; 16;

on this occasion, there was no representation harmful to the dignity of the *campus sollemnis*. In fact, the ritual was celebrated in Rome, not elsewhere, on the basis of a foreign imitation and of a *ius simulatum*.

In contrast, the fiction – legal as well as ceremonial – and the *ius simulatum*, to which Claudian alludes, are (albeit only implicitly) at the centre of Ausonius's composition. For the Gallo-Roman rhetorician,[155]

17 and 18), the poet writes in the same *Panegyricus dictus Honorio Augusto consulati sexti* vv. 11-17: *Qualis erat terris, quem mons Euandrius offert / Romanis auibus, quem T<h>ybris inaugurat, annus? / Quamquam omnes, quicumque tui cognominis, anni / semper inoffensum dederint successibus omen / sintque trop[h]aea tuas semper commitata secures, / hic tamen ante omnes miro promittitur ortu, / Urbis et Augusti geminato nomine felix*. Claudian imagines that the auspices taken for the sixth consulate of Honorius foretell a year of happiness and successes. Finally, in verses 11 and 12, there is an explicit allusion to the *augurium* of the twelve vultures appearing to Romulus on *mons Euandrius* (common synonym to indicate the Palatine): cf. Liv. 1.7.3; Verg. *Aen*. 8.51 ff.; Statius, *silvae* 4.1.7-8: see Charlet, 'Notes complémentaires' (n. 151) 365. In this regard, also Salvian (*de gubernatione Dei* 6.2.12-13 *Quid enim? Numquid non consulibus et pulli adhuc gentilium sacrilegiorum more pascuntur et uolantis pinnae auguria quaeruntur, ac paene omnia fiunt quae etiam illi quondam pagani ueteres friuula atque inridenda duxerunt? Et cum haec omnia ipsi agant qui annis nomina tribuunt et a quibus anni ipsi exordium sumunt, credimus nobis bene annos posse procedere, qui a rebus talibus ordiuntur? Atque utinam sicut haec propter consules tantum fiunt, ita illos tantum incestarent propter quos fiunt!* 13. *Illud est feralissimum et grauissimum quod, dum consensu publico aguntur, honor paucissimorum fit crimen omnium, ac sic, cum singulis annis bini inaugurentur, prope est ut in omni mundo nullus euadat*) clearly refers to the divinatory and augural practices that each year celebrated the assumption of office of the two new consuls. Perhaps Salvian was alluding, when speaking of *uolantis pinnae auguria*, to Cic. *de div*. 1.15; 2.35. When looking at the so-called *auspicia ex tripudiis*, it must be considered that the *pullarii*, custodians of the chickens used for consultation of the auspices, were included in the organization of the city's civil service at least until the period of Marcus Aurelius, precisely up to 173 CE, the year of the last epigraphic testimony on the subject. However, it is evident, in light of Salvian's testimony, that these practices continued for centuries: in any case, see G. Foti, 'Funzioni e caratteri del 'pullarius'in età repubblicana e imperiale', in Acme 64 (2011) 90-121.

[155] Cf. *Gratiarum Actio*, 9.42 *tu, Auguste uenerabilis, districtus maximo bello, adsultantibus tot milibus barbarorum, quot Danuuii ora praetexitur, comitia consulatus mei armatus exerces. tributa ista quod in urbe Sirmio geruntur, aut quod in procinctu, centuriata dicentur? an ut quondam pontificalia uocabuntur, sine arbitrio multitudinis sacerdotum tractata collegio? sic potius, sic uocentur, quae tu pontifex maximus Deo participatus habuisti*. On this point, see J. Rüpke, *Tra Giove e Cristo. Trasformazioni religiose nell'impero romano* (It. transl. Brescia 2013) 279. For a discussion, see Amm., 14.6.6 *Et olim licet otiosae sint tribus pacataeque centuriae et nulla suffragiorum certamina* (…).

Gratian presided over the *comitia* that approved the election of his former tutor, *in urbe Sirmio*, while, one year after the defeat of Hadrianopolis on 9 August 378, he was leading an expedition against the barbarians along the banks of the Danube.[156]

According to a passage from the text of the *epistula* of appointment[157] – which the rhetorician reported *verbatim* in his *Gratiarum Actio* – Gratian did not merely pronounce (*designaui*) the names of the consuls but also provided for their formal proclamation (*et declaraui et priorem nuncupaui*), giving rise to a ritual coinciding, in effect, with the *renuntiatio*, the solemn and public announcement of the results of the elections, and thus with the only act able to attribute to the nominee the fullness of his *potestas* and of his auspices:[158]

---

[156] He wonders if these comitia should be defined as *tributa*, since they took place *in urbe Sirmio*, or *centuriata quod in procinctu* (i.e. among the troops in battle), or *pontificalia*, such as those which, *sine arbitrio multitudinis*, this priestly college had once practised. Ausonius – perhaps thinking of the *comitia curiata* presided over on some occasions by the *pontifices* – in his rhetorical construction, accepts this last solution.

[157] *Gratiarum Actio*, 9.43. In this case, we are not dealing with *codicilli* of appointment in the proper sense, but with a mere communication to the interested party of his election to the consulate *in absentia*. Although at times, even in testimonies from the end of the first or second century CE, the term *codicilli* was used to indicate a short letter with which, for example, information was given to the recipient about his designation to the praetorship (Marotta, *Esercizio e trasmissione* [n. 43] 52 f.), this expression was more properly used to indicate those documents used to appoint officials – *praefecti* and *procuratores* of equestrian rank or *legati Augusti pro praetore* of senatorial rank – directly subordinate to the *principes*: see S. Panciera, 'Le virtù del governatore provinciale nelle iscrizioni latine da Augusto a Diocleziano', in S. Demougin, X. Loriot, P. Cosme, P. Lefebvre (eds.), *H.-G. Pflaum un historien du XXe siècle* (Genéve 2006) 457-484, with other information. Also see S. Segenni, 'Appunti per uno studio sulla corrispondenza imperiale. Il problema dei 'codicilli' imperiali', in Acme 58.2 (2005) 100-109.

[158] Also in Late Antiquity, attention was paid to these aspects and there was full awareness of the fact that the consul was, at least virtually, the holder of an *imperium* of the same nature as that of the *princeps*. All this emerges, with some clarity, from an episode recounted to us by Amm. 22.7.1-2 *Allapso itaque Calendarum Ianuariarum die cum Mamertini et Neuittae nomina suscepissent paginae consulares, humilior princeps uisus est, in officio pedibus gradiendo cum honoratis, quod laudabant alii quidam ut affectatum et uile capebant. 2. Dein Mamertino ludos edente circenses, manu mittendis ex more inductis per admissionum proximum, ipse lege agi dixerat, ut solebat, statimque admonitus iuris dictionem eo die ad alterum pertinere, ut errato obnoxium decem libris auri semet ipse multauit.* Mamertinus was officiating the circus games to celebrate the start of the judiciary. Iulianus, who had followed the consular procession on foot together with the officials of the *officia*, after taking his place in the circus, proceeded personally, due to an error of the *proximus* of the *officium admissionum*, to the manumissions, pronouncing the usual ritual formula (*ipse lege agi dixerat*). Realizing his

Gratiarum Actio, 9.43 *Non est ingenii mei, piissime imperator, talia comminisci. Uerba sunt litterarum tuarum, quibus apud me auctoritatem summi numinis et tuae uoluntatis amplificas. Sic enim loqueris: "cum de consulibus in annum creandis solus mecum uolutarem, ut me nosti, atque ut facere debui, ut uelle te sciui, consilium meum ad Deum re<t>tuli. Eius auctoritati obsecutus te consulem designaui et declaraui et priorem nuncupaui.*

Gratiarum Actio, 12.57–58 *Cum prior renuntiatus sim, satis est tuum tenere iudicium: interpretes ualete meritorum. Neque autem ego, sacratissime imperator, in tenui beneficio gradum nuncupationis amplector. Non est haec gloria ignota Ciceroni, "Praetorem me", inquit, "populus Romanus primum fecit, consulem priorem". Ex ipsa eius sententia intellegitur commendabilius ei uideri <uni> quam pluribus esse praepositum: nulla enim est equidem contumelia secundi, sed in duobus gloria magna praelati.*

Instead, Claudian wished to underline that, on the occasion of the sixth consulate of Honorius, there was no *ius simulatum*, based, we can presume, on the principle that "Rome is that place where the emperor is",[159] almost as if the city where the *princeps* was staying became *pro tempore* and by fiction an *altera urbs*. In 404, the assembly of the *campus sollemnis* took place – observes the poet – in full respect of the ancient tradition and forms.[160]

For almost four centuries now, the assemblies of the *comitia* seemed a mere ritual, not able, as such, to conceal the fact that each magistrate, even a consul, assumed a representation that was vicarious with respect to the *princeps* and thus, by this manner, somewhat dignitary.[161] On the political level – even more so in Late Antiquity – this was undoubtedly

---

inadvertent infraction, i.e. having learned that, on that day, in the presence of the consul, he should have refrained from performing any judicial act involving the exercise of his *imperium*, Iulianus imposed upon himself a fine of ten librae of gold. Hence, it is difficult, but certainly possible, to identify testimonies attesting to the commitment of some *principes* to comply with the rules of Republican legality. In this regard, see Marotta, *Esercizio e trasmissione* (n. 43) 60 f.

[159] Herod. 1.6.5: *supra*, p. 243.

[160] Perhaps according to the example followed at the time by Trajan (cf. Plin. Min. Pan. 63), hence opposed to the practice adopted by Gratian, to which Ausonius alludes: *Gratiarum Actio*, 3.13 *Romanus populus, Martius Campus, equester ordo, rostra, ouilia, senatus, curia, unus mihi omnia Gratianus*. On the text and its ideological implications, see M. Vitiello, 'Blaming the Late Republic: Senatorial Ideology and Republican Institutions in Late Antiquity', in Classical Receptions Journal 7 (2015) 31-45.

[161] I refer the reader, in this regard, to Marotta, *Esercizio e trasmissione* (n. 43) 48-54.

so. Yet, on the juridical level, the reference that had to be taken into account – through the effective fiction by which Rome, the *communis patria*, moved by means of the *oikouménē* wherever the *princeps* moved – were still those of the *civitas* and its institutions.

Chapter 10

ASPECTS OF THE CRITICAL EDITION OF ROMAN JURISTIC WORKS. THE EXAMPLE OF ULPIAN'S *DE OFFICIO PROCONSULIS*

Dario Mantovani

SUMMARY: 1. Introduction. – 2. Mommsen's edition of the Digest (I): ecdotic criteria – 3. (II): textual emendation. –4. (III): reaching the textual layer of classical jurists. – 5. The edition of Ulpian's *De officio proconsulis*: purpose and method. – 6. D. 48.18.1.23: mechanical errors and glosses. – 7. D. 48.18.1 pr.-4: error by haplography. – 8. D. 1.16.6pr.-2: mechanical errors and intentional alterations. – 9. Coll. 3.3.1 and D. 1.6.2: dual tradition and emendation. – 10. Paratext. – 11. Juristic books as 'Literature'

1. Introduction

The typical aim of a critical edition – to restore a text as faithfully as possible to its "authentic" state, that is the one intended by its author but altered to varying degrees in the course of its transmission – also applies to the edition of works of Roman jurists. This principle is at the core of the considerations that follow below and which draw on my experiences with the edition of Ulpian's *De officio proconsulis*, accomplished with Mario De Nonno. Our edition began in 2007 as part of the then *Csir* project directed by Aldo Schiavone and continued at the pace of a few weeks of work every year. The edition is now completed, as regards both the constitution of the text and to the preparation of the critical apparatus, and it will be published as soon as our commitments will allow it.[1] I present here a small sample thereof, repre-

[1] The edition was realized jointly, working at the same table, bringing together our respective expertise and perspectives. Hence, the text and apparatus of the examples here discussed must be attributed to both authors. I thank Mario De Nonno for allowing the use of our shared work; responsibility for the article and any errors are mine. Part of the present study was conducted within the Redhis - ERC AdG 2013 Project ("Rediscovering the Hidden Struc-

sentative of aspects that may have some specific interest in terms of methodology.[2]

2. Mommsen's edition of the Digest (I): ecdotic criteria

Ulpian's *De officio proconsulis*, likely written between 212 and 217, has a richer textual tradition than other works of Roman legal science. In addition to the Digest, some extensive fragments are found in the *Collatio legum Romanarum et Mosaicarum*, whose transmission in turn depends on at least three medieval manuscripts housed in Berlin, Wien and Vercelli.[3] There are other rare and occasional indirect witnesses to Ulpian's treaty on the provincial governor's duties: an Ephesian inscription, Lactantius, and the glossary attributed to Philoxenus.[4] Precisely because we set as our task to produce a critical edition, our goal has been to restore the text according to Ulpian's intent.

This objective implied at the outset and above all (for quantitative reasons) a reflection on the transmission of juristic works via the Digest. Since this is an issue that applies to all the works of the classical jurists directly excerpted by the compilators of the Digest, it is useful to expound on it at the start and at some length (§ 2-4). The topic must be discussed on two levels, proceeding, so to speak, *à rebours*: we will deal first with the relationship between the *codex Florentinus* and the Digest (i.e. between the main witness available to us and Justinian's 'original') and second, going backwards, with the relationship between the Digest

ture. A New Appreciation of Juristic Texts and Patterns of Thoughts in Late Antiquity").

[2] The Latin text we prepared is accompanied by an Italian translation; however, we have not provided a commentary on the legal contents, except when essential to justify our choices concerning the critical constitution of the text.

[3] *B* = Berlin, Staatsbibliothek-Preussischer Kulturbesitz, Lat. fol. 269, ff. 157v-182v (ninth century); *W* = Wien, Österreichische Nationalbibliothek n. 2160, ff. 162v-184v (ninth century); *V* = Vercelli, Biblioteca Capitolare n. 122, ff. 13vb-15rb + 159vb + 162ra-186ra (tenth-eleventh century). Cf. recently R.M. Frakes, *Compiling the Collatio Legum Mosaicarum et Romanarum in Late Antiquity* (Oxford 2011). An updated study conducted by Matthijs Wibier is forthcoming, as part of the Redhis project (also with reference to the discovery of a further manuscript).

[4] C. Börker, R. Merkelbach (eds.), *Die Inschriften von Ephesos*, II (Bonn 1979) 30 (nr. 217); Lact. *Div. Inst.* 5.11.18; *Gloss*[L] *Philox.*, ed. Laistner 1926 = *CGL* II Goetz 1888. See also Patrikios and Eudoxios in Sch. 2 ad Bas. XXI, 3, 4 (Thalel.) = C. 2.11.4

and the classical works used by the compilers.[5] Exploring both of these relationships leads us necessarily to the *editio maior* by Th. Mommsen of 1866-70; therefore, it is advisable to point out the main ecdotic criteria Mommsen has followed.[6]

For the constitution of the text, in addition to relying on the *codex Florentinus*, Mommsen obviously collated the few, and particularly important, remnants of manuscripts contemporary with the one now in Florence or at least dating from the early Middle Ages (a new fragment of the Digest from the sixth century has been published recently).[7] He also used medieval manuscripts and Greek witnesses, i.e. the *Basilika* with their respective scholia, the use of which had been virtually eschewed by his predecessors.[8]

---

[5] The *codex Florentinus* (*F*) is reproduced in *Justiniani Augusti Digestorum seu Pandectarum codex Florentinus olim Pisanus phototypice expressus*, ed. by Commissione ministeriale per la riproduzione delle Pandette (Roma 1902-1910) and in A. Corbino, B. Santalucia, *Justiniani Augusti Pandectarum codex Florentinus* (Firenze 1988); on the manuscript, now see D. Baldi, 'Il codex Florentinus del Digesto e il Fondo Pandette della Biblioteca Laurenziana (con un'appendice di documenti inediti)', in Segno e Testo 8 (2010) 99 ff.; S. Ammirati, *Sul libro latino antico. Ricerche bibliologiche e paleografiche* (Pisa-Roma 2015) 96 (the eastern, indeed Constantinopolitan, origin of the *codex Florentinus* is still the most reliable hypothesis). On the question whether it is correct to speak of an "original of the Digest", see *infra*, note 8.

[6] From now on, I will refer exclusively to the *Grundlage* of 1862 [*infra*, note 9] and to the *Praefatio* issued upon completion of the work in 1870: *Digesta Iustiniani Augusti*, recognouit adsumpto in operis societatem Paulo Kruegero, Th. Mommsen, I (Berolini 1870). The provisional short *Praefationes* are now translated by G. Hillner: 'Digesta Iustiniani Augusti, Praefationes minores von 1866 und 1868', in ZSS 126 (2009) 461 ff. A review of the main ecdotic criteria, also with references to subsequent studies, is presented in F. Bartol Hernández, *Criterios teleológicos de la editio maior (Th. Mommsen)* (s.l. 2007) (albeit not exhaustive); I have dealt with this issue in 'La critica del Digesto fra passato e futuro', in *Problemi e prospettive della critica testuale (Trento, 14 e 15 dicembre 2007)*, ed. M. Miglietta, G. Santucci (Trento 2011) 151 ff., part of which I use here, with some updates.

[7] They are described e.g. in B.H. Stolte, 'Some Thoughts on the Early History of the Digest Text', in SGron 6 (1999) 103 ff., esp. 109 ff. A new fragment, chronologically close and only a few copies removed from the original of the Digest, has been published by M. Fressura, D. Mantovani, 'Un frammento di una nuova copia del Digesto di età giustinianea: P. Berol. inv. 14081', in Athenaeum 105 (2017) 685 ff.

[8] For Mommsen, passages where the *Basilika* and the first hand of the Florentine manuscript are in agreement should be considered as bearing "*ipsam archetypi Iustiniani scripturam*". Therefore, should this shared reading be erroneous, this implies an error in the Justinianic original itself or in the copies of the works of the jurists available to Justinian's commissioners. The existence of a single "original" of the Justinianic Digest is now being questioned (in my opinion, unduly): Mantovani, 'La critica del Digesto fra passato e futuro' (n. 6) 151 ff.

While recalling the steps he took, it is crucial, however, to be aware of Mommsen's purpose. His aim, which he explicitly stated, was not to restore the "original" text, at Justinian's level (what he calls *archetypus Iustiniani*), but to provide the most complete representation of the extant manuscripts,[9] among which the *codex Florentinus* obviously holds the most prominent place.

To grasp the centrality of this manuscript, around which the other witnesses just revolve as satellites, it is sufficient to note that, where the reading accepted by Mommsen in the text of the *editio maior* diverges from the one attested to by the *codex Florentinus* (going back either to the original scribe or to subsequent hands), it is recorded in italics, even when the variant reading is drawn from another contemporary and independent manuscript. Moreover, as a basic reference text, Mommsen delivered to his typographer the printed edition produced in 1553 by Lelio Torelli,[10] which is fully based on the *codex Florentinus*. From this perspective, it could be said – forcing somewhat the issue – that Mommsen's edition is the result of a new collation and correction of Torelli's edition with the *codex Florentinus*.[11] The formula

[9] Cf. Mommsen's 'Über die kritische Grundlage unseres Digestentextes' (1862), now in Id., *Gesammelte Schriften*, II (Berlin 1905) 108. On the *archetypus*, see e.g. Mommsen, *ed. mai.*, *Praef.* 1870 8n. 6) XI-XII. Even more so, Mommsen's goal was not to reach the layer of the classical works collected in the Digest: see *infra* §§ 4-5.

[10] Mommsen, *ed. mai.*, *Praef.* 1870 (n. 6) XVII-XVIII. Lelio Torelli's edition: *Digestorum seu Pandectarum libri quinquaginta ex Florentinis Pandectis repraesentati*, Florentiae in officina Laurentii Torrentini ducalis typographi, 1553 (repr. *Editio taurelliana digestorum. Littera Florentina*, ed. Laelius et Franciscus Taurellius. Mit einer Einleitung von H.E. Troje, Frankfurt am Main 2004). On the attempts prior to Torelli, see H.E. Troje, 'Zur Historia Pandectarum. Vorläufer der Editio Taurelliana', in *Festschrift für Rolf Knütel zum 70. Geburtstag* (Heidelberg 2009) 1301 ff.

[11] In addition to the edition of Torelli, Mommsen used the one of G. Chr. Gebauer of 1776 (in turn based on the collation of the *codex Florentinus* carried out by H. Brencmann in 1711): Mommsen, *ed. mai.*, *Praef.* 1870 (n. 6) XVIII. The autopsy of the *codex Florentinus* was performed not by Mommsen himself but by Adolf Kiessling (1837-1893) and August Reifferscheid (1835-1887), then young collaborators but who would pursue brilliant careers as philologists (particularly renowned is the commentary on Horace by Kiessling – who in 1889 would succeed Friedrich Leo in Göttingen –, as is his edition of Seneca the Elder). Among other things, Kiessling and Reifferscheid were entrusted with distinguishing the hands of the many copyists at work on the manuscript (and with ascertaining the periods to which they belong). See Mommsen, *ed. mai.*, *Praef.* 1870 (n. 6) XIX; further investigations were subsequently assigned to Paul Krüger. According to W. Kaiser, 'Schreiber und Korrektoren des Codex Florentinus', in ZSS 118 (2001) 170 ff., eight correctors at work on *F* can be distinguished on palaeographical grounds (Mommsen thought of two ordinary correctors).

used by Mommsen in his provisional preface of 1866 is eloquent: "*Ante omnia textum quem edo ad Florentinam lectionem siue priorem siue posteriorem quam fieri potest accedere uolui*" (VIIII).

Aside from its greater precision in recording the reading of the *codex Florentinus* (and the use of a larger set of witnesses), the major difference between Mommsen's edition and Lelio Torelli's lies in the fuller collection and recording of textual variants. In fact, in places where the Florentine manuscript has been corrected, the sixteenth-century editor avoided recording the manifestly erroneous reading of the two (regardless if this was the *lectio prior* or, as may happen, the *posterior*).[12] This stance, as Mommsen pointed out, sacrificed important critical information. Recording all the textual variants is crucial, first of all, to ascertain the relationship between the *codex Florentinus* and the late medieval manuscripts belonging to the *Vulgata*, since some of the errors borne by those latter manuscripts can be explained precisely by taking into account the presence of two different readings in the *codex Florentinus* (a correlation that can be established only if both are recorded).[13]

Above all, the complete recording of the readings of the *codex Florentinus* – including the openly mistaken ones – is necessary (and it is not sufficient to instead include only the right reading in the main text) because many corrections (those that Mommsen notes in the apparatus as F^2) derive from the use of another manuscript, different from the one initially used by the scribes (F^1). Therefore, the *codex Florentinus* itself can be considered "a single manuscript witness to two" ("*unus*

---

[12] The case is exemplified *infra*, § 7, by Ulp. 8 *off. proc.* D. 48.18.1pr.

[13] Mommsen, *ed. mai.*, *Praef.* 1870 (n. 6) XIX. Also see H.E. Troje, 'Ubi in libro Florentino duae lectiones inveniuntur ...: zur Geschichte der Digesteneditionen (16.-19. Jh.)', in TvR 72 (2004) 61 ff. As known, the dependence on *F* of the medieval *codices secundi ordinis* (the so-called *Vulgata* tradition or *littera Bononiensis*) is proven by a great number of *errores coniunctiui*. However, some superior readings than those of *F* (e.g. D. 17.1.27-D. 17.2.27) show that the copy taken from the latter (which gave birth to the *Vulgata* tradition) was collated with a different manuscript (see *infra*, note 16). Nevertheless, according to Mommsen, *ed. mai.*, *Praef.* (n. 6) LXVIII-LXXI, many of these superior readings of the *Vulgata* are the result of medieval conjectural emendations, progressively increasing as legal exegesis took root in law schools. A recent discussion, based on several examples, is in W. Kaiser, 'Besserlesungen in den Vulgathandschriften gegenüber Codex Florentinus und Basiliken? Zur Genuinität der erneuten Inskription vor D. 3.5.30.3 (Pap. 2 *resp.*) in den Handschriften des Digestum vetus', in *Römische Jurisprudenz. Dogmatik, Überlieferung, Rezeption. Festschrift für Detlef Liebs zum 75. Geburtstag*, K.-H. Mischeler (Hg.) (Berlin 2011) 293 f.

liber duorum instar"),[14] i.e. a witness both of the manuscript used for the first writing and of the different manuscript used for the revision (these operations, writing and revision, were performed in the same environment and in the same period).[15] The quality of this second manuscript can only be appreciated by recording the whole set of readings of the *codex Florentinus*.[16]

That said, what matters most to our discussion is the relationship between the *codex Florentinus* and the text of the Digest,[17] first in terms of the quality of the manuscript, and second with respect to Mommsen's approach to its errors.

To gauge the reliability of the *codex Florentinus* as representative of the Justinianic original, it is enough to compare it with the few remnants of contemporary or early medieval manuscripts. In particular, Mommsen had highlighted that the manuscript of the Digest now in Naples[18] and even more so the Gudian (and Palatine) manuscript of the *corpus agrimensorum Romanorum* (which includes excerpts of the title D. 10.1 *finium regundorum*)[19] bear some readings that are definite-

---

[14] Mommsen, *ed. mai.*, *Praef.* 1870 (n. 6) XIX.

[15] "*Sine dubio eodem tempore eodemque loco codex et scriptus et emendatus est*": Mommsen, *ed. mai.*, *Praef.* 1870 (n. 6) XXXVIII.

[16] The demonstration that the correctors of F^1 used a different antigraph is provided by Mommsen, *ed. mai.*, *Praef.* 1870 (n. 6) XXXV ss. Doubts are raised mainly by the fact that some major gaps, highlighted as such by the F^1 copyist himself, were not filled on the basis of F^2, as would be expected if the correctors had had a different antigraph available. On the largest of these gaps, see now W. Kaiser, 'Die Lücken in D. 48, 20 und D. 48, 22', in *Festschrift für Christoph Krampe zum 70. Geburtstag*, I. Reichard, M. Armgardt, F. Klinck (Hgg.) (Berlin 2013) 147 ff., esp. 148-149.

[17] The relationship between *F* and the medieval manuscripts belonging to the so-called *Vulgata* is also relevant to the textual constitution of the Digest. In fact, manuscript *X* (abbreviation proposed by Stolte, *Some Thoughts* [n. 7] 104), on the basis of which the hyparchetype *S* (forerunner of this family of medieval copies) was corrected, was partially independent of *F* (see *supra*, note 13). Therefore, also (the reconstruction of) *X* would be of importance to then reach a higher textual level than that represented by *F*, irrespective of whether this level coincides with the Justinianic original or not.

[18] Ms. Napoli, Bibl. Naz. IV.A.8 (*CLA* III 402), uncial, saec. VI^2, Italy (*N*). These are four leaves of a manuscript later reused, in the seventh/eighth centuries, in the *scriptorium* of Bobbio, for Flavius Sosipater Charisius' *Ars grammatica*. For example, the erroneous *adiectum eo* in D. 10.2.7 is lacking in ms. *N* (Mommsen, *ed. mai.* [n. 9] 310, 7).

[19] Mommsen directly used only ms. Gudianus (*G*), i.e. Wolfenbüttel, Herzog-August-Bibliothek, Guelferb. 105 Gudianus Latinus 2°, which however derives from

ly better than those of the *codex Florentinus*. It follows – writes Mommsen in the provisional preface (ed. 1866, VIII) – "how wrong are those who believe that we read the Digest in the form in which its compilers published it" ("*quantopere errent qui talia nos legere opinantur qualia emiserunt eorum (scil.: Digestorum) conditores*").[20]

To this criterion of comparison, we can add the one recently provided by Otto Zwierlein, who – following Mommsen's footsteps – contrasted the version of the *constitutio Tanta* preserved in the Florentine manuscript with the version of the same constitution conveyed by the manuscripts of the *Codex Iustinianus*. His conclusions are the following: the scribe at work on the Florentine manuscript abounded in mechanical errors (skip of the nasal consonant, as in *sa<n>ction*; omission of the prefixes, as in *<com>positio*; exchange of consonants *b/u*, e.g. *belle/uelle*, *r/l*, e.g. *alma/arma*, *r/p*, e.g. *insertae/inseptae*, *t/n*, e.g. *tam/nam*); he was responsible of particularly frequent omissions by homeoteleuton.[21] For a fair assessment of the merits of the *codex Florentinus*, one should also remark that most of these errors were corrected by F^2. On the other hand, the specificity of this very case must be considered, i.e. that here the revisor probably used the updated version of the constitution *Tanta* included in the second edition of the Code of Justinian (the same could not apply to the text of the Digest itself).[22]

Therefore, although chronologically close to the date of creation of the Digest, the *codex Florentinus* is already burdened with a significant number of errors generated, as in any other manuscript tradition, by the very process of copying (a condition too often forgotten in the days of "interpolationism", the scholarly stance which attributed any inco-

---

ms. Città del Vaticano, BAV, pal. lat. 1564: cf. W. Kaiser, 'Spätantike Rechtstexte in agrimensorischen Sammlungen', in ZSS 130 (2013) 332 ff. For example, D. 10.2.4.1 (Mommsen, *ed. mai.* [n. 9], 306) non inique *G*, inique *F*; D. 10.2.4.10 (Mo. 307, 14-15) nam in confinio praediorum urbanorum *G*; urbanorum *F*.

[20] Also see Mommsen, *Ueber die kritische Grundlage* (n. 6) 111 (about *N*); 112 (about *G*); B.H. Stolte, 'Finium regundorum and the Agrimensores', in SGron 5 (1992) 61 ff.; Id., 'Some Thoughts' (n. 7) 115 ff. *(Appendix: Ms. Naples IV.A.8 foll. 36-39 rescr.)*; Kaiser, 'Spätantike Rechtstexte in agrimensorischen Sammlungen' (n. 19) 273 ff.; Fressura, Mantovani, 'Un frammento di una nuova copia del Digesto' (n. 7) 685 ff., esp. 699 ff.

[21] O. Zwierlein, 'Textkritisches zu den Digesten Justinians', in H. Altmeppen, I. Reichard, M.J. Schermaier (Hgg.), *Festschrift für Rolf Knütel zum 70. Geburtstag* (Heidelberg 2009) 1493 ff.

[22] This is the view expressed by Mommsen, *ed. mai.*, *Praef.* 1870 (n. 6) XL-XLII (ibid., XLII note 1, list of readings of F^2, on the basis of the revised version included in the Code of Justinian).

herence in the text to an intentional alteration). Such is the number of errors that Mommsen blamed the excessive faith in the quality of the Florentine manuscript as "*timidorum hominum praua religio*".[23]

3. (II): textual emendation

Making the quality of the *codex Florentinus* (and its limitations) clear is fundamental to the edition of juristic fragments handed down by the Digest. However, as mentioned before, there is a second (and even more weighty) factor very much in play, namely the ecdotic criteria of the *editio maior*. As underlined above, Mommsen's purpose was to produce the most faithful representation possible of the manuscripts themselves, and primarily of the *codex Florentinus*. For this reason, he resorted to conjectural emendations only sparingly, i.e. he did not only avoid making the most immediate grammatical corrections but also refrained from systematically reporting and correcting more serious errors. In fact, and he reiterated it upon completion of his work just as he had stated it at the beginning, his objective was to provide reliable and full "equipment" needed to accurately establish the wording of the Digest ("*ut instrumentum ad uerba digestorum recte et apte constituenda pararetur certum et plenum*").[24] Hence, it could be said that he aimed to prepare an edition prodromal to the edition of the Digest. By his own admission, he gave only a sporadic attention to emendation of the text ("*subitariam magis et prout res incidit operam ei impendi*"). However, even when he did make emendations, his objective still remained reaching the Justinianic layer of the text, certainly not the deeper layer of the juristic works collected in it: "*in digestis non respicimus nisi eam operis formam, quam edi iussit Iustinianus*".[25]

In pursuing this aim, even where the text of *F* is certainly or most likely corrupted, emendations were inserted by Mommsen in his first apparatus, not in the main text. This depends on the fact that it is almost always uncertain whether the error occurred in the tradition sub-

[23] Mommsen, *ed. mai.*, *Praef.* 1870 (n. 6) LV; apparently more optimistic at LXXVIII.

[24] Mommsen, *ed. mai.*, *Praef.* 1870 (n. 6) LXXVIII. His refrain from conjectural criticism was promptly highlighted in the review by E. Zachariä von Lingenthal, 'Digesta Justiniani Augusti recognovit, adsumpto in operis societatem Paulo Kruegero, Th. Mommsen. in Voll. I-II', in ZRG 10 (1872) 177 f.

[25] Mommsen, *ed. mai.*, *Praef.* 1870 (n. 6) LXXVIII.

sequent to the original Justinianic text or it was already in that original ("*in ipso Digestorum archetypo*": *Praef.* 1866, VIIII). In the latter case, the defective reading must not be eliminated if one aims at producing an edition of the Digest.[26]

Mommsen also eschewed systematic discussions of the proposals of emendation made by previous scholars. In doing so, he stated his conviction that in the nineteenth century, the conjectural criticism on the Digest was flagging, and that this condition has endured since the time of Cujas.[27]

4. (III): reaching the textual layer of classical jurists

Therefore, Mommsen considered premature to intervene systematically on the text of the Digest, and deemed it preferable to provide useful tools to resume the work later on. From this perspective, the preparation of the *Vocabularium Iurisprudentiae Romanae* was also aimed at laying the foundations for this new phase.[28] On the other hand, his re-

[26] The difficulty of distinguishing between the errors in the Justinianic original and those due to the copyists of the *codex Florentinus* is highlighted in Mommsen, *ed. mai.*, *Praef.* 1870 (n. 6) LVII.

[27] *Op. lc. cit.*: "*nescio quomodo digestorum emendatio plus quam credas iacuit post Cuiacium in hac quidem re non tam maximum quam unum scientiae nostrae lumen, et iacet etiamnunc. Philologi enim ii quoque qui a Gaio et Ulpiano non abhorrent a digestis abstinent: iuris autem auctores optimi quique, quos propter prudentiae acumen suspicimus, ubi uerba auctorum tractare incipiunt, mirum in modum et artis philologicae expertes se probare solent et saepe adeo ne mediocri quidem linguae Latinae notitia imbutos, ut peruersissima quaeque et quouis auctore non inscito uel infante plane indigna nescio quibus eculeis tormentisque adhibitis defendant, denique si quando ad emendationem ipsi accedunt, monstra fere parturiant et prodigia mirifica: quamquam rarius hoc faciunt et frequentius peccant uetustis ineptiis defendendis quam proferendis nouiciis*".

[28] Cf. Mantovani, 'La critica del Digesto fra passato e futuro' (n. 6) 151 ff. Dissenting view in M. Varvaro, 'La storia del 'Vocabularium iurisprudentiae Romanae' 1. Il progetto del vocabolario e la nascita dell'interpolazionismo', in Quaderni Lupiensi 7 (2017) 251 ff.; on the other hand, E. Stolfi, 'Protagonisti e percorsi dell'interpolazionismo a proposito di una recente indagine su Gradenwitz e Riccobono', in SDHI 84 (2018) 325 ff., esp. 341-346, shares my view of a link between the rebirth of interpolationism and the renewal of philology in the second half of the XIXth c. (notably, set in motion, as far as Roman legal sources are concerned, by Mommsen's *editio maior* of the Digest); he also remarks that Varvaro misconstrues some of my statements. Other remarks on this latter author's method in D. Mantovani, 'I professori di diritto romano a Pavia dalla Restaurazione alla Prima guerra mondiale. Un laboratorio della modernità', in L. Gagliardi (ed.), *Antologia giuridica romanistica ed antiquaria*, II (Milano 2018) 455 ff., esp. 488 nt. 105.

fusal to resort to emendations provided by contemporary scholars was also affected by the consideration that the Digest is a document with a particular status, having become the subject of interpretation and application in the medieval and humanistic traditions: hence, every intervention on the text creates tension with the previous interpretations.

All that has been said thus far on the relationship between the *codex Florentinus* and the Justinianic layer of the text, highlighting the flaws of the Florentine manuscript and the boundaries Mommsen imposed on himself regarding conjectural emendation, obviously has an impact on another issue, that is, the adherence of the texts of the jurists collected in the Digest to the intentions of their authors.

On the one hand, what has been argued above urges caution against excessive trust (which would become indeed "*praua religio*") in the quality of the *codex Florentinus*; on the other hand, it explains the attitude Mommsen took vis-à-vis this further textual level (i.e. that of the jurists' books used by Justinian's commissioners). If Mommsen believed that it is almost always impossible to ascertain whether the mistaken readings in the *codex Florentinus* can be attributed to the Justinianic original or to the copyists of subsequent manuscripts, he felt even more incapable to state whether such mistakes were present in the copy of the classical works used by the compilers. In any case, as stressed above, his goal as editor of the Digest was not to proceed beyond the Justinianic layer. Therefore, Mommsen did not point out, if only rarely ("*plerumque non indicaui*"), the changes made by the compilers to the texts of the jurists, precisely because – he commented – this was not a task that belonged to the editor of the Digest but to those who study Roman law ("*ea enim opera [...] non tam digestorum editoris est, quam eorum qui in iure antiquo inuestigando opera dant*").[29] Obviously, Mommsen nevertheless flagged places where the Justinianic text presents gaps or other errors, that often depend on the editing process and changes performed by the compilers of the Digest.[30]

To make clear where he drew the line between modifications performed by the compilers and interventions extraneous to the editing process, we can look at how he handled Paul. 1 *sent.* D. 4.4.48: *Minor se in id, quod fideiussit uel mandauit, in integrum restituendo reum principalem non liberat.* The Visigothic version of the same passage of the *Pauli Sententiae* reads: *Minor se in his, quae fideiussit uel fidepromisit*

---

[29] Mommsen, *op. cit.* (n. 6) LXXVIII-LXXVIIII.

[30] *Op. cit.* (n. 6) LXXVIIII.

uel spopondit uel mandauit, in integrum restituendo reum principalem non liberat. The latter is obviously the author's version, but Mommsen (*ed. mai.*, 138) limited himself to inserting it into the apparatus, as a parallel tradition.

Mommsen's ecdotic approach becomes even clearer if compared with Lenel's approach in his *Palingenesia Iuris Civilis*. To give just one example among very many similar ones: *F* reports Ulp. 14 *ad ed.* D. 2.8.7pr. as follows: *Si fideiussor non negetur idoneus* [...]. Lenel puts forward the emendation "fideiussor] sponsor", while Mommsen purely and simply records the reading of the *codex Florentinus*, without any annotation.[31]

Lenel's objective was to reach the textual layer of the classical works, while Mommsen's was to reach the level of the Digest. This difference cannot be better explained than by observing the inverted positioning the two editors respectively granted to a passage from Ulpian's *libri ad Sabinum* conserved both in the *Fragmenta Vaticana* and in the Digest: Lenel adopts the version of the *Vaticana* as the main text and puts that of the Digest in a note, while Mommsen does the opposite.[32]

Hence, Mommsen's *editio maior* is the indispensable reference point for those who are interested in accessing Justinian's Digest, but it presents specific limitations for those who wish to use it as the basic text for the edition of a classical juristic work.

5. The edition of Ulpian's *De officio proconsulis*: purpose and method

Our own experience in providing the critical edition of Ulpian's *De officio proconsulis* has confirmed that errors occurred in the transmission of the Digest (i.e. down to the *codex Florentinus*) are numerous and must be emended, all the more so when the editor's intention is to recover not the Justinianic text but rather, as far as it is possible to do so, Ulpian's.[33] Thus far I have mainly focused on the Digest, because it is the primary (and often sole) witness for most of the classical jurists'

[31] O. Lenel, *Palingenesia Iuris Civilis*, II (Leipzig 1889) 492 note 4; Mommsen, *ed. mai.* (n. 6) 49.

[32] Lenel, *Palingenesia*, II (n. 31) 1061 note 4; Mommsen, *ed. mai.* (n. 6) 222 notes 2-4.

[33] In general, on the unavoidability of conjectural emendation, see E. Fraenkel, 'Zum Texte römischer Juristen', in Hermes 60 (1925) 415 ff., now in Id., *Kleine Beiträge zur klassischen Philologie*, II (Roma 1964) 417 ff.

works. However, a critical edition of the *De officio proconsulis* has to face further and specific issues, related to the presence of other witnesses, the variety of which has already been mentioned.[34]

Therefore, I will now present some examples of how we proceeded to establish the text: the examples are chosen not for the sake of their contents, but because they highlight various types of errors and different modalities of tradition. The texts and editorial choices are self-explanatory, the critical apparatus providing all information: therefore, I will just add a few comments where they can help clarify the type of error detected and the proposed solution.

As a premise, I bring forward the working hypothesis Mario De Nonno and myself adopted as aim and guideline of our edition, i.e. the "philological reconstruction of the preserved fragments and/or extracts[35] of Ulpian's text – which may be of different kinds and sizes – to the extent made possible by the nature (and the uneven intention of fidelity to the authentic text) of the available witnesses: (1) Digest alone, (2) *Collatio* alone, (3) Digest + *Collatio*, (4) other witnesses. This aim is pursued in the light of an overall evaluation of Ulpian's *'usus scribendi'* and of the legal contents.

Fragments and extracts of type (3) are the most interesting from a methodological and critical point of view, due to the presence of two sources that were compiled at different times and with different editorial intents. As far as fragments of this kind are concerned, our goal to restore the authentic Ulpian's text is pursued by merging the passages attested both in the Digest and the *Collatio*. As far as the sections they share are concerned, these two witnesses are delt with philologically, i.e. as *Variantenträger*. As a matter of fact, this variance does not usually show signs of far-reaching editorial activity, but falls within the ordinary range of variability that affects any classical Latin text transmitted by several *auctores* or witnesses in an indirect (or even direct + indirect) form.

In rendering the text of fragments and extracts of type (1-3), the usual diacritical signs are used for additions and deletions. We have italicized letters that depart from the reading attested by *F* (for the pas-

---

[34] See *supra* § 1.

[35] By "extracts" we mean the parts of a single fragment handed down in different places of the same source (typically the Digest) or in different sources; in such cases, interruptions between one extract and another cannot be ruled out. For the sake of simplicity, in what follows I will often refer to both categories of texts by the term "passage".

sages of type 1) or by the archetype of the *Collatio* (for passages of type 2). *A fortiori* the expressions we have attributed to Ulpian, replacing those that have undergone systematic reformulation by the compilers of the Digest (e.g. *ad libertatem proclamare* > *in libertatem adserere* and similar), are italicized. For texts of fragments or extracts of type (4) alone, the symbol [ ] indicates a physical lacuna in the witness.

The edition has a dual critical apparatus. The first reports the corresponding passages of the *Basilika* and their scholia, the duplicate texts (*leges geminae*), and parallel or similar passages of importance for the reconstruction of the original text. The second apparatus records the variants, provides very brief critical observations and points to parallels deemed useful to support the editorial choices”.[36]

6. D. 48.18.1.23: mechanical errors and glosses

To illustrate the different instances that may occur in the critical edition of a classical jurist’s book, I shall start with the case of a text passed down only by the *codex Florentinus* of the Digest. It is an example of mechanical errors and glosses that have infiltrated the text. The fragment is taken from book VIII of *De officio proconsulis* (fr. 2211 Lenel):

> [D. 48.18.1.23] Quaestioni fidem non semper nec tamen numquam habendam constitutionibus declaratur: etenim res est fragilis et periculosa et quae ueritatem fallat. Nam plerique patientia siue duritia [tormentorum] ita tormenta contemnunt, ut exprimi eis ueritas nullo modo possit; alii tanta sunt inpatientia, ut *pot*ius mentiri quam pati tormenta uelint: ita fit, ut etiam uario modo fateantur, ut non tantum se, uerum etiam alios criminentur. [24] Praeterea inimicorum quaestioni fides haberi non debet, quia facile mentiuntur; nec tamen sub praetextu inimicitiarum detrahenda erit fides quaestion*i*, [25] sed causa cognita habenda fides aut non habenda. [26] Cum quis latrones tradidit, quibusdam rescriptis continetur non debere fidem haber*i* eis in eos, qui eos tradiderunt; quibusdam uero, quae sunt pleniora, hoc cauetur, ut neque destricte non habeatur <neque ita habeatur>, ut in ceterorum persona solet, sed causa cognita aestimetur, habenda fides sit necne. Plerique enim, dum metuunt, ne forte adprehensi *ips*os nominent, prodere eos solent, scilicet impunitatem sibi captantes, quia non facile eis indicantibus proditores suos creditur. Sed neque passim impunitas eis

[36] I am citing the editorial premise, written in its provisional form by M. De Nonno, stating the criteria to which we abide in our work.

per huiusmodi proditiones concedenda est, neque transmittenda allegatio dicentium idcirco se oneratos, quod eos ipsi tradidissent; neque enim inualidum argumentum haberi debet mendacii siue calumniae in se instructae.

Cf. Bas. 60.50.1 (p. 3059,20-3060,4) *cum schol.* (p. 3856,13-3857,4)

23 tormentorum *deleuimus (cf. Cic. de or.* 3.62 Anthisthene, qui patientiam et duritiam in Socratico sermone maxime adamauerat*; Tac. ann.* 6.34.2 Hiberi Albanique saltuosos locos incolentes duritiae patientiaeque magis insueuere*)* || potius] quouis *F, correximus coll. schol. Bas. (*ὥστε μᾶλλον βούλονται ψεύδεσθαι ἤπερ ὑποφέρειν βασάνους*),* quo<d>uis *uulgo edd.* || ut non] *scribendumne* et non*?* || criminentur F^2 *(*comminentur F^1*)* || § 24 quaestioni] quaestionis *F, corr. edd.* || § 25 sed causa F^2 *cum schol. Bas. (*ἀλλὰ κατὰ διάγνωσιν τῆς αἰτίας*):* causaque F^1 || § 26 haberi] habere *F, corr. edd.* || <neque ita habeatur> *suppl. Momms.* || ipsos] eos *F, correximus.*

We shall return below to this passage to examine its style (§ 11); but for now, concerning the textual issues, I will only note that it cannot be determined at what stage of the transmission the gloss [*tormentorum*] infiltrated the text. It may have already entered the copy of *De officio proconsulis* available to Justinian's commissioners, but it may as well have been inserted by the commissioners themselves, or even have entered the Digest at some point in the transmission chain that relies the *codex Florentinus* to the Justinianic original text. The first hypothesis seems to me the most likely.

7. D. 48.18.1 pr.-4: error by haplography

The second passage I will dwell upon exemplifies an error by haplography, which explains the absence of the subject of the infinitive in the sentence *posse uerum scire iudex crediderit* (a fault that other editors propose to rectify as *uerum sciri*, less justified on palaeographical grounds). Moreover, the passage carries an example of the floating relationship between the readings due to the main scribe and those of the corrector of the *codex Florentinus*: contrary to expectations, the reading of the corrector is not always the best. In our case, the superiority of F^1 over F^2, already spotted by Mommsen, is proven by a scholion of Dorotheus. The text comes from book VIII (fr. 2209*a* Lenel):

[D. 48.18.1pr.] In criminibus eruendis quaestio adhiberi solet. Sed quando uel quatenus id faciendum sit, uideamus. Et non esse a tormentis incipiendum et diuus Augustus constituit neque adeo fidem quaestioni adhibendam, sed et epistula diui Hadriani ad Sennium Sabinum continetur. [1] Verba rescripti ita se habent: «Ad tormenta seruorum ita demum ueniri oportet, cum suspectus est reus et aliis argumentis ita probationi admouetur, ut sola confessio seruorum deesse uideatur». [2] Idem diuus Hadrianus Claudio Quartino rescripsit; quo rescripto illud expressit, a suspectissimo incipiendum et a quo facillime posse <se> uerum scire iudex crediderit. [3] Ad quaestionem non esse prouocandos eos, quos accusator de domo sua produxit, nec facile credendum subiectam eam quam ambo parentes dicuntur caram filiam habuisse rescripto diuorum fratrum ad Lucium Tiberianum emisso declaratur. [4] Idem Cornelio Proculo rescripserunt non utique in serui unius quaestione fidem rei constituendam, sed argumentis causam examinandam.

Cf. Bas. 60.50.1 (p. 3058,4-11) *cum schol.* (p. 3857,25-3858,11)

Pr. eruendis F^1, seruandis F^2 *obstantibus schol. Bas.* (ἐν τῇ τῶν ἐγκλημάτων ἀναζητήσει) || § 2 <se> uerum scire] uerum scire *F, suppleuimus* (uerum sciri *edd. aliquot).*

8. D. 1.16.6pr.-2: mechanical errors and intentional alterations

The following case provides the example of two aetiologically different errors: one is mechanical, while the second was produced by the compilers of the Digest in the editing process. The fragment comes from book I (fr. 2144 Lenel):

[D. 1.16.6pr.] Solent etiam custodiarum cognitionem mandare legatis, scilicet ut praeauditas custodias ad se remittant <a>ut innocentem ips*i* libere<n>t. Sed hoc genus mandati extraordinarium est: nec enim potest quis gladii potestatem sibi datam uel cuius alterius coercitionis ad alium transferre, nec liberandi igitur reos ius, cum accusari apud eum non possint. [1] Sicut autem mandare iurisdictionem uel non mandare est in arbitrio proconsulis, ita adimere mandatam iurisdictionem licet quidem proconsuli, non autem debet inconsulto principe hoc facere. [2] Legatos non oportet principem consulere, sed proconsulem suum, et is ad consultationes legatorum debebit respondere.

Cf. Bas. 6.2.8 (p. 167,9-18) || pr. *cf. legem geminam* D. 50.17.70 *(*Nemo potest gladii potestatem sibi datam uel cuius alterius coercitionis ad alium transferre*)*

Pr. aut innocentem ipsi liberent] ut innocentem ipse liberet *F obsequentibus quodammodo Bas., correximus praeeuntibus Huschke* (aut innocentes) *et Schulting* (ut ~ ipsi liberent).

To better frame the textual problem, it is helpful to recall the legal background. The proconsul (the main judge in the province, μείζων δικαστής in the words of *P. Euphr.* 3, l. 12) possessed the *ius gladii*, the authority to inflict the death penalty or other punishments depriving a person of liberty and citizenship (except the authority to deport a criminal to an island, *ius deportandi in insulam*).[37] The proconsul could delegate the jurisdictional functions (*iurisdictio*) to his legate, but within narrow limits in the punitive sphere, for the legate had no right to apply the death penalty or to inflict a corporal punishment or severe flogging: *neque enim animaduertendi coercendi uel atrociter uerberandi ius habet* (Venul. 2 *off. proc.* D. 1.16.11). As Ulpian states in our passage, the proconsul can entrust the legate with the interrogation of prisoners; however (so the text of the *codex Florentinus* goes) after the examination the legate must still send the prisoners back to the proconsul, who will arrange not only to condemn the guilty but also to liberate those whom the legate's interrogation has shown to be innocent (*ut praeauditas custodias ad se remittant, ut innocentem ipse liberet*).

After describing this kind of mandate and its (limited) scope, the text in the Digest shows a telling inconsistency, first declaring that this mandate is *extraordinarium*, i.e. outside of the system (we may say illegal), and then explaining why it must not be accorded. Just as he cannot delegate the power to punish – this is Ulpian's justification –, the proconsul cannot transfer to his legate the authority to release (*liberandi reos ius*) people who could not even be accused before the legate himself. In short, punishment and liberation are inseparable facets of the same power. As clear as it is, this explanation is however inconsistent with the first part of the passage, which – as we have seen – deals with a mandate to the legate which – correctly – does *not* contain the power to release the prisoners (*ipse liberet*, i.e. the proconsul).

The lack of coordination undoubtedly derives from the editing or alteration of Ulpian's text. Originally, it must have discussed a *mandatum* formulated in a way opposite to the one we now read in the Digest, i.e. a mandate which entrusted the legates with a power deemed to be

[37] Cf. Ulp. 1 *opin.* D. 1.18.6.8; 9 *off. proc.* D. 48.22.6.1. See in general A. Berenger, *Le métier de gouverneur dans l'empire romain, de César à Dioclétien* (Paris 2014).

too broad (*ut praeauditas custodias ad se remittant aut innocentem ipsi liberent*), thus deserving the criticism that Ulpian elaborates upon in the second part of the text.

Another textual feature, not seen by Mommsen, but noticed by Huschke[38] further complicates the restitution of the original reading. In fact, originally the text must have presented a disjunctive (*aut* where we now read *ut*), thus stating the two possible choices left open to the legates according to the outcome of the interrogation, i.e. that the legates returned to the proconsuls the prisoners they considered guilty (*ad se remittant*) or directly released those they believed to be innocent.[39] The alternative no longer made sense after Justinian's commissioners had changed the scope of the *mandatum* by depriving the legates also of the power of releasing the prisoners (just as the power of punishing them, which they never had). Hence, the compilers of the Digest had to revise the disjunctive conjunction *aut*, transforming it into the subordinating *ut*.

Once the text is restored, the aetiology of the mistakes is clear: the compilers modified the first part of Ulpian's passage, thus making it positively enunciate the mandate in its lawful formulation; then they

---

[38] Mommsen, *ed. mai.* (n. 6) 33 n. 6 (on the precedent of Schulting); Ed. Huschke, 'Weitere Beiträge zur Pandektenkritik (aus Ed. Huschkes Nachlass)', in ZSS 9 (1888) 331 ff., esp. 340 (*aut innocentes ipsi liberent*).

[39] Therefore, interpretations of this text that fail to take into account the alternative are not acceptable. On the text, see e.g. T. Spagnuolo Vigorita, 'Imperium mixtum. Ulpiano, Alessandro e la giurisdizione procuratoria', in Index 18 (1990) 113 ff., esp. 120 and 146 note 53 (he also believes that what follows in Ulpian's text makes the emendation *ipsi liberent* necessary; he does not comment upon *aut*); V. Marotta, *Mandata principum* (Torino 1991) 166; Id., *Ulpiano e l'impero*, I (Napoli 2000) 196 f. (accepting the emendation *ipsi liberent* but maintaining *ut*); F. Botta, 'L'iniziativa processualcriminale delle 'personae publicae' nelle fonti giuridiche di età giustinianea', in S. Puliatti, A. Sanguinetti (ed.), *Legislazione, cultura giuridica, prassi dell'impero d'Oriente in età giustinianea tra passato e futuro (Atti del Convegno, Modena, 21-22 maggio 1998)* (Milano 2000) 285 ff., esp. 302 f. (who, in my opinion rightly, accepts both *ipsi liberent* and *aut*); A. Lovato, *Il carcere nel diritto penale romano. Dai Severi a Giustiniano* (Bari 1994) 44-46 (he keeps the reading of F, denying it contradicts the qualification of *mandatum extraordinarium*); L. Fanizza, *L'amministrazione della giustizia nel principato. Aspetti, problemi* (Roma 1999) 94-95; 136 (who seemingly believes that *cognitio custodiarum* was in itself not transferable); A. Bérenger, 'Le gouverneur de province et ses légats: délégations de pouvoirs et de compétences sous le Haut-Empire romain', in A. Bérenger, F. Lachaud (ed.), *Hiérarchie des pouvoirs, délégation de pouvoir et responsabilité des administrateurs dans l'Antiquité et au Moyen Âge* (Metz 2012) 179 ff., esp. 191 (she keeps the reading *ipse liberet* but construes it as if it were *ipsi liberent*).

failed to eliminate the following part, where the criticism of the mandate in its original and excessive scope (which Ulpian qualified as *mandatum extraordinarium*) remained.[40]

That Justinian's version was the one we read today in the *codex Florentinus* is confirmed by the *Basilika* (*F*: *ipse liberet* – Bas.: ἵνα αὐτὸς ψηφίσηται). It is noteworthy that, confronted with a contradictory text, the Greek interpreters, rather daringly indeed, sought nevertheless to make sense out of it they attribute to *mandatum extraordinarium* the meaning of "outside the rules" but not "against the laws" (Τοῦτο δὲ τὸ πρόσταγμα ἔξω τῶν ὡρισμένω καὶ οὐ παρὰ τοῖς νόμοις ἀκρίβειαν).[41] In this way, the contradiction disappears.

This analysis prompts some remarks on the manner in which the compilers of the Digest proceeded. They edited Ulpian's passage in a manner which perfectly fits their legislative task, positively enunciating the content that the proconsul's mandate to the legate can lawfully assume (rather than negatively criticizing an unlawful formulation, as Ulpian did). Therefore, all in all, the modification did not distort Ulpian's own legal assessment, an indication of the respect with which the commissioners handled the classical books they used. From an editorial perspective, the oversight of Justinian's compilers lies in the failure to delete the continuation of Ulpian's text. This occurred – if we may venture to step further into their workshop and try to see them at work – because the compilers were distracted by another operation they were performing on this very passage, that is, to extract from it the principle *Nemo potest gladii potestatem sibi datam uel cuius alterius coercitionis ad alium transferre*, placing it for greater evidence (also) in the title *De regulis iuris antiqui*, where it stands as a *lex gemina* (D. 50.17.70).

---

[40] In the light of the justification, the adjective *extraordinarium* cannot be construed as referring to the rarity of the mandate (after all, the verb *solent* indicates that it was a widespread practice) but rather qualifies its opposition to *ordo*.

[41] Bas. 6.2.8 (p. 167,9-18 Sch.): Ἐπιτρέπει δὲ τῷ λεγάτῳ ἀκροᾶσθαι τῶν ἐγκληματικῶν καὶ ἀναφέρειν αὐτῷ, ἵνα αὐτὸς ψηφίσηται. Τοῦτο δὲ τὸ πρόσταγμα ἔξω τῶν ὡρισμένων ἐστὶ καὶ οὐ παρὰ τοῖς νόμοις ἀκρίβειαν· οὔτε γὰρ δύναταί τις, ἣν ἔχει ξίφους ἢ τιμωρίας ἑτέρας [ἐξουσίαν] μεταφέρειν εἰς ἄλλον. Εἰκότως οὖν οὔτε τὸ δίκαιον τοῦ ἐλευθεροῦν καὶ ἀφεῖναι τοὺς μετὰ ἐξέτασιν ἀναιτίους εὑρισκομένους δύναται τῷ λεγάτῳ ἐντέλλεσθαι, καθ' ὃ μήτε κατηγορεῖσθαι κατὰ ἀκρίβειαν δύναταί τις παρ' αὐτῷ (Hb.: *Mandat [scil.: proconsul] autem legato, ut audiat causas criminales et ad se referat, ut ipse sententiam ferat. Hoc autem mandatum extraordinarium est et non contra rigorem in legibus obtinentem: neque enim potest quis, quam habet gladii uel alius coercitionis potestatem, in alterum transferre. Merito igitur neque ius liberandi et dimittendi eos, qui post cognitionem innocentes reperti sunt, potest legato mandare, cum neque accusari stricto iure quis apud eum possit*).

D. 1.16.6 deserves a final comment concerning the different ways it should be handled in the framework of a critical edition. For an edition of the Digest, the text must be maintained as it reads in the *codex Florentinus* (and is confirmed by the *Basilika*), in its mistaken form, because this is how it stood in the Justinianic original. Conversely, for the edition of *De officio proconsulis* the text must be amended and brought back to Ulpian's wording, by restoring the mention of the too broad mandate some provincial governors used to bestow on their legates, criticized as excessive by the jurist.

9. Coll. 3.3.1 and D. 1.6.2: dual tradition and emendation

The texts of *De officio proconsulis* preserved in the *Collatio legum Romanarum et Mosaicarum* provide opportunities for further reflections. As aforementioned, such texts are particularly enlightening in the case of a dual tradition (*Collatio* and Digest), as occurs in the following example taken once more from Ulpian's book VIII, the one that has survived most abundantly (fr. 2213 + 2214 Lenel): [42]

> [Coll. 3.3.1 (≈ D. 1.6.2)] | Dig. Si dominus in seruos saeuierit uel ad inpudicitiam turpemque uiolationem compellat, quae sint partes praesidis, ex rescripto diui Pii ad Aurelium Marcianum proconsulem Baeticae manifestatur.
>
> Cuius rescripti uerba haec sunt: «Dominorum quidem potestatem in suos seruos illibatam esse oportet nec cuiquam hominum ius suum detrahi: sed dominorum interest, ne auxilium contra saeuitiam uel famem uel intolerabilem iniuriam denegetur his, qui iuste deprecantur. [3] Ideoque cognosce de querellis eorum, qui ex familia Iulii Sabini ad statuam confugerunt, et si uel durius habitos quam aequum est uel infami iniuria affectos cognoueris, uenire iube ita, ut in potestatem Sabini non reuertantur; qui si meae constitutioni fraudem fecerit, sciet me admissum seuerius executurum». [4] Diuus etiam Hadrianus Vmbriciam quandam matronam in quinquennium relegauit, quod ex leuissimis causis ancillas atrocissime tractasset. | [5] Item diuus Pius ad libellum Alfi Iuli rescripsit <in> haec uerba: «Seruorum obsequium non solum imperio, sed et moderatione et sufficientibus praebitis et iustis operibus contineri oportet. [6] Itaque et ipse curare debes iuste ac temperate tuos tractare, ut ex facili re*tin*ere eos

[42] Regarding the *Collatio*, each manuscript is referred to in the apparatus according to the usual abbreviations (listed *supra*, note 3); the initial *C* indicates the archetype of the *Collatio*, which can be reconstructed by way of *recensio*, while the abbreviation *Coll.* (analogous to *Dig.* and *Inst.*) indicates the original of the *Collatio*.

possis, n*e*, si apparuerit uel inpare*m* te inpendiis esse uel atrocior*e* dominationem saeuiti*a* exercere, necesse habeat proconsul u.c., ne quid tumultuosius contra <te> accidat, praeuenire et ex mea iam auctoritate <te> ad alienandos eos conpellere. G*lab*r*i*one et H*o*mu*ll*o consulibus».

Cf. Bas. 31.1.2 (p. 1519,12-16) *cum* 19.7.11 (p. 938,13-21) – *Ad* §§ 1-3 *cf.* Ad §§ 1-3 cf. Inst. 1.8.2 (Sed et maior asperitas ecc.…

Inst. 1.8.2 (Sed et maior asperitas dominorum eiusdem principis constitutione coercetur. Nam consultus a quibusdam praesidibus prouinciarum de his seruis qui ad aedem sacram uel ad statuas principum confugiunt, praecepit, ut si intolerabilis uideatur dominorum saeuitia, cogantur seruos bonis condicionibus uendere, ut pretium dominis daretur: et recte; expedit enim rei publicae, ne quis sua re male utatur. Cuius rescripti ad Aelium Marcianum emissi uerba haec sunt: «Dominorum quidem potestatem in suos seruos illibatam esse oportet nec cuiquam hominum ius suum detrahi. Sed dominorum interest, ne auxilium contra saeuitiam uel famem uel intolerabilem iniuriam denegetur his, qui iuste deprecantur. Ideoque cognosce de querellis illorum, qui ex familia Iulii Sabini ad statuam confugerunt, et si uel durius habitos quam aequum est uel infami iniuria adfectos cognoueris, ueniri iube ita, ut in potestatem domini non reuertantur. Qui Sabinus, si meae constitutioni fraudem fecerit, sciet me admissum seuerius exsecuturum»).

1 seruos *Dig.,* seruum *Coll.* || Aurelium *Coll.,* Aelium *Dig. et Inst.* || manifestatur *Coll.,* manifestabitur *Dig.* || § 3 eorum *Dig. et W nec non Inst.,* illorum *BV* || si uel *Dig.,* siue *C* || habitos *Dig. Inst.,* (h)abiti *C* || est *om. BW* || infami iniuria *Dig. et V nec non Inst.,* infamiae iniuria *B,* infamem iniuriam *W* || iube ita *V (*iubeta *F),* iube intra *W*, iubet *B* || potestatem *B nec non Inst.,* potestate *FVW* || qui *Dig.* (qui Sabinus *Inst.),* quod *Coll.* || § 4 Vmbriciam *Dig.,* Vmbram *Coll.* || tractasset *Dig.,* tractaret *C* || § 5 <in> *suppl. Huschke* || § 6 debes *W (Pithou),* debet *BV* || temperate tuos *W (Pithou),* temperate et uos *BV* || ex facili] et facili *BV,* et facile *W (Pithou), corr. Lachmann* || retinere] requirere *C, correximus (cf. e.g. Ter. ad. 58* liberalitate liberos retinere satius esse credo quam metu*)* || possis *W (Pithou)*, -it *BV* || ne si] nisi *C, corr. Pithou* || inparem te] in parente *BV* (-tem *W*)*, corr. Pithou* || atrociore dominationem saeuitia] atrociorem dominationem seuitiam *C, corr. Lachmann* || contra <te> *suppl. Lachmann* || praevenire et *WV,* praevenire se et *B* || auctoritate <te> *suppl. Lachmann* || Glabrione et Homullo] grauione et romulo *C, corr. Pithou.*

A key aspect which deserves special mention here is that, in preparing an edition of the *De officio proconsulis* with the purpose of coming as close as possible to Ulpian's original work, we chose not to merely juxtapose the two parallel witnesses, the *Collatio* and the Digest. We present the text as one, as a result of both witnesses, treated philologically as bearers of variant readings. The critical apparatus is obviously denser, given that the *Collatio* has been handed down to us by (at least) three manuscripts, which present numerous variant readings. Lenel's choice was different, presenting separately the version of the Digest as the main text and the variant readings of the *Collatio* in footnotes, without choosing between the two versions: therefore, Lenel's *Palingenesia* cannot be used as though it were an edition presenting what had stood in Ulpian's original.[43]

Turning now to the contents and form of text, I will focus on *Coll.* 3.3.6 (which convey a part of the text not incorporated in the Digest), where our edition significantly departs from the one presented by Lenel (and by the editors of the *Collatio*). The textual transmission of Antoninus Pius's rescript to Alfius Julius (on the means used to obtain the obedience of slaves) is clearly defective. In particular, the reading *requirere* is questionable: it is attested by all the manuscripts of the *Collatio*, but its meaning is not acceptable in the context. For the emendation *retinere*, a passage by Terence (one of the cornerstones of school education in the imperial period) offered us the starting point and direction to follow. It belongs to "The Brothers" and dwells on the different ways to obtain obedience from children, and contrasts – just as the *princeps* would do later in his rescript – *imperium* with reasonable generosity (Ter. *ad.* 57-67): *pudore et liberalitate liberos / retinere satius esse credo quam metu. / Haec fratri mecum non conueniunt neque placent / uenit ad me saepe clamitans: «Quid ais, Micio? / Cur perdis adulescentem nobis? Cur amat? / Cur potat? Cur tu his rebus sumptum suggeris? / Vestitu nimium indulges; nimium ineptus es!» / Nimium ipse est durus praeter aequomque et bonum, / et errat longe mea quidem sententia, / qui imperium credat grauius esse aut stabilius / ui quod fit, quam illud quod amicitia adiungitur* ("I believe that it is better to discipline children by gaining their respect and showing generosity than through fear. My brother doesn't agree with me on this; he just doesn't approve. He often comes to me shouting "What are you doing, Micio? Why are you ruining our boy? Why is he having a love affair? Why is he drinking? Why are you supplying him with money for these things? Why are you spoiling him with expensive clothes? You're being all too silly about it." Well, he's being all too strict,

[43] Moreover, the readings of the *Collatio* are reported without taking into account the existence of textual variants in the three medieval witnesses of the work.

well beyond what is fair and right; and he's making a big mistake, in my opinion at least, if he thinks that authority imposed by force is stronger or surer than one based on affection". Transl. John Barsby).

10. Paratext

The critical edition of the work of a Roman jurist must strive to restore not only the text, but also the paratext, in particular the intermediate titles, i.e. the *tituli* or *rubricae* (these are equivalent terms, which emphasize respectively either the function or the form). Concerning paratext, one is confronted with an amazingly contradictory scholarly landscape. Lenel's *Palingenesia Iuris Civilis* is replete with with *tituli/rubricae* (and subtitles), the true backbone of Lenel's colossal undertaking. *Tituli/rubricae* and subtitles mark the different arrangements of legal materials Lenel reconstrued (edictal system, Sabinian system, etc.) and within which he then replaced each fragment. Nevertheless, despite Lenel's authoritative reconstruction, and almost independently of it, the opinion that the Roman jurists did not provide their works with a paratext is widespread. Especially from the middle of the twentieth century, most of the scholars insist that *tituli/rubricae* were added to the juristic texts only later, during the "passage from scroll to codex", i.e. only in the copies of classical books that were produced in this latter format in Late antiquity.

Therefore, one must wonder if, in preparing the edition of a classical jurist's work, it is appropriate to follow Lenel's example or if the *tituli/rubricae* must be excluded.

Elsewhere I have collected the sources attesting to the early presence of the paratext in the writings of the jurists, also in the form of *rubricae* written in red ink, that are already to be found in an anonymous juristic papyrus in the scroll format dating from the first or second century CE (*P. Mich.* VII 456 + *P. Yale* inv. 1158r).[44]

The early presence and spread of paratext is confirmed by the characterization of the legal books put forward more or less around the same period by one of the commensals of Petronius's *cena Trimalchionis*, who with deliberate barbarism called them *libra rubricata*, "books with red-letter headings" (Petr. *sat.* 46.7).[45]

---

[44] TM 63275; LDAB 4481; MP^3 2987. Edition for Redhis by Serena Ammirati and Eleonora Nicosia in *Digital Corpus of Latin Papyri* online.

[45] Sources are discussed in D. Mantovani, 'Tituli e capita nelle Institutiones di

Headings (i.e. *rubricae/tituli*, intermediate titles) are in fact also attested for Ulpian's *De officio proconsulis*, preserved by the *Collatio*. I present them all here (omitting the critical apparatus):

- *De sicariis et ueneficis* (*Coll.* 1.3.1)
- *De mathematicis et uaticinatoribus* (*Coll.* 15.2.1)
- *Ad legem Iuliam de ui publica et priuata* (*Coll.* 9.2.1)
- *De poena legis Corneliae testamentariae* (*Coll.* 8.7.1)
- *De dominorum saeuitia* (*Coll.* 3.3.1)
- *De naufragiis et incendiariis* (*Coll.* 12.5.1)
- *De abigeis* (*Coll.* 11.7)
- *De furibus* (*Coll.* 7.4.1)
- *De termino moto* (*Coll.* 13.3.1)
- *Ad legem Fabiam* (*Coll.* 14.3.1).

The general picture, attesting to the use of intermediate *tituli* since the first/second century and in the *uolumen* format, fosters trust that this kind of paratext goes back to Ulpian himself (or to whoever first dealt with the dissemination of his *De officio proconsulis* in the first decades of the 3rd c. CE). Naturally, it cannot be excluded that there were later additions or modifications, all the more so because intermediate titles are particularly exposed to editing not only by the copyists but also by the owners of the copies.

All this taken into account, as far as the wording of the *tituli* of *De officio proconsulis* is concerned, the above list shows good homogeneity, which seems to confirm their unitary conception, thus going back to Ulpian's original work. The titles refer mostly to the agents, defining the crime with regard to its perpetrator. Reference to the *leges publicae* seems instead secondary (two instances: *ad legem Fabiam*; *ad poenam legis Corneliae testamentariae*); it is noteworthy that reference to the statute is not made for the *lex Cornelia de sicariis et ueneficis*. Being an handbook for the administration of justice in the provinces, in *De officio proconsulis* the *leges iudiciorum publicorum* were less central than they were for Rome, especially in determining punishments and procedures (they remained instead essential for the definition of the offence). Moreover, the choice to favour criminal agents over the *leges* in the wording of intermediate titles seems consistent with Ulpian's exhortation to the proconsul to work "conscientiously at ridding the province

Gaio e nell'Epitome Gai. Contributo allo studio del paratesto negli scritti dei giuristi romani', in SCDR 28 (2015) 545 ff.; Id., *Les juristes écrivains de la Rome antique. Les œuvres des juristes romains comme littérature* (Paris 2018) 241 ff. (*App.* 1).

of wicked men" (*ut malis hominibus prouincia careat*).[46] In short, as far as we can judge from the remaining evidence concerning *De officio proconsulis*, a well-calibrated relationship, both formal and substantial, between text and paratext stands out.

11. Juristic books as 'Literature'

Prompted by this last remark, we can conclude that providing new critical editions is crucial to restoring the works of the jurists to the Roman literary sphere. Treating juristic books as 'literature' certainly must not be reduced to a quarrel about names and notions (i.e. what should be meant by this term).[47] More concretely and less ideologically, treating the works of the Roman jurists as literature means asking of jurists' books the same questions usually asked of other Latin prose texts and applying the methods already experimented in the study of the latter. To exemplify an interpretative approach that focuses on the relationship between content of thought and textual organization, we can return to a fragment of *De officio proconsulis* we already commented upon from the point of view of textual criticism (§ 6), and read it from this other angle (D. 48.18.1.23-26):

> Quaestioni fidem non semper nec tamen numquam habendam constitutionibus declaratur: etenim res est fragilis et periculosa et quae ueritatem fallat. Nam plerique patientia siue duritia [tormentorum] ita tormenta contemnunt, ut exprimi eis ueritas nullo modo possit; alii tanta sunt inpatientia, ut *pot*ius mentiri quam pati tormenta uelint: ita fit, ut etiam uario modo fateantur, ut non tantum se, uerum etiam alios criminentur. [24] Praeterea inimicorum quaestioni fides haberi non debet, quia facile mentiuntur; nec tamen sub praetextu inimicitiarum detrahenda erit fides quaestion*i*, [25] sed causa cognita habenda fides aut non habenda. [26] Cum quis latrones tradidit, quibusdam rescriptis continetur non debere fidem haber*i* eis in eos, qui eos tradiderunt; quibusdam uero, quae sunt pleniora, hoc cauetur, ut neque destricte non habeatur <neque ita habeatur>, ut in ceterorum persona solet, sed causa cognita aestimetur, habenda fides sit necne. Plerique enim, dum metuunt, ne forte adprehensi *ips*os nominent, prodere eos solent, scilicet impunitatem sibi captantes, quia non facile eis indicantibus proditores suos creditur. Sed neque passim impunitas eis per huiusmodi

[46] Ulp. 7 *off. proc.* D. 1.18.13pr.

[47] For further discussion on this topic, we refer the reader to Mantovani, *Les juristes écrivains* (n. 45) 17 ff.; see also B. Colot (dir.), *La littérarité latine, de l'Antiquité à la Renaissance* (Rennes 2019).

proditiones concedenda est, neque transmittenda allegatio dicentium idcirco se oneratos, quod eos ipsi tradidissent; neque enim inualidum argumentum haberi debet mendacii siue calumniae in se instructae.[48]

Ulpian's discourse shows a strong coherence, provided by a main theme, which takes the form of a principle expressed through the litotes *non semper nec tamen numquam*. It is the principle of moderation, of case-by-case assessment, *causa cognita*. This main theme is carried out by Ulpian in a series of symmetrical negations and antitheses, which in some way resemble and imitate the swinging psychological process of someone struggling with a weighty decision: *plerique patientia/alii tanta sunt inpatientia*; *non debet/nec tamen detrahenda erit fides/sed* [...] *habenda fides aut non habenda*; *quibusdam rescriptis/quibusdam uero*; *neque destricte non habeatur <neque ita habeatur> ut* [...] *solet*; *habenda sit necne*; *sed neque passim impunitas eis per huiusmodi proditiones concedenda est neque transmittenda allegatio*. This relentless oscillation is also reflected in the chiastic pattern: *quaestioni fides haberi non debet* [A], *quia facile mentiuntur; nec tamen sub praetextu inimicitiarum detrahenda erit fides quaestioni* [B] ... *habenda fides* [B] *aut non habenda* [A].

[48] I present here, with a few adaptations, Alan Watsons' translation (48.18.1.23): "It is stated in constitutions that reliance should not alwavs be placed on torture, but not never, either; for it is a chancy and risky business and one which may be capable of distorting the truth. For there are a number of people who, by their endurance or their toughness [under torture], are so contemptuous of torture that the truth can in no way be squeezed out of them. Others have so little endurance that they would rather lie than suffer torture; so it happens that they confess in various ways, incriminating not only themselves but others also. 24. Moreover, you should not place confidence in torture applied to (a person's) enemies, because they readily tell lies. Not, however, that [all] confidence in torture should be lost where enmity is alleged, 25. but it is only after evaluating the situation that you can have confidence or not. 26. In a number of rescripts the principle is found that when someone has betrayed brigands, reliance should not be placed on the latter's (allegations) against those who betrayed them; but in certain rescripts that deal with the subject more fully there is the proviso that you should neither make it a rigid rule not to rely on them, <nor rely on them> as you would in the case of other kind of witnesses; but it should be considered only after evaluating the situation whether to trust them or not. For most people, when they fear that (others), on being arrested, may perhaps name them, are accustomed to betray those (others first), naturally to obtain immunity for themselves; for it is not easy to believe those who inform on their own betrayers. But immunity should not indiscriminately be allowed to those making betrayals of this kind, nor should the (counter) allegations of those who say that they were accused solely because they themselves had handed over men (who have now denounced them) be disregarded; in fact the argument of falsehood or calumny deployed against them should not (always) be treated as invalid".

The figurative formulation *etenim res est fragilis et periculosa et quae ueritatem fallat* can be compared with a well-known definition of *aegritudo* proposed by Cicero (*Tusc.* 3.25): *taetra enim res est, misera, detestabilis, omni contentione, uelis, ut ita dicam, remisque fugienda* ("For distress is loathsome, wretched, execrable, to be avoided so to speak with full spread of sail and reach of oars". Transl. J.E. King). Both phrases are explanatory, introduced by *etenim/enim*. Given the similarity, we can nevertheless appreciate their differences: Ulpian uses a trinomial, distinctive of juridical language (e.g. *urere frangere rumpere*), and, as typical of rhythmic prose, his three cola are of increasing length. Cicero uses a quadrinomial, also of increasing length and with the last phrase verbal (here with the gerund). In the orator-philosopher's discourse, a methaphor stands out: *aegritudo*, distress, must be avoided by means of sails and oars (*ut ita dicam* is the sign of the metaphor); the jurist, although in a (rare) figurative context, does not go as far as resorting to a true metaphor (although *fragilis* applied to *veritas* in the context of torture comes close to it). Cicero indulges in the asyndeton, while Ulpian structures the text with conjunctions.

The comparison between the two quotes demonstrates how far jurists could go in exploiting stylistic resources and what the boundaries they set for themselves were. It also hints at the usefulness of restoring juristic texts to the wider Latin literary sphere, in order to acquire a broader and more solid basis of assessment of their distinctive nature.

Chapter 11

THE CODE SYSTEM. REORGANIZING ROMAN LAW AND LEGAL LITERATURE IN THE LATE ANTIQUE PERIOD *

Detlef Liebs

Summary: 1. The digest system. – 2. Pseudo-Paul's *Sententiae*. – 3. *Codex Gregorianus*. – 4. *Codex Hermogenianus*. – 5. Hermogenian's *Iuris epitomae*. – 6. Pseudo-Ulpian's *Opiniones*. – 7. *Codex Theodosianus*. – 8. *Codex Iustinianus*. – 9. Justinian's *Digesta*. – 10. Summary.

1. The digest system

The late antique collections of legal pronouncements of the emperor, called imperial constitutions, the *Codices Gregorianus*, *Hermogenianus*, *Theodosianus*, and *Iustinianus* all include a large quantity of short and also longer constitutions covering all fields of law. They are all arranged in a similar manner generally identyfied with the so-called digest system. This system derived from the edict system, and is apparent in juristic works since Hadrian, who had ordered the praetorian edict's definitive edition. Whoever arranged statements on law extending over all of its fields from then on, i.e., on all those hitherto treated in the law literature, arranged it according to the digest system. It helped practicing lawyers already familiar with the praetorian edict to find information in these works quickly about just interesting topical points of law. These works were often entitled *Digesta*, originally meaning 'arranged'. Works with this title are known from Celsus *filius*, Julian, Marcellus, Cervidius Scaevola, and Papinian, in his case *Digesta responsa*. It was especially chosen when the single statements, arranged in a work, were of a different nature: authoritative replies to legal cases from the author's practice (*responsa*), legal discussions of cases in detail (*quaestiones*), explanations of individual legal rules, and minor teaching treatises. According to Paul Krüger's elaboration in 1886, the legal

* Translated by *Carole Gustely Cürten*.

works of the 2nd and early 3rd centuries entitled *Digesta* contained heterogeneous texts arranged by and large in the same manner; for these he coined the term 'Digestensystem'[1] (digest system). "System" is a term that is actually too lofty. Krüger chose the term to distinguish this arrangement from others as in the Gaius, Sabinus, or Mucius systems; the term became established.[2] The digest system obviously applied as well to collections of only *responsa*, *quaestiones*, or *disputationes* covering all fields of law. Shortly after Krüger's publication, Otto Lenel expounded it in detail in his *Palingenesia iuris civilis.*[3]

The digest system consists of two parts. Roughly the first two thirds of the relevant works were arranged according to the praetorian edict, whose order and wording had been fixed by Hadrian once and for all.[4] Already then, some non-edictal topics had also been incorporated into this first part of the digest system when convenient, e.g. *fideicommissa* followed the law of legacies,[5] and possession, including acquisition by adverse possession was inserted between the edicts *XXXII De publicanis* and *XXXIII De praediatoribus.*[6] The second part, covering about the last third, was dedicated to those fields of law that were not covered by the first part; a certain sequence in that became conventional. Krüger and Lenel did not entirely agree on this second part. Lenel maintained that, as the first part mainly contained the *ius honorarium*

---

[1] P. Krüger, 'Ueber die Zusammensetzung der Digestenwerke', in ZSS 7 fasc. 2 (1886) 94-106, table 103; Krüger, *Geschichte der Quellen und Litteratur des Römischen Rechts* (München 1912²) 143 f. The *Digesta* of Celsus *filius*, who was older than Julian, possibly have been edited only posthumously; the doubly quoted book titles in D. 4.4.3.1; 28.5.9.2; and 34.2.19.6 may be interpreted in that sense.

[2] Cf. F. Schulz, *History of Roman Legal Science* (Oxford 1946) 225 f.; F. Wieacker, *Römische Rechtsgeschichte* II (München 2006) 93; D. Liebs, *Hermogenians iuris epitomae. Zum Stand der römischen Jurisprudenz im Zeitalter Diokletians* (Göttingen 1964) 26-28, 110; Id., 'Das Codexsystem. Neuordnung des römischen Rechts in nachklassischer Zeit', in ZSS 134 (2017) 409-43.

[3] O. Lenel, *Palingenesia iuris civilis*, 2 vols. (Leipzig 1889) (in the following Lenel, *Pal.*).

[4] Formally by Hadrian; it was done by Julian, then imperial *quaestor*, cf. e.g. K. Wachtel, in *Prosopographia Imperii Romani²* VII 2 (Berlin 2006) 45 f. Julian's rearrangement of the praetorian edict was reconstructed by O. Lenel, *Das edictum perpetuum. Ein Versuch zu seiner Wiederherstellung* (Leipzig 1927³; 1st ed. 1883).

[5] See Julian, *Digesta* 39/40 in Lenel, *Pal.* I 419–27; Celsus, *Digesta* 20/21 in Lenel ibid. 155 f.; Marcellus, *Digesta* 15 in Lenel ibid. 616-18; Papinian, *Digesta responsa* 8/9 in Lenel ibid. 916-25. Cervidius Scaevola, *Digesta* 14-23 in Lenel, *Pal.* II 227-59, treated legacies and *fideicommissa* together.

[6] See Julian, *Digesta* 44 in Lenel, *Pal.* I 435-40; Celsus, *Digesta* 33 in Lenel ibid. 157-59; Marcellus, *Digesta* 17 in Lenel ibid. 620; Scaevola, *Digesta* 25 in Lenel, *Pal.* II 262 f.; Papinian, *Digesta responsa* 10 in Lenel, *Pal.* I 928 f.

(law created and formed by the praetor), the second would contain essentially those topics of the old *ius civile* (statute law) that had not been addressed already in the first part, and for that he assumed the chronological order of the underlying statutes.[7] On the other hand, Krüger stressed that the digest system should comprise the entire legal order including customary law, both old customs such as *patria potestas* (paternal authority) including adoption and emancipation, repatriation law (*postliminium*), and Rhodian law of jettison (*lex Rhodia*), as well as new customs inspired and coined by the emperor as the law of appeal, new penal law, fiscal law (*ius fisci*), and military law.[8] In late classical collections of *responsa* and in Ulpian's *Disputationum libri*, criminal law was followed by *ius fisci*, the law of appeal and military law. This sequence reveals no logic; although it was generally observed, Krüger rejected any internal connection between the main chapters.[9]

2. Pseudo-Paul's *Sententiae*

Were the constitution codes really arranged according to the digest system? The oldest of these, the *Codices Gregorianus* and *Hermogenianus*, whose first editions must have been compiled in 291/92 and 295 AD, not survived, not even in part. There are only: a short epitome of the *Gregorianus* and a very short one of the *Hermogenianus*, quotations, and the codes' echo in the *Codex Iustinianus*. One can seldom read from that how the topics were originally arranged; sometimes it can be inferred.[10] Much more has survived of Pseudo-Paul's *Sententiarum libri V* which was just a few years younger. Among other remnants, we have an extensive epitome with about a fifth of the original text and over half of the arrangement in books and titles, although not all of their headings seem to be original. Besides that, tradition has passed down many quotations from the *Sententiae*. Taken all together, we

[7] Lenel, *Pal.* I 464 nt. 10; II 1255 f.; Id., *Das edictum* (n. 4) 6 near nt. 3.

[8] Krüger, *Geschichte* (nt. 1) 143 f., also criticizing Lenel, *Pal.* II 1255 nt. 1, who had noticed these topics among the twelve considered works in only three late ones, doubting a fourth.

[9] Krüger, 'Ueber die Zusammensetzung' (n. 1) 104.

[10] On reconstruction of the *Gregorianus* from the preserved relics and from books 2 to 9 of the *Codex Iustinianus* which rely especially on the *Gregorianus*, see G. Rotondi, 'Studi sulle fonti del Codice Giustinianeo', in Id., *Scritti giuridici* I (Milan 1922) 110-265 (first 1913); S. Corcoran, *The Empire of the Tetrarchs.* Revised Edition (Oxford 2000) 25-28; Id., 'The Gregorianus and Hermogenianus assembled and shattered', in Mefra 125-2 (2013, http://mefra.revues.org/1772), no. 1-23.

probably have almost a third of the original text.[11] Thus, the sequence of the individual topics observed at that time can be followed quite well in the *Sententiae.*[12] The older literature on Roman law, also Krüger and Lenel, let Paul be the *Sententiae*' author and regarded the work as belonging to those arranged according to the digest system.[13] In their view, all post-Hadrian juristic works comprising all fields of law were arranged according to that system. Modern literature on Roman law is still biased about this concept. But a critical inspection of the tables of Krüger and Lenel[14] reveals that this concept regarding the *Sententiarum libri V* is inappropriate. According to these tables, the especially numerous remnants of this work say nothing neither *de intestatorum successione*, nor *ad legem Falcidiam*, nor *ad leges de manumissionibus latas*, nor *de adoptionibus*, nor *ad legem Rhodiam*, nor *de sponsoribus et fideiussoribus*, nor *de usuris*. However this view of theirs, shortened by scrutinizing only the digest system's second part, is deceptive. It ignores the fact that all these topics are addressed adequately in the *Sententiae* elsewhere, just not there where they maintain they should be addressed in line with their concept. The old second part of the digest system, occupying a third there, is reduced here to less than a seventh of the whole.[15] Nevertheless, criminal law plus the law of criminal procedure

[11] My calculation starts from the average length of a *liber* in Roman law literature. Nearly completely preserved are only the four *libri* of the Institutes of Gaius. In Ph. E. Huschke / E. Seckel / B. Kübler (edd.), *Iurisprudentiae anteiustinianae reliquiae*, vol. 1 (Leipzig 1906^{6}) 141-396, these cover 53+71+67+65 = 256 pages, resulting to an average of 65 Huschke-pages a *liber*. The five *libri* of the *Sententiae* cover in vol. 2, part 1, 1908, 14–161 (the *Pauli Sententiae* are quoted in the following as PS according to that edition), 148 pages, but from this number one must subtract wasted space to insert many headings, one or two on each page, and more space for footnotes than in Gaius; thus only about 20 Huschke-pages a *liber* remain.

[12] Discussed by G. Scherillo, 'Teodosiano, Gregoriano, Ermogeniano', in *Studi in memoria di U. Ratti* (Milan 1934) 247-323 = Id., *Scritti giuridici* I (Milan 1992) 263-332; D. Liebs, 'Die pseudopaulinischen Sentenzen. Versuch einer neuen Palingenesie', in ZSS 112 (1995) 151-71; Id., 'Die pseudopaulinischen Sentenzen II', in ZSS 113 (1996) 132-242; F. Grelle, 'I giuristi, il diritto municipale e il Codex Gregorianus', in *Iuris vincula. Studi in onore di Mario Talamanca* IV (Naples 2001) 317-42; M. U. Sperandio, *Codex Gregorianus. Origini e vicende* (Naples 2005) 301-375.

[13] Krüger, 'Ueber die Zusammensetzung' (n. 1) 102 and 103 (table); also the table of Lenel, *Pal.* II 1255 f., und since then almost all; critically G. Scherillo, 'L'ordinamento delle Sententiae di Paolo', in *Studi in onore di S. Riccobono* I (Palermo 1936; the off print 1931) 39-69; Liebs, *Hermogenians* (n. 2) 26-28, 110.

[14] Krüger, 'Ueber die Zusammensetzung' (n. 1) 103; Lenel, *Pal.* II 1255 f.

[15] PS 5.11-37.

and law of appeal are given much space.[16] Apart from these fields of law, the *Sententiae* preserved from the old digest system's second part *donationes* (gift law) and *ius fisci* in their final part, both before criminal law.[17] This ended with military criminal law; it seems bold to deduce from that a general chapter *De re militari.*[18] Military law, *ius fisci*, and law of appeals did not become part of works arranged according to the digest system until the early 3rd century.[19] The classical jurists had discussed these three fields only late in their literature, beginning with monographs.[20]

Most topics of the old second part were moved into the first part: *donatio mortis causa* after legacies,[21] intestate succession after succession by will (and connected topics),[22] *manumissio* (release from slavery) before *De liberali causa* (proceedings on one's enslavement or liberty),[23] adoption and emancipation after *De agnoscendis liberis* (law of

---

[16] Criminal law: PS 5.14-31; it was discussed broadly earlier (leaving aside the pertinent monographs including Ulpian, *De officio proconsulis* et similia) only in Papinian's *Digesta responsa*, books 15 and 16, Lenel, *Pal.* I 941-44. Papinian was praetorian prefect from 205 until the beginning of 211, and in that function he had to hear many criminal cases, e.g. that of Bulla Felix, Cassius Dio-Xiphilinus 76 (77).10.7. – Appeals: PS 5.32-37.

[17] PS 5.11 and 12 f.

[18] Krüger, 'Ueber die Zusammensetzung' (n. 1) 102 f., and Lenel, *Pal.* II 1256, both regarding PS 5.31 *De poenis militum*; D. 48.19.38.11 f. and 49.16.16 generally are taken as pieces of this title, rightly.

[19] Military law in Papinian's *Digesta responsa* and Ulpian's *Disputationes*; *ius fisci* in Papinian's *Responsa*, Ulpian's *Disputationes*, Paul's and Modestin's *Responsa*; and law of appeals in Papinian's *Responsa*, Ulpian's *Disputationes*, and Paul's *Responsa*. For evidence see Liebs, 'Codexsystem' (n. 2) 416 and notes 28-31.

[20] Military law by Taruttienus Paternus, Arrius Menander, and Aemilius Macer; *ius fisci* by Callistratus, Paul, and Marcianus; and law of appeals by Paul, Ulpian, Marcianus, and Macer. On these cf. shortly D. Liebs, 'Jurisprudenz', in *Handbuch der lateinischen Literatur der Antike* IV (München 1997) 136-38 = § 419.6 f.; 168 = § 423 W.63; 184 = § 424 W.22; 202 = § 428.1 W.1.3; 211f. = § 430.1 W.1; 215 f. = § 430.3 W.4 f.

[21] PS 3.7 *De mortis causa donationibus* after 3.6 *De legatis*.

[22] PS 4.8 *De intestatorum successione* after 3.4A *De testamentis* until 3.8 *Ad legem Falcidiam* and also *fideicommissa* (4.1–3), contesting a will (4.5 *De inofficiosi querella*), inheritance tax (4.6 *De vicesima*), and forgery of a will (4.7 *De lege Cornelia*).

[23] PS 4.12 *De manumissionibus*, 4.13 *De fideicommissis libertatibus*, 4.14 *Ad legem Fufiam Caniniam*; to insert all that before 5.1 *De liberali causa* made sense, see already Cervidius Scaevola, *Digesta* 23/24, Lenel, Pal. II 259-62 no. 102–106, and his pupil Papinian, *Responsa* 9 f., Lenel, *Pal.* I 926-28 no. 622–35.

father and child),[24] jettison (*Ad legem Rhodiam*) after *De exercitoribus* (contractual liability of shipowners),[25] suretyship (*De fideiussore et sponsore*) in the first book,[26] and interests (*De usuris*) after *fiducia* (fiduciary transfer of ownership, especially by way of security).[27] The *Sententiae* even treated some crimes within private law in order to consider their consequences in private law, thus the duties of the *pater familias* in case of punishable sexual practices[28] and the private consequences of a forged will.[29]

By moving many subjects away from the second part of the digest system (which had obviously been poorly arranged) into the first part, the second one was not just shortened, it was also made more coherent.

3. *Codex Gregorianus*

To determine the original order of the individual topics in the *Codex Gregorianus*, we have at our disposal the modest epitome in Alaric's Breviary and the quotations from outside the Breviary,[30] in addition the fact that the contents and arrangement of the *Codex Iustinianus* depend in large parts on the *Gregorianus*, especially the books 2 to 8, and 9 in part.[31] The *Gregorianus* consisted of at least 14, probably 15 *libri*. The first twelve were arranged according to the praetorian edict and the rest, books 13 until presumably 15, contained what Gregorius had left for the second part of the old di-

[24] PS 2.24A, probably *De adoptionibus*, and 2.25: *Quemadmodum filii sui iuris efficiuntur*, both after 2,24 *De liberis agnoscendis* from the title *De liberis et de ventre*, Lenel, *Das edictum* (n. 4) 311 ff.

[25] PS 2.7 *Ad legem Rhodiam* after 2.6 *De exercitoribus*.

[26] PS 1.20; cf. Lenel, *Das edictum* (n. 4) 214-218.

[27] PS 2.14 *De usuris* after 2.13 *De fiducia*.

[28] PS 2.26 *De adulteriis*, exceptionally preserved almost in full.

[29] PS 4.7 *De lege Cornelia*; preserved of that title are mainly elements of the offense, originally probably meant just introducing into those consequences. Ps.-Paul treated this crime anew within the section 'criminal law', now stressing the penal elements of it, PS 5.25 *Ad legem Corneliam testamentariam*.

[30] A clear utilization of the relevant data offers Rotondi, 'Studi' (nt. 10) 154-57.

[31] Not book 1 and 10-12, formed mainly on the model of *Codex Theodosianus*. Book 9 partly depends on book 9 of the *Theodosianus*, partly on book 14 of the *Gregorianus* (probably C. 9.1, 2. 6. 9. 16. 20. 22. 23. 32–35. 41. 43. 45-47. 50. 51); already book 9 of the *Theodosianus* had been formed on the model of book 14 of the *Gregorianus*, cf. Rotondi, 'Studi' (nt. 10) 146-69.

gest system. There is no known reference to the 15th book, but it can be inferred.[32] A 16th book is discussed.[33] One argument is the location of municipal law (*ius rei publicae*) in this code. The 10th book of the *Codex Iustinianus* presents 40 titles with 72 constitutions on municipal law taken from the *Gregorianus*[34] and another 11 titles with 19 constitutions on it in the 11th.[35] In the digest system, municipal law was traditionally addressed at the beginning, according to the praetorian edict's first title. But the remnants of book 1 of the *Gregorianus* show that there was too little space for an extensive treatment of this subject. Already the 10th title of the first book was devoted to *pacta*,[36] the 3rd title of the praetorian edict; the title on *transactions*,[37] a branch of that, must have followed; and the 12th was entitled *De postulando*,[38] coinciding with the 5th title of the edict.[39] In the 15th book of the *Gregorianus*, however, there is enough space. Without municipality law, this book would comprise only *ius fisci* and military law, both less broadly expanded subjects in the *Gregorianus*, to judge by their reflexion in the *Iustinianus*: 10 titles with alltogether 23 constitutions and 4 with 18.[40] The three known com-

---

[32] Rotondi, 'Studi' (nt. 10) 167–69, but it is incorrect to maintain (168 nt. 2): "il XV e XVI (sc. as number of books) figurano assai più spesso del XIV". Known are two works on Roman law of 14 *libri* (by Iavolenus and Maecianus), and three of 15 (by Iavolenus, Neratius, and Gaius) as of 16 *libri* (by Maecianus, Paul, and Marcianus); only later is there also the *Codex Theodosianus* (16 *libri*).

[33] Rotondi, 'Studi' (nt. 10) 168 f., but according to him the 16th book is less probable; of different opinion Sperandio, *Codex Gregorianus* (nt. 12) 346.

[34] C. 10.32.1-5; 10.33.1 f.; 10.39.1-4; 10.40.1-5; 10.41.1 f.; 10.42.1-7; 10.43.1-3; 10.44.1 f.; 10.46.1; 10.47.1; 10.48.1-4; 10.50.1–3; 10.51.1 f.; 10.52.1-4; 10.53.1-4; 10.55.1-3; 10.57.1; 10.59.1; 10.60.1; 10.61.1 f.; 10.62.1-4; 10.63.1; 10.64.1; 10.65.1-3; 10.67.1; 10.68.1; 10.69.1; 10.70.1.

[35] C. 11.30.1-3; 11.31.1; 11.32.1 f.; 11.33.1; 11.34.1 f.; 11.35.1; 11.36.1-4; 11.37.1 f.; 11.38.1; 11.39.1; 11.40.1.

[36] Lex Romana Visigothorum (in the following LRV), Appendix 1.3 *De pactis* from book 1, see App. 1.1; Consult. 9.17 adds that this was the 10th title; from this, C. 2.3 took its constitutions no. 1-19.

[37] Consult. 4.6 and LRV Cod. Greg. 1.1: 1st book; from this title, C. 2.4 took its constitutions 1-15.

[38] LRV Appendix 1.1; from this title, C. 2.6 took its constitutions 1-3.

[39] The 1st and the 2nd titles of the praetorian edict, according to Lenel, *Das edictum* (n. 4) 51-57, turned out to have been just one, R. Domingo, *Estudios sobre el primo título del Edicto pretorio*, 3 vols. (Santiago de Compostela 1992-1995); thus Lenel's 4th title had been the 3rd and Lenel's 6th the 5th.

[40] On *ius fisci*, the 23 constitutions of 10th book of the *Codex Iustinianus* taken

pendia of Roman law from that time – 5 to 35 years younger than the *Gregorianus* (see below) – all nevertheless follow in this subject the praetorian edict's traditional order and treat municipal law at the beginning,[41] whereas in the *Codex Theodosianus*, *Codex Iustinianus*, and Justinian's *Digesta* we find it at the end also, as a part of public law.[42]

To return to private law, interest-law problems had a special title *De usuris* not only in the *Pauli Sententiae*,[43] but must have had it already in the *Codex Gregorianus*, placed in the first, the edict part as well, here after the edictal subtitles *Ad senatus consultum Vellaeanum* and *De compensationibus*, to judge by their reflexion in the *Iustinianus*.[44] In Justinian's *Digesta*, a corresponding title is missing, instead *usurae* are treated there together with four related subjects in a title *De usuris et fructibus et causis et omnibus accessionibus et mora*.[45] Almost all the *Digesta*'s titles begin by excerpting a leading work from classical law literature, but in this title it is missing; the traditional digest system not seems to have had a special chapter *De usuris*. Paul published a *De usuris liber singularis*,[46] but he seems to have been alone addressing interests as a special subject; he did so in the 25th book of his *Quaestionum libri* as well,[47] near the end of the second part of that work which is generally arranged according to the digest system.[48] In the *Gregorianus*

---

from the *Gregorianus* are: C. 10.1.1-5; 2.1-3; 3.1-4; 4.1; 5.1; 7.1; 8.1 f.; 9.1; 10.1; 11.1-4; and the18 on military law: C. 12.33.1 f.; 35.1-8; 36.1-4; 62.1-4.

[41] Liebs, 'Die pseudopaulinischen Sentenzen II' (nt. 12) 133-35; Id., *Hermogenians* (n. 2) 117-19; Id., 'Ulpiani opinionum libri VI', in TR 41 (1973) 279-310 (2008 revised version: https://freidok.uni-freiburg.de/data/5085), here 305.

[42] CTh 12.1-5, but see also 1.29 f. (and 32 ed. Krüger); C. 10.32-78 (and 11.30-40); D. 50.1-12.

[43] PS 2.14.

[44] C. 4.32.1-17 after 4.29.1-13 and 4.31.1-9 (4.32.18-24; 4.29.14-20; and 4.31.10-13 from the *Hermogenianus*). Between the latter two, C. 4.30.1-8 reflect another extra-edictal subtitle: *De non numerata pecunia*.

[45] D. 22.1.

[46] D. 22.1.17 is taken from that work which is attested also in D. Index auctorum 25.28.

[47] D. 22.1.11 according to Krüger, 'Ueber die Zusammensetzung' (n. 1) 101 and 103; less appropriate Lenel, *Pal.* I 1220 no. 1422 f.: *Ad leges de fenore latas* with question mark.

[48] The traditional topics of the second part of the digest system ended in Paul's *Quaestiones* in book 23; the topics treated in book 24, Lenel, *Pal.* I 1219-21, cannot be assigned for now, and from book 26, attested by D. Index auctorum 25.2, nothing is preserved, it may not have even existed.

a short title *De nautico fenore* seem to have followed,[49] possibly already in Paul's *Quaestiones*;[50] in cases of *fenus nauticum*, disputes about interests were frequent. These titles were placed in the *Gregorianus* within contract law, as *De usuris* later in the *Sententiae*. There, the third preserved *sententia* of the title *De usuris* seems to be an epitome of a constitution of the *Gregorianus*, here placed in the following title *de nautico fenore*.[51] This code may have contained three further titles on problems of interest but placed in different chapters: on guardianship,[52] legacies,[53] and civil procedure.[54]

Also the chapter 'intestate succession' must have been placed already in the *Gregorianus* in the first part, arranged after the edict titles on testate succession;[55] here the special titles *Ad senatus consultum Tertullianum* (intestate succession of a mother to her child) and … *Orfitianum* (… of children to their mother) precede the general title *De legitimis heredibus* instead of following it.[56] *Donatio mortis causa*, however, was apparently presented in the *Gregorianus* only in the second part,

[49] The probable model of C. 4.33 *De nautico fenore*, whose first four constitutions are taken from the *Gregorianus*.

[50] D. 22.2.6 (Paul. 25 *quaest.*) may be taken from a corresponding title.

[51] In the *Iustinianus* C. 4.33.2, cf. D. Liebs, *Römische Jurisprudenz in Africa mit Studien zu den pseudopaulinischen Sentenzen* (Berlin 2005^2) 97.

[52] The probable model for C. 5.56: *De usuris pupillaribus*, as the first three constitutions there seem to have been taken from a corresponding title of the *Gregorianus*.

[53] Model of C. 6.47: *De usuris et fructibus legatorum vel fideicommissorum*, whose five constitutions seem to have been taken from a corresponding title of the *Gregorianus*.

[54] The possible model C. 7.54: *De usuris rei iudicatae* with one constitution from the *Gregorianus*; the other two are Justinian's, the second from 531 AD, thus added only in the second edition.

[55] Cf. C. 6.55-59. Model of C. 6.55-58 was probably the *Gregorianus*, as the first constitutions of these titles are taken from this code, whereas in C. 6.59: *Communia de successionibus*, the first ten constitutions are taken from the *Hermogenianus*; there is also Cons. 6.18: *ex corpore Hermogeniani tit. de successionibus* after 6.17: *Eodem* (sc. *Hermogeniani* as in 6.14) *corpore tit. de testament.*; see furthermore C. 6.23: *De testamentis* ... with five constitutions taken from the *Hermogenianus*; 6.30: ... *de adeunda vel adquirenda hereditate* with eight; 6.37: *De legatis* with five; 6.42: *De fideicommissis* with nine; and 6.50: *Ad legem Falcidiam* again with five; Rotondi, 'Studi' (nt. 10) 54 f. (book 8); Liebs, *Hermogenians* (n. 2) 23 f. and 30; A. Cenderelli, *Ricerche sul Codex Hermogenianus* (Milan 1965) 106-110 and 167 f.

[56] See C. 6.56 and 57, each with one constitution taken from the *Gregorianus* (and one and two from the *Hermogenianus*).

regarding it as a part of the chapter on gifts,[57] as once Julian and Papinian had done. On the other hand, also the title *Ad legem Falcidiam* already in the two older codes was put in the first, the edictal part after the titles on legacies and *fideicommissa*.[58]

Immediately after intestate succession, the law of release from slavery (*manumissiones*) followed in the *Gregorianus* broadly subdivided.[59] This chapter seems to have followed immediately intestate succession also in the *Sententiae*, but it was not as broadly extended there.[60] Suretyship in the *Gregorianus* was placed in the 12th book under the heading *De sponsoribus et fideiussoribus*,[61] as a branch of the law of *stipulationes*[62] (contracts by *verba sollemnia*). That chapter had arisen from the final title in the praetorian edict on special praetorian stipulations.[63] In the *Sententiae*, the title on suretyship, entitled *De fideiussore et sponsore*, was placed in the first part also, but among its first titles,[64]

---

[57] Thus, at any rate C. 8.56 with two constitutions taken from the *Gregorianus* after 8.53 *De donationibus* with eight (and 16 taken from the *Hermogenianus*); 8.54 *De donationibus quae sub modo ... conficiuntur* with four; and 55 *De revocandis donationibus* with three constitutions taken from the *Gregorianus*.

[58] Cf. C. 6.50 with 12 constitutions taken from the *Gregorianus* and five from the *Hermogenianus* after C. 6.37-49, titles of the *Iustinianus* on legacies and *fideicommissa* with (except 6.41, 43, and 48) a lot of constitutions taken from the *Gregorianus* and *Hermogenianus*.

[59] This can be deduced from its reflexion in the *Iustinianus*, namely C. 7.1 *De vindicta libertate* ... with one constitution from the *Gregorianus* (only because of the fourth constitution of Constantine, the heading was lengthened by *et apud consilium manumissione*); C. 7.2 *De testamentaria manumissione* with nine; C. 7.4 *De fideicommissariis libertatibus* with ten; C. 7.8 *De servo pignori dato manumisso* with seven; C. 7.9 *De servis rei publicae manumittendis* with two; C. 7.10 *De his qui a non domino manumissi sunt* with five; C. 7.11 *Qui manumittere non possunt* ... with five; C. 7.12 *Qui non possunt ad libertatem pervenire* with two; C. 7.13 *Pro quibus causis servi praemium accipiunt libertatem* with one; C. 7.14 *De ingenuis manumissis* with three; Rotondi, 'Studi' (nt. 10) 54–56: book 9. There may have existed two additional titles *Ad leges Fufiam Caniniam* and *Ad legem Aeliam Sentiam* which laws Justinian abolished, C. 7.3 and 7.15.2.

[60] PS 4.12-14A.

[61] Lex Romana Burgundionum 14.7. Justinian abolished *sponsio* and approached the mandate providing credit to a third person to securityship, D. Liebs, *Die Klagenkonkurrenz im römischen Recht* (Göttingen 1972) 38-44; consequently C. 8.40 was headed *De fideiussoribus et mandatoribus* instead of the above mentioned heading of the *Gregorianus*; the 18 first constitutions are taken from this code, but only 8.40.7 concerns a matching mandate.

[62] This can be deduced from the position of C. 8.40 between 8.37-39 and 8.41.

[63] Lenel, *Das edictum* (n. 4) 514-53.

[64] PS 1.20.

not at its end; the praetorian edict had already had its proper chapter on suretyship located in this earlier place.[65] The constitutions on *patria potestas* including *adoptio* and *emancipatio* in the *Gregorianus* were not yet integrated in the digest system's first part;[66] they are found only in the 13th book,[67] followed by a title on adoption, another on emancipation,[68] and a third on *postliminium* and *redemptio ab hostibus*.[69] Apparently, with this 13th book the – here still moderately – shrunken second part of the digest system in the *Gregorianus* began. This book 13 must have contained more, probably on gifts,[70] the detriments of celibacy and childlessness,[71] and the advantages of having more than two respectively three children (*ius liberorum*).[72] Book 14 was devoted to criminal law and the law of criminal procedure,[73] and 15, as explained above,[74] to *ius fisci*, military law, and municipal law. The law of appeals, in the *Sententiae* addressed broadly at the end of the second part and thus the entire work,[75] in the *Gregorianus* seems to have been placed already in the first part, inserted between *res iudicata* (or *confessa*)[76] and the chapter on the law

---

[65] Lenel, *Das edictum* (n. 4) 214-219.

[66] But some years later the *Pauli Sententiae* have it integrated, at least adoption and emancipation, above nt. 24.

[67] LRV Cod. Greg. 13 *De patria potestate* preserves the heading and one constitution; C. 8.46 *De patria potestate* further six constitutions from the *Gregorianus* (and three from the *Hermogenianus*).

[68] This can be deduced from, immediately after C. 8.46, 8.47 *De adoptionibus* with five constitutions taken from the *Gregorianus* and 8.48 *De emancipationibus liberorum* with two.

[69] Apparently, the model of C. 8.50 *De postliminio et de redemptis ab hostibus*, where the first eight constitutions are taken from the *Gregorianus*.

[70] Probably the model of C. 8.53-56.

[71] Instead of C. 8.57, before Constantine's and Honorius' abolition of the pertinent Augustan laws, C. 8.57.1 and 2; on this subject must have existed more than one title.

[72] Cf. C. 8.58 *De iure liberorum*, but now only with Theodosius' II. devaluation of these advantages a. 410.

[73] Cf. Coll. Mos. 1.8: *Gregorianus libro XIIII Ad legem Corneliam de sicariis et veneficis*; 3.4: *Gregorianus libro XIIII sub titulo De accusationibus*; and 15.3: *Gregorianus libro XIIII sub titulo De maleficis et Manichaeis*.

[74] Text to above nt. 40.

[75] Text to above nt. 16; similar in D. 49.1-13, whereas the *Iuris epitomae* must have placed this chapter as had Gregorius, which we can conclude from D. 49.1.27 and 49.10.2, both already from Hermogenian's book 5.

[76] Lenel, *Das edictum* (n. 4) 404-10, titles 36 and 36a of the praetorian edict; cf. C. 7.52-59 with many constitutions from the *Gregorianus*.

of execution.[77] In the *Gregorianus*, the digest system's second part had not yet become as brief as in the *Sententiae*, only about six years younger.

The *Gregorianus* became the model not just for the *Sententiae*, but also other small law books at that time containing statements on all fields of law followed that practice of arranging single subjects more convincingly than they had been in the old digest system with its less satisfactory second part; they put as many single topics of the second part as possible to related topics in the first (the edict part), and revised how the relatively small rest was arranged.

4. *Codex Hermogenianus*

The first edition of the *Codex Hermogenianus* must have been compiled in 295 AD. It was not subdivided in books, but only titles. Nevertheless, it was not just as large as a classical *liber singularis*, but as four of even five traditional *libri.*[78] Alaric's Breviary had epitomized this code also, but the result was an especially tiny epitome consisting of two titles, each with one constitution and *Interpretatio*. This epitome does not reveal much about this code's original structure. The middle piece of the so-called *Consultatio veteris cuiusdam iurisconsulti* yields more; this piece was once a separate work[79] which cited eight titles from the *Hermogenianus* together with its original headings.[80] Giovanni Rotondi arranged these titles and the quotations found elsewhere according to their arrangement in the *Codex Iustinianus*,[81] but his result is not completely satisfactory, especially not his inverting of the Breviary's two ti-

---

[77] Lenel, *Das edictum* (n. 4) 411-46, titles 37-42, cf. C. 7.71-75 with their constitutions from the *Gregorianus*. Law of appeals: C. 7, 62 and 64-68 with many constitutions from the *Gregorianus*; Rotondi, 'Studi' (nt. 10) 165: "rimane per me incerto".

[78] Information on that is scattered, Rotondi, 'Studi' (nt. 10) 157 nt. 1; add Thalelaios, Scholion zu C. 2.4.18. On its original extent Liebs, *Hermogenians* (n. 2) 23 f.; at that time there were other extensive works on law not subdivided in *libri*, for instance the original of the so-called *Fragmenta* (*iuris*) *Vaticana*.

[79] The so-called part A (Cons. 4–6), a little older than part B (Cons. 1-3 and 7-8, perhaps in addition 9), see e.g. D. Liebs, *Römische Jurisprudenz in Gallien (2. bis 8. Jahrhundert)* (Berlin 2002) 138-41.

[80] Cons. 4.9 (–11): *De pactis et transactionibus* (and 6.19); 5.6 (+7): *De calumniatoribus et plus petendo* (and obviously 6.13); 6.10 (+11): *De donationibus inter virum et uxorem* (and 12); 14: *Ad exhibendum*; 15: *Ubi agi debeat*; 16: *De instrumentis*; 17: *De testamentis*; 18: *De successionibus* (meant *ab intestato*).

[81] Rotondi, 'Studi' (nt. 10) 158 nt. 1.

tles.[82] On the other hand, he correctly deduces a title *De successionibus* on intestate succession from the *Iustinianus*,[83] following the titles on testamentary succession[84] and not placed, as in the old digest system, at the beginning of the second part. A special argument is C. 6,59,4; this constitution was originally part of a larger one,[85] another part is transmitted by *Consultatio* 6,18 *ex corpore Hermogeniani tit. de successionibus*. At any rate, this title's probable original location in the *Hermogenianus* is the same as that of the corresponding title in the *Gregorianus*.[86] The *Hermogenianus* would not have existed had the *Gregorianus* not already, therefore, when Hermogenian got down to arranging the single topics of his code, it must have seemed obvious to him to follow the *Gregorianus* model wherever it was convenient.

5. Hermogenian's *Iuris epitomae*

The same Hermogenian composed some years later the *Iuris epitomarum libri VI*. This work was not arranged according to the old digest system either but rather to its modernized version as the *Gregorianus* and *Pauli sententiae*. 107 mostly short pieces from the *Iuris epitomae* are preserved, among them the author's own statements on the system.[87] Moreover, there is a strong indication of that: Justinian's commission composing his *Digesta* excerpted from that work and the *Pauli Sententiae* together, beginning with the *Sententiae*'s first *liber* minus its end, then the *Iuris epitomae*'s first *liber* and after that, the first *liber*'s end and the second *liber* of the *Sententiae*, followed by the *Iuris epitomae*'s second *liber*, and so on.[88] Doing it in this way only made sense if the single topics in the

---

[82] LRV Cod. Herm. 1 and 2.

[83] Attested by Cons. 6.18.

[84] This can be deduced from C. 6.59 *Communia de successionibus*, as all ten of its pre-Justinian constitutions are taken from the *Hermogenianus*, cf. Liebs, *Hermogenians* (n. 2) 23 f., 29 f.; and the palingenesia of Cenderelli, *Ricerche* (nt. 55) 167 f.

[85] Originally containing also C. 3.31.8 and 7.16.27, all four with the same addressee and connected contents.

[86] Above, text to ntt. 54 f.

[87] D. 1.5.2, see *infra*. This is very seldom, comparable is only Gai, *inst*. 1.8 (together with 2.1 and 4.1).

[88] See Paul Krüger, 'Ordo librorum iuris veteris in compilandis Digestis observata' in P. Krüger/Th. Mommsen (edd.), *Corpus iuris civilis editio stereotypa*, vol. 1: Institutiones. Digesta, (Berlin 1928[15]) 927–31, here 930, no. 205-214; Liebs, *Her-*

two (or more) commonly excerpted works had been arranged in the same or nearly the same manner.[89] Thus the *Iuris epitomae* must also have been arranged in a manner at least resembling the *Sententiae*. Hermogenian described the structure of his *Iuris epitomae* as follows:[90]

Cum[91] hominum causa omne ius constitutum est, primo de personarum statu ac post de ceteris, ordinem edicti perpetui secuti et his proximos atque coniunctos applicantes titulos, ut res patitur, dicemus.

As all law is constituted for the sake of men, we shall first speak on personal status and thereafter on the other topics, following the order of the permanent edict, and adding to them the most related and connected titles, as matters allow.

Krüger had interpreted this passage as referring to the digest system,[92] as Lenel interpreted it also.[93] Both related *his proximos atque coniunctos applicantes titulos* to the second part of the digest system. But this is compatible with neither the plural *his* nor with *proximos atque coniunctos*. *His* refers to *ceteris* (six words in front) and *ceteris* to the other topics after *de personarum statu*. The plural *his* does not refer to the edict as a whole, but refers to the individual subjects or titles arranged according to the edict. By that, Hermogenian states that he would attach to the edict's single titles the most closely related titles with non-edictal subjects, that is to insert every title with a non-edictal subject there in the edictal order, where an edictal title is closely related. Already in the digest system, single non-edictal subjects had been inserted here and there into the first, the edictal part if it seemed convenient, e.g. *fideicommissa* or *possessio* and *usucapio*.[94]

---

mogenians (n. 2) 109 f.; T. Honoré, *Justinian's Digest* (Oxford 2010) 57, 71, 83, and 155 f., no. 205-214.

[89] As were for example the three commentaries on Sabinus' *Iuris civili libri III*, see Krüger, 'Ordo' (nt. 88) 927, no. 1-3; the commentaries on the praetorian edict, Krüger, ibid. no. 4-9, and 928 f. no. 95-123; others: 928, no. 57 f. and 64-66; 929, no. 134 f.; 930, no. 162-67 and 194-204.

[90] D. 1.5.2.

[91] Justinian's compilers inserted *igitur* here, a particle in order to smoothen the transition from D. 1.5.1.

[92] Krüger, 'Ueber die Zusammensetzung' (n. 1) 105 nt. 1.

[93] Lenel, *Pal.* I 265 nt. 2.

[94] On *fideicommissa*, see e.g. Iul. 39 f. *dig.* and Lenel, *Pal.* I 419-27; Cels. 20 f. *dig.* and Lenel ibid. 155 f.; Marcell. 15 *dig.* and Lenel ibid. 616-18; Pap. 8 f. *resp.* and Lenel ibid. 916-25. On *possessio* and *usucapio* Iul. 44 *dig.* and Lenel, *Pal.* I 435-40; Cels. 33 *dig.* and Lenel ibid. 157-59; Marcell. 17 *dig.* and Lenel ibid. 620; Scaev. 25 *dig.* and Lenel, *Pal.* II 262 f.; Pap. 10 *resp.* and Lenel, *Pal.* I 928 f.

Lenel's embedding of all preserved passages of the *Iuris epitomae* (less the first twelve and the last five) into the edictal system[95] is being put into a Procrustean bed. That has led to inconsistencies which is clearly shown by his headings of the passages on the law of succession in books 3 and 4. He allocated two Hermogenian passages from book 3, in Justinian's *Digesta* placed in D. 29.2 *De adquirenda vel omittenda hereditate*, to the last heading of the edictal chapter on the praetorian law of succession, the *bonorum possessio*.[96] This section he had initially headed *De successorio edicto*,[97] later preferring *Quis ordo in possessionibus servetur*.[98] But neither the first nor the later heading are convenient to Hermogenian's relevant passages. Nor are convenient the parallel passages quoted by Lenel in order to strengthen his heading. For the first Hermogenian passage he had placed under this heading, he quoted a passage from Ulpian's commentary on the praetorian edict,[99] and a constitution from the *Codex Iustinianus* for the second.[100] But this constitution has a different heading: *De iure deliberandi et de adeunda vel adquirenda hereditate*, a heading from Roman civil law of succession, whereas Lenel, relying on his theory, felt forced to a heading from the praetorian law of succession. Concerning the passage from Ulpian, parallel passages cannot be found in his commentary on the edict; however, there are appropriate parallel passages in his commentary on Sabinus' *Ius civile* and in the corresponding commentary of Pomponius.[101] Both these passages in Justinian's *Digesta* come from the same title as Hermogenian's passage, D. 29.2, as they all were probably already in their original context.[102] Yet this heading is no edict heading, but rather that of a *proximus atque coniunctus titulus* to an edict title, in this case one from the *ius civile* on testamentary succession.[103]

---

[95] Lenel, *Pal.* I 266-276, no. 13-99; the last five, 276 f. no. 100–104, according to him represented the second part of the digest system.

[96] D. 29.2.94 and 96, Lenel, *Pal.* I 272, no. 64 f.

[97] Lenel, *Pal.* I 272 before no. 64 and II 1252 § 165, following his original reconstruction of this paragraph of the *edictum perpetuum*, obviously according to D. 38.9.

[98] Lenel, *Das edictum* (n. 4) 361, there according to D. 38.15; in nt. 1 he provided reasons for his change of opinion.

[99] Lenel, *Pal.* I 272 nt. 1: D. 38.9.1.6 (Ulp. 49 *ed.*).

[100] Lenel, *Pal.* I 272 nt. 2: C. 6.30.12.

[101] Pomp. D. 29.2.27 (3 *Sab.*) and Ulp. D. 29.2.21.2 (7 *Sab.*) for Hermog. D. 29.2.94; and Ulpian D. 29.2.34 pr. (8 *Sab.*) for Hermog. D. 29.2.96.

[102] Lenel, *Pal.* II 90, no. 408; and II 1034 f., no. 2482.

[103] R. Astolfi, *I libri tres iuris civilis* (Padova 2001^2) 205 f.; see also 9 f. and 75.

A third passage from book 3 of the *Iuris epitomae* has been put by Lenel under the heading *Ad senatus consultum Silanianum*,[104] an edict heading as well; in its entirety it would have continued as did the D. 29.5 heading: *Ad senatus consultum Silanianum: quorum testamenta ne aperiantur.*[105] In later editions of his *Das edictum perpetuum* – the first edition came out a few years before the *Palingenesia iuris civilis* –, he reduced this heading to its second part: *Quorum testamenta ne aperiantur.*[106] But in Justinian's *Digesta*, this Hermogenian passage is placed under the heading *De his quae ut indignis auferuntur*. In this case too, there is no reason to think Justinian's compilers would have taken the passage from a different title in the *Iuris epitomae*; apparently the *Codex Gregorianus* had a corresponding title as well,[107] and the *Sententiae* possibly too.[108] And as this code and this law book had done, so also the *Iuris epitomae* addressed intestate after testamentary succession.[109]

To sum up, in Hermogenian's *Iuris epitomae* the majority of the non-edictal titles are integrated into the edict system, as they had been in the *Sententiae*. Those not integrated, at any rate criminal law and *ius fisci*[110] amount to about a tenth of the whole, less than in the *Gregorianus* and also in the *Sententiae*. Gregorius, Hermogenian, and the *Sententiae* author, they rearranged the old digest system more and more

---

[104] D. 34.9.20: Lenel, *Pal.* I 273, no. 69.

[105] Cf. Lenel, *Pal.* II 1252 § 169, and D. 29.5.

[106] Lenel, *Das edictum* (n. 4) 364.

[107] We can conclude this from C. 6.35 *De his quibus ut indignis auferuntur et ad senatus consultum Silanianum*. The first ten constitutions concern the first part of the heading, nine taken from the *Gregorianus* and one from the *Hermogenianus*; only the last two from Justinian himself, a. 531 and 532, thus not yet in the first edition, concern that *senatusconsultum*. Therefore the heading's second part was an addition of the second edition of that code.

[108] Liebs, 'Die pseudopaulinishen Sentenzen II' (nt. 12) 178, referring to App. Visig. 2.15 and LRV PS 3.6.10. Transmitted are different headings for both passages, but modern editors doubt this, see P. Krüger, in *Collectio librorum iuris anteiustiniani* II (Berlin 1878) 85, and E. Seckel / B. Kübler, in *Iurisprudentiae anteiustinianae reliquias* II 1 (Leipzig 1908) 77; but they do not propose a heading instead.

[109] Liebs, *Hermogenians* (n. 2) 66 and 125 on D. 38.7.6. But different from p. 47 and 125 there, D. 48.4.9 did not belong to that title either; this passage's transmissed book number 5 should not be changed, a title *De commissis* in book 5 after the title *De vectigalibus*, p. 126, fits better. Lenel, *Pal.* I 274 no. 86, gave to that passage the heading (*Ut in possessionem eatur eius,*) *Qui capitali crimine damnatus erit*, a stopgap to save his theory.

[110] Lenel, *Pal.* I 275-78; Liebs, *Hermogenians* (n. 2) 128-30.

thoroughly; first Gregorius (and Hermogenian) in their constitution codes, then the author of the *Sententiae* in his summary of the established law, and still more definitely Hermogenian in his one. This rearrangement of law fields and topics should have its own designation. Gregorius had introduced that by his *Codex Gregorianus*; the *Codex Hermogenianus* probably followed that example, and later followed them the *Codex Theodosianus* and finally the *Iustinianus*. Thus the proposition of the term *Codexsystem* (code system). [111]

6. Pseudo-Ulpian's *Opiniones*

65 short and longer passages in Justinian's *Digesta* are taken from allegedly Ulpian's *Opinionum libri VI* from which is preserved approximately as much text as from Hermogenian's *Iuris epitomae* with its 107 passages. Lenel stated that these texts cannot have come from Ulpian's pen, but rather from an author from a later period. Nevertheless, he was trying to reconcile that observation with Ulpian's alleged authorship, and assumed that the author of these texts would have excerpted Ulpian's opinions from his writings. [112] As "later period" (*posterior aetas*) Lenel must have meant a time, when legal Latin had diverged strongly from Ulpian's which had occurred by the time of the *Codex Theodosianus*. A jurists expressing himself clearly differently from another, however, does not simply excerpt from him, he writes something new; whoever epitomizes adopts the language of the original. The many known epitomes of legal texts are never stilistically as far from their original as the *opiniones* texts are from Ulpian's writing. Nevertheless, Lenel insisted that the legal content of the *Opiniones* were taken from Ulpian's writings. He was baffled as well when he tried to reconstruct the work passage by passage according to the digest system. That attempt failed completely, already in book 1. [113] The writing would have covered less than a quarter of the whole, ending with the 15th of the 45 titles of the edict, that system's first part. He concluded that the *Opiniones* had either never been finished or were

[111] Liebs, *Hermogenians* (n. 2) 26-28, 110, and 115-30.

[112] Lenel, *Pal.* II 1001 nt. 2 (*sent.* 5): "Mirum est, quantum hi libri distent dicendi genere a ceteris Ulpiani libris: posterioris aetatis auctorem has opiniones ex Ulpiani libris excerpsisse credideris."

[113] Lenel, *Pal.* II 1001, nt. 2 (*sent.* 2): "Agitur libro I de officio praetoris et praesidis, sed praeterea de multis aliis argumentis, quae nescio qua ratione inter se conexa sint".

passed down to Justinian incompletely.[114] These two further auxiliary hypotheses weaken his theory once more.

Young Lenel was unaware of the many misattributions of writings to famous authors, so-called pseud-epigraphy flourishing especially in late antiquity,[115] a factor that should be kept in mind in the field of legal literature also. If we disregard Lenel's auxiliary constructions – his basic idea had already misled him with the pseudo-pauline *Sententiae*[116] – the path is free to determine the date, place of origin, and character of the *Opiniones*. The result is: a work reflecting Roman law practice in a province[117] in the early 4th century.[118] But it is difficult to state whence the author got his legal rules. Ulpian's writings have been shown as the probable source just once,[119] and imperial rescripts hypothetically two or three times.[120] More than a third of the passages preserved from the *Sententiae* and Hermogenian's *Iuris epitomae* can be traced back to a certain passage by a late classical jurist[121] an or imperial rescript.[122] Rescripts by provincial authorities are another potential source of his knowledge of which pratically nothing has survived;[123] those of the author's province are most probable. However, the interesting point here is, how the author arranged the material. Dating the work into the 4th century and free from Lenel's obsession with the digest system, the code system turns out to have been the most satisfactory means of ordering the preserved passages from books 1 to 6 in that

---

[114] Lenel, *Pal.* II 1001 nt. 2 *sent.* 3 f.: "Inde a libro II edicti perpetui ordo servari videtur. Cum tamen libri sexti quae supersunt fragmenta ultra edicti perpetui titulum XV (Lenel) non procedant, suspicari licet aut non perfecisse auctorem hos libros aut partem eorum ad Iustiniani aetatem non pervenisse".

[115] Cf. W. Speyer, *Die literarische Fälschung im heidnischen und christlichen Altertum* (München 1971).

[116] Liebs, *Africa* (nt. 51) 42-44 and 58-111.

[117] Liebs, 'Ulpiani' (nt. 41) 306-308.

[118] Liebs, 'Ulpiani' (nt. 41) 280-94.

[119] Liebs, 'Ulpiani' (nt. 41) 298.

[120] Liebs, 'Ulpiani' (nt. 41) 299 f.

[121] Liebs, *Africa* (nt. 51) 42-94; Id., *Hermogenians* (n. 2) 39-86.

[122] Liebs, *Africa* 94-111; Liebs, *Hermogenians* (n. 2) 92-97.

[123] See the papers of F. Hurlet, A. Jördens, R. Haensch (2), S. Strassi, and B. Kelly, in Rudolf Haensch (ed.), *Recht haben und Recht bekommen im Imperium Romanum* (Warschau 2016); esp. P. Yale 61, cf. H. Horstkotte, in ZPE 114 (1996) 189-93. An example not from Egypt is a *subscriptio* by the Palestine governor from 22 Jan. 150 AD on a petition of veterans in the 10th legion, asking him to attest to their service, R. Cavenaile (ed.), *Corpus papyrorum Latinarum* (Wiesbaden 1958) no. 117.

work.[124] It's true there is no passage preserved on *ius fisci* nor on *iudicia publica*. That, however, does not necessarily indicate that these fields were completely absent originally.[125]

7. *Codex Theodosianus*

The aim of *Codex Theodosianus* was to compile the general Roman imperial laws issued since Constantine; it was to follow the example of the *Codices Gregorianus* and *Hermogenianus*, that is, to arrange them as the older imperial laws had been in the older *codices*.[126] Thus the general laws issued in the last circa 120 years in both the Eastern and Western Roman Empire had to be arranged according to the code system. But the modern general laws did not address the same subjects as the older codes had with mostly imperial rescripts to private people. In addition to topics familiar from those codes, they contained recent legislation related to many new fields, namely new constitutional law, administrative law, status law, law of the public services, and ecclesiastical law; these were fields lacking in the older codes. These codes mainly contained imperial information on points of the law in force; the quarrels of the private people involved mainly questions of private law, whereas the new code was meant to document only laws claiming general validity from now into the future; each of the new laws established a new legal situation by either amending established law or regulating something for the first time; it contained only *leges novellae* after the Gregorian and Hermogenian codes, in this case not just from three decades (like after the Theodosian and Justinian codes), but from twelve. And new public law was the main subject of these *novellae*. The change from principate to late antique absolutism had yielded completely different laws which had to be amended permanently. Thus public law fills books 1 and 5 to 16, although 5 and 8 only partly, private law is found in 2 to 4 and parts of 5 and 8. Private law usually is not amended as often as public law is.

Although the Roman praetor's edict concerned private law essentially,

[124] Liebs, 'Ulpiani' (nt. 41) 300–305.

[125] Some criminal law was addressed in the 1st book, cf. D. 1.18.6 and about that Liebs, 'Ulpiani' (nt. 41) 301 and nt. 93.

[126] CTh 1.1.5 (Constantinople, a. 429): *Ad similitudinem Gregoriani atque Hermogeniani codicis cunctas colligi constitutiones decernimus, quas Constantinus inclitus et post eum divi principes nosque tulimus*; sent. 2 of this text ordered expressly to arrange them as well according to their system.

it began with an extensive title on judicial organization.[127] Likewise, the works arranged according to the digest or code system generally began like that as well. But some put in advance a short chapter on the sources of the law[128], as did the *Theodosianus* in the first fifth of book 1 dealing with imperial constitutions (1,1–3) and the writings of the classical jurists (1,4). The large remainder of the 1st book (1,5–34) is devoted to the contemporary judicial organization. Thus only the first quarter of this *Codex* was arranged according to the code system's edictal part,[129] whereas those topics were spread out across three-quarters of the whole which covered a fifth or sixth in the first five works treated earlier. Public law was now given overwhelming emphasis; it had also penetrated fields of law that had been regulated until then by private autonomy and private law, even the law of succession. Members of the town councils and of certain professional bodies could no longer make a will at their discretion;[130] which had till then been called *successio ab intestate,*[131] it was now *legitima hereditas*, and the transposition of that field of law from the digest system's second part into the edictal part, after testamentary succession, has been given up; the chapter on *legitimae hereditates*[132] now leads to the new status law. Legal succession is followed by *postliminium* (repatriation by return from wartime captivity)[133] and new law of civil status,[134] then the farming of abandoned land and awarding of public farmland,[135] finally the late antique colonate system with its regional pe-

---

[127] R. Domingo, *Estudios* (nt. 39).

[128] E.g. Hermogenian in his *Iuris epitomae*, Lenel, *Pal.* I 265 no. 1-3; Liebs, *Hermogenians* (n. 2) 116 no. 1-4; cf. Id., Gnomon 80 (2008) 755 f. (2012 supplemented version: https://freidok.uni-freiburg.de/data/8595). Among the transmitted texts from Roman law literature, a similar chapter appears first in Gai inst. 1.1-7, and later in Ulpian 1 inst. D. 1.1.1,4,6 and 1.4.1.

[129] Approximately, as the size of the *libri* in this code varied heavily; especially thin were books 13 to 15; book 11 has nearly as much text as these three *libri* have together, books 9, 12, and 16 each has more than books 13 and 14 together. Unfortunately, books 1 to 5 are incompletely preserved, only an epitome and fragments, comprising roughly a third of the original, a little more has survived of book 1.

[130] CTh 5.2-6 *ed.* Paul Krüger, Codex Theodosianus, fasc. I liber I–VI, Berlin 1923, 163–66.

[131] Cf. PS 4.7: *De intestatorum successione*; and *Codex Hermogenianus* (Cons. 6.18): *De successionibus*, sc. *ab intestato*.

[132] CTh 5.1-4.

[133] CTh 5.7 f. ed. Krüger.

[134] CTh 5.9 f. ed. Krüger.

[135] CTh 5.11-14 ed. Krüger.

culiarities,[136] and new public real-estate law.[137] This sometimes incorporated regional traditions may be the reason why book 5 ends with a title on customary law: *De longa consuetudine*. To put this title so far away from the chapter on the sources of the law at the beginning of book 1, reflects that this, a relic of the ancient regional laws, in late antiquity was not considered to be a fully adequate source of law.

Book 6 contains mainly new status law, book 7 military law, book 8 rules for lower officials;[138] then gift law,[139] a topic which, as mentioned above, had remained in the annex also in the older works arranged according to the code system; the end of book 8 contains once more new status law and law of succession.[140] In book 9, criminal law and the law of criminal procedure follow, 10 to 13 the law of taxes, levies and charges, among those also the organization of important professional groups, thus the law of compulsory corporations of late antiquity and their public service. Book 14 was devoted to the publicly organized distribution of basic food, free or at low prices in Rome and other large cities in the empire. Book 15 addressed publicly organized entertainements, and 16 ecclesiastical law.

This somewhat clear arrangement of the *Theodosianus* was a remarkable work, although imperfect in many details. The general imperial laws of the last 125 years were both extremely numerous and wordy. Ever more areas of life then were statutorily regulated, and the emperors exploited them for rhetorically overblown imperial propaganda as well.[141]

8. *Codex Iustinianus*

The structure of the *Codex Iustinianus*[142] and of Justinian's *Digesta* is closer to that of the works from about 300 AD than to the structure

[136] CTh 5.15-20 ed. Krüger.

[137] CTh 5.21-26 ed. Krüger.

[138] CTh 8.1-11.

[139] CTh 8.12-15.

[140] CTh 8.16-19.

[141] Cf. R.M. Honig, *Humanitas und Rhetorik in spätrömischen Kaisergesetzen* (Göttingen 1960).

[142] Cf. recently S. Corcoran, 'The Codex of Justinian: The Life of a Text through 1500 Years', in B.W. Frier et al. (edd.), *The Codex of Justinian. A New Annotated Translation with Parallel Latin and Greek Text* (Cambridge 2016) I, xcvii–clxxxi.

of the *Theodosianus*. The *Iustinianus* combined the essentials from the three older *Codices Gregorianus*, *Hermogenianus*, and *Theodosianus*, and of the amendments that had been issued meanwhile in the Eastern Empire. But it restricted itself to the still valid regulations more resolutely than did the *Theodosianus* in particular. The compilers of the *Iustinianus* selected more rigorously, shortened the individual texts more strongly, and even updated them if necessary; only the laws from Justinian himself were adopted unchanged. The private law part of the *Iustinianus* (books 2 to 8) was dominated by the older imperial rescripts on private law from the *Gregorianus* and *Hermogenianus*. For these books, the *Gregorianus* had furnished also the pattern for the titles' scaffolding. As to public law, books 1 and 10 to 12, these were arranged according to the *Theodosianus*. As to book 9 (criminal law), both gave the model; almost all of book 9's headings in the *Iustinianus* seem to have been taken from the *Theodosianus*, but most of the constitutions in his book 9 were taken from the *Gregorianus*,[143] where criminal law was addressed in book 14.[144] Its titles' staffolding must have been the pattern already in book 9 of the Theodosian code.[145] This code apparently kept silent on private penal law; thus the *Iustinianus* took that only from the *Gregorianus* and the *Hermogenianus*.[146]

The arrangement of the *Iustinianus* combined both versions of the code system, its older one of the two first codes and the younger one from the *Theodosianus*.

---

[143] Book 9 of the *Iustinianus* has 51 titles. 19 thereof lacking preconstantinian constitutions have a heading, equal or similar (≈) as has the corresponding title of book 9 of the *Theodosianus*: 3, 4, 7, 10, 11, 14, 15, 17, 24, 26–28, 30, ≈31, 36, 38, 39, 44, 48; four have only constitutions of Justinian: 5, 13, 29, 37. Among the remaining 28, 16 have headings equal or similar to those of the *Theodosianus*: 2, 8, 9, 12, 16, 18–20, 22, 41, 42, ≈43, 46, 47, 49, 51, but as they also contain preconstantinian constitutions, already the *Gregorianus* must have had corresponding titles; almost certainly this code had them in the case of 12 titles with only or mainly preconstantinian constitutions, only: 1.6.21, 23, 25, 32–34, 45, 50, mainly: 35, 40, but except one: 25, taken from the *Hermogenianus*.

[144] We have five passages from that: Coll. Mos. 3.4; 1.8-10; and 15.3.

[145] Cf. Rotondi, 'Studi' (nt. 10) 146-85, on book 9 shortly 167 and 169.

[146] C. 9.32 and 34 took its constitutions only from the *Gregorianus*, 33 mainly from the *Hermogenianus*, and 35 also from it with a Zenonian addition: 9.35.11 (a. 478).

9. Justinian's *Digesta*

When the *Digesta* were being planned, Justinian ordered that they be arranged as his code was and according to the praetorian edict, as the compilers found more convenient.[147] This is evidence that the code and edict systems were not one and the same for him either; the compilers had to decide from title to title to follow either the Justinian code or the edict, as the context suggested. In fact, they made use of the improvements of the code system, and developed it further, even at the expense of the edict system.[148] The old digest system's second part, shrunk to a mere annex in the older code system, likewise occupies only the last four *libri* in Justinian's 50 books *Digesta*, seemingly a twelfth of the whole, but as they are longer they occupy a little more than an eighth of the whole text. Nevertheless, these four books incorporated a long chapter previously placed in the edictal part, the *actio furti* together with some similar *actiones*.[149] The compilers had for the first time united all of private penal law, placing it in the annex before criminal law; until then the chapter *furtum*, traceable back to an edict title,[150] was placed in turn within the edict part in every pertinent work.[151] With this afford, they had accomplished that which seems to have been started in the Justinian code but probably originated in the *Gregorianus*, the code that had already placed single offenses of private penal law near criminal law.[152] All penal law is placed together in Justinian's *Digesta* for the first time, beginning with private penal law, book 47, introduced by a general title *De privatis delictis* (unknown till then); book 48 continues with criminal law. The *Digesta*'s compilers distanced themselves further away from the edict in this point. But with their

---

[147] D. const. Deo auctore (= C. 1.17.1, a. 530) § 5: ... *oportet eam* (see before: *haec materia ... collecta) pulcherrimo opere extruere ... et certos titulos totum ius digerere tam secundum nostri constitutionum codicis quam edicti perpetui imitationem, prout hoc vobis commodius esse patuerit, ...*; from this Krüger, 'Ueber die Zusammensetzung' (n. 1) 105, only cited the compilers' second model *edicti perpetui imitatio*, referring it to his digest system, thus neglecting *nostri constitutionum codicis*, the first named model.

[148] Krüger, *Geschichte* (nt. 1) 376-79.

[149] D. 47.2-7.

[150] Between guardianship and patronate law, Lenel, *Das edictum* (n. 4) XIX f. and 322-38, title XXIII.

[151] In the *Sententiae*, PS 2.31; in the *Iuris epitomae*, book 2 title 17 according to Liebs, *Hermogenians* (n. 2) 123; in the *Gregorianus*, probably book 7, Rotondi, 'Studi' (nt. 10) 163 f.; and in the *Iustinianus*, C. 6.2.

[152] See above (sub 8.), the constitutions noted in nt. 146, and their place in the *Iustinianus*.

wordings of the individual titles' headings, they indulged in widespread classicism; their wording is often more archaic in the *Digesta* than in the four codes, probably following the wording of the edict.[153] Another tribute to especially law-school classicism had been the revival of private penal law. Punishing minor offenses by fines to be paid to the injured party was hardly practiced any more in the 6th century, a fact that is only revealed at the end of book 47's two main titles.[154]

The new constitutional, administration, military, and status law extended in the *Codex Iustinianus* appears at best sparsely in the *Digesta*, and not at all ecclesiastical law. This reflects the composition of the *Digesta* through excerpts from the writings of the classical jurists; only the few most recent, essentially the aforementioned epi- and postclassical works contained a bit of the new law, just some basics.[155] Hermogenian's cited passage on the structure of his *Iuris epitomae* therefore could immediately be taken to describe the *Digesta*'s structure at a similarly prominent place as in the original, namely in the first book.[156]

10. Summary

Late antique works containing statements on all at that time relevant fields of law were arranged according to the code system. This absorbed the old digest system and developed it further; the latter had been a similarly further-developed edict system. The high and late classical jurists arranged their works comprising all then statutorily-regulated fields of law according to the digest system. Its first part was arranged according to the edict of the praetor in Rome (the provincial governors had essentially corresponding edicts); it was familiar to all practicing lawyers. The second part, about half as long, contained the topics not placed in the first, as a kind of collecting tank.[157] New fields of law which over time had been regulated, were annexed there, and the second part gradually lost shape.

---

[153] This had been a leading idea of Lenel, *Das edictum* (n. 4).

[154] On *furtum* D. 47.2.93 (Ulpian 38 *ed.*); and on *iniuria* D. 47.10.45 (Hermogenian 5 *iur. ep.*).

[155] Excerpting these works as well, the compilers, strictly speaking, disobeyed Justinian's order D. const. *Deo auctore* § 4. Besides the *Sententiae*, there are further works wrongly attributed to Paul, among them the *Liber singularis de cognitionibus* with much public law, Liebs, 'Jurisprudenz' (nt. 20) 174 = § 423 Ps. 1.

[156] D. 1.5.2.

[157] Krüger, 'Ueber die Zusammensetzung' (n. 1) 104, stressed that.

Towards 300 AD, the *Codex Gregorianus* began to place many topics from the second part into the first; Hermogenian did likewise in his *Codex*, as did the author of the pseudo-Pauline *Sententiae*, and Hermogenian again in his *Iuris epitomae*, as well as the *Opiniones*' author, allegedly Ulpian. That made the second part shrink to a relatively small annex, containing mainly public and criminal law. In the 5th century, all imperial general laws issued since Gregorius and Hermogenian had to be collected and arranged similarly, culminating in a *Codex Theodosianus*. To arrange these laws turned out to be a major challenge. These general imperial laws concerned mainly new public law; only a quarter thereof related to private law which had occupied three-quarters of the older codes. As public law had even infiltrated fields of private law, the *Theodosianus* reclamed some topics again into the second part which the earlier codes had transferred into the first. Thus two versions of the code system need to be distinguished. The older version containing not much more than the traditional fields of law is represented mainly in the works from about 300 AD and again in Justinian's *Digesta*, and the younger of the *Theodosianus*, whereas the *Codex Iustinianus* represents a combination of the two versions. The differences not only have to do with the fact that the four codes cover 250 years, three times as long a period as the *Digestorum libri*'s referred to above, but also that the imperial constitutions collected in the individual codes had different aims. The works arranged according to the digest system differed now and then also,[158] if not as much as in the codes. Every jurist publishing a legal work on different fields of law rearranged individual topics within the chosen system's framework, which could have been the digest, Gaius-, Sabinus-, or another system; they did so even in their commentaries on the praetorian edict.[159]

Later medieval and modern jurists disregarded this system. The edict system's authority was less due to a solid logic than to tradition and its blessing by the emperor. During the Middle Ages until the 16th century, only small collections of laws and brief law books were written. Later, emphasizing private law as had the Roman jurists, they preferred the shorter and more convincing system of Justinian's *Institutiones*, a revised version of the Gaius-system. The imperial splendor of the edict system paled in comparison to that, and thus the digest and code systems as well. The tradition of the Roman jurists' familiarity with the edict merely by practicing disappeared in the Early Middle Ages.

---

[158] See Lenel, *Pal.* II 1255 f.

[159] Lenel, *Das edictum* (n. 4) 6 and 11-13.

INDEX *

* This index and the following have been compiled by Dr. Roberta Soscia.

M

N

O

P

Q

R

S

NAMES (ancient and modern)

D

E

F

G

H

M

N

O

P

Q

R

For Product Safety Concerns and Information please contact our EU
representative GPSR@taylorandfrancis.com
Taylor & Francis Verlag GmbH, Kaufingerstraße 24, 80331 München, Germany

www.ingramcontent.com/pod-product-compliance
Ingram Content Group UK Ltd.
Pitfield, Milton Keynes, MK11 3LW, UK
UKHW020018200926
475702UK00014B/1942
* 9 7 8 1 0 3 2 0 4 7 5 7 7 *